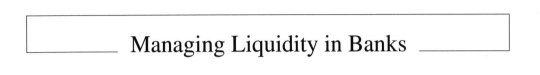

Managing Liquidity in Banks

For other titles in the Wiley Finance series
please see www.wiley.com/finance

Managing Liquidity in Banks

A Top Down Approach

Rudolf Duttweiler

A John Wiley and Sons, Ltd., Publication

© 2009 John Wiley & Sons Ltd

Registered office
John Wiley & Sons Ltd, The Atrium, Southern Gate, Chichester, West Sussex, PO19 8SQ, United Kingdom

For details of our global editorial offices, for customer services and for information about how to apply for permission to reuse the copyright material in this book please see our website at www.wiley.com.

Library of Congress Cataloging-in-Publication Data

A catalogue record for this book is available from the Library of Congress.

British Library Cataloguing-in-Publication Data

A catalogue record for this book is available from the British Library.

ISBN 978-0-470-74046-0(H/B)

Typeset in 10/12pt Times by Aptara Inc., New Delhi, India.
Printed in Great Britain by CPI Antony Rowe, Chippenham, Wiltshire

To My Children
Jan and Alexandra

Contents

Foreword

Exact timing is essential for a good treasurer – and this book arrives right on time! In his book, Rudolf Duttweiler presents the sum of 24 years of professional experience, gathered in positions of responsibility at several banks, 14 years of which include working for Commerzbank. He is definitely no theoretical analyst, but a practitioner with high standards for logical and structured thinking.

This book appears at a time of probably the most severe financial crisis since the Great Depression of 1929. One of the many lessons learnt from the 'subprime' crisis is without doubt that liquidity risks were underestimated across the board. Possibly the intensive debate over the last few years on default risks, solvency and Basel II has distracted too much attention from these kinds of risks. With hindsight they should have been considered as a grave threat to the financial sector, and it is clear that liquidity is crucial: for individual market participants, for the markets and for the whole financial system.

Another thing to note is that products, markets and financial institutions are more closely connected by the new financial innovations that have been created. At the same time, the worldwide ramifications of such developments are not sufficiently transparent to both market participants and supervisory authorities. The reasons are, amongst other things, international differences or 'loopholes' in regulatory frameworks, as well as differing transparency standards – consider, for example, conduits and similar arrangements.

In a nutshell, liquidity management has become more important than ever for banks.

There are two conclusions in this book which I think are especially important. One conclusion is that securing and managing bank liquidity is not merely a supporting, back office task which can be easily delegated. Since there is a strategic dimension, it needs to be done at top management level. It is only at such a level that decisions can be made on exactly what measures need to be taken, to what extent and at what costs, in order to deal with any kind of situation threatening the liquidity of a bank.

The other conclusion, masterfully illustrated here, is not just to fulfil all liabilities completely. This would also be possible to do at the price of breaking up a bank, albeit not punctually. No, it is primarily about preserving a bank, its reputation and thus its ongoing client and investor connections. Otherwise, its business network would be lost, a network built on hard-won trust, sometimes over centuries.

Another great achievement of the author is the provision of clear definitions and practical explanations, including the big picture.

Over the years, I have come to know and hold Ruedi Duttweiler in high esteem both personally and as a professional. I am deeply grateful to him – not only personally, but also on behalf of the shareholders, clients and colleagues of Commerzbank.

Ruedi Duttweiler has in particular been responsible for skilfully securing the liquidity, and thus helping to preserve the continued existence, of Commerzbank. For the first time, the related stress situations are revealed in detail for a professional audience in Chapter 7. Special attention is devoted to the intentional, yet completely unfounded rumours of liquidity shortages in 2002 which put the bank in a precarious position. The author was able to calm markets then, thanks to a conservative, high-liquidity strategy that he and his colleagues in the treasury department pursued. With his long professional experience and the steady hand of a 'veteran' (he is, by the way, a reserve officer in the Swiss Army), he exuded the necessary credibility amongst his peers worldwide. Consequently, he was able to convey the message that there was no reason to believe these rumours. The public support of the German banking supervisory authorities at that time can without doubt be attributed to a significant extent to his calm strategy and the good liquidity management he employed at Commerzbank.

To summarise: this book and its conclusions merit a large number of readers, thoughtful reading, and consideration as a textbook for daily treasury practice. Once this happens, the author will have provided an invaluable service to the whole financial community.

Klaus-Peter Müller
Chairman of the Supervisory Board, Commerzbank AG
President of the Association of German Banks

Preface

Liquidity risk and its management have become public focal points in the course of the US subprime mortgage crisis, when state intervention was necessary on a large and unprecedented scale to avoid the collapse of the financial system. The response is understandable given the severe implications when lacking control over it. And control over it seemingly has been lacking in many cases, as illustrated by well-known names in many countries: Bear-Stearns, Fannie Mae, Freddie Mac, Lehman Brothers, Fortis, Kaupthing, Northern Rock, Royal Bank of Scotland, UBS, Hypo Real Estate or IKB, to mention but a few. Yet it is surprising how little seems to have been known or applied in the banking industry when it comes to dealing with liquidity risk. We do not necessarily refer to the handling of the crisis, but mainly to the apparent shortcomings in the preparation to keep this type of risk within manageable levels. After all, next to downside risk, it is the most important risk elements immediately endangering solvency.

Why then has the banking industry been affected so strongly – in fact, more severely than in any liquidity crisis in the last 50 years or so when considered on a global basis? It is obviously neither the lack of general knowledge about the subject nor any disregard on a large scale which caused it. Based on rules and regulations agreed by the members of the Bank for International Settlements (BIS), national supervisors have put such principles into national legislation, not in a uniform manner but with their essence preserved and adjusted for local conditions. At the turn of the millennium in 2000 the Basel Committee on Banking Supervision set out principles in respect of 'Sound Practices for Managing Liquidity in Banking Operations'. More detailed recommendations have been delivered since. The banking industry thus had time to familiarise itself with the subject and to put legislation into concrete action.

My personal assessment relates much of the impact to having failed to read the equivalent of the 'small print' in a contract. Liquidity is an extremely complex subject and liquidity risk has many dimensions. Board decisions on business policies such as dynamic internal growth or a substantial acquisition can drastically alter the liquidity structure of a bank. Substantial losses will impinge on capital ratios and hence on the financial health of a bank, which in turn may affect the attitude of lenders and thus funding capacity. Or the funding markets may have turned less liquid, thus reducing or eliminating the level of borrowing at normal spreads and volumes, and the effects may have occurred despite an unaltered structure in liquidity or financial health of an institute. Any cautious bank management will have provided for such events by establishing liquidity buffers in the form of tradable assets. However, how liquid are liquid assets when they actually have to perform their duty? The answers to each question have found their way into modern liquidity management and the quantitative part into the respective measurements.

For bank management entrusted with securing and furthering the commitment to shareholders and stakeholders, staying liquid cannot be regarded as an isolated goal. It has to be brought into a balanced equation of further business and financial aims, as there are additional elements endangering solvency. Considering the latter point, the expectations of bank management exceed the primary goal of liquidity management, which is: to ensure that all payment obligations are fulfilled as and when they fall due. Taking the latter goal *in extremis*, it includes fulfilling all obligations till the last transaction is off the books leaving a skeleton of a bank with no customers left. Surviving a crisis thus means keeping the core of the business and customers, i.e. the franchise, intact. Defining it and determining the degree and duration of protection are the prerogatives of bank management.

Considering the high-level implications of liquidity as well as the management's respective responsibilities, it is advisable not to begin with technicalities, however. What is required is the application of a top-down approach. Derived from set business and financial goals, we are going to formulate a policy framework for liquidity based on which specific aspects of liquidity management and measurement are evaluated. Taking this route will permit us to embed the subject within the overall frame of decision making applicable to bank management. The approach is based on practical experience put into concepts, with the understanding that, without working in conceptual frames, the 'small-print' syndrome cannot be avoided.

We start in Chapter 1 by defining liquidity, its risk and its relation to solvency. This serves as an introduction to the basics and lists at the end elementary but vital principles to be applied to any liquidity scheme with a chance of success. Since policy aspects of liquidity related to banking have been rather neglected until recently, Chapter 2 evaluates traditional concepts including schemes applied in corporate finance. In view of the difference in complexity between 'corporates' (i.e. non-financial firms) and banks, the key financial determinants for banks are evaluated by using a technique developed to deal with complex structures.

The key determinants are then integrated into a conceptual framework in Chapter 3. The two dominant financial risk factors in banking – loss and liquidity – are analysed and the possibility of applying to liquidity the widely accepted methods for calculating downside risk is evaluated. The chapter concludes with a conceptual framework integrating all relevant points concerning liquidity policy in banking. We then formulate the elements of the latter in Chapter 4, including contingency planning and securing the franchise of a bank. Given the significant diversity in size, structure, complexity and environment within the banking industry, we abstain from uniform recommendations. Instead, whenever possible, alternatives are presented, their pros and cons discussed and personal preferences stated if applicable.

The following two chapters address the aspects of liquidity management derived from the conclusions drawn when discussing policy elements. The subject is divided into a more qualitative and a rather quantitative part. Chapter 5 covers the former. For the purpose of presenting the key elements within the liquidity status in an aggregated high-level form, the instrument of the liquidity balance sheet is introduced. Franchise, security buffers, assets at risk, stable and non-stable funding are all defined and their interaction and relevance to liquidity management discussed, followed by specific recommendations with regard to policy as a form of feedback. Chapter 6 brings in the quantitative aspects. New mathematical methods proposed for managing liquidity risk are presented and their value assessed. For determining the size and structure of buffers, our own approach is introduced and put forward. The chapter ends with limit-related aspects and two concepts referring to transfer pricing.

In Chapter 7, dealing with stresses is analysed from the point of view of an insider. Although having inevitably encountered quite a few stressed conditions as treasurer, the author has selected both a shock (9/11) and a chronic type (name-related stress in late 2002). Preparations to withstand such occurrences as well as actually dealing with them are outlined in a real-life manner in the case of Commerzbank. Furthermore, a preliminary assessment of the subprime crisis is added. The chapter concludes with generally valid recommendations derived from the experiences.

The final chapter takes a broader view and extends this to supervisors and their role with regard to controlling liquidity risk. The issues covered address their perception vis-à-vis banks and the stability of the financial system as well as the concepts applied. This is followed by an assessment of whether and to what extent supervision is or is supposed to secure goals defined by bank management.

Rudolf Duttweiler

Acknowledgements

Any practical experience is enhanced by in-house and external communication in discussions and presentations. Many of these have formed my present view and understanding of dealing with liquidity risk and thus contributed indirectly to the book. I wish to thank my former team at Commerzbank as well as the members of the European Bank Treasurer Group of which I had the pleasure to belong for more the 10 years. Namely, ABN Amro: Rolf Smit and Karl Guha; Allied Irish: Nick Treble; BPH: Miroslaw Boniecki and Ryszard Petru; Intesa Sanpaolo: Giovanni Gorno Tempini and Stefano del Punta; Bank Austria Creditanstalt: Heinz Meidlinger; Barclays Bank: Chris Grigg and Jonathan Stone; BNP Paribas: Michel Eydoux; Danske Bank: Jens Peter Neergaard; EIB: Anneli Peshkoff; KBC Bank: Patrick Roppe; and UBS: Andreas Amschwand and Stephan Keller.

Special thanks go to Dr Kai Franzmeyer, my former head of liquidity and subsequent successor with whom many of the basic principles have been developed; to Peter Bürger and Dr Peter Bartetzky for their suggestions and critical review of specific subjects; as well as to Sandra Appelt and Sandra Hartmann who patiently and diligently transformed these ideas into graphical presentations.

Presenting the view from inside a bank requires information and consent to use it for publication purposes. My thanks for this go to the CEO, Martin Blessing and to the Executive Board of Commerzbank, represented by its member Michael Reuther.

Rudolf Duttweiler

About the Author

Rudolf Duttweiler is an economist by training with a PhD from the University of St Gallen, Switzerland. Liquidity has played an important part in all his professional life. His first practical experience of banking was gained in Zurich and London as Treasurer of the Swiss Bank Corporation (now UBS) and Credit Suisse. From 1993 until 2006 he headed the Group Treasury of Commerzbank at its headquarters in Frankfurt. This was the formative period during which a comprehensive understanding of liquidity policy and respective concepts for managing liquidity were developed. Throughout his professional life he has continued to publish and lecture on market- and liquidity-related subjects. His last publication in 2008 referred to liquidity as part of banking-related financial policy, in which the basis was laid to integrate liquidity into the framework of business policy for banking. Dr Duttweiler is a lecturer on Bank Treasury Management at the University of St Gallen.

1
Liquidity and Risk: Some Basics

The term 'liquidity' is anything but well defined. In any meaningful discussion with treasury colleagues in other banks or with controllers on liquidity, one can be confident that everybody will have a solid knowledge of liquidity and risk as terms. Often, however, it is well into the discussion before one encounters a common understanding of the specific elements on liquidity being addressed. This is somewhat surprising given the fact that the issue has been around for a very long time. Back in the nineteenth century, Knies (1876, page 249) stressed the necessity for a cash buffer to bridge negative gaps between payment inflows and outflows in cases where their timing cannot be completely regulated. In the last century the issue was also taken up and intensely discussed, as for example initiated by Stützel (1959, pages 622–629). The further discussions primarily centred on basic considerations such as the relationship between liquidity and level of solvency (Stützel, 1983, page 33f.) or the distinction between the level of liquidity reserves and its structure (Witte, 1964, page 770f.), for example.

Around the mid-1990s a new wave started, became intensified after the turn of the millennium and is still continuing. It is clearly distinct from former discussions. Its focus is on specific issues of liquidity management, but only touches policy issues related to liquidity. A selection of publications covering wider aspects, in addition to the numerous papers on very specific issues, may illustrate the point made: namely, Matz (2002), Zeranski (2005), Matz and Neu (2007) and Bartetzky, Gruber and Wehn (2008).

1.1 SOME UNDERSTANDING OF LIQUIDITY

Why then can we not relate to clearly defined terms after the subject has been dealt with for well over 100 years? The long intervals certainly have not helped. More importantly, however, banks, as one of their basic functions, are collecting points of money for the various groups within society. Thus, for most of the time, getting funds has been of little concern in itself, and this especially so if compared with employing these funds as assets in a secure and profitable manner. Furthermore, liquidity has many dimensions. The term is used to express a specific condition for a product, an institution, a market segment or even an economy, just to mention some important applications, as can be seen in Figure 1.1.

As a starting point we take the basic and most narrow definition (Box 1.1).

Liquidity thus is neither an amount nor a ratio. It rather expresses the degree to which a bank is capable of fulfilling its respective obligations. The opposite would be 'illiquidity', i.e. the lack of the respective capability to fulfil them. In this sense, liquidity represents a qualitative element of the financial strength of a bank (Duttweiler, 2008, page 30).

1.1.1 What do we know about liquidity?

The understanding of how liquidity is affected under different circumstances has improved significantly within the last decade. This is not so much because many of the aspects have been

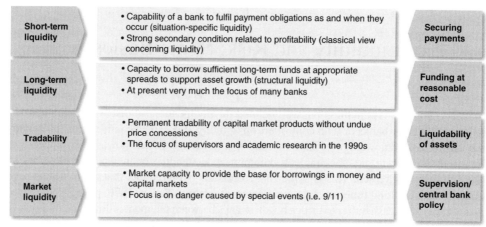

The different types of liquidity are related to each other

Figure 1.1   Different meanings of liquidity
(*Source*: Adapted from Bartetzky, 2008, page 9)

Box 1.1 Definition of liquidity

- Liquidity represents the capacity to fulfil all payment obligations as and when they fall due – to their full extent and in the currency required.
- Since it is done in cash, liquidity relates to flows of cash only. Not being able to perform leads to a condition of illiquidity.

---

known for much longer, but it is only relatively recently that methods have been developed that allow a more precise quantification. By following a selected and illustrative list of known facts, a commonly used segregation into risk types can be made:

- Volume and tenor of assets depend largely on business policy.
 - The more the long-term assets are financed with short-term liabilities, the bigger the liquidity gap will be.
- The more stable deposits do come from the retail sector, but they are structurally short term in nature. Usually, their volume is not sufficient to finance all assets on the balance sheet.
- Banks do write options to their customer base. They can differ in name, like committed lines of credit; backup lines for issuers in the commercial paper (CP) market; drawdown facilities in the mortgage finance sector; or early repayment facilities. But they are similar in character: the option may or may not be executed, or partly only; and the timing of the event is very much open to an agreed timeframe.
- If one allows for liquidity gaps to stay, the initial funding matures before the respective asset falls due. Thus, the bank will have to go into the market at a later date to finance the old asset for the remaining time till maturity.
- How easy the later financing can be executed in the market and the price one has to pay at that date in the future are not known in advance.

- Some assets are generally marketable, i.e. they can be turned into cash through selling or entering into a repo transaction for example. As conditions of instruments and markets can change, their value as liquidity is subject to alterations.
- The willingness of the market to provide funding will depend on the financial solidity of the borrowing institution, as assessed by the market at that future date.
- The financial status of a bank itself, as well as its perception by the market, are made up of various interrelated business data such as quantity and quality of risk taken on the book, capital and capital ratio, earning power and expected future trend, to mention just a few.
- There is no guarantee that one can forecast today what one's own financial status will be a few years down the road. Furthermore, one does not know how this status will be perceived by the market at that time.

When it comes to the characteristic of liquidity sources, the following distinctions are generally made: availability, maturity structure, cost structure and liquidity risk. Structurally they are usually grouped into the following four blocks:

1. Call liquidity risk: This relates to both assets and liabilities. Drawings under an option facility may be executed. Deposits can be withdrawn heavily at the earliest date possible instead of being prolonged.
2. Term liquidity risk: Payments deviate from the contractual conditions. Repayments may be delayed for example.
3. Funding liquidity risk: If an asset has not been financed congruently, the follow-up financing may have to be done under adverse conditions, i.e. at a higher spread. In extreme cases, funds may even be withdrawn heavily as explained under call risk.
4. Market liquidity risk: Market liquidity relates again to assets and liabilities. Adverse market conditions may reduce the capacity to turn marketable assets into cash or to fund the required quantity. A combination of both effects is possible as well.

Furthermore, we know that liquidity is just one element to be watched and managed within a bank. Applying a categorisation as is common in the business literature, one can start with business risk, go to customer risk, add the trinity of market, credit and operational risk, and close the circle with auxiliary risks (Figure 1.2).

As all the other items have a formative influence on liquidity status, it follows that liquidity is not a driving element but is of a subsequent nature. The question then arises about the importance of its role within the large frame of issues and risks.

1.1.2   What is the issue about liquidity?

Experience shows that most of the time it is plentiful. There are periods when it is somewhat scarce and thus at a premium pricewise. As soon as we start to consider longer periods, these differences in price will average out. Movements in spreads are not dissimilar from what a bank may experience in its other market segments. This cost is sustainable by a bank and rather a question of optimising return than securing survival.

However, it is a characteristic of liquidity that it has to be available all the time and not on average or most of the time. Payments have to be executed on the day when they are due, or the bank is declared illiquid if it fails to perform. Statistically, the chances of this happening are very low. But if it happens, the effects will be severe and could be fatal to the bank. No manager can sensibly take such a risk and play with the investments of shareholders.

Figure 1.2   Liquidity risk as one element of banking risk
(*Source*: Adapted from Bartetzky, 2008, page 11)

When talking about potential illiquidity, one should not concentrate on just the extreme case. Clearly, the ultimate stress model one can think of has to be analysed. However, this case should not be the main concern of a liquidity manager for the following reasons:

- Firstly, it is hard to imagine a single liquidity controller who would miss this. The ultimate stress case is definitely on the risk report.
- Secondly, the chances are that this stress will closely resemble something like the biblical Flood. Should one therefore build the financial equivalent of Noah's ark for this?
- Thirdly, if one did, business would be greatly restrained and earnings curtailed. This again cannot be in the interest of management.
- And lastly, liquidity strains occur more frequently on a level less severe than the Flood but still sufficiently dangerous to interrupt business for a while, making it necessary to alter the business strategy of the company, or at least elements of it.

Those people and committees responsible for securing an appropriate liquidity status in a bank will aim to keep the various types of risk at acceptable levels as well as in the form of a weighted equilibrium. Taking these goals into account, any liquidity policy has to consider the aspect of securing payment obligations on the one hand as well as allowing a subsequent earning-related business strategy on the other hand. In other words, the extremes of total neglect and the equivalent of the Flood cannot be part of the policy applied.

In the process of formulating any policy it is helpful if one can refer to the experience of similar institutions, or, better, to adapt generally agreed rules. For some aspects of banking significant progress has been made in this respect. On the question of capital adequacy, the systematic to rate customers that the bank is exposed to or the principles applied to assess market risk for example, rules exist which are comparable beyond national borders. As these rules are similar, it helps banks to refer to an accepted standard while allowing them to compare institutions against each other. Unfortunately, that stage has not yet been reached regarding liquidity. National rules applied by the respective supervisors can still differ greatly from country to country. Endeavours towards reaching an effective and comparable systematic for liquidity as well are on their way, but for the time being it means adhering to national rules and, in case they do not keep up with the complexity of one's own institution, developing liquidity concepts which appropriately cover in-house needs.

1.1.3   How to look at liquidity

As stated earlier, liquidity represents a qualitative element of the financial strength of a bank or institution. Although true, management looks at liquidity in a more practical way and generally differentiates the following aspects (Figure 1.3).

1.1.3.1   Level of aggregation

In our case, aggregation incorporates several dimensions (Box 1.2) such as amount, currency and time factor. Which level to choose is not easy to advise. Supervisors or controllers seem to have a preference for rules on an aggregated level. No doubt the latter has the advantage of concentrated information with few figures to deal with. It is almost inevitable that the highest possible level will be aggregated if one wishes to use ratios. They have become very popular. Ratios are relatively easy to benchmark and to compare. Moreover, there is no need to look at many details. What weight do we then put on the question of currency mix?

- For a bank hardly extending its activities outside its own currency area the answer is easy. There will be the odd payment in foreign currency. It has to be taken care of within the frame of correspondent banking. Moreover, we do not seriously distort reality if small amounts are shown in local currency equivalents.
- It is a different matter in the case of large multi-currency banks. They may have sufficient liquidity overall, but concentrated in one or a few currencies. As long as markets work in

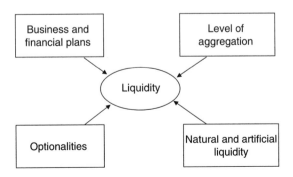

Figure 1.3   Aspects of liquidity

> **Box 1.2 Principle to be applied for aggregation**
>
> Keeping all the possibilities and the respective implications in mind, one can only advise maintaining information on liquidity as detailed as possible, even if it is not required by supervisors and controllers.

a satisfactory way, balances can be closed in time through short-dated foreign exchange transactions. At the moment disturbances occur, the system may no longer work smoothly, however.

- In cases where geographical locations are far apart, we may be acting in two different time zones. Clearing deadline in Tokyo tends to be at midnight in New York, i.e. outside working hours. Furthermore, amounts may be out of the general pattern from time to time. In both cases a proper infrastructure as well as working relationships with banks in foreign centres are required to cover larger liquidity needs in a short period of time.
- The potential danger of illiquidity is not limited to main currencies. Failing to perform can also stretch to modestly used currencies and still be followed by severe repercussions.

1.1.3.2   Natural and artificial liquidity

Natural in this sense relates to flows from maturing assets or liabilities. Artificial liquidity is created through the capacity to transform an asset into cash before the maturity date is reached. The process can be achieved, for example, through a sale or a repo transaction with the market or by using the instrument as collateral with the central bank. Technically, it is known as shiftability and marketability. Assets with these characteristics are thus generally called 'marketable'.

There are two points which we should introduce now. They will be important when we address the question of forecasting implications under various scenarios:

- For most of the time a specific security may easily be transformed into cash. The market for this product is mostly deep and wide. As long as a single firm wishes to turn a security into cash the market is capable of absorbing the transaction. Even the price of the security will not be negatively affected. As soon as large groups of investors are faced with the same needs, the market may become out of balance. It may take longer to execute the desired volume. At the same time, sellers may be faced with a shift in pricing against them.
- Natural liquidity refers to the legal maturities. Especially in banking, a transaction with a customer at maturity is often rolled over, either for the same amount or a smaller/larger one. The customer base in total behaves mostly in a rather predictable way. For specific portfolios one will experience a pattern in prolongation. This is true not only for assets but also for liabilities.

The main point is that customers expect certain behaviour from their chosen institution. They want to be sure they can reinvest or borrow again after the prior transaction has matured. Commercial customers need working capital. The nature of each drawing may be short term but the line will be used frequently. The relationship they keep with the specific bank includes a basic understanding of reliability: namely, that business will be continued. The legal view

---

Box 1.3 The term 'optionalities'

The term 'optionalities' expresses the commitment of a bank equal to that of an option seller.

Optionalities can relate to assets or liabilities; on- or off-balance-sheet transactions.

---

on maturities to assess future gaps in liquidity neglects all these expectations. Leaving your customers out in the rain undermines your franchise and thus your own future as a bank. If any liquidity policy aims at surviving not only as a legal entity but also as a bank with its customer base intact, a different approach is required. We call it the 'business view', in contrast to the legal or accounting perspective, an approach which takes into account that the franchise is too valuable to be neglected.

1.1.3.3 Optionalities (Box 1.3)

The option market, whether exchange traded or over the counter (OTC), has increased impressively in the last few decades. The number of option buyers has spread through all markets. They are willing to pay a premium for the right to choose whether or not to execute the contract at the agreed respective date. Simultaneously, their counterparts have grown in numbers as well. Ready to wait for the decision of the buyer, they receive compensation from the buyer in the form of a premium. The magnitude of some markets has reached levels which have made it advisable for supervisors to introduce controls and some restrictions.

The risk is asymmetric between counterparts in options. The buyer of a contract for paying a premium can choose whether to execute the deal or not. The buyer's maximum cost is defined by the premium paid. The earning potential, if the market goes the buyer's way, is only limited by the extent of the market move. For the seller of an option it is the reverse. First the seller gets a premium but then price movements of the respective product determine the seller's earnings or losses. Such earnings are limited to the premium received. Losses are a result of market moves against the seller. That is the principle, although any position will be managed and not left to the mercy of the market.

Liquidity in this segment can be affected in three ways:

1. The pure cash element: Whatever is 'paid' for premiums or losses, it will be an outflow of cash. And whatever is 'received' as premium or profit is an inflow of cash. To compute the effects on liquidity after options have been revalued may be cumbersome but is not difficult. To assess the future flows to be generated by options is, however, a challenge. Flows will depend on market price behaviour, which in itself is not predictable. The best one can go for is approximation. Today there are techniques available to do this. They are not perfect but give an acceptable degree of information on what might happen.

2. The seller of options may feel uncomfortable with the position held and thus will try to reduce or even square it. The principle one is working with is based on the assumption of moving quickly and with negligible loss, i.e. assuming a perfect or at least an absorbing market. A tightening in the derivative market could pass through to the cash market if too many position takers were to undo their exposure at the same time. The reason could also lie in the cash market itself due to systemic liquidity problems. Either way, risk parameters are no longer the same. It will take longer to get out of a position and almost certainly

prices will move against the seller. As a consequence we will have to cater not only for normal but also for stressed market conditions as well.

One may argue that the respective implications on profit and loss just mentioned should not be related to liquidity but to earnings. This is a valid point, but only in principle. Where margin calls are standard there is a specific injection of liquidity required, be it at the end of the day or during the day. It does not help to create earnings somewhere in the bank and compensate them with margin requirements. Earnings may not be followed by a corresponding flow of cash. Depending on bookkeeping and market rules, accounting for earnings may deviate from the actual flow of cash in timing. Furthermore, even if cash does actually flow, it may not be available at the place and time needed. Thus margin accounts have to be managed properly and separately to avoid failing to fulfil payment obligations. This point was addressed earlier when we discussed the proper level of aggregation (1.1.3.1).

 For many institutions it is the third aspect related to liquidity which can alter cash flows significantly as well as abruptly. Banks and in particular commercial banks support and service their client base with standby facilities. Clients need them for possible and unforeseeable events when cash need rises beyond the normal credit lines granted. Lines of credit for working capital are one channel. Depending on seasonal fluctuations in sales of goods and services as well as payment patterns, utilisation of the line may oscillate within a wide band. The movements may be smooth or jumpy and volatile. Standby letters of credit and CP backup lines belong to the same group of standby facilities. It is common to both that they are not used for primary financing. Utilisation of these lines will be triggered only when the channel of primary financing is closed for whatever reason. Over the years banks have rarely been called to back up. To provide and develop this kind of service became attractive. Without actually lending and using much capital, income was still received in the form of fees. However, the magnitude of the risk involved for many a bank materialised during preparations for Y2K (switching computers to the year 2000). On looking into the matter it soon became apparent how a simple technical failure in IT could trigger an injection of liquidity by the guaranteeing bank. And the potential sums involved often were not at all small.

Security settlement and clearing as well as correspondent banking services are further areas. Within limits customers can draw on the bank at their discretion and debit or credit their account respectively. In various countries borrowers in the mortgage market are given the right to early amortisation and repayment. In other words, the cash can flow earlier than originally agreed.

From a purist's point of view, this definition may have stretched the term 'option' somewhat. There are, however, good reasons for putting all these banking products under a single heading. They have one thing in common: once the bank has agreed to provide the service, it has largely put itself into the position of an option seller. Whether or not, when and to what extent the option will be utilised are solely at the discretion of the option buyer – the bank's customer. The amounts of required cash can be very substantial, but hardly predictable.

1.1.3.4   *Business and financial plan*

Within the planning process of a firm, strategic decisions concerning short-, medium- and long-term goals are made. Elements can be enlarging or reducing investments, entering new markets or market segments, or changing finance-related business activities on assets as well

---

Box 1.4 Liquidity and business policy

Business policy impacts strongly on the liquidity structure of a bank. The former has thus to be looked at as a 'driving' force.

---

as liabilities. They are an important source and should not be neglected when anticipating future needs for liquidity (Box 1.4).

For our later analysis we must stress two vital principles that we get from this process:

- Firstly, liquidity is too often looked at from a static point of view. To a certain extent it has to do with both the need to collect data and to report them to banking supervisors. What one gets is the outlook based on the accounting data from yesterday or the last month end. It is similar to planning a trip and basing the weather forecast on the conditions prevailing during the previous week. However, what is needed is a dynamic approach where actions affecting the future status of liquidity are incorporated to the largest extent possible. The process of business and financial planning supports this need – at least for effects derived from management decisions.
- Secondly, when net earnings are calculated a firm will follow accounting rules. Accruals, revaluation earnings/losses on assets and liabilities, amortisation, just to mention some of the items, are taken to arrive at the result. Not all of them trigger a corresponding flow in cash. In fact it works in two ways: some of the income and cost of the accounting period presented will induce a flow in cash at a later date. In the case of long-term credit lending, for example, earnings are calculated on an accrual basis. In accounting terms, for each day and thus each month, the precise income is computed and shown. According to the contract, interest will be paid in intervals of 3 or 6 months. Cash thus flows only in longer intervals and not daily or monthly. When bought securities are revalued, the result is reflected in the profit and loss statement of the period under consideration. The cash will flow later, either at maturity or when the security is sold. Conversely, we will recognise cash from payments made and received from transactions already considered by accounting in earlier periods. As a consequence, as much as integrating planned activities help to assess future flows, a high-level view is not sufficient. One has to work with a precise time schedule.

1.2   THE MEANING OF LIQUIDITY RISK

In the previous section we looked at liquidity and some of its major determinants. We recognised how important it is to be clear about the strategic goals: the franchise one wishes to protect puts limits on flexibly adjusting exposures in order to lower the cash needed. Acting as an option seller opens up a whole range of channels through which cash may be drawn. Whether or not, to what extent and when cash is called for are largely open. Planning in the sector of option-related products requires the use of methods of approximation and probability. We also fully appreciated that liquidity is flow of cash. The term does not include any monetary value if it is not turned into cash in the period under consideration. The change in one's status of cash and flow of cash does not, however, necessarily imply any risk at all. As an institution you may still be in a position to fulfil your obligations to pay as, when, where and in the currency and amount needed.

Box 1.5 Definition of liquidity risk

Liquidity risk represents the danger of not being able to fulfil payment obligations, whereby the failure to perform is followed by undesirable consequences.

So the danger is that you cannot fulfil your obligations and the failure to perform may have undesirable consequences. The term 'danger' has been used on purpose, although the condition is usually expressed by the term 'risk'. The expression 'risk' in many understandings simply means a deviation from the expected outcome. The concern in our case is limited to an undesirable deviation, because, if it were not undesirable, why should we concern ourselves? Thus, our general understanding will be: liquidity risk is the possibility that the capacity may not be sufficient to fulfil payment obligations when and where they fall due (Box 1.5); that not performing the duties in full will have undesirable consequences up to and including company failure.

Before entering more deeply into liquidity risk let us review some strongly related items, namely solvency, interest rate risk and market risk. Each one has its own characteristics. At the same time they correspond partly to each other but definitely with liquidity risk. In later chapters we will refer to them time and again. Therefore, we will start with a common understanding of how to use these terms.

1.2.1 Liquidity versus solvency

To be solvent signifies being able to cover losses. They may occur for various reasons like too high a cost base compared with earnings (business risk); loans may not be repaid as some of the customers have failed (credit risk); trading positions may have gone wrong (market risk). On the operational side (operational risk) significant costs may have occurred through legal compensation or fallout from technical systems, to mention a couple of possibilities.

The risks may materialise singly or in combination. In any case, if for any of these reasons the profit and loss account turns negative, payments have to come out of a buffer, which is the capital of the company. The Basel Committee emphasises the importance of capital in particular as it declares the ratios of credit and market risk to capital as key elements of supervisors' control. Does that mean the lower the risk ratios and thus the bigger the capital buffer, the better the quality of solvency and hence the smaller the liquidity risk? Is it a possible chain reaction?

 In a certain way, yes it is, but with some reservations. Reserves in the form of capital are available to bear for the losses. As long as capital can cover losses the company is solvent. Can it also pay the bills? Not necessarily. Capital may be invested in assets which cannot be turned easily into cash. Payments are to be made in cash, however. If payments cannot be fulfilled the bank will be illiquid, with all the consequences following that situation. Obviously, a company can be solvent and illiquid at the same time.

What then is the relationship between solvency and liquidity (Box 1.6)? Solvency is a condition of having sufficient capital to cover losses. In a narrower sense solvency is an expression of capital adequacy. In a wider sense solvency requires additionally having ready money available when payments have to be fulfilled. In other words, a sound capital base is a necessary condition but is not sufficient in itself. A link also exists the other way around. To be liquid requires being solvent in the first place. If a firm is left without capital it will not have ready money to pay the bills.

Box 1.6 The relationship between solvency and liquidity

A positive status of solvency is a precondition for being liquid. As liquidity, in contrast to solvency, is solely cash related, it is possible to be solvent and illiquid at the same time.

There is a third link as well. Liquidity as flows of cash is very much determined by the behaviour of the customer base and business counterparts in general. For them, the status of solvency indeed influences their relationship with the bank. This is not limited to their considerations of whether to invest with your bank in whatever form, e.g. deposit with you, buying bonds issued in your name or holding shares in your company. Your status also affects your asset side. The customer base, for the sake of its own financial stability, inevitably watches and assesses a bank in respect of willingness and ability to secure their own financial needs – at least within a certain framework.

In one way or another, we touched upon these elements when dealing with the customer franchise. The angle then was a different one. There we put forward the question of how flexibly management can act on restricting cash outflow, when it wants to protect its customer franchise. This time, we will have a look at the customer base and ask how it will react in the light of status regarding solvency.

How then do counterparts form a view about the condition of solvency and liquidity? It is too early to go into details at this time. At the moment there is only one fact we should keep in mind. No outsider, whether customer or market, knows the liquidity status of an institution. A view will be formed based on various information but not on detailed knowledge. Thus one could say that it is not so much the actual status, but the perceived status, which directs their actions. Whether or not the perception reflects the truth has no immediate impact on their behaviour. As we stated earlier, liquidity is neither an amount nor a ratio. It is a qualitative element of a firm's financial position.

1.2.2 Liquidity versus interest rate risk

We covered this subject briefly when referring to the business and financial plan (1.1.3.4), stressing why focusing on cash is crucial.

At first sight, both liquidity and interest rate risk can be viewed in a similar way when it comes to gapping. If, from lending to customers, one has got an interest exposure 6 months long in an amount of 20 million euros, the risk manager has various choices on how to handle the risk. But let us assume that the decision enters into a compensating transaction, e.g. borrowing the same amount for 6 months. Now the interest rate (IR) risk position is fully closed. That is the example on interest rate risk. On liquidity it works the same way. As long as borrowing and lending are equal in amount, currency and tenor, the positions are closed and any gap is eliminated. In a way, a systemic relationship exists between gaps in interest rate and in liquidity, given certain conditions. We will now evaluate the conditions by adding further instruments related to on- and off-balance-sheet transactions.

In the following example (see Figure 1.4 and Table 1.1) we enter into a few money market transactions in cash and compare the gaps in the interest rate and liquidity positions respectively.

In order to distinguish clearly the effects on the liquidity and interest rate sensitivity reports respectively, we will address the issue in three steps. We start with some short-term transactions

Assets:	(1) 100 units 6 months of advances to customers
	(2) 50 units 3 months of CP bought
	(3) 30 units 5 years of floating rate loans with 6 months of rollovers
	(4) 20 units 2 years of floating rate loans with 3 months of rollovers
Liabilities:	(5) 70 units 3 months of customer deposits
	(6) 20 units 3 months of customer deposits
	(7) 80 units 1 month of interbank deposits
	(8) 30 units 6 months of CP
Hedge:	(9) FRA bought 100 units 1–6 months
Current:	(10) The sum of assets to be financed, i.e. (1) till (4)
	(11) The sum of liabilities to be financed, i.e. (5) till (8)

Figure 1.4   The transactions used

and later add long-term commitments with interest rates adjusted during the lifetime of the contract. Finally, we hedge part of the interest rate position with a derivative contract (FRA = Future Rate Agreement).

We recognise the gaps on both sides as being equal. The lack of deviation derives from the fact that interest rates are fixed for the same period as applies for liquidity. If we take transaction 5, for example, the interest rate is fixed for the period of 3 months. In this case it coincides with the contractual period, which is the determinant for liquidity.

In Example 2 (Table 1.2) we continue using cash transactions only, with one alteration added. Some of the transactions are of longer maturities with interest rates fixed in shorter intervals (so-called floaters).

Although we still stick exclusively to cash transactions, the systemic relationship recognised in the prior example is broken. Gaps are not equal. While liquidity is using as its parameter the tenor when cash actually flows, interest rate gaps are determined by the structure of interest payments. When taking transaction 4, for example, the underlying commitment relevant to liquidity is for 2 years; the interest rate is, however, fixed for 3 months only.

When interest rate risk is managed in a commercial or financial institution it is not done with cash instruments alone. Very often cash may not even be used primarily. Interest derivatives such as futures, swaps, options, swaptions, etc., play an accepted role in risk management.

Table 1.1   Example 1: transactions 1, 2, 5 and 7

Month	Liquidity Report		Net	IR sensitivity Report		Net
Current	−150 (10)	+150 (11)	0	−150 (10)	+150 (11)	0
			—			—
1		−80 (7)	−80		−80 (7)	−80
3	+50 (2)	−70 (5)	−20	+50 (2)	−70 (5)	−20
6	+100 (1)		100	+100 (1)		100
			—			—
Balance			Nil			Nil

Table 1.2   Example 2: adding transactions 3, 4, 6 and 8

Month	Liquidity report		Net	IR sensitivity report		Net
Current	− 200 (10)	+ 200 (11)	0	− 200 (10)	+ 200 (11)	0
			────			────
1		−80 (7)	−80		−80 (7)	−80
3	+ 50 (2)	−70 (5)	−40	+ 50 (2)	−70 (5)	−20
		− 20 (6)		+ 20 (4)	−20 (6)	
6	+ 100 (1)			+ 100 (1)		100
		−30 (8)	70	+ 30 (3)	−30 (8)	
2 years		+ 20 (4)	20			
5 years		+ 30 (3)	30			
Balance			Nil			Nil

Irrespective of their risk behaviour, when utilising them, no payments of principal are involved. The differences between interest rate and liquidity gaps may thus be even more accentuated.

For illustrative purposes we leave physical deals as in Example 2. However, to reduce the interest rate risk, the interest rate gaps beyond 3 months' maturity are to be closed with a derivative transaction (Table 1.3).

The interest hedge of transaction 9 has eliminated all gaps in interest exposure beyond the 3 months' period. As no principal and thus no cash are flowing, the liquidity status has not been affected at all.

The three examples tell us that the systemic relationship between risk in interest rates and liquidity exists under very restrictive conditions only. Transactions need to be in cash and with the interest rate fixed for the whole contractual period. Adjustments of rates during the lifetime of the contract and using derivatives cause gaps to differ.

In the extreme case where interest rate risks were created solely through derivatives, no position of payments of principal would occur on the liquidity balance sheet. Would that also mean that no cash would flow at all? Not necessarily, as there may be subsequent flows of cash. Transactions after conclusion undergo changes in value whenever the actual market price moves up or down. The trading instruments are usually valued mark to market on a daily

Table 1.3   Example 3: hedging part of IR position of Example 2

Month	Liquidity report		Net	IR sensitivity report		Net
Current	− 200 (10)	+ 200 (11)	0	− 200 (10)	+ 200 (11)	0
1		− 80 (7)	−80	+ 100 (9)	− 80 (7)	20
3	+ 50 (2)	− 70 (5)	−40	+ 50 (2)	− 70 (5)	−20
		− 20 (6)		+ 20 (4)	− 20 (6)	
6	+ 100 (1)	− 30 (8)	70	+ 100 (1)	− 30 (8)	
				+ 30 (3)	− 100 (9)	N/L
2 years		+ 20 (4)	20			
5 years		+ 30 (3)	30			
Balance			Nil			Nil

basis. Contractual agreements between the parties involved may demand compensation to each other daily for the balances accrued. To do so, cash payments are involved. Official exchanges have worked on this principle since the inception of derivative contracts. In the OTC market, compensating positive and negative values during the lifetime of a deal is not obligatory. Many participants nevertheless see the benefit in joining netting systems with margin calls attached. In this way credit risk exposures may be significantly reduced.

However, under any circumstance and if no intermediate compensation had been agreed, the required payments have to be fulfilled at the end of the contractual period, and this has to be done in cash. True, the amounts are small compared with volumes generated by cash instrument, where the principal is exchanged as well. With many of the big players the sum of cash changing hands every day due to margin calls alone can still be substantial and thus relevant for liquidity management.

There are further asymmetric conditions one can find when optionalities come into play.

We do not refer to the standby facilities, the group of options which, when utilised, trigger an outflow of cash. Assume that a customer suddenly and quite unexpectedly can no longer draw funding from the CP market. For this case the customer would have gained an assurance from the bank of a backup line. The customer will now utilise his or her right and the bank will pay on the basis of the agreement. In this case the bank's interest position will immediately be affected according to the specifications of the transaction. So also will the liquidity position, as the loan is a cash outflow with the specifications of the same transaction. Both the interest and the liquidity balance sheets carry risk as shown in Example 1 where the condition is a symmetric one.

What we are referring to is an asymmetric pattern as, for instance, with early amortisation. The mortgage loan may have been granted many years previously. Final maturity is still some years ahead. The bank at the beginning of the contract had secured funding and eliminated any interest rate risk. If the mortgage is paid back earlier, the bank has a new risk position in interest rates. The financial implications will depend on how far the present rates for the remaining period differ from the contractual ones. It could result in unexpected income or cost. Early amortisation also means having the cash back already, although the related funding has still not matured. In our definition of liquidity risk, there is none in this case. We certainly have the capacity to fulfil the payment obligation when it falls due, as cash has already been returned. In the short term, or till the maturity date of the funds borrowed, we are indeed over-liquid.

To sum up: based on typical bank transactions we compared implied risk on liquidity and interest rate in some detail. We found singular types of transactions where a symmetric condition is inherent. Indeed, there are also many types where it is not. What does this imply? Let us visualise a typical balance sheet of a bank, consisting of short- and long-term assets as well as liabilities. Then we look at the lines below the balance sheet with all the derivatives to hedge the interest rate risks and at the optionalities granted and properly listed. What are the chances of arriving at a predictable relationship between the two risks? One would say close to zero. Thus again it is advisable to have separate and detailed calculations. One should not be tempted to derive liquidity from interest rate gaps, for the sake of simplicity only.

1.2.3 Liquidity risk versus market liquidity risk

When we asked about how to look at liquidity, among other issues we differentiated between natural and artificial liquidity (1.1.3.2). The latter, we concluded, is created through the capacity to transform an asset into cash before the maturity date is reached. The term used to state the level of how easy or difficult the transformation may be is 'level of marketability'. Depth, breadth and resilience of a market seem to be helpful indicators to judge a market's capability of turning assets into cash at negligible cost (Schwartz and Francioni, 2004, page 60f.).

The market size is a good first indicator. Marketable securities for example, be it stocks or bonds, generally are held by a large number of investors. The more there are, the greater is the interest declared to buy and sell close to above and below the prevailing price. The markets for German Bunds and US Treasury Bills fit well into this category. If larger orders are put into the market there are sufficient bids and offers in the pipeline to restore a reasonable market value.

Even if markets are liquid, prices are affected by specific determinants. A large portfolio manager for example or a group of market participants may decide to buy or sell an influential portion of a financial commodity over a very short period. The disparity in supply and demand will cause prices to move up or down. As long as a new level of market price equilibrium is found within a short space of time, the market has proven to be liquid.

More likely, markets are affected by news. Economic data may indicate future pressure on interest rates. Committee members of a central bank's policy body talk in a hawkish manner. A company's chief executive is delighted to announce increased earnings beyond market expectations. Whatever is said, the information will be analysed, digested and the new market price will incorporate the news. Indeed, most likely not at the level it was before.

To call an asset liquid does not imply a stable value irrespective of the period under consideration. Even the most liquid markets over time will see prices rise and fall. Nevertheless, the market has depth and width all the time. Larger sums could be placed short term.

Negligible in our understanding refers to execution cost. These costs are expressed in small or wide spreads and the accepted size of a single transaction. In other words, they reflect the level of liquidity of the market. When spreads are low, the market is liquid and capable of absorbing larger orders. Whether the market price stays at historic highs or lows is not the point. In a large market with no dominant or oligopolistic groups, the process of making decisions is widely decentralised. Whenever prices deviate from equilibrium a new sustainable level will be found. In a large, decentralised and transparent market the process of reaching the new equilibrium will take a short period of time. In other words, the market is resilient as new orders are soon available.

The shorter the period that the market maker has to wait for other orders, the more he or she will feel comfortable in quoting and holding resulting positions temporarily. In these market conditions the market maker can then lower his or her risk protection, of which the tightening of the bid-offered spread is one indicator. The volume of orders taken follows the same principle. A market maker who can assume the ability to replace larger volumes quickly in the market can also offer a fixed price for larger orders. If spreads are thus tight and transaction volumes large, a market can be said to be highly liquid. Execution cost then is low and therefore negligible for a liquidity manager.

But how liquid is liquid? Up to now we have referred to market liquidity in relative terms. Our assessment was based on how much the market can absorb in a given period of time. Implicitly one talks about a share or a percentage of the market volume outstanding: 1%, 2% or 5%? When it comes to volumes, equity markets cannot be compared with large debt markets. Even the company with the largest market value is small in comparison, and one has to look at each single stock. The same is true for regional debt markets or segments like small sovereign and company debt markets. In addition, when we consider that only a fraction of the total outstanding is available in the marketplace at any given time, we are talking about significant differences in amounts. Liquidity managers at times require large quantities, however. Here again the restriction applies: to hold assets of markets which are liquid is a necessary condition;

however, this requirement may not be sufficient when considering the volumes demanded and compared with the absorptive capacity.

From experience everybody will accept that small markets with only a few participants and low average daily turnover in relation to total outstanding are not liquid. If it takes days and weeks to absorb the holding it is definitely not prime liquidity in the view of a liquidity manager. The chances that this may change for the better soon are quite slim. What about liquid markets then – may they change for the worse all of a sudden?

The bigger the market and the better the quality of the issuer(s), the less likely this is to happen. However, it cannot be fully excluded. For a liquidity manager this is especially critical if the need for cash is primarily triggered by general market circumstances, such as a crash. In extreme conditions it may affect this manager's funding capability as well as using marketable assets in order to create cash. In such a case the problem is caused by the segments on which the liquidity manager relies for cash.

1.2.4   Ways to close the gap

Liquidity gaps do arise in the normal course of business activity. Referring to the examples presented above, we considered some normal business transactions to illustrate the respective effects on both the liquidity and the interest risk position. Now we will address the question of the form in which they may present themselves and how to deal with them.

1.2.4.1   General observations

Liquidity risk was defined as the possibility that the capacity may not be sufficient to fulfil payment obligations when and where they fall due, and that not performing the duties in full will have undesirable consequences up to company failure.

For commercial companies it is natural to have a surplus of assets over self-created liabilities in the form of capital, reserves and retained profits. In a stage of growing the business fast it would hardly be possible to accumulate in-house financing at the speed and volume necessary to keep up with assets. Even if it were possible, management in these companies would have learnt a long time ago not to do so for economic reasons. Going for capital is an expensive way to get financed. Mixing the company's own means with external financing from the market or a bank produces improved return on capital, at least for companies with a reasonable level of profitability.

Is this method of argumentation applicable to banks as well? When one raises the point with colleagues in the banking sector the answers are mixed. There are three basic lines of argumentation leading to the answers, as follows.

Many bankers are of the opinion that applying the argument to banks would be like comparing apples with pears. The reasoning refers to the different types of products employed. A chemical company buys the raw materials and sells chemical products. A car maker largely buys semi-produced components and sells finished cars. Even the travel industry partly buys hotel rooms for a season as well as airline tickets and sells holiday packages. The banks, in contrast, buy 'money' (borrow) and sell 'money' (lend). The distinction between money as a product and money as a part of finance is blurred and applying the argument to banking is thus not useful, so they say.

Representatives from large and in particular internationally active banks understand the distinction between money as a product (borrowing/lending as part of business in operating units) and money as a part of finance (closing the remaining gaps through shareholder capital and wholesale funding). They tend, however, to disagree with the conclusions, i.e. to search for the optimal mix. Their business-induced balance sheet also carries assets that are much larger than the self-created liabilities. They argue that their product is money and not goods, but just like commercial companies they have to secure their financing through third parties because capital is too small a part to close the gap.

Savings banks, the third group, usually cannot follow this chain of argumentation. They stress their special client base in the retail sector. According to their experience, they claim that the behaviour of retail customers is stable. Deposits placed with them can be relied on. In fact, if they are driven at all, they are rather liability driven, quite in contrast to large and international banks.

If by and large the assessments of the various factions in the banking industry are correct concerning the position they are in, the majority in terms of numbers, i.e. the savings banks, would be in a comfortable position. Liquidity for them seems to be a non-event. Large banks on the other hand seem to be in the same boat as industrial companies. If this is indeed true, we may learn from the long experience from the latter.

1.2.4.2 The liability approach $\Rightarrow$ *The bank's borrowing + deposits*

The Comptroller of the Currency's handbook (2001, page 13f.) calls it liability liquidity. The institutions in this case are asset driven. Typically, their loan portfolio is a large, if not a dominant, item on the balance sheet. To close the financial gap, the banks refer to external financing. To do this, various channels and numerous products are available for tapping. Basically, one distinguishes between private customers, corporate customers and the financial market. Products range from savings accounts to money-market-related deposits, from CDs (Certificates of Deposits) and CPs to bonds and equities issued. In order to avoid becoming dependent on a single market segment, any funding policy has to be based on diversification. It might be done by products or investor type (Box 1.7).

When it comes to investor behaviour the funding sources available cannot be taken as one coherent group. The sensitivity to credit risk and interest rates, the reaction to economic and market conditions, as well as to the financial conditions of the funding bank, differ. The line drawn from experience is between retail and wholesale. The latter comprises funds from corporate customers and the markets. Tapping a specific market largely determines the maximum tenor of funds available. In the money markets a maturity of longer than 3 months is available but the vast majority of deals and volumes is performed in the short end. Investor sensitivity and maturities of funds will now be considered in more detail.

Retail funding *deposits* Retail bankers and liquidity managers both value retail funds highly, but not for the same reasons. For the retail banker they are an important element of customer franchise. Once a customer keeps funds with the bank a relationship exists. Information at least about some of the means available for possible investments in securities or funds is at

---

Box 1.7 Determinants of liability funding

Liability funding is determined by the behavioural attitudes of the types of lenders. They may respond to name or institution as well as market-related conditions.

hand. In addition, these types of liabilities are relatively cheap and a source of income to the manager of the operative unit, if an interbank-related transfer price system with the treasury exists. Nevertheless, the natural focus of a retail banker is not funding.

The retail banker will endeavour to offer clients attractive investment products. They may be funding vehicles of the banker's own institution and thus mean only a liability switch. In all other cases, funds are redirected to third-party issuers or investment funds, causing a reduction in liability liquidity. As markets change, so do attractive investment opportunities. In periods of booming markets parts of retail funds will find their way into alternative products. On the other hand, when markets turn negative the more secure deposits may become attractive again – even at the price of lower nominal return.

Liquidity managers value retail funds for their relative stability and resilience. No doubt the market cycles just mentioned do affect the volume available, but over periods and usually not all of a sudden. The cost factor as well presents itself as somewhat different for liquidity managers. Funds may be cheaper for the retail manager, but if transferred at market-related prices the advantage to wholesale funds is rather negligible for liquidity management. Conversely, retail customers are less likely to withdraw deposits or fail to renew them because of some adverse developments or publicity at the bank. The reasons for this behaviour are manifold, whereby the deposit insurance scheme existing in many countries definitely plays a part which should not be underestimated. For the liquidity manager this relative stability is important as it provides a basis for assessing funding need.

On the other hand, it would not be appropriate to take the stability for granted. The rules set by German supervisors, for example, define a possible outflow for saving deposits under severe circumstances of up to 10%, although they are included in the deposit insurance scheme. We have to assume further that intensity of customer contact and geographical proximity have an impact as well. Retail customers in regions where the bank is less known will probably act faster than those in its prime domain where it may have been established and present for a hundred years or more.

The policy of attracting new retail customers has intensified in the last few years. In Europe, for example, interest rate levels at one point were extremely low, persisting over a long period of time. To attract this customer base, some of the banks offered deposit rates above the level in the interbank market. The volumes accumulated in a short period of time were impressive. Even a strongly performing equity market was not detrimental to the trend in Germany. Nevertheless, it poses some questions for the liquidity manager: What is the probability that rapidly accumulated retail flows will be as resilient as normal retail deposits? Can one put them in the same category as the traditional stock of retail funds? From a liquidity manager's point of view, a distinction and separation is crucial. A customer segment that has already shown a high level of flexibility is very likely to be equally agile.

In the introduction to this section we referred to diversification of funding by products or investor type. Regional proximity and intensity of relationship indicate an emphasis on customer type rather than on products. The application of this principle nevertheless requires detailed analyses and differentiated application.

Wholesale funding   For many banks it is the wholesale market from which they get most of their funding. Their business strategy involves accumulation of assets for which there is not sufficient retail funding or their own means available. Providers of wholesale funds typically are large industrial and commercial corporations, banks and other financial institutions, government agencies and some smaller groups.

Using the wholesale market has benefits for the liquidity manager. The markets are made up of professionals and amounts offered can be large. It is an easy and quick way to cover substantial needs. Having to deal with professionals requires knowledge and consideration of the prevailing rules and specifications. Compared with the retail sector, specifications are more complex and often structured.

Professional managers act on behalf of their institution (commercial or financial corporation or bank) or their clients (funds). Being assessed on net return, they are highly sensitive to any deterioration in credit quality of the institution they invest in. Adverse movements in interest rates will also reduce the value of financial assets. Especially with the principle of valuing mark to market of more and more items on the balance sheet, the sensitivity to changes in interest rates has grown simultaneously.

Actual drops in wholesale funding can be substantial, even fatal. According to studies, including one from the Federal Reserve Bank of New York, four of the banks analysed each lost sensitive funding in the region of 25% of total liability within about 6 months (Matz, 2002, page 83f.). In the end all of them failed. This demonstrates that wholesale funds can be highly volatile and the consequences extremely harsh. We will thus follow up the question of whether there are marked differences and, if the answer is positive, how they impact funding policy:

- Unsecured funding: Depending on the bank, much if not most of the funding is done on an unsecured basis. Money market maturities range up to 2 years, but concentrate on periods up to 3 months. Most of the flows stem from daily cash management of companies and banks. In the process of managing daily payment in- and outflows, positive and negative balances do occur. What is required is an efficient and uncomplicated market where the balances can be squared without large administrative effort.

  The market for unsecured funds covers this need. The credit risk is managed and monitored through limits. Whether they are set generously or tightly is determined by the financial health of the institution one is ready to place deposits with. The nature of business requirements does not allow for accepting larger risks. Any deterioration in credit standing will immediately cause a respective downward adjustment in limits set for that institution. From a borrower's point of view, this type of funding can thus diminish rapidly.

  Unsecured funding can also be obtained by tapping the capital market, be it in the form of medium-term notes or bonds. The main purpose is not to use them as an instrument for managing cash but to finance longer term assets on the balance sheet. Because of the long maturities it will take years until repayment of these assets is due. Assessing the future financial health of the borrower so many years ahead is more difficult than gaining a perception of the money market instruments with a range of up to 3–6 months. The element of uncertainty as well as anticipation of the borrower's trend in financial strength is compensated by the spread to be paid. As a benchmark top-rated issues like Bunds and US Treasuries are taken. The more the perceived quality of a borrower deviates negatively from the benchmark, the wider the spread and the higher the interest to be paid will be.

  Textbooks usually list the credit quality of the borrower and also developments of interest rates as qualitative elements. Our observations indicate that interest rate moves no longer play such a vital role. True, if interest rates rise, bonds acquired before and at a lower rate will face a drop in market value. Their price will fall below the issue price. Portfolio managers for this reason do not invest as much in rates as in spreads. By hedging the underlying risk with a swap transaction, for example, their position is neutral and not subject to interest rate fluctuations. The attitude of asset managers with a view to total return might be different. The value of their portfolio suffers whenever there is an interest rate hike. But take the case of a pension insurance company. Its long-term assets are set against long-term liabilities. Whenever interest rates move either way during their lifespan, at maturity, when payments have to be made to the insurer, the investment will be repaid at nominal value.

For a liquidity manager tapping the capital markets, interest rates do not seriously impair his or her funding capability. If the quality of the manager's institution is still perceived to be sound, he or she will get the funds. Indeed, because of higher rates, funding costs will not be as advantageous as before. Although wider spreads are thought to compensate for the higher risk, deterioration in the financial health of the respective institution is a different matter. This is especially so if the market perceives the deterioration to be the beginning of a trend to the worse; the willingness to invest in this borrower will diminish or even completely disappear. Even offering higher spreads may not compensate for the anticipated risk of the company failing.

- Secured funding: In the case of unsecured funding it is the status of the issuer which counts. In contrast, secured funding primarily relates to an asset which contains a risk value of its own, independent of the institution issuing it. The generic term 'asset-backed securities' (ABS) covers a wide range of assets and structures. Securitisation of credit cards, commercial loan portfolios or mortgage financing are just some of them. The issue may be plain or structured. The principles and effects will be explained using the commonly known and internationally actively used mortgage-backed securities.

A bank financing borrowers in the property market inevitably will carry mortgage loans as an asset on its balance sheet. Without any further steps being taken they will be funded like any other general asset of the bank. Spreads to be paid will depend on the financial health, expressed as a rating. The mortgage loan itself is covered by the property it is financing. Its risk quality depends on the value of the underlying property. First-tranche mortgages (e.g. in Germany up to 60% of the property value) are assessed as a high-quality asset for which the market asks a low-risk premium and accordingly a small spread.

A bank can choose whether or not to put secured assets into specific portfolios and get direct financing for it. Whenever the standing of the bank is rated as inferior to the security, it then makes economic sense to securitise the asset and not finance it through general, unsecured liabilities. In this case, costs for secured funding are lower, which is a benefit in itself. Improved price competitiveness is a further advantage, permitting the bank to grow without suffering in margin income. Benefits also exist even for highly rated banks. Markets for secured and unsecured funding are segregated. The bigger the part of the balance sheet financed on a secured basis, the lower the need for general financing in the unsecured market. For this reason many a bank enhances the rating of riskier portfolios in order to reach specific investors. The amounts may still be large but could be excessive otherwise.

Despite the benefits the liquidity manager would do better to watch the particularities involved. As we have learned, a securitised portfolio gets its financing and the terms related to it on the back of its quality. It follows that deteriorating economic conditions of the bank will impair its funding capability in the unsecured market. As long as the assets in the securitised portfolios are still sound, their funding should not be negatively affected in any serious way. Actual cases support this conclusion. But what about the other way around? The market condition may decline in the segment that the securitised portfolio belongs to. Its funding may become negatively affected in price and also in quantity. If this is serious the bank will have to step in. As ultimate owner of the portfolio it may also be affected economically and its unsecured financing may suffer as well. As we can see, segregating markets do bring benefits; if things become tight, however, it is not a universal remedy.

- Rating-related funds: It is a generally practised policy of investors to relate volume and duration of limits to the financial health of the borrowing institution. The stronger the borrower in financial terms, the higher the volume and the longer the maturities are the general principles applied. Within a wide band the scales usually follow a gradual line. There are exceptions, however.

  Supervisory boards and boards of directors may decide to put a threshold at the lower end to reduce credit risk further. The policy can often be observed in state-related firms but equally in commercial and financial companies. The threshold is expressed in a form of the minimum rating acceptable. If a borrower falls below the required rating level, the borrower's name is deleted from the credit limit list.

  A comparable system exists in the US CP market. It is firmly structured according to the ratings of agencies like Moody's and Standard & Poor's. The top market segment which demands top short-term ratings (e.g. A1/P1) combines the vast majority of all CPs invested in. The remaining grades get the small balance. In all of these cases the process is no longer gradual but dualistic. Above the threshold the borrowing capacity is large. If one falls below, the source will be drastically reduced or even dry up completely.

- Additional considerations: Funding, as one of the means to get liquidity, cannot be regarded in absolute terms. It would be wrong to believe that any strategy could ensure the protection of a company against adverse liquidity conditions irrespective of the severity and length of negative circumstances. It is particularly obvious when we define minimum growth and acceptable profitability as indispensable goals.

  The absolute best one could achieve would be to fund all assets congruently. The funding of each single transaction would be secured till maturity. But if the worse came to the worst, we could not replace maturing assets fully or even at all, depending on the severity of the condition. Thus, at best, one could be liquid at any point but at the same time be permanently taking assets off the balance sheet. In an extreme case, a skeleton of a legal entity would remain, but the bank as an active institution would surely have gone.

  Any liquidity policy therefore should aim at bridging short-term strains. In the case of prolonged negative conditions it should give management time to make and implement business decisions which are aimed in the long run at convincing the market to invest again.

  The terms 'secured' and 'unsecured' funding do not at all imply any maturity spectrum. The timeframe ranges from overnight to, say, 30 years. In a serious liquidity crisis, from experience the first week is the most critical period. If one can get through the first 90 days, the chances of survival increase. The aim therefore has to be to secure locked-in funding for these periods. On the liability side three measures are at the forefront to support the endeavour:

  - Since retail funds are to be judged as relatively stable, it pays to put management effort into keeping the share of retail funds to the total as large as possible. Finding ways of making it attractive for the retail manager to focus not only on assets but also on liabilities will benefit the liquidity manager at the same time.

  - Most liabilities from third parties are based on a contractual obligation to keep them invested till maturity. It is therefore very much in the hands of the borrower to decide on the periods to be locked in. Admittedly, there is a price to be paid for liabilities with longer maturities. However, it is a way of gaining time, either to bridge short-term disturbances or to allow management to take the necessary steps in case of prolonged negative economic conditions.

– When dealing with optionalities we discussed standby facilities. Liquidity might be scarce for any institution under specific conditions. Many of these conditions are not foreseeable and the need for additional funds might suddenly arise. To conquer such circumstances it helps to have reserves in place. In contrast to commercial companies, a bank should abstain from relying on backup lines committed by other financial institutions. If the trigger is caused by market-related circumstances they may be of a nature which is also affecting the provider of the facility.

It would be a serious misunderstanding to believe that the measures discussed above could be the solution to any liquidity problem potentially facing a liquidity manager. They are elements to support the *endeavour*, to prevent and if necessary to overcome a liquidity crisis.

Much will depend on whether difficulties are restricted to a single institution or concern wider market segments, such as in the case of a flight to quality, i.e. when flows are directed to best qualities only, even avoiding good quality expressed as an investment grade.

It is a comfort to know that reserves in the form of marketable assets are available in case of difficult circumstances. But will they still qualify to be turned into cash in the actual event?

One should aim to diversify funding and even consider having it balanced in such a way that not too many sources respond in the same way under a specific market condition. But how well does this anticipate potential occurrences and behaviour?

Before dealing with these aspects in detail we will first take a closer look at the assets side and evaluate its contribution in respect to closing the gaps.

1.2.4.3 *The asset approach*

Liquidity gaps are not just determined by actions on the liability side. Assets play an equally important part. In many, if not most, cases assets are the primary force behind gaps. How does this come about?

The overall and supreme goal of a private company is to produce net earnings. Banks are no different in this respect. Moreover, in banks earnings are primarily attributable to asset and fee income. Business policy is thus a driving force in determining the volume as well as the type and maturity structure of assets. As self-created liabilities (own means and liabilities collected by operating units) do not match assets, and in the case of international banks they miss it by far, the commercial-related balance sheet is one-sided. In other words, once all transactions of operating units are transferred to the liquidity manager, he or she will be faced with a funding gap which needs to be closed.

If one could assume the immediate availability of funds all the time and in the structures and maturities required in relation to liquidity management, funding could be called a non-event, of interest to a liability manager only, who would have to find ways and means to keep funding costs as low as possible. Unfortunately, the analyses of the various types of funding do not support the assumption of unlimited and stable funds under all circumstances.

After this short detour we will now focus on the assets themselves (Box 1.8). We deal with them in two ways. Firstly, as business policy is a driving force in determining the vital aspects of the asset structure on the balance sheet, the aspects will be dealt with separately. The following assets will be segregated according to their degree of being liquefiable.

Business-policy-induced assets   Most probably, the biggest single impact derives from business decisions. The board may decide to strengthen the firm's market penetration on a

---

Box 1.8 Behavioural attitudes of asset liquidity

Within the asset structure, which is predominantly determined by business policy, the degree of asset liquidity is additionally influenced by market-related conditions. Protecting the core business and thus the franchise defined by business policy will clash with liquidity related to maturities.

---

diversified basis. One way to achieve this is through a strategy of growth. The focus may be on a region not yet covered or on a segment often reserved for specialised institutions like direct banking – offshore or mortgage banking, for instance. Whatever the way taken, the more pronounced the path of growth, the greater the need for additional funds. Most probably, part of the gap might be covered through issuing additional equities in order to keep the capital ratio at an acceptable level. The larger part has to be obtained from the market, however. The implications are similar if the expansion concentrates on regions and product groups that are already part of business policy. As assets grow, so do the liquidity gaps and hence funding need.

Naturally, the contractual maturities are important. How does the tenor of the new business compare with the relative stability of liability segments? When assessing and monitoring liquidity risk it makes a difference whether the new demand for funding hits a stable or a highly volatile funding segment. In the process of evaluating proposals and taking business decisions these questions have to be analysed and answers must be integrated into the planning process.

From a wider perspective there is a further aspect worth analysing. It is one we touched on earlier when we discussed the meaning of liquidity: customer franchise. It would be brave to assume that all business activities relate automatically and exclusively to the group of core clients. Even with a sound and coherent strategy, there will be opportunistic business done to increase earnings. Opportunistic in this context means that business is done outside the formally defined and declared group of core customers. The opportunity will be attractive from a financial point of view as there is room on capital and funding to pick up the additional earnings. At times the amounts involved can be substantial, and can tie up remarkable resources. A securitised loan where one takes over a portion from the arranging bank is a classic example. No core relationship can be built in this way as the borrower has no contact with the ultimate investor. Conversely, when funding becomes extremely difficult there are these investments which are potentially available for reducing assets as no core relationship will be endangered. No doubt earning implications will be felt, but the franchise with core customers will not be touched.

There may even be some room with selected core customers. With normal funding conditions a bank may be willing to offer substantial sums for cash management purposes to large corporations on an uncommitted basis. If it gets tight the question is then: can we reduce the volume? As we deal with uncommitted facilities the answer is definitely yes, we can. If we do, what is the risk of endangering the relationship? The answer may be: it depends.

We can sensibly assume that a customer will be happier if the bank acts generously. The various degrees of contentment will hardly affect the bilateral relationship established. Producing a feeling of being dissatisfied on the other hand will probably have negative consequences. Within this range there is some room for manoeuvre, when push comes to shove. The degree of flexibility will differ from customer to customer. It must be sounded out in a sensitive manner if this route is to be followed.

Cash and marketable assets   At first sight both cash and marketable assets could be decisive tools for any liquidity manager. Cash in hand can be employed to fulfil payment obligations at any time. Marketable assets can either be sold without delay or be repossessed in the market and generate cash on a secured basis. As for liquidity status, selling the asset makes funding obsolete and repossession means getting it financed through a repurchase agreement whereby the asset serves as collateral for the benefit of the lender. Either way, to the extent realised it will reduce the liquidity gap and thus present funding needs; that is, if all other things are unchanged.

In order to get a sound level of equilibrium, based on our present information we could derive the following principles.

Paid-in capital and accumulated reserves (own means) can be utilised for funding without restrictions. We also understand that a large part of (short-term) retail funds can be called stable – not absolutely stable and not under all circumstances, but with a high probability. In addition, funds with a long maturity locked in are stable funds till the final date.

The principle for equilibrium could therefore be as expressed in Box 1.9:

Box 1.9 'Long-term' funds versus 'long-term' assets

Own means + Longer-term funds ≥ Non-marketable longer-term assets.

The expression indicates a simple correlation: as long as liabilities with a longer-term character are equal or exceed longer-term assets, funding for the period under consideration is secured. The period defined can be shorter than the lifespan of the contracts. For practical reasons we will apply a separation at the 1-year level, which is a commonly used period for segregating long from short term. Funding sources can be longer term due to contractual specifications, because they stay most probably longer term despite being contractually of a shorter-term nature, or simply stay as no automatic payback is envisaged.

Or we can address it from a different angle, which is more appropriate as we are presently dealing with assets. Shorter-term funds should not exceed the sum of primary liquidity and marketable assets combined. The reasoning behind this relates to the following consideration: in case liabilities maturing within the defined timespan are not prolonged or cannot be replaced with other funds, assets need to be converted to cash in one way or another. Three alternative routes are open to achieve the required effect: the bank already holds cash; it can rely on short-term assets maturing soon and not being prolonged; or marketable assets can be turned into cash before the maturity date is reached. That is, concluding in Box 1.10 from the expression above:

Box 1.10 'Short-term' funds versus 'short-term' assets

Short-term funds ≤ Primary liquidity + Marketable assets.

This expression states that if the equation is fulfilled, any reduction in short-term funds can be compensated by utilising primary liquidity or taking marketable assets as a means to create the cash needed. The principles contain an element of logic. However, at this stage we will not enter into details, although the delineation of each parameter would be quite a challenge. Instead, for the time being we will accept the principle and focus on the types of assets involved and their behaviour.

Primary liquidity   What we called cash or ready cash is known under the technical term 'primary liquidity'. It is defined as reserves from cash in hand and all the deposits due which are held with central banks and other banks. As banks are not generally known to hold substantial quantities of banknotes in their vaults, we will neglect them in the further discussion. Cash is deposited with the institutions mentioned on the basis of being available on call. For practical purposes we will thus treat primary liquidity and cash/ready cash as equivalent.

Holding cash is not a way to employ resources in a profitable way. Maturities are the shortest one can imagine, and cash is placed with professionals and monetary authorities and not with customers ready to pay a credit spread. Cash holdings for these reasons are kept at a minimum level. Regulatory requirements and clearing needs are the two main elements which determine the volume to be held.

Some impact arises from the clearing process. Banks can clear either directly with the respective central bank or indirectly via another bank with the licence to do so. In either case one has to keep appropriate amounts with them as both of them execute payment orders within a strict regime of rules. Limiting credit or counterparty risk is one of them. Apart from a relatively small overdraft limit granted, orders will only be executed if cash is in the account. If payments received from third parties are not sufficient to fulfil the bank's own orders, cash has to be kept at or injected to the level necessary to guarantee the outgoing payments. In countries where minimum reserve requirements are applicable the regulatory amount held may exceed the one for clearing because, for the latter, the larger part of holdings with clearers is kept in the form of marketable assets. Furthermore, 'window dressing' also plays its part. The term means demonstrating to the community that the bank has got sufficient cash at hand. Thus at external reporting days, month end, quarter end and even more at year end, the amounts held are lifted for external purposes.

The cash amounts so employed during the day are already quite substantial for normal conditions. Earning considerations prevent banks from keeping significantly bigger volumes and thus from covering stressed situations as well. As a result, in case of lack of new funds the liquidity manager should not utilise this pot for asset financing. If so, he or she risks endangering the fulfilment of payment obligations with the potentially severe consequences up to illiquidity and failure of the institution.

From a practitioner's point of view, one may object to defining primary liquidity so rigidly. The question could be posed of whether including deposits due from parties other than central banks and banks as well would be more appropriate. When all is said and done, cash is cash, irrespective of the source.

But is cash really cash irrespective of the source? Technically speaking it would be, if it were not for the customer franchise. The money market among banks serves very much as the vehicle for cash management. Surpluses are deposited and shortages are borrowed among the community within the limits granted to each other. There, no relationship exists comparable with the one between a bank and its commercial clientele. Broking and electronic broking have established themselves as strong pillars in this market. Anonymity among the dealers involved is relatively high. Needs are covered with whoever in the community has got a matching requirement. The system works because of the multitude of participants and not because there are established financing agreements.

The commercial clientele, whether corporate or private, expects to be served according to its needs – at least within an agreed and established frame. The strategically defined core group makes up the bank's franchise. Individual demand for overnight money will fluctuate daily as it concerns a specific client. Looking at the group, however, the behaviour is rather predictable. Generally, the liquidity manager will sensibly integrate this portfolio into the planning process. To reduce the amount would imply the bank's declining at least part of the new customer requests. If that is done the franchise established over many years will suffer immediately. For this reason it is not advisable to touch this portfolio for urgent asset reduction – at least not as long as sustainable earnings is a policy goal.

Secondary liquidity or marketable assets   Secondary liquidity reserves combine the stock of marketable assets that the bank or institution holds. The term 'secondary' declares marketable assets as the second most liquid asset class. In volume terms it is much bigger than primary liquidity.

There is a wide range of marketable assets known on the balance sheet. As products they can be equities, bonds, money market instruments like CDs and CPs, consumer lending, corporate loans, etc. They can be sold, used for repo transactions or taken as collateral. The transactions can be concluded with the market or with central banks. The assets can be kept on the bank's own balance sheet or put into a special purpose vehicle (SPV).

Marketable assets are the generic term for assets which are near cash, and can be switched into cash if required. Unfortunately, this does not say much about the time factor required to turn an instrument into cash. Some of them, like Bunds, US Treasuries, CDs, CPs, etc., are trading products with a respectable local or even global market. In case of need, the asset can be sold or repossessed. The same is true for other sovereigns (i.e. state issues), company bonds, etc. The market size of a product will differ depending on the quantity issued. So will the amount one can turn in a functioning market at negligible cost.

This latter point is very pronounced when it comes to equities. The size of the total equity market, expressed either in market value of the companies registered on an exchange or as the daily turnover of the shares, can be enormous. However, the market is very much fragmented. What counts is the volume available for a single equity, which is only a fraction of the total market. The amounts to be turned at negligible cost are thus significantly lower than in the case of Bunds and US Treasuries, for example. If one holds equities of non-registered companies, a bilateral buyer has to be sought. This will prolong the time to execution even more. There may be a comparable condition even if the company is registered on an exchange. If larger portions are held by strategic investors as in the past in Germany (the so-called Deutschland AG), very little of the total will find its way onto the market. Thus, despite potentially large volumes based on equities issued, the relevant ones meeting the marketplace can still be mediocre or small.

Declaring securitised loans as marketable in some cases can also be misleading. In certain parts of Asia, for example, it has not been uncommon to structure a simple loan as a securitised one, because it fitted the client's balance-sheet structure. The contract at the same time was enhanced with an understanding not to sell the securitised loan into the market. So-called 'lock-up' agreements have also been known in the CD market. In all these cases the label does not match what it promises.

Marketable assets can be of a plain vanilla (straightforward) or a structured nature. The structure may contain a range of credit qualities and/or derivatives. The less straightforward a portfolio, the more difficult it is for the potential buyer to assess the risk involved. Assets with low ratings pose similar uncertainties. The assessment of risk takes time. Additionally, the market of potential investors for these types of assets usually turns out to be small. For these reasons the liquidity manager has to keep in mind that marketable assets of complex structures and thus of higher risk will not find a deep and wide market. To create liquidity from this source is most likely to be time consuming.

The diverse aspects of marketable assets regarding time needed and volumes possible, when it comes to creating liquidity, have to be considered in the course of ordinary business. True, this asset class is substantial in size but cannot be taken as one single block for all purposes. When setting up a liquidity grid with the gaps in the different time periods, one cannot assume structured assets to be available to cover short-term or even daily needs. If we wish to place collateral with the central bank to secure the execution of payment orders, we need sufficient assets of the type, minimum risk quality and to the extent required. These considerations already apply for normal conditions in the ordinary conduct of business.

If it were just for normal conditions, the amount of marketable assets generally kept would not be as large as it is. At times, liquidity may be extremely short. This may happen abruptly, triggered, for example, through larger amounts of standby credits drawn or a sudden reduction in deposits available to the bank in the market. In any case, it would be a bank-specific and not a systemic problem of the market itself. In such cases the liquidity buffer in the form of marketable assets would come into use. Which assets to choose is then a question of availability on the balance sheet and amounts required.

The picture presents itself differently if the market is faced with a systemic problem. Fortunately, such crises occur rarely. Nevertheless, even in the recent past we have seen a lemming-type flight to quality. Best qualities were assessed as good enough to get and keep; lower-rated marketable assets were avoided by almost everybody. In such cases a large part of the assets kept for creating liquidity when needed may no longer be marketable in reality. Such a systemic crisis, if lucky, may be short-lived. But even this is not much consolation to a bank if it coincides with its own specific needs.

To round off this section, marketable assets with all the considerations and restrictions can help to overcome or at least smooth the effects caused by short-term liquidity stress. In the case of any longer-lasting imbalance their utilisation at best can serve as a supporting measure, but the solution to the problem has to come from different quarters. Besides, any marketable asset needs to be of an unencumbered nature to be usable as a cash generating vehicle.

1.2.5 Intermediate Summary

The goal of this chapter was to constitute the basis for the subjects to come: liquidity as part of financial policy, followed by liquidity policy and management. In order to get a common understanding we had to go into considerable detail. It is an experience liquidity managers are used to. The terms 'liquidity' and 'risk' are used in various segments of banking and their interpretation has many facets. As far as possible we have tried to use terms that are commonly understood. We may not have succeeded in every instance.

As explained earlier, liquidity and liquidity risk still have not yet been developed into a coherent framework with generally accepted terms and methods. To penetrate the subject and get a better understanding of it resembles mapping hardly known territory. It is not so much the management aspect which has been neglected. This subject has been the focal point of recent publications mentioned at the beginning. Management of any subject cannot stand alone but has to be embedded in a frame of strategy and policy, as emphasised by Duttweiler (2008,

Box 1.11 Summary of relevant parameters affecting liquidity status

- Cash and its flow are the decisive items to compute and assess. They have to be brought into a frame of time sequences. Neither net earnings nor interest rate gaps correctly reflect balances from actual payments and receivables in the period considered.
- Liquidity risk concerns the future and not the past. Any concept or method applied needs to integrate prospective developments, whether directly or indirectly related to liquidity. From today's perspective some of them are predictable with a relatively high level of certainty, e.g. contracts falling due. Others can only be assumed, e.g. customer response, investor behaviour.
- Business policy is easily the most impacting single issue determining asset volume. The effects are not predictable but at least can be planned.
- In this context optionalities like standby facilities etc. are a special case. They are of a dichotomist nature, which means the effects are neither predictable nor able to be planned. Most probably, one will have to use scenarios.
- The power to attract liabilities for funding purposes depends partly on the price offered. In case the prospective credit risk perceived by the investor falls below a certain threshold, and which cannot be predicted, even wider spreads offered may not convince investors to take on the risk. Key business data such as capital ratio, sustainable earnings and asset quality will be taken as indicators to build perception.
- Liquidity policy ought to be integrated into the framework of business and financial decisions. Liquidity management can and must support the endeavour to achieve business goals.
- Any liquidity policy needs to focus on both assets and liabilities. Each one determines the size and shape of liquidity gaps. In the end, both sides of the balance sheet have to match, which is the minimum required.
- Not all groups of investors respond in the same manner to the problems of a bank. Retail customers react in a less volatile manner in speed and volume, but they do react. The group of wholesale fund providers, i.e. corporate and financial institutions, responds quickly and sometimes drastically. Nevertheless, some funds will remain stable and be prolonged. To enlarge the more stable segment and diversify funding in the second pillar should be envisaged in any policy.
- Stress on liquidity can arise from various sources and corners. Thus, one should not aim for a standard solution to the diverse problems. Specific situations require specific approaches. For example, having to deal exclusively with a bank-specific problem is a matter to be distinguished from dealing with it within a systemic crisis at the same time.
- Lengthening the maturities on market funding is a way to buy time. It does not solve the problem in the case of any long-term distress. Yet, gaining time gives management the opportunity to take and implement measures with the aim of rectifying the underlying cause.

pages 39–44). This framework has hardly been touched when it comes to banks, either by academia or otherwise. Yet personal experience has shown it to be of the utmost importance, for liquidity management is just one of the elements to be performed in a bank. As such it has to fit into a general business concept. Above all, its double function as protector and supporter of business as a going concern requires its integration in a balanced way. It is for this reason that understanding the basics has to be achieved.

Going forward we have to keep in mind the essential knowledge gained when discussing the basics. In order to have a comprehensive and easily readable set of parameters for reference, we attempt to filter them from the multitude of detailed observations discussed (Box 1.11).

Even when discussing basics only, it is obvious that business policy plays a part that is largely underrated in liquidity management. Experience leads to an attitude where being involved in business and financial planning is step number 1. Whatever the outcome of this process, it determines the basic liquidity structure in the future; that is, the structure which can be assumed to arrive within liquidity management from the activities of the operating units. Advancing the subject in this way allows a forward-looking approach to be applied on the one hand, and assessing the feasibility of such a route, given the funding capacity applicable to the institution, on the other hand. Liquidity management then has to follow and relate more to the proper doing, given a business-determined liquidity structure and possible conditions facing the liquidity managers.

Integrating the subject of liquidity into the business and financial framework of a bank has not been one of the strong elements in banking. Corporate finance is much more advanced in this respect. The following chapter will thus evaluate the possibilities to apply proven knowledge in the corporate sector to our question. Although we cannot assume to formulate a theoretical framework, we may at least be in a position to arrive at a practical perception.

2

Liquidity in the Context of Business and Financial Policy

2.1 INTRODUCTION

Liquidity policy and management do not exist in a vacuum. They are neither ultimate goals in themselves nor do they represent a value in itself. Liquidity policy and management can only be understood as an integral part of the business and financial goals of a company. In this context they can fulfil two major roles: firstly, to take all steps necessary to secure funding at the highest possible level; secondly, to support operating units in their efforts to achieve business goals.

Both of these functions cannot be achieved without interacting with business and financial policy as well as the targets of a company. On a management level sometimes the different goals are complementary. More often, however, they are contradictory. Buying security costs, and the higher the level secured, the more expensive it will be. Cost, on the other hand, is one of the key determinants which decide on whether producing specific goods and services is economically feasible. The endeavour to support business departments in their efforts to achieve business goals must consider market attitudes, either those of equity investors or those of the providers of retail and wholesale funds. Less credible business and financial policies, for example, are limiting constraints when it comes to convincing lenders of any kind to take the risk when investing in the firm.

Achieving the main goals requires an organisational setup which, among other tasks, coordinates the various elements necessary for success. In cases where at least some of the elements contradict, this setup is even more important. Coordination does not suffice. Following a process in which the conflicting items are evaluated and brought into line, decisions have to be made. The various targets must be communicated and progress made must be supervised and monitored.

Moreover, liquidity policy has to fit into the frame of business and financial goals set by management. In business management this process would be called dealing with a magic polygon: polygon, since there are several goals linked together; and magic because at least two of them are competing against or contradicting each other – especially if each of them was followed unilaterally and extensively

The aim of this chapter is to be in a position to evaluate the necessary elements, within which a coherent liquidity policy can be formulated. We approach it in two steps. Firstly, traditional rules and newer concepts applied in corporate finance will be analysed and reviewed with respect to their adaptability for banks. Secondly, principles will be formulated considering the special environment of banks. The findings in the previous chapter will be of value in this respect. And within them, the points summarised at the end of it will have to be integrated.

The decision to address the subject in two steps is based on practical considerations. In the introduction about how to close the gap between commercially induced assets and liabilities one relevant distinction was raised and which has now become significant to us. Commercial companies produce tangible goods. A segregation between production and finance is easily made in their case. If it is money, it is finance. Goods belong to production. With banks it is not that clear cut. Corporate, retail and investment banking departments use money as a 'product' to a large extent. The line drawn is often blurred and not recognisable without further explanation.

The clarity between finance and production in commercial companies, actually, is only one reason to follow this approach. One cannot ignore that research in corporate finance has been concentrating for quite some time on the issue of integrating liquidity into the general policy framework. By taking this route we may get some insight into the mechanics which we can employ when addressing the subject in relation to banks. It is for these reasons that we are going to assess the relevance for banking in this section. In other words, we take the systemic approach from corporate finance but evaluate its value for banks simultaneously.

Regarding commercial companies, the setup follows the traditional approach of major readings in corporate finance such as Spremann (1996), Vormbaum (1995) and Volkart (2003). We will start with the conditions of financial equilibrium as a basis and the role of liquidity within its framework

2.2 EQUILIBRIUM AS A TOOL WITHIN FINANCIAL POLICY

Financial equilibrium deals with the relationship between the structure of assets and liabilities. The knowledge gained serves to formulate and implement the funding policy of the company.

There is further relevance to this item. Over the years, concepts have been developed that are used to assess the quality of the balance sheet and, among others, the credit quality of a borrower. The subject thus is not relevant to internal optimisation of the funding structure only, but has practical implications when it comes to the quantity available from and the price paid to external lenders.

2.2.1 The weakness of the traditional approaches

Most of the funding rules are based on balance-sheet items. The basic structure follows the principle of maturity on the one hand and shareholder capital versus outside borrowing on the other hand (Figure 2.1).

Fixed assets are defined as long term, so is capital. Current assets are items which liquidate themselves in a relatively short period of time.

The next step will help to evaluate the extent to which different rules can be practically used as a basis for liquidity management. Although a 'corporate' (i.e. a non-financial firm) differs in many respects to a bank, the definition of liquidity does not: payments have to be fulfilled as and when they fall due and in the currency required.

Assets	Liabilities
Current assets Fixed assets	Short-term liabilities Long-term liabilities
Total sum	Total sum

Figure 2.1   The balance-sheet structure of a 'corporate' (*Source*: Spremann, 1996, page 252)

Box 2.1 Cash-related liquidity ratios (*Source*: Spremann, 1996, page 220)

$$\text{Liquidity first grade} = \frac{\text{Cash}}{\text{Short-term liabilities}}$$

$$\text{Liquidity second grade} = \frac{\text{Cash and short-term claims}}{\text{Short-term liability}}.$$

2.2.1.1 Cash and near cash

For the purpose of securing payments obligations, the focus is very much on short-term conditions. To fulfil payment obligations in the near future requires cash in hand or coming in soon. Thus, the time horizon of short term is subdivided again, taking degrees of cash into consideration. The ratios in Box 2.1 relate to this emphasis.

First-grade liquidity is not expected to reach a ratio where cash covers 100% of the short-term liabilities. The range is at about 20% or more. Second-grade liquidity, where short-term claims are added to cash, is expected to cover at least 100% of short-term liabilities.

Both of the ratios are related to cash management and are useful for this purpose. They give a helpful indication as to the capability to fulfil payment obligations now and in the immediate future. However, their value for financial equilibrium is negligible: within the total of assets and liabilities they cover only a part. Financial equilibrium, however, contains a view of the total balance sheet.

2.2.1.2 The golden rule of funding

In order to cover the needs of financial equilibrium one has to refer to the main elements of the balance sheet; that is, to the structure as presented in Figure 2.1. The thinking behind it is to segregate short- from long-term liquidity considerations; or to put it in another way, distinguishing between payment-related or situation-specific liquidity on the one hand and structural liquidity on the other hand. The ratios reflecting these aspects are presented in Box 2.2.

The equation, called the golden balance-sheet rule, represent a concrete form of the golden rule of funding – to many readers probably better known as the golden rule of banking.

The rule states that assets have to be financed congruently. If their lifespan is long term, the funds attached to them have to be of long maturities as well. Fixed assets do not liquidate

---

Box 2.2 Balance-sheet-related liquidity ratios (*Source*: Spremann, 1996, page 252)

$$\text{Liquidity third grade: } \frac{\text{Current assets}}{\text{Short-term liabilities}} \geq 1$$

$$\text{Golden BS rule: } \frac{\text{Fixed assets}}{\text{Capital} + \text{Long-term liabilities}} \leq 1.$$

---

themselves in a short period of time. Thus, funding them short term carries the risk of not being able to repay the loan at maturity as the funding may not be prolonged or cannot be replaced.

From a static point of view, the principles are logical and coherent. Assets financed short term do leave the balance sheet early and produce the necessary cash in time to repay the accompanied debts. The remaining assets are financed either through capital or long-term borrowing from banks and the capital markets. The maturities of assets and liabilities concur.

2.2.1.3 *Considerations*

We mentioned that the principles are logical and coherent from a static point of view. On the other hand, companies are not static organisations. Moreover, any proper policy and management of liquidity has to be forward looking. By doing so, one is considering likely and possible events in the future. In addition, the company's franchise and power to produce earnings have to be maintained. The question then arises of whether the rules can uphold these principles:

- The rule implies that, to secure a healthy liquidity status, capital and long-term liabilities have to be equal or bigger in amount than fixed assets. However, at least the external portion of long-term funding is limited in time. If the specific long-term asset is still on the books when the corresponding long-term liability matures, the funding need does not cease. The prior borrowing will have to be replaced, either through prolongation or by borrowing from alternative sources. Although causing potentially critical conditions, the facts are compatible with the principles of the rule.
- Consequently, funding is assessed as neutral and thus not critical for liquidity purposes, and it is implicitly assumed that the necessary prolongation is possible without any problems. However, if the assessment holds true, what is the need to follow the golden rule? If the replacement of maturing funds does not pose any liquidity risk, then there is no need at all to fund congruently (Vormbaum, 1995, page 87f.).
- According to the rule, it is permitted to fund current assets short term. The thinking behind this sees these assets turning into cash in a relatively short period of time. For example, raw materials are processed into semi-finished products. They will be processed into final goods which, when sold, will produce the necessary cash to pay back the short-term loans related to them. Here again, the thinking is compatible with the principles applied for liquidity.
- Admittedly, the current assets on the balance sheet are congruently and thus securely financed. Referring to the example just mentioned, current assets contain vital resources for future production. They need to be replaced and funded as well. In other words, the rule implicitly assumes that future funding is a given and does not contain any liquidity risk.

This brings us to what we called franchise and power to produce.

In corporate finance they call it capacity. The power to produce, i.e. the capacity of a company to produce at maximum level, is determined by the technical as well as the financial capacity. Financial refers to funding, while technical contains the efficient use of staff and tangible resources as well as the quality of the organisational structure. It follows that shortcomings in any of the elements are the limiting factor restricting the capacity of the company.

We stated in the summary of the previous chapter that liquidity management can and must support the endeavour to achieve business and financial goals. If one wishes to uphold this aim, funding should be appropriate; that is, vital resources determining the technical capacity, such as raw materials, although grouped in current assets, should be financed long term. Neglecting this requirement in many cases has been the reason for companies failing (Vormbaum, 1995, page 89f.).

In banking, franchise also plays its part – in fact a vital one. For example, if we replace raw materials with short-term advances to customers for cash management purposes, the condition that one is in is the same. True, lending is done on a short-term basis, but it is a continuing process. When looking at the customer base as a whole, a certain amount will always be outstanding. If a bank were to decide not to replace the maturing advances, its franchise would suffer severely.

2.2.1.4 Summary

We must conclude that none of the funding rules we looked at fulfil the requirements we set; nor do they do so in corporate finance. Some capture only part of the balance sheet. The others show significant weaknesses when a dynamic view is taken.

As soon as protecting the level of present capacity of a company is introduced, funding and thus liquidity risk become unavoidable, even when adhering to the presented liquidity rules. In the case of banks the effects would be similar. When funding problems occur, cash from maturing assets would be available to pay back liabilities falling due; however, the capacity to produce or, related to banking, the franchise would be impeded.

To overcome the risk in corporate finance one could fund all vital assets, both fixed and current, with shareholder capital. This has been proposed, but was dropped after calculating the effects on profitability. Equity holders would not have supported the approach. Neither would bank shareholders.

Nevertheless, this does not mean that the rules are useless. Adhering to them supports the endeavour to manage liquidity risk properly, and they are still commonly in use. For our purpose, however, they fall short of requirements.

2.2.2 The alternative approach: financial equilibrium

The traditional definitions discussed above definitely have their value. At a glance they give an indication of where the company stands concerning liquidity at the present and most likely in the immediate future. The weaknesses manifest themselves in the longer term, when a dynamic approach is required.

We can generally assume that businesses are supposed to be managed as going concerns. Thus a long-term view on strategies and policy decisions is appropriate. In a market economy and without subsidies any privately owned company has to fulfil some minimum conditions to secure its existence in the long run.

Demands on management can build up from three basic directions. Firstly, the owners and other financial stakeholders wish to see a positive total return on a relatively secure basis. Secondly, changes in customer preferences and in the competitive environment affect the company's own competitive position and consequently the income achievable. Thirdly, the question of how resources are employed within the company will have a bearing on cost, progress in product development and the level of security. In order to secure existence in the long term the various demands have to be brought into balance.

2.2.2.1   Financial goals and business values

The demand on management is manifold and complex. To make it manageable one has to reduce the multiple requests to some basic key elements which make up the value for shareholders. Traditionally, they consist of the parameters of profitability, liquidity and security, the so-called magic triangle, for both the corporate and the banking sectors.

The various financial goals are not necessarily complementary but contradict each other quite often. Increasing the level of liquidity, for example, brings about higher funding cost. Improving security implies taking less risk. From experience, it means subsequently lowering expected profitability. The relationship between the goals is particularly important in periods when the company is growing rapidly. The various parameters tend to change in a rather erratic manner and there is a good chance of upsetting the previously stable structure. Keeping an acceptable financial equilibrium alive can easily become a real challenge. The significant impact that changes in volume can play in this respect has in recent times been taken into consideration in corporate finance. Growth has been added, thus creating the magic quadrangle as shown in Figure 2.2.

Before analysing the relationship of the four aims, it may be helpful to clarify a few points.

A company will obviously follow many more goals than the ones listed in the polygon. Staying independent, following social aims, protecting the environment, enhancing the image and prestige of the company may be just some of them. They are important in any context of managerial leadership of a firm. In our case we can exclude them as we deal exclusively with the financial elements, and restrict ourselves to the impact on liquidity.

Referring to Rappaport (1986) and Copeland, Koller and Murrin (1995), shareholder value could also have been called company value. The first term is better known in the English-speaking parts of the world, but loaded with some narrow interpretations. The term refers to the methods to be applied when: (1) the value of a company is assessed based on discounted cash flows; (2) measuring the benefits of business decisions made; and (3) calculating effective financial success in a period against accounting results. If the word is used in this way, there is no difference with the term 'company value'.

This narrow interpretation refers to the last statement of the concept, i.e. the duty of the management to follow only the goal of increasing shareholder value (Spremann, 1996, page 461f.). It would not pose a problem for us, because we stay within the financial compound. Actually, shareholder value in the sense stipulated last is only one of several approaches applied today. As there is no need, we will not enter into a discussion concerning general management theory, but turn to the contents of the magic quadrangle.

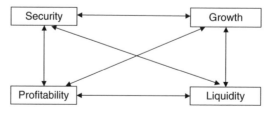

Figure 2.2   The magic polygon in corporate finance (*Source*: Volkart, 2003, page 123f.)

2.2.2.2   The concept and its elements

In a first step, the foreseeable interrelationship is looked at in a one-dimensional way, followed later by an interrelated view.

Growth   Growth, most probably, is the biggest single item determining the liquidity status and the volume of funding needed. Within a policy framework of business as usual, demand will mainly be limited to replacement of borrowings maturing. If the company is reasonably profitable, future funding may even be reduced. As there have been sufficient earnings generated, the potential to pay back some of the debts exists. Expanding business on the other hand requires additional investment and thus an increase in funding. If the expansion takes the form of an acquisition, funding needs may augment abruptly and in substantial quantity.

Telecommunications companies in the 1990s, for example, followed a remarkably fast growth path, including taking over foreign competitors. As a result, their funding needs exploded and their indebtedness reached levels which were assessed by potential investors as becoming critical. The subsequently introduced policy to reduce debts significantly bore fruit in two ways. Interest payments were reduced and added to improve profitability. At the same time, debts came down to more reasonable levels, thus reducing the risk premium to be paid on new borrowings and enlarging the funding potential. All these benefits showed the way to a more balanced financial equilibrium.

Growth can be triggered internally or externally (Volkart, 2003, pages 68ff. and 801ff.). When the route of internal growth is taken, the power to produce more is built up within the company. The elements are in nature either quantitative (capacity enlarged) or qualitative (to improve product know-how and product development). Internal growth is a long-term process and the financial implication to build it up is more gradual and continuous in character. Expenses related to the process, according to accounting rules, are largely debited directly to current expenses and affect the profit and loss of the respective period. Many expenses cannot be capitalised and therefore are not put as assets on the balance sheet, although the inner value of the company has improved. Only the components of investment are capitalised and amortised over time. Internal growth usually starts with a prolonged period of investing in a tangible infrastructure and know-how, while earnings from it will start to flow albeit delayed.

Quantitative and qualitative growth alternatively can be achieved through the external route. Acquiring another company in part or in full is a common way to do it. Funding the extension is not stretched over a longer period. The payment for the takeover is due at the date it takes place. But so are the benefits. From the day after the acquisition the current returns flow to the new owner, without the delay characteristic of internal growth. Moreover, the investment this time can be fully capitalised and put as an asset on the balance sheet, including intangible assets in the form of goodwill, if accounting standards permit. The amortisation will occur over time, as for investments in the case of internal growth. Over a period of time, once goodwill is written off, the values on the book will be equal, irrespective of which route is taken.

The amounts involved and consequently the drain on liquidity can be substantial. Whenever possible, companies endeavour to build up a war chest in order to dampen the effect. The sums involved may, however, be too big to be financed out of a war chest, or cash payments to the old shareholders may not be feasible. To overcome these obstacles, the purchasing company may issue new equity capital and offer the new shares to the owners of the old company as payment. To soften their potential resistance to the deal, a combination of shares and cash payment is quite common as well.

Within the frame of our polygon, growth inevitably will affect the other three goals of security, profitability and liquidity, as each one of them in turn will again impinge on the rest.

Security   In the context of business activity, security can be no more than a goal and never a basic status. Any strategy approved, any decisions made, any plans implemented contain an element of uncertainty about the outcome. The degree of uncertainty can vary, but it always signifies the absence of security. The deviations from the goals are called risk and may be positive or negative. Generally speaking, management tends to be less concerned about a positive deviation – the chances – than about negative ones. As a consequence, under the headline of security one rarely finds terms like certainty, sureness or assurance, but all variations of risks, which are to be reduced, limited or eliminated (Volkart, 2003, page 666f.). The attitude is understandable at first sight, although security represents two sides of a coin: reducing the negative implications of risk is one side; but simultaneously reducing the chances to overperform through these measures is the other side.

The primary goal of management is to generate value to a company on a relatively secure base, i.e. with a long-term perspective for the share- and stakeholders. Security can be threatened in almost any way, as each decision bears the risk of not reaching expectations. To bring the various types into a structured form thus becomes necessary, in order not to lose sight. For our purposes we distinguish between the following (Box 2.3):

Box 2.3 The distinction of risk types (*Source*: Adapted from Volkart, 2003, page 666f.)

Dimension

Strategic risk:	The basic business approach
Volatility risk:	Range of expected outcome
Downside risk:	Expressed as Value at Risk

Origin

Market risk:	Price, interest rate, currency and market liquidity risk
Credit risk:	Counterparty risk
Operational risk:	All internals risks caused by systems, procedures, personnel, etc.

Area of influence

Cash flow:	Liquidity
Economic result:	Profit and loss account
Capital base:	Own means

Not all of the risks are equally relevant to us. Some will knock straight through into other items of our polygon, others will work in an indirect way or may be negligible for our purposes.

Profitability   Profitability is a relative term. In this context it is not a value defined by itself, but based on an amount of profit which is brought into the relation with other business data like sales, total investment or equity capital. There is an existential minimum which profitability has to achieve on average over several years, covering the full costs. Otherwise, the company will produce losses to be born by the capital. If the negative trend holds sufficiently long, the company one day will have lost capital to such an extent as to become non-operational.

In the longer term, covering costs, actually, cannot even be a theoretical approach. If followed, suppliers will hesitate to deal without prepayment and potential lenders will be concerned about the security to see loans repaid. Additionally, shareholders will have alternative investments at hand with a reasonable return. Such a company would not be considered attractive by stakeholders and customers alike. Management thus follows a policy of maximising returns as much as possible, in order to be competitive in the various segments of resources.

To achieve the overall aim, all departments have to make their contribution and maximise their profitability and cost efficiency. The finance department within the company is not exempt from these requirements. Its contribution concentrates mainly on two aspects: to optimise the funding structure and to have liquidity secured, but cost efficiently. Vormbaum (1995, page 91f.) calls this overall requirement elasticity or flexibility. For the finance department it is broken down into optimal levels of indebtedness and liquidity.

Although demonstrated on a corporate level, it basically applies for financial institutions as well. Losses erode the capital base and may lead to a state where the requirements of capital adequacy are no longer fulfilled, with the risk of losing the banking licence. But even well before that stage is reached investors, lenders and customers may lose trust and consequently reduce their engagements with the bank.

Liquidity   Within the polygon, the function of liquidity is a subordinate one. That means it is not to be maximised but to be kept at a level which is sufficient to secure payment obligations in an optimal way. Optimal thereby refers to quantitative as well as to cost-related aspects. In the previous section we touched briefly upon some characteristics of liquidity, without going deeper into the subject. We will now make up for it and try to present the full picture (Figure 2.3).

• **Liquidity in the form of assets** has been dealt with before under marketable assets. Apart from cash, which is ready and at hand, all other assets have to be turned into cash first before they become usable for fulfilling payment obligations. How easily the assets can be turned into cash determines their ranking within the liquidity structure. In the case of a corporate, the structure does not necessarily follow a given pattern, but is very much dependents on the strategy to be followed. If all business lines are supposed to work on the basis of a going

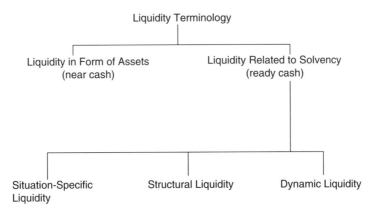

Figure 2.3   Different aspects of liquidity (*Source*: Adapted from Vormbaum, 1995, page 113)

concern, semi-finished products, for example, are nearer to liquidity than raw materials. The latter have to pass through two more processes to become final goods, while semi-finished goods need only go one step further. If a line is to be discontinued, the respective raw materials can easily be sold. Semi-finished products, on the other hand, have to be turned into final products first and additionally require demand in the market before being turned into cash (Vormbaum, 1995, page 113f.). In banks we find a similar pattern. A marketable asset with a long maturity can be turned more easily and faster into cash than a shorter-term but non-marketable asset.

- **Liquidity related to solvency** refers to cash payments when they fall due. Solvency on this understanding is not the critical point and reflects our previous statement that solvency is a precondition for liquidity and is given and reasonably assured. What is relevant within this frame is the time structure of liquid means. As we concluded earlier, an institution can be solvent and illiquid at the same time.
- **Situation-specific liquidity**, as stated earlier, concentrates on securing short-term and thus imminent payment obligations. Due to the short timeframe, cash at hand and instantly available is the key, as there might not be sufficient time to create the necessary means.
- **Structural liquidity** on the other hand refers to the liquidity composition of the balance sheet. All business concluded, but still on the books, is evaluated under the aspect of liquidity. The contractual dates when cash will flow are taken and potential gaps computed. Structural liquidity thus presents a complete overview of an institution's liquidity status till the longest maturity, but only for transactions already booked.
- **Dynamic liquidity** tries to overcome the deficiency of relying solely on booked transactions. According to accounting rules, not all commitments are booked. Some of them are similar to what we called optionalities in the previous chapter. They can be arranged in the form of a right to be drawn at any point within an agreed period, or a contract with future delivery. It may add to or drain the cash in hand at a date in the future. In either circumstance, they are not visible on the accounts. Moreover, with the exception of gone concerns, business continues well into the future. Foreseeable activities in the weeks and months to come will have a bearing on flows in cash. Liquidity managers should and cannot neglect them.
- According to the dynamic approach, the assessment of liquidity needs can thus be based neither on specific items of assets or liabilities, nor on the present balance sheet in total. What is required is a financial plan which includes those activity-related flows most likely to materialise within the next year at least. In this way, potentially severe and critical changes and unwanted excesses of liquidity become evident. As mentioned, it means keeping deviations on both sides within acceptable levels. Within financial equilibrium, liquidity is not a goal to be maximised but rather one to be optimised.

2.2.2.3 *Financial equilibrium and its relevance for liquidity*

In the corporate case, financial equilibrium serves as a tool for reaching an optimal balance based on two criteria: to achieve as high an economic success as possible while not letting other relevant parameters drop below a minimum level set by management. Profitability and growth related to it are items to be strengthened as much as possible. Considering security implies setting risk limits (Box 2.4); even so, the introduced restrictions reduce the otherwise achievable levels in profitability and growth. Security, within the understanding of both corporate finance and banking, includes all risks except liquidity; only in banking is the term named risk – the downside risk.

Box 2.4 'Drivers' and 'brakes' in financial equilibrium

Drivers	Growth and profitability: These elements tend to be maximised for the benefit of long-term success.
Brakes	Security/risk and liquidity: These limit the maximisation of the 'drivers'. Through them, management protects 'drivers' to reach excessive and destabilising levels.

A balancing approach, and incorporating both groups, will secure long-term success at a relatively stable level.

The thinking behind segregating general risk from liquidity risk reflects a special circumstance: the characteristic of liquidity. To the extent that it cannot be generated internally or through shareholder capital, it has to be created via external funding. These funds have to be financed by banks (especially important for a corporate) or from participants in the money and capital markets. Whatever channel is used, funding to the extent required by the institution is neither guaranteed nor available to an unlimited extent. If this fact is not considered properly, the institution may end up with insufficient means to fulfil payment obligations. The severe implications of such a state, which in the end could result in the failure of the firm, make it advisable to integrate liquidity as a separate item within the frame of the equilibrium.

Although banks differ in many ways from a corporate, the principle just outlined applies for them as well. To the extent that funding needs cannot be covered by shareholder capital and through special measures, whereby the asset is going to finance itself, a bank also is dependent on external means. In case the expansion of assets outweighs the incoming means, the fulfilment of payment obligations is at stake with the same consequences as for a corporate.

From a purely liquidity point of view, there are several traps to be avoided:

- For example, in the case of internal financing, when cash-related profit is turned into equity to bolster financial health, the total amount of funds stays unchanged and cannot be counted twice. The effects will be shown in the capital ratio, which will improve.
- In an alternative scenario, management may decide to put maximising profitability as the main goal. The ratio of share capital to external funding could then be driven to extremely low levels. On the other hand, the aspect of solvency cannot be neglected.
- Capital is not just an element of funding and thus liquidity. It is also the buffer which, if necessary, absorbs losses. When the stock is not sufficient as a comfortable cushion in relation to the risk taken, the financial standing of the company is going to suffer. Where exactly to draw the line is difficult to say.
- Commonly accepted ratios give an indication. By their very nature they refer to the immediate present at best. External perceptions about the future may differ, in the positive as well as negative sense. And the attitude of future lenders is more geared towards perception.
- Given certain minimum standards of financial strength, companies of all sizes can relate to external financing through banks. This is not so when borrowing in the money and capital markets, which are the main sources for banks. These are highly professional wholesale markets. Investment decisions are not made after time-consuming bilateral negotiations. Instead, ratings from professional agencies like Moody's and Standard & Poor's play a decisive role.

- Moreover, for wholesale markets flexibility to buy and sell the instruments from specific issuers and thus market size and depth are important. It is for these reasons that the market favours rather larger and well-known companies with a rating within the investment grade. Companies and banks belonging to this group have a wide new range of additional lenders at hand.
- Tapping the different markets enlarges the funding available, without being burdened with the risk inherent when borrowing is concentrated. Generally speaking, diversification achieved in this way is accompanied by a larger potential of funds at hand. The ones which spring immediately to mind are fixed and floating rate bonds and those attached with caps and collars or CP programmes – not that large, but still sufficient to generate investors' interest in near-equity instruments such as convertible loans and subordinated debts.
- When shareholder capital is partly substituted by external funding, there is a price to be paid. The flexibility in using instruments with the appropriate maturity to cover specific needs not the least originates in the characteristic of having a due date attached. Even continued funding at only the present level demands addressing lenders again at a later stage. It means being aware of the risk that circumstances either in the market or with respect to one's own financial status may have turned against oneself.

2.2.3   Liquidity in focus

Financial equilibrium comprises four elements and contains no less then 12 relationships, if we review each element relative to the other pillars. However, our focus is exclusively on liquidity. The question therefore centres on whether financial equilibrium is an appropriate instrument to allow us to formulate a policy for liquidity related to banks. To concentrate on this particular issue we will narrow the analysis to liquidity aspects only.

2.2.3.1   *Growth related to liquidity*

Growth touches liquidity directly as well as indirectly. Growth produces income, which adds to liquidity. On the other hand, expenditures not qualifying as investments will impact on current expenses and drain liquidity accordingly. In contrast, the portion which according to accounting rules is accepted as an investment augments long-term assets and can be financed by equity capital, external borrowing or by falling back on a built-up war chest. As far as external funds are needed from shareholders or lenders in the market, some questions arise: What mix is preferred between share capital and other funding from a business point of view? What is its extent and the price at which the favoured funds are available? Furthermore, what is the appropriate maturity to be chosen considering the calculated payback period of the investment, the cost implications of different alternatives and, not least, the risk taken if funding is not done congruently?

Funding in the market for the full amount needed, cost-wise, may be the favoured route to follow. As a result, the capital ratio may fall to a level which raises questions about the solvency of the company. To opt for relatively short funding periods may be cheaper. But how certain can one be to get the prolongation at favourable rates and, even more important for a liquidity manager, will the market and internal conditions be such that one gets the funds at all? This brings us to indirect links.

Liquidity management and funding are like a set phrase with two elements: turning the screw on one side affects the other side immediately and congruently. To know what to do in liquidity management is one issue; to have investors who get along with you is another one. Lenders do not care about a company's need. For them, avoiding unnecessary risk is at the forefront of their thinking.

Their perception about the financial solidity of a firm is made up of items like capital ratio, level and solidity of earnings and debt ratio, just to mention some key financial issues. To strike a sound balance is the first priority. At the moment, it would not be fitting to go deeper into the matter. It is more appropriate first to get a proper overview and understanding of the interrelationship from various positions. We will come back to it when we summarise the findings at the end of the section.

2.2.3.2   *Profitability related to liquidity*

The link between profitability and liquidity is simultaneously both complementary and contradictory. The latter refers to cost implied when liquidity is generated and held. Spremann (1996, page 198f.), for example, segregates situation-specific and structural liquidity. On this understanding, planning to secure payments at the due dates is situation specific. As all plans contain an element of uncertainty, a buffer is required in the form of a reserve. Keeping reserves is expensive and the higher the reserves, the more expensive they are.

Structural liquidity refers to the composition of the balance sheet. How far are long-term assets financed with fixed rate long-term liabilities instead of usually cheaper, short-term ones? Or is the liquidity secured for longer periods, based on floating rates and thus possibly subject to extremely high interest costs? Is the funding structure geared more towards usually more expensive share capital or does other external funding dominate?

Whether viewed as situation-specific or structural, increasing liquidity in quantitative and qualitative terms inevitably has a contradictory effect on profitability. Yet the timeframe considered differs and so does the character. When necessary measures are taken to secure that payments are fulfilled correctly on the date due, it is cash which counts: in the currency required, the amount demanded and at the clearer charged with the execution.

Cash at hand or at the ready does not play any relevant function in structural liquidity. We deal with the future and not with imminent payments. The focus is on flows which have already been determined but will hit the cash accounts in coming periods, sometimes years away. In other words, one part of cash surpluses and deficits at any future date has already been decided. Reducing potential risk to come is accompanied by and large with increased cost over the whole lifespan and not just at the payment date. Therefore, one faces a conflict of interest which has to be solved. Where then is the complementary aspect between liquidity and profitability? Admittedly, there is no way to increase liquidity, either in quantitative or qualitative terms, and avoid the cost related to it. The benefit is indirect, protecting the business case in difficult times.

2.2.3.3   *Risk related to liquidity*

The term 'security' contains many facets, as we have seen. Contrary to the belief of many managers, there are far fewer cases than expected where liquidity can contribute. Often, terms like solvency are used in a somewhat blurred way, and not applied as clearly distinct from liquidity. It may, therefore, be helpful first to get the facts clear, before analysing the links.

Any business activity and decision which directly affects the profit and loss account, or the capital, in the first instance are not related to liquidity. The second instances we will deal with later. As we are dealing with first instances now, the origin of risks like economic and capital risk can be excluded. The former relates solely to profit and loss, the latter to one's own means. Liquidity can somehow relate to them indirectly, but it never can be part of them. Terms like capital liquidity, profit and loss liquidity against liquidity simply do not exist – and this is for good reason. On the level of the risk dimension, liquidity cannot compensate for potential negative effects stemming either from strategic and volatility risks, or from downside risks.

What use then is liquidity for security reasons? In a first instance, only to secure that payment obligations can be fulfilled. This may be a little disappointing at first sight. Nevertheless, if it is not secured, the consequences will be felt severely and can lead to the failure of the company.

In a second instance, the room for manoeuvre is larger, although with a more indirect character. The elements of financial equilibrium have been determined in a process following and strongly interrelated with business planning. In the course of action, all essentials have been analysed and weighed against each other. At the end, a result has been achieved where all decisive issues are properly defined, with the overall frame in balance, including the desired level of security or risk accepted. Experience has shown many times that reality too often deviates from the plan, either positively or negatively. The investments needed to develop a new product or to establish the infrastructure in a new market turn out to be larger. The starting date of sale as well as the reception that the product is going to receive in the early phase may have been planned too optimistically. Or, on the contrary, expectations and planning have been exceeded, by so much, in fact, that capacity has to be enlarged earlier than foreseen. In such circumstances, management will have to adjust the liquidity plan. If actual need is lower than anticipated, the solution is probably easy: planned funding requirements will be used to a lesser extent. If the level required is augmented, it will be necessary to draw on fund providers.

There should be no serious obstacles to this, provided the institution's financial standing is sound at that time in the future, its debt ratio is not close to critical levels, the individual business perspective is positive and, last but not least, the lender's view of the respective industry that the company belongs to is not affected critically when the additional liquidity is asked for.

None of them may occur. We just do not know. As a precaution it makes sense always to secure a buffer to draw on, in case of unexpected need. It can take the form of cash or near-cash portfolio, committed lines not utilised or any standby facility. The choice is a question of principle as well as of financial cost and availability. Following this approach directly strengthens the issue of security within the equilibrium generally. No specific condition is anticipated, except the 'what if' case, whatever it may be. If something happens outside the plan, the buffer helps to bridge and dampen the effects as long as liquidity is the bottleneck.

2.2.3.4 *Liquidity related to growth*

Whether grown internally or externally, resources are required at the initial stage, including financial ones. The financial requirements are derived from a business plan. Liquidity is part of it. Within the relationship it plays a supporting role, to make growth both possible and sustainable. Unfortunately, liquidity does not exist in a vacuum. In-house and market conditions impact on the range of means and their available price.

Even diligent business planning cannot be more than an assessment of the most likely developments, covering the period ahead. That reality deviates from the anticipated path, on either side, is highly likely. With this in mind, potentially realistic scenarios around the planned development are set up. Otherwise, the liquidity plan may be boxed into a corner, which may be advantageous only if reality and plan coincide. In case of deviations, it may be a rather bad alternative which has been chosen.

To follow the plan but keep potential business alternatives within a wider spectrum bears fruit in several ways. Creating liquidity can be done by either reducing (other) assets to be funded or increasing liabilities to shareholders and external lenders. Which way and what mix to select depends on various conditions.

The cost analyses may indicate that financing growth should be done through external borrowing. Economically, it is the most viable route to follow. On the other hand, the capital ratio might already be tight. Letting it fall further may raise concerns about the solvency of the company, which in turn will limit the amount lenders are willing to invest. The planned level of growth could now be reduced to the extent at which solvency, investors' risk appetite and funding needs are again in balance. Alternatively, at least part of the amount could be contributed by shareholders increasing their capital with the company. It may not be the optimal way but it is a practical approach.

At the moment we will not follow the question of how shareholders would respond to the call, because we will turn to it later. Yet there are two important findings that we can already refer to. Firstly, once capital is involved, the flexibility for management is rather limited. No doubt shares can be bought back, as we experience every day. But this is a strategic measure and not accepted by shareholders and the wider markets as a tactical tool.

Further funding is viewed in a similar way; nevertheless, the handling could be done more flexibly. In relation to a bank, the full amount could be agreed on a committed basis and drawn only according to need. Although this generates commitment fees, the company would not be boxed into a corner.

The second finding refers to the economic value of being flexible. Uncertainty is an inherent part of any business. Taking final financial decisions related to uncertain economic developments can produce an inappropriate balance-sheet structure or at least turn out to be costly. To remain flexible within a suitable range of liquid means adds value to the business. That again brings us back to the significance of a dynamic liquidity approach, permitting us to define the range within which management can utilise alternatives.

2.2.3.5 *Liquidity related to risk*

With respect to security, it is the subject of reserves which deserves special attention. There are two questions that arise immediately. If reserves are supporting security against dangerous events, what then are the characteristics of the events? In addition, are there recognisable priorities in order to quantify the reserves to be held?

If done properly, all known facts are integrated into the liquidity scheme and taken care of. Payments following known maturities are catered for and planned business data are incorporated as well. Nevertheless, we cannot exclude that reality will deviate from the plan. There are almost as many terms for this condition as there are experts, but let us simply call it danger (Box 2.5): that is, the danger that events will not turn out in the way anticipated and the outcome will be undesirable.

The events themselves may be predictable and considered, predictable and not considered, or not predictable at all. Again, one can find a multitude of terms to characterise the conditions. To use modern and market-related terms, for our purposes we call them neglected danger, risk and uncertainty.

Box 2.5 The term 'danger' and its mouldings

Danger is an undesirable deviation from expectation, taken as:

- Neglected: that is, outside of one's own control.
- Risk: the deviation is quantifiable based on probability.
- Uncertainty: it cannot be assessed and quantified.

Neglected danger refers to events which are beyond the control of an institution and the impact on business is not controllable with any of the means at hand. Earlier we called them the equivalent of the biblical Flood, and they include severe war activity within the main area of business or natural disasters of immense proportions. If the world around us falls to pieces, nobody can plan and secure.

Risk, within the frame of action, is quantifiable, based on probability. In banking, we know for example about the likelihood or probability of experiencing losses stemming from customers which fail. The same is true for almost any other market exposure. The effects on rating-related funds, in case the company falls below the threshold, is another example. Danger of this kind can and must be computed and the effects on liquidity taken care of in the form of reserves. Deviation from other items on business plans can be treated in a similar fashion. There is only one critical point: where to put the limit for calling the effect expected – at 2σ, 3σ or 4σ? In others word, would you be satisfied with a probability of 95% or one up to 99.9%? These questions are significant but do not give the full answer. Wherever one puts the threshold, there is a reality beyond.

Uncertainty, as it is called in technical terms, means one simply cannot assess the risk. To continue with the example above, the distance between the limit set beforehand, wherever it is, and 100% is unknown. We know the worst case experienced. However, is it also the maximum one can face in the future, or does it go beyond, even far beyond? Because of the severe implications, neglecting the possibility is not the remedy. To cater for an unknown quantity, however, is not the remedy either. This brings us to the second question: are there recognisable priorities to limit the amount?

If all parts and subparts of a business are equally important and if security is taken as the main goal, there is no alternative but to finance the company with shareholder capital both exclusively and generously. The means are then available to absorb losses, and there are no legal obligations to guarantee dividends or repayment of capital. Suboptimal profitability and consequently hesitant shareholders to finance the whole part – they may have more profitable alternative investments available – usually hinder rather than make this strategic route feasible.

Security could also be enhanced through a combination of shareholder capital and long-term external financing. Here again, the obstacle is profitability, which would suffer too much as long-term funds generally trade at higher rates compared with shorter periods. In addition, the risk for investors rises, the longer they have to wait for repayment. This is compensated by higher spreads which come on top of the basic rate related to maturity.

A further point concerns flexibility. To keep a company in business in the long term means running it in a profitable way. In a changing environment this can only be sustained by constantly adapting to the new challenges and opportunities. When going through these processes, the composition of assets and liabilities changes and hence the optimal liquidity structure has to be adapted as well.

Box 2.6 Prioritising present business activities

Based on business policy, present activities can be subdivided into:

- Core business: This includes all present activities which are seen by management as the cornerstone of the business.
- Business expansion: If the expansion is related to the cornerstone of activities it is also called 'future core business'.
- Attractive investments: These are profitable business opportunities, but not judged essential for upholding the business concept.

The degree to protect the business under severe conditions declines in falling order.

A clearly defined strategy is the basis whenever security is considered. In this respect, the traditional segregation between fixed and current assets does not take us any further. Accounting rules distinguish between types of assets but not the strategic value they are given by management. What is declared as 'core business', in which areas will the capacity be expanded and become core business in the future, and what is seen as an attractive investment for its own sake may have the future potential to diversify into a new business area (Box 2.6).

Core business, as the cornerstone of sustained profitability, has to be financed in a secure way, by capital or long-term funding. It includes not only fixed but also current assets, as long as they are vital for keeping the power to produce. In relation to banking, one would include short-term assets belonging to the franchise of the bank.

Capacity expansion can take various forms. Present production centres can be enlarged or new subsidiaries in the home country or abroad can be founded. To decide on the appropriate funding structure further questions have to be answered. What stage of planning and implementation has the project reached? Is the investment essential for the financial stability of the company? If the project were abandoned at this stage, what would the financial implications be? The answer concerning optimal funding is no longer given as for core business. Evaluating the inherent risks and formulating the risk appetite for oneself will lead to different solutions.

Attractive investments with no decisive links to the core business are a different matter. Under stable business conditions the extra earnings are a favourable addition. If, however, the going gets tough, usually liquidity status and the financial status suffers. To ease the pressure, non-core business is the first to be made over to cash. Funding should thus not be long term, but at least ought to cover the time it takes to conclude the transaction.

2.2.3.6 *Liquidity related to profitability*

In certain instances liquidity, security, profitability, and growth are so strongly interweaved that one should not segregate them artificially. It is for this reason that we put some aspects under the previous heading. Nevertheless, they remain valid for this section, although we will not repeat them.

Liquidity is an important issue, but should be optimised and not maximised, not least because of cost implications. There is still one open question. It focuses on measures which first enhance profitability and indirectly benefit liquidity. A typical example within the production stream is the decision on stock keeping. Traditionally large stocks were kept in order to secure availability. On the other side, apart from respective storage cost, liquidity was required to finance the large stock. If the turnover is increased, there is less volume which has to be kept in stock and the funding required will be lower as well. Delivery just in time is a further development which reduces storage to an absolute minimum and requires almost no liquidity at all.

There are also other ways and means in the financial sector. The chain of effects in these cases starts with liquidity effects benefiting profitability and not the other way around as before. Leasing instead of purchasing reduces the payment per period, although at the end of the lifetime the cash spent might not differ greatly. To receive early payments from debtors means cash at hand which does not have to be borrowed. Factoring is one way, pay as we go is another. The latter is quite common for example in housing and ship construction. Offering discounts on early payment serves the same objective.

To complete the circle we will refer to further measures that affect liquidity: for example, sale of licences; special sales actions; or delaying full investment for maintenance. The impact on liquidity in all these instances is felt immediately. The result on profitability beyond the period of direct action is unclear. A mere shift of future earnings into the present cannot be excluded.

There are comparable links in banking. Assets may be bought with a view to structuring and securitising them. Funds needed to bridge the time between collection and sale can then be of a short-term nature and thus cheaper as congruent financing when kept on the balance sheet. A similar effect is achieved when keeping longer-term marketable assets on the books. Doubtless, they are on the balance sheet but impinge on liquidity in different ways than non-marketable ones: although of a long-term nature based on the underlying maturity, they can be either employed for self-financing through repo transactions etc., or kept as unencumbered and financed short term on an unsecured basis and sold whenever wished or required. There is, however, a residual risk involved when markets turn less liquid: the assets may no longer be marketable under such circumstances and short-term funding can turn out to be inappropriate as the needed subsequent financing may no longer be possible.

2.2.4 Summary

From a purely financial point of view, it would make sense to aspire to a mixture of share capital and external financing which promises a maximum return for the owner of the company. In other words, as long as the costs for borrowing do not reach the level of the return on investment, further needs should be covered through external funds. The decision might then be reduced to the question of preferred sources, structures and tenors. In the process of evaluation and planning, the considerations and requirements discussed above would be integrated and weighted before the final plan was decided on and implemented.

By doing so, financial equilibrium might become out of balance. From Figure 2.2 we can easily see how much the pillars are actually interrelated. Prioritising any of the other three goals, namely growth, security or profitability, will inevitably affect liquidity. Some policy decisions influence more the quantity needed than the structure of funding.

An ambitious growth target, for example, usually requires heavy investments, thus absorbing liquidity accordingly. For liquidity status, it does not matter whether it is financed out of liquidity reserves (what can be called the war chest) or by additional borrowing externally. In both cases, the measure will initially lower the level of liquidity. The difference is in the outcome. If liquidity, after financing the investment out of reserves, is still at an acceptable level, no further measures are required. Yet the buffer is smaller or even eliminated. Room for further measures or counteracting unexpected events is thus reduced or gone altogether, if it is intended not to depend solely on investors. If reserves are to be restored or are not available at all, funding is needed to replenish them to the required level.

The quantitative aspect also plays its part by changing the level of security. This time, the measures and adjustments required are not initiated by investment as before. Security, as one of the goals within the frame of equilibrium, has its own genuine aims. And they compete with the other pillars of the equilibrium. Thus, the chosen degree of security itself determines the level of liquid funds made available. Once again, however, the impact is limited to the amount required and does not go any further.

Profitability is different in this respect. We have moved away from liquidity level and reached gap financing. The quantity needed is given. The question is which channels to use and what mix of shareholder and external funds to envisage. If profitability in the sense of return on equity is the focal point, share capital will be kept at such a level, which maximises the return for its holders. With capital and its respective level, we deal with one of the operative key elements within the frame of liquidity management. It does not just serve as the denominator in the equation given in Box 2.7:

Box 2.7 Profitability and its equation

$$\text{Profitability} = \frac{\text{Net profit}}{\text{Share capital}}.$$

Indirect impacts on 'credible policy' should also not be neglected. More important, capital determines solvency, signifying the level up to which a company is able to cover losses. Through these two routes capital is most probably the most important single determinant for the assessment of a 'credible policy'.

The latter in turn is taken by investors as a key indicator when it comes to forming an attitude towards a specific investment, i.e. whether to choose the company or an alternative one. This, of course, on the basis of comparable market-related returns – comparable in the sense that differences in risk are reflected. This is true for shareholders and external investors alike. The plan to maximise profitability through the perfect mix of funding might therefore find its constraint. Apart from various non-financial and 'soft' facts, there are some financial ratios which are not missed when evaluating the financial standing of a firm, as in Box 2.8:

Box 2.8 Defining the debt ratio

$$\text{Debt ratio} = \frac{\text{External borrowing}}{\text{Shareholder funds}}.$$

This reflects the capital gearing applied. It is significant primarily as an indicator for solvency. In difficult circumstances, when the going gets rough, it is shareholder capital that has to take the burden. If it is too low, i.e. the debt ratio too high, solvency is at stake and an investment may be charged as risky beyond acceptable levels. As inherent risk differs from one branch of industry to another, there exists no unanimous ratio. Nevertheless, for any industry, a benchmark does exist. The ratio indirectly reflects also the capacity to absorb risk-related losses, if potential danger becomes a reality.

The capital gearing, however, leaves out the composition in respect of fixed and current assets. While the debt ratio may be at an acceptable level, on the basis of cost considerations external funds with rather short durations may be taken. As a result, parts of fixed assets are funded incongruently. Funding thus has to follow the 'golden balance-sheet rule' as defined above (2.2.1.2).

To the extent that the ratio stays above 1.0, long-term assets are not fully covered by liabilities with respective maturities. As discussed earlier, this constellation puts the company at an undue risk of not being able to replace the maturing funds in the future. For our purpose, at this stage, we have no need to go deeper into the subject. We thus neglect what type of assets to add under fixed assets. Some assets may be of shorter maturity but prolonged in character, like raw materials and personnel, which are to be kept continuously at a minimal level to assure production; or in the case of banks, short-term assets being part of the franchise. It is important to recognise that any unacceptable deviation from the rule bears negatively on 'credible policy' and thus on investor attitude.

As soon as liquidity aspects are taken into consideration, maximising return on earnings (ROE) might be constrained. It is most likely that implications of investor attitude become detrimental before the ideal mix of external and shareholder funds is reached. Whether shareholders are willing to make the necessary additional contribution is not guaranteed at all. With this in mind, it cannot be excluded also that funding may not meet requirements under the present planned business policy. In such a case, business parameters already set have to be reviewed and adjusted. It may be frustrating to stretch or even abandon the implementation of a very promising business plan. However, the alternative in too many cases has been the origin of illiquidity and ultimate company failure.

2.3   THE CONCEPT ENLARGED TO FIT BANKS

The concept of the magical polygon developed in corporate finance is a big step forward when compared with the traditional approaches and covers a wide range of banking aspects as well. On that basis one could apply the principle directly to banks, were it not for some observations made during the discussion of specific relationships within the polygon. One of these is capital, another refers to financial health or rating. Within an economy, banks still play a vital role as intermediary between lender and borrower, although corporate borrowing directly in the markets has increased over time. Financial institutions thus could also be called the 'piggybanks' of an economy. When it comes to funding itself, their dependency on wholesale markets is much more pronounced compared with a corporate, however. The latter always has the possibility to refer to bank credits at the end of the day. This route is closed to financial institutions. Their bilateral contact does not follow the characteristic of a lender–borrower relationship but is shaped by an attitude known as 'at arm's length'. Especially when related to borrowing in the wholesale markets, and this is the biggest part being tapped by large and internationally orientated banks, risk sensitivity is a distinctive feature. It is in this context that financial stability and capital as one of the pillars determining it need to be incorporated in the financial equilibrium for banks.

Although the findings discussed above remain valid, it would be inappropriate simply to add the missing elements to the four pillars of the magic quadrangle. What is required is a concept which puts all elements into a sequence and shows their direct dependences in a concrete manner. Unfortunately, to achieve this goal we have to return to a few issues dealt with before, but in a very concentrated form.

2.3.1   Introduction

It is often declared that liquidity aspects in banks, as against corporate ones, differ too much to be comparable (Zeranski, 2005, page 2f.). The reasoning behind these statements refers to observations such as:

- Banks have easy and sufficient access to the money and capital markets; for corporates it is much more difficult to get funding, and specifically at short notice.
- For banks, the flow of liquidity is less predictable. Within the contractual agreements their customers can and will make arrangements (particularly) for their deposits, according to their needs and without consulting the bank in advance. Non-banks have the benefit of being able to determine the flows to a much greater extent. Their flows are rather internally than externally determined.
- Through their customer base, banks, to some extent, can count on a rather stable base for funding, which corporates cannot. It is understood that the relatively stable element is a minor part of the total borrowed. Nevertheless, where deposit insurance schemes are in place, the stability of these funds is assessed as rather high. The observed behaviour has found its way into national rules concerning liquidity requirements, as for example in Germany.

The diverse statements seem to be somewhat contradictory. Thus, we will now evaluate the differences, analyse them, and see whether they are significant for our purposes. Yet, it must be assumed that we cannot restrict ourselves to differences only. If we refer again to short-term assets as part of the franchise, according to the understanding and principles of accounting, they are short term by nature. The reality looks different, if the going concern of a specific firm is taken as policy. If necessary, we will have to adjust to new realities.

2.3.2   Business policy as a starting point

Any policy with a chance of succeeding will have to be based on some basic findings, as we stated in the intermediary summary at the end of Chapter 1. The points listed were concluded from the findings of the prior discussion on liquidity and liquidity risk. In the sections to come, the knowledge gained up to now will be evaluated in the light of the principal requirements for banks. This relates to policy, relevant parameters and indicators alike. The conclusions will then serve as the bases for a liquidity policy of a banking institution.

We start with policy.

According to Volkart (2003), there is a general understanding about the goals that companies are striving to achieve and get into balance (Figure 2.4).

Generally speaking, and at a first glance, there is nothing which could not apply for a privately owned bank. For community, county or otherwise state-owned banks, the accents and weights may have different priorities. Some non-financial aims may be put before profitability. Nevertheless, they have to be profitable if their purpose is to be fulfilled in the future as well.

The range of business goals is wide. Many of them are not financial at all, but still contain an aspect related to it. In order to avoid having too many goals to deal with, we will see whether we can drop at least some of the non-financial ones. Compatibility is not to be limited to the principles as defined at the end of Chapter 1. For our purposes, the elements of the enlarged financial equilibrium are equally important.

Company goal	Finance-related aspects
Profit/profitability	Economical way of funding Minimise tax obligation Increase return on equity
Value of company	Increase value of company Focus on shareholder aims Maximise shareholder value
Growth and size of company	Financing of internal or external growth Analysing potential for growth Balancing growth and financial policy
Liquidity	Secure payment obligations Secure solvency Analyse cash flow effects of shareholders and external financing
Security	Protect value and shareholder capital Limit downside risk Minimise liquidity risk Financing congruent with lifespan of assets Keep shareholder capital in line with risk taken Assure appropriate liquidity policy
Independence	Autonomy against third parties Creating liquidity reserves Supporting internal financing
Flexibility	Ability to adjust to external and internal changes Financial flexibility through various funding sources
Social aims/environment	Staff-related social security Environmental protection
Image, prestige	Informative publication of financial items
Personal aims of stakeholders	Taking measures to judge the company as a going concern

Figure 2.4   Business goals and financial aspects (*Source*: Adapted from Volkart, 2003, page 124f.)

The aspects of non-financial aims, relevant for our purposes, have all been dealt with within our framework. That is:

- The company as a going concern (stakeholder aims).
- Measures to be in place to tap various funding sources (flexibility).
- Focusing on shareholder aims, including maximising value (value of the company).
- Creating liquidity reserves and supporting internal financing (independence).

The remaining two pairs of items (social/environmental aims as well as image/prestige) are important in themselves but hardly influenced significantly by our financial aims – at least not in a direct way. We therefore neglect them and move forward to the next level, the parameters.

2.3.3 Financial determinants and their description

A first link from business to financial policy has been made. As we can detect, the majority of all business goals are financial or finance related. But how do financial items link to each other? To list them simply in any order or combine them with each other will not enable us to get the answer. What is required is a solid understanding of the directional effects that each financial item is subjected to, both received and made, and a qualitative assessment of its position within the frame of the relationship.

2.3.3.1 A graphical view of banking business

Financial relationships within banking are diverse and rather complex. Production (private, commercial and investment banking, asset management, etc.) can take the form of balance-sheet or off-balance-sheet contracts. To reduce risk exposure, part of the original position is hedged. Shareholder capital performs its various functions, such as absorbing potential losses, serving as a means of financing, impacting solvency, etc., or the resulting financial gaps have to be funded according to business activities and risk considerations. Each of the items is both an initiator and receiver of relationships, but not to the same degree. The number of links may differ at both ends of contact.

In order to get a clearer picture, it may be helpful to present the interaction of a bank in a visual form. For practical reasons, we will limit activities to the most relevant ones. Otherwise, the level of complexity one tries to avoid in this way will be reached again, although in the form of a different outline. The approach to be employed is based on a technique used to deal with solving complex problems (Probst and Gomez, 1989, page 9f.), where arrows signify the direction of the relationship between two items.

The principle of the method requires all relevant elements to be taken and a sequence found with no crossing of arrows. The result differs significantly from the structure shown in Figure 2.2. Instead of simply stating each element as being interrelated to any other one, we now learn how they are linked together: whether directly or indirectly; who is an initiator and a receiver, and with whom; and last but not least, whether there are single or multiple contacts. As no crossing of arrows is permitted, the sequence is determined by the methodological approach only. In other words, no individual interference is possible to get a preferred shape without producing a crossing of arrows. As can be seen in Figure 2.5, the sequential approach results in a sort of dynamic flowchart. Beginning with commercial items on the left side, gradually links to financial determinants are established whereby the latter, as we move to the right, take over completely.

The scheme clearly shows the various individual links, which in Figure 2.2 have been presented by four parameters and 12 combinations in total, but without showing degrees of intensity. One can also recognise the circular course of effects. For example, the required funding of the gap demands an increase in capital which, if not or only partially provided by shareholders, determines the level of external financing.

Furthermore, the ratio between capital and external funds is again significant. If capital is kept low to enhance ROE or for any other reason, solvency and consequently credible policy/rating will be negatively affected. The latter in turn impacts on investor attitude. Assuming that rating has been falling to critical levels, external funding will become sparse or cease completely.

Each position in the scheme can reach limits which in turn then impinge on prior ones. In such cases we follow the route backwards. An example may illustrate the point. By sounding

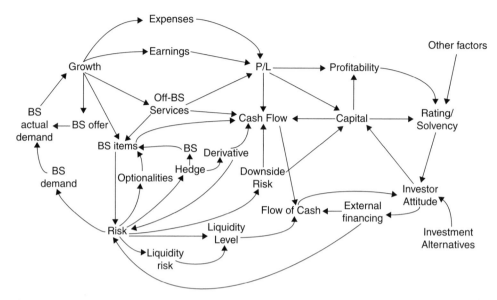

Figure 2.5   Graphical overview of related financial items in a bank

out the attitude of envisaged investors in the course of the budgeting process, it may turn out that the gap planned for cannot be funded – at least not to the full extent. The route backwards passes flow of cash, liquidity level and then risk. If funding reductions in other areas are not acceptable, it leads through balance-sheet items, and ends in growth, one of the pillars of financial equilibrium. Thus, an ambitious aim, although sensible in many ways, must be adjusted for funding realities.

When bringing the polygon into equilibrium, not all positions are equally relevant. Having to deal with a limited number of key factors also eases the complexity within the planning process. One can sensibly assume that key positions must be linked up stronger than other ones. Here again the scheme can help, regarding growth, profit/loss, acceptable level of risk, flow of cash, liquidity level desired as well as level of capital and rating. Any adjustments in any one of the key factors affect in sequence the preceding ones and the ones to follow, respectively. And because of the many links, the flows of non-key positions undergo respective adjustments simultaneously

2.3.3.2   Assessing the key factors

Based on the chart in Figure 2.5 we select the items which are linked up stronger, as a concentration of several links on one single item is a first sign of its relevance. Either the financial aspect is a multi-receiver and thus determined by several other items, or it is strongly influential on related matters (Box 2.9). In some cases it may be a mixture of both of them. We will start on the left side and gradually move to the right.

2.3.3.3   Summary

Based on our detailed discussions in the context of the general financial equilibrium, we soon recognised its limited meaning in the case of banks. As a means for a better understanding

Box 2.9 Key factors of financial equilibrium for banks

Growth: Being the initial determinant of business policy decisions, growth affects several further items. They can be related to balance-sheet or off-balance-sheet businesses from where new effects emerge. Growth also plays a vital part when it comes to creating net earnings (P/L), through both of the lines mentioned above. Indirectly it determines risk through various channels.

Profit/loss: Net earnings contain several dimensions on both sides. Without doubt, P/L is a vital factor for any business. In itself P/L is not exactly meaningful. Any given figure can be judged as a successful or mediocre result. A significant assessment requires a comparison with the necessary shareholder capital employed in order to achieve the respective result. For these reasons it makes sense to evaluate net earnings expressed as *profitability* and not just in itself.

Risk: It is largely growth which determines the level of risk a bank is burdened with initially. Risk policy thus plays a key part in deciding about the level seen as appropriate to keep. Hedging is a way to reduce it; limiting potential exposures stemming from optionalities is a means to contain it, for example. Risk can take the form of either losses (downside risk) or liquidity exposure.

Flow of cash: The term is used in the following way. Liquidity is based on cash elements. The respective flows originate from balance-sheet and off-balance sheet transactions, from services provided to customers and the cash element of profit and loss. If it could be assured to have in- and outflows of cash in balance, that is every single day and during the day, even per currency, the item would be a non-event for our purposes. As the assumption is not valid, balances add to the financial gap and affect risk as well.

Liquidity: As stated earlier, risk is neither an amount nor a ratio. It is a level of capacity to fulfil payment obligations when they fall due. As such, liquidity is not expressed in its own terms but as a financial cash gap. The latter is determined by the difference between the envisaged level of liquidity necessary to fulfil the obligation and the balances stemming from the flow of cash. The financial or funding gap can be financed through capital and, to the extent lacking, by means of external financing.

Capital: Except as a vehicle to close the funding gap at least partly, shareholder capital also is one of the two elements determining profitability. The second strong string relates to its effect on solvency and thus indirectly on the rating of the bank. As the buffer which can absorb losses in case they occur, it plays a vital role in the assessment process of rating agencies.

Rating: The rating of a bank primarily is made up of the capital strength and the outlook on profitability. Other factors play an adjusting role and relate to the sustainability of the two items just mentioned, the quality of management judged in the form of a coherent business and risk policy etc. The rating itself is a key factor when it comes to the attitude of investors regarding their willingness to invest in the specific bank, be it through shareholder capital or repayable short- and long-term funds.

of links and the importance of the various financial items within the grid we referred to a technique used to solve complex problems. Using a sequential approach, with principally no crossing of arrows, we arrived at a sort of dynamic flowchart. Beginning with commercial items on the left side, gradually the link to financial determinants was established, and the latter, as we moved more to the right, took over completely.

When analysing the graph, not all positions are equally relevant. Consequently, we selected those with many links, as receiver, initiator or a combination of both of them. The scheme clearly shows the various links, which otherwise have to be expressed verbally, and due to the enlarged concept is spread over seven key functions and no less than 42 combinations in total.

One can also recognise the circular course of effects. For example, securing a defined liquidity level demands a specific structure in the flow of cash. If it is not already given, the gap determines the level of additional external financing. However, if funds are not available to the level required the risk element is augmented, and if this is not acceptable, growth will be negatively affected. Furthermore, the ratio between capital and external funds is again significant. If capital is kept low to enhance ROE or for any other reason, solvency and consequently the rating will be negatively affected. The latter in turn impacts on investor attitude. Assuming credibility has been falling to critical levels, external funding will become sparse or cease completely.

But how will they interrelate on a high level view? If a policy for liquidity is formulated, this question has to be answered. Before addressing this point, however, we need to deal with a few loose ends.

2.3.4   Towards a financial equilibrium for banks

We have learned that for corporate management, achieving or at least keeping a high level of the company and shareholder value is the supreme goal. If management succeeds in the endeavour, the owners are satisfied; the outlook for the company looks promising, products as well as services provided find a positive response from the customer base and management is valued highly. In order to reach the financial status aimed for, the financial elements of growth, security, profitability and liquidity are brought into equilibrium.

The management of banks also strives to achieve, or at least keep, a high level of company and shareholder value. The financial element of growth is missing, however. As Volker (2003, page 124) states (Figure 2.6):

> A classical view regarding financial policy for banks is the one relating to the magic triangle: liquidity, security and profitability. (Author's translation)

Schierenbeck (2003b, page 1) also leaves growth out of the equation. According to him:

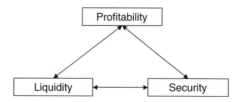

Figure 2.6   The classical triangle in banking

Managing the value of the company means integrating profitability and risk – controlling explicitly into the policy frame. (Author's translation)

When risk controlling is dealt with in more detail, risk exposure is separated into 'value at risk' and 'liquidity at risk'. In this indirect way, growth is included, although not as one of the pillars of the equilibrium. For us, two questions arise: Can and will we exclude growth as one of the pillars within financial policy? And are there significant unwanted implications if liquidity is summed under risk, at the same level as value at risk?

2.3.4.1 A case for growth

In a relatively static environment and from a practitioner's point of view, one could hardly oppose having growth excluded from the financial equilibrium as a main pillar. Gradual movements and minor changes could be taken care of within the management process. The necessary measures would be performed on a level below the pillars. Looking at this from another angle, implications stemming from liquidity most probably would not impinge greatly on the principal goals.

Most banks do not live in a stable environment, however. Over the last two decades, the industry has gone through remarkable changes. Three of them are especially relevant to liquidity managers:

- Pressure on profitability has led to business expansion and will continue to do so. Expansion through acquisition is one of the ways to cost saving measures, if internal growth seems not to be the appropriate route to follow. While mergers at the beginning were limited to acquisitions within a country, lately they have expanded to cross country dimensions.
- Expansion is not limited to a growing balance sheet. Banks for example provide services in asset management, wealth management for individuals and payment execution on behalf of clients. Besides, most of them are engaged in trading activities. Growth in most of these areas will hardly affect the balance sheet significantly. Yet they all produce flows of cash to a significant degree.
- At a time when balance sheets were less sizable and the investment attitude of the retail sector much more conservative, relatively stable saving and related deposits in many an institution were a solid and prime funding source. The range of investment vehicles for this group has been enlarged over the years and banks have been successfully directing saving deposits away from their balance sheets into various types of asset management portfolios. A policy for growth in one specific area can thus affect the volume in another business segment, including the relative stable funding just mentioned.

The examples only illustrate the graphical presentation in Figure 2.5. From a practitioner's point of view and one responsible for liquidity management in a bank, growth cannot be treated as a financial goal of secondary importance. The implications on liquidity are too severe. Growth has to be part of financial equilibrium; it has to play the role of a pillar.

2.3.4.2 The planning process and aspects of growth to be considered

Growth has many aspects (see Figure 2.7). And within the business plan, they all have to be considered. For our purposes, we pick the ones which at the end affect 'profit and loss' on the

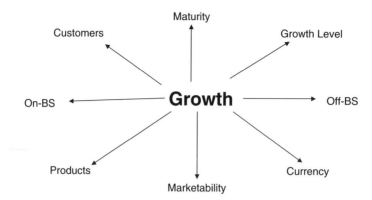

Figure 2.7 Aspects of growth

one hand and 'risk danger' on the other hand. Both of them have a bearing on liquidity, either directly or indirectly.

To start with, it may be helpful to comprehend the term itself. It is understood that growth can be positive or negative. Zero growth is an option as well. Growth can relate to balance-sheet or off-balance-sheet transactions. Even in the case of zero growth, the structure within can change. Lending to customers in long-term maturities may be planned to increase to the extent at which short-term advances are to be curtailed, or vice versa. The total volume then stays unchanged, yet demand on liquidity will differ, due to an altered maturity spectrum. That is what we mean when we talk about growth level.

Products and customers in many cases go very much hand in hand. Specific customer segments have specific potential needs. Or, to put it another way, certain products are not within the requirements of all bank customers. The retail sector will hardly ask for standby credits in order to secure funding in case the CP market fails to provide the means. On the other hand, a corporate does not belong to the client base asking for consumer loans. It may sound trivial. Nevertheless, plans have to be broken down into great detail. It is the detailed information which is required to permit the liquidity manager to structure his or her most likely flowchart for the coming periods.

It also includes the time factor. Business goals are defined for a period. The duration will depend on the time horizon of the planning phase. Long term covers a time of 3–5 years; medium term goes down to 1 year; and below this is short term and budget related. Whatever timespan we take, even if the focus is on the budget period of 1 year, growth targets are usually set for the end of the period or defined as the average of the year. Yet being liquid is not defined as having the cash available at the end of the period or on average. It is the capacity to fulfil payment obligations each and every day. To secure against imponderables, the liquidity manager can be pushed to build up a cushion, in the form of inflated liquidity reserves. To act economically, it is advisable also to quantify the most likely drawdown over the period, broken up into phases and currencies as precisely as possible.

Whenever one deals with positions on the balance sheet, and in particular when they are set with fixed maturities, two critical points are to be focused on. Both relate to a possible deviation from the plan, either as to contracts concluded in volume terms or as to effective drawdown. Periodic and frequent assessments of progress made compared with targets should give a good enough basis to adjust the future flows.

It is not uncommon to put investment banking and trading-related investments and products into a special purpose vehicle – a so-called SPV. Whether or not the SPV is legally integrated into the mother company and in this way part of the stated group balance sheet is not so much the point; in some cases it can be treated both ways. What really matters is how these investments are treated organisationally. To include all transactions on the group balance sheet in the liquidity profile goes without saying. An SPV is not on it in all circumstances, and quite often it is financed externally. In other words, one easily can 'forget' about SPVs. In the absence of stressed conditions related to markets as well as the assets in the SPV, group liquidity management will not be asked for its funding service as the portfolio is financed externally. Although not required under normal circumstances, liquidity management remains the ultimate lender, the lender of last resort within the bank. Thus, the stress case has to be catered for and ought to become part of the planning in liquidity management. To neglect the function as lender of last resort is easily done. The implications are often severe, as the amounts involved can be very substantial. Moreover, time to action is mostly short and the event may coincide with a general shortage of funds which also affects the group funding capacity.

The mechanics is not limited to an SPV but equally applies to all investments in the form of participations. Normally, the units function on their own, smoothly and efficiently, until the day of stressed circumstances. Sometimes a subsidiary or a legally independent company within the group might take a substantial portion of all the funding for the group. Investors of any type will judge the group as a whole and not treat each single unit as independent and unrelated to the parent company and its subsidiaries. Problems in one end will rush through the group's organisation chart and affect everybody. Consequently, preparing for the stress case, with very few exceptions, is not sufficient. What is required is a full organisational integration of all the liquidity-related elements of the group.

Off-balance-sheet business and transactions have to be treated differently. Those with potentially the most severe implications have been treated under the term 'optionalities'. Standby facilities in the form of lines of credit for working capital, letters of credit and backup lines for securing the CP issuer are examples. Letters of credit serve as a secured buffer for unforeseen funding needs by corporates; rating agencies take them as an element when assessing the financial strength. CP backup lines protect the respective issuer, as the bank will step in should the market not provide the funding for whatever reason. It is assumed, and largely confirmed by experience, that the latter two facilities are rarely drawn on. The effects in time and magnitude are, however, similar to the implications in the function as lender of last resort when taken, often without much early warning and in large sums – at least, that is the risk. In contrast to the SPV, there is no funding demanded in normal situations, whether external or internal. Nevertheless, it has to be taken care of.

As above, off-balance-sheet transactions include all types of trading and services. Trading is not a relevant liquidity absorber, so long as no positions are taken either as cash or forward. As most cash transactions have a value date 2 days later than when the trade is concluded and forwards can be of maturities of 10 years or more, not even intra-day liquidity plays a noticeable part. The picture turns as soon as positions are taken. The word used by traders is 'carrying' a position and it usually absorbs and sometimes creates liquidity. Especially if trading aspects are combined with investment portfolios on own account, the sums reached can be considerable. Thus the magnitude has to be integrated into the planning.

This brings us to the services like asset, wealth and portfolio management in general. Provided it is third-party money that is managed, funds are provided from and returned to persons and institutions that are not part of the balance sheet. Effects, if any, may be experienced through payment executions as clearer in currencies. As we have seen before, the clearing function requires the means in cash or cash substitutes in order to secure the execution of payments. Depending on how extensively the service is developed, reserves kept with the ultimate clearing institution, mainly the respective central bank, add up, and more so as major international currencies are added. It implies, however, that flows of cash are segregated into different currencies – also in the planning process.

We will round off this section by addressing two elements which create funding or at least liquidity. One relates to assets, the other to liabilities, but both of them are balance-sheet items of great importance to a liquidity manager. Within a policy framework for retail banking, customer deposits that are of a more stable nature than wholesale funds should not be missed. Promoting these liabilities not only augments business-related funding, but can serve as a measure to bring depositors closer to the bank for asset- or off-balance-sheet-related services. Despite being of short maturities legally, their greater stability actually brings them closer to longer-term funds, or at least a bigger portion of it.

Even with a long legal maturity attached, assets can be close to cash. From an economic or business point of view, a 3-month advance to a corporate is moved more away from cash than a 30-year US Treasury bond, for example. The difference lies in the degree of being marketable. Basically, marketable assets have the potential to 'finance' themselves, if the holders wish to do so. The process can be transacted through outright selling, securitisation, repo transactions or by using the asset as collateral. In any way, marketable instruments can be highly effective means to ease and reduce funding requirements. As such, they have to be segregated, separately budgeted for and brought to the attention of the liquidity manager.

When excluding self-financing, in all the discussions we implicitly assume general or unsecured funding. Unsecured means that no independent instrument serves as security, other than the financial standing of the bank. If the bank fails to perform its duties towards the investor, no regress to an alternative value is possible. Secured funding indeed reaches beyond securitisation, repo transactions and collateralisation. The probably biggest market in this context refers to mortgages. In Germany, for example, the market is governed by strict rules. However, if the mortgage fulfils the requirement and the bank has been authorised, first-tranche mortgage-secured bonds (so-called *Pfandbriefe*, which cannot exceed 60% of the property value) can be issued, with the property serving as security on and above the standing of the bank. Other countries have equal or similar setups. From a liquidity manager's point of view, it means not only diversification of resources, but also greater stability. As these funds are secured additionally through the related assets, the respective market segment traditionally responds relatively little to a temporary weakening of the financial strength of the bank.

Having dealt with the aspects of growth, the results have to be transposed to profit and loss as well as risk danger. Calculating the expected cost related P/L is laborious, but for us the result, whatever it may be, can be taken at face value and does not need further liquidity-related analyses.

We started with business policy, moved to financial policy and defined the role of liquidity within the frame of equilibrium; now it is liquidity policy that we are going to address.

3

Liquidity as an Element of Banking Risk

Under this heading we will address the subjects which are related to liquidity policy. The chapter deals with the risk aspects in banks and distinguishes liquidity risk (LAR) from downside risk or, as it could be called, the danger of losses (VAR). The terms LAR and VAR are synonyms for liquidity and downside risk respectively. The aim of the chapter is to come up with an integrated concept in which liquidity is incorporated into a wider frame of business and financial policies. It will serve us as the basis needed to formulate elements of a liquidity policy.

3.1 SOME CLARIFICATIONS

Within business and financial policy, the approaches for banks and corporates distinguish themselves gradually but not fundamentally. The process and the key elements are not exactly the same, but at least they are comparable. The differences relate to the dissimilar purposes they serve: providing goods in the case of corporates and offering financial services when it comes to banks. Although the distinction may look obvious and thus trivial, its relevance for policy and the management of liquidity should not be neglected.

A bank is a financial intermediary. As such, its 'production' relates to money, but the 'goods' used are money as well. Production in commercial companies is also related to money. Whatever is produced or provided as a service finds the equivalent of value in the form of a price and consequently can be expressed in money terms. There the correspondence between banking and non-banking industries ends.

For a corporate, the basic 'material' used is goods at any stage of refinement and in every form. For banks, the 'material' used is cash. It may have different names such as project financing, mortgage financing or overdraft within cash management. As a result, maturities differ, the instrument may qualify for covered funding, it may be accepted by central banks as collateral or not, but the 'material' used is money; and for the purpose of liquidity it is money in the form of cash. For the moment it is sufficient to keep the distinction in mind. We will come back to it later in the section.

The other distinction relates to risk. All firms, whether engaged in the corporate or financial sector, are exposed to markets. Both groups are affected by the ups and downs of the economy. Directly, it is due to changing demand, failure of debtors or shortage in supply, which is followed by rising cost. Indirectly, it is due to secondary effects on their infrastructure which may be either strained or left with unused capacity. Both businesses again can relate to a historic record of the respective industries and thus roughly assess the potential implications. However, it is in banking alone where independent supervisory bodies determine which methods to use, what parameters to employ and what minimum standards to adhere to regarding risk.

Before we turn to the two concepts of VAR and LAR it may be helpful to look at the term 'risk' again. As stated earlier, in the proper understanding of the word, risk stands for an uncertain development which could end in a better or worse result than the planned or anticipated result. The first one is called chance in the form of upward potential, the other one means danger (Spremann, Pfeil and Weckbach, 2001, page 321). As both terms, VAR and

LAR, relate to a potentially negative development, we look at danger and use the word at the same time as the generic term mutually for both of them.

3.2   THE CONCEPT OF DOWNSIDE RISK (VAR) AND ITS CIRCLE OF RELATIONSHIPS

3.2.1   A basic understanding of VAR

In several instances we treated risk as an integral part of business activities. For banks, risk as a business category has a special dimension. As a financial intermediary it is one of its principal functions to take over and manage risk in many ways. For its customers and counterparts, a bank is the business partner onto which they can offload any risks they do not want to carry themselves. The driving forces relate to the assets as well as liabilities of a bank. Although downside risk focuses on assets when it comes to balance-sheet transactions, the initial force relates to liabilities. Loans to the customer base, for example, are financed through the funds of depositors and investors which prefer bank risk compared with corporate or consumer credit risk. Were it not for this reason, the function of a bank as financial intermediary would be much reduced. Customers will also optimise undesirable imbalances in interest maturities, currencies and so forth through respective off-balance-sheet transactions with banks. For taking over the risks, the bank is compensated in the form of margins or fees, whereby the professional knowledge in managing risk allows dealing with it at a cost below the compensation received.

In our terminology, danger is the generic term for the fact that events may not turn out in the way anticipated. They may be predictable and considered (called risk), predictable and not considered (called neglected danger) or not predictable at all (called uncertainty). Following Schierenbeck (2003b, page 17) VAR is defined as:

> the estimated, maximum loss occurring either in a single position or within a portfolio. It is assumed to happen under normal circumstances, within a specific time frame or holding period, and with a defined probability. (Author's translation)

VAR as such is predictable as well as considered and thus qualifies for the category risk. Before entering deeper into the subject, we will try to understand the function of VAR in comparison with liquidity.

For the moment we will accept a simple version. It states that VAR computes the loss potentially occurring, based on a predefined probability. The areas covered are credit, market and operational risk (Figure 3.1). When losses become effective, they show up in the profit

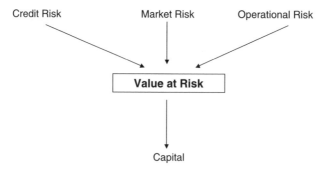

Figure 3.1   The elements of downside risk

and loss account, the net balance of which is again an integral part of shareholder capital. The size of the potential loss is determined by three main facts: firstly, the volumes at risk involved, e.g. billions of credits outstanding, open trading positions, etc.; secondly, the fallout rate in the respective credit risk bucket or in case of trading positions, the estimated adverse price movements, both of them at least partly taken from mathematical back testing; and thirdly, the level of probability which has been chosen. The higher the level of confidence, which states the number of cases taken out of the sample, the more the severe losses are included. As a rule, for credit risk one can thus say: the bigger the volume of lending and trading positions at risk, the lower the quality of the creditors; and the higher the level of confidence, the greater the potential loss. This amount is calculated and must be taken as the assessed maximum loss which has to be expected under defined conditions and, if it materialises, needs to be absorbed by the capital. Naturally, management does not aim for these losses, quite the contrary, but prudent policy does not exclude them.

The computed loss potential in itself is not really meaningful. The question is whether or not it can be absorbed, should the potential risk become effective. Against the risk potential there has to be at least an equivalent of capacity to carry the risk. As the buffer for losses is one's own means, the latter, expressed as a ratio in comparison with risk potential, becomes a closely watched indicator of financial health. A reduction in the same triggers a change in investor attitude. How restrictive market participants will act by further providing cash to the respective bank depends on the impact on the overall assessment of how credible the policy still is. The reaction can vary between asking for a higher risk premium, simply shortening the maturities till the volumes are additionally reduced, drastically or absolutely in the worst case. Against this background it might be advisable to understand the mechanics of downside risk in somewhat more detail. Nevertheless, we will limit our discussions to the points relevant to liquidity policy.

3.2.2   The mechanics of VAR

VAR is generally based on assumptions about the distribution of future results. Except for special products like currency, interest rate or equity options, for example, a normal distribution of the financial outcome is supposed (Box 3.1). Technically, the relationship between changes in price and changes in result are of a linear nature. Leaving the special cases aside, it follows that, given a certain quantity of a trading position or lending within a specific quality bracket, results of 5% and 10% will be produced if the determinants of the market change by either 5% or 10%.

Box 3.1 The distribution of losses

- If a normal distribution applies, losses (profits) of specific instruments respond in a linear pattern to price changes.
- A significant group of instruments are characterised by a nonlinear pattern: options and related instruments belong to this group.
- The mathematical methods chosen need to replicate the actual behaviour.
- The selected level of confidence applied to a predetermined database permits the maximum potential loss to be assessed under the given restrictive conditions.

With a given position in the specific instrument, potential earnings or losses will increase in amounts, the higher the probability chosen. As stated earlier, in this regular form it only applies to instruments which respond linearly to changes in the respective determinant. Options follow a different, nonlinear pattern. Accordingly, the methods applied to calculate the effects in monetary units cannot be the same. Three different mathematical approaches have been generally accepted and are widely used. Two of them, namely historic and Monte Carlo simulations, can be taken for linear and nonlinear behaviour. Monte Carlo, however, consumes so much computer time to reach the result that it is reserved for special and complex cases.

The third widely used mathematical basis, variance–covariance, is only applicable for cases characterised by a linear pattern. Whichever of the three concepts is taken, as long as they fit the linear or nonlinear character of the instrument, an appropriate result will be achieved.

Once the linear or nonlinear distribution is known, the question arises of where to draw the line between expected and unexpected loss. As VAR is concerned with the loss risk, the earning potential, which is the favourable side of risk, is neglected. Referring to the principles developed originally by K.-F. Gauss, it becomes obvious that potential losses rise in line with an increasing probability. The reasoning behind it is rational. Losses are put in an upward-moving order. Assuming that one standard deviation covers the probability of losses up to 5000 monetary units at 84.14%, by taking a probability of 99.87%, however, losses up to 15 000 monetary units cannot be excluded. In practical terms it simply states that, taking a full year of 256 days when markets are open, two standard deviations includes all of them except 6 days; at 99.87% probability, only 1 day is left out. A glance at graphs of daily movements in any instrument will confirm the basic statement: small changes in value are much more frequent than large ones, or high volatility is rare and extremely high volatility the exception – but with severe effects. For our further discussion, we prefer a different graphical illustration (see Figure 3.2).

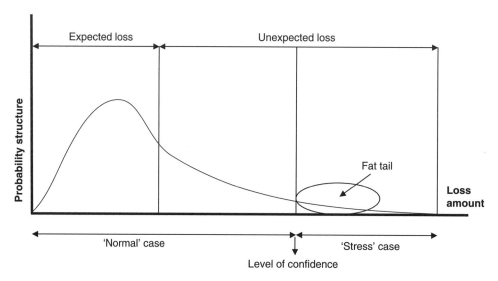

Figure 3.2 Losses in relation to level of confidence

(*Source*: Adapted from Schierenbeck, 2003b, page 233)

Looking at the losses to be considered, the question is where to draw the level of confidence. Will it be at 100% or below, and, if below, how distant from 100%? Following some principles may bring us closer to the answer:

- Firstly, the result should be relevant for policy decisions. To jump too short will produce relatively moderate loss figures. At the same time, many of the really bad days within the base period of usually 1 year are excluded. Consequently, the number of days not included should be kept low and treated as exceptions. Following the argument, 1–3 days, the equivalent of 99% probability or higher, could be a sensible range.
- Secondly, as the risk concept applied and the results of VAR are usually made public, the probability taken as a basis should fit into the general pattern of the industry. Of course, the underlying principles of the method allow any third party to adjust the figures to the relevant degree. Psychologically, most probably a prima facie artificially low figure will not boost confidence with investors. How much other window dressing is going on, they may ask?
- Thirdly, where supervisory authorities and rating agencies demand specific confidence levels, the choice is restricted – at least for external use. Internally, one may work with different probabilities if one wishes to do so. Even so, they should follow sensible principles. Otherwise, one is cheating oneself, with the danger of believing that one's own figures are comparable to reality.

Once the threshold is defined, the potential loss up to the level can be calculated. It is known as loss under 'normal' conditions. 'Normal' signifies the amount at risk which is achieved by applying the level of confidence to the underlying database. The result taken from each product and adjusted for correlations gives the total VAR under normal conditions. The part beyond the level of confidence covers the remaining potential losses. One may be tempted to assume that the range covers the difference to 100%. Yet the systematic nature of VAR does not allow for doing so.

The probability underlying the VAR calculation is founded on a time-related sample of usually 2 years. In other words, the expected losses are derived from the real historic data of the underlying period taken. If by chance it were to be a period with no significant upheavals, the biggest calculated loss could be comparatively moderate in relation to experiences in the distant past. Therefore, the 100% base which is related to the underlying period need not be the utmost loss to be considered. There have been occurrences that are not covered by the underlying database and which can produce losses beyond the normal case. The conditions producing such exceptional losses are called 'stress'. For stress, the timeframe is no longer limited to the base of VAR. Market shaking upheavals of the recent and more distant past are taken as a basis. Scenarios can include the terrorist attacks of September 2001, the Asian crises of 1997, the Russian crisis of 1998, the equity crash of 1987, the credit crunch of 1994 or the interest and currency upheavals in the aftermath of the UK pound leaving the EMS in 1992, just to name some prominent occurrences. There are no fixed rules which one ought to follow. Nevertheless, it is important to select at least one occurrence affecting each of the businesses in which the bank is significantly engaged. The requirement relates to products as well as to geographical areas.

The respective calculations for normal and stressed situations are done for each product. When added and adjusted for compensating items, one arrives at the risk or loss potential of the bank under normal and stressed conditions. How much of the potential then is to be taken against capital depends on budgeting and accounting rules. Some of the potential losses are already accounted for in the budgeting process; that is, they are expected. At least the part of credit risk believed to become effective as real is budgeted as such. As these expected losses are treated as already 'real', the amount is no longer to be accounted for as unexpected. It has already found its way into the budgeted profit and loss. The sum of the net overall risk potential beyond the amount already taken into the budgeted profit and loss is then taken as the potential threat for shareholder capital.

3.2.3 VAR as an element within an integrated circuit

Experience tells us that elements of any business do not exist as unrelated but are linked to other parts. The difficulty then arises of how to evaluate the relevant items. Bringing them into a logical sequence and defining the starting point is the second complexity one is faced with.

The answer is covered in our flow diagram for financial items of banks in Figure 2.5. As a starting point we take VAR expressed as downside risk (risk potential) and its relation to capital as the buffer (risk capacity). Growth has been recognised as a main driver for VAR as well as for P/L, whereby the latter defines the level of profitability once it is linked to capital. We now have a circle made up of the five elements mentioned earlier: VAR, capital, growth, P/L and profitability. When evaluating the starting point we ask for the ultimate driver, the one with the strongest impact on the circle as a whole.

Our graph indicates that it must be growth. Growth is the only overall driver within the circuit. As the determining force behind the size and structure of balance-sheet, off-balance-sheet as well as service activities, it is the key to the elements of VAR and thus VAR itself. In addition, through the impact on P/L, growth affects the level of capital. However, its force leads well beyond the circle of VAR, either directly or in an indirect way. Through its bearing on the size of the balance sheet, there is a link to liquidity and its volume, currency and maturity structure. Yet it is not limited to this type of business. Off-balance-sheet activities like trading can also have a significant bearing on liquidity. Even in the case of an overall zero-growth policy, the structure within the balance sheet may change sufficiently to alter the liquidity status of a bank markedly.

We can thus conclude that growth can be the starting point for both the VAR and the LAR circles. Starting with growth coincides also with the view of Reichmann (2006, page 31) who, in a similar context, takes growth separately and segregates it from structural components. We now will set up the VAR circle (Figure 3.3).

3.2.4 The elements within the circle and their relationship

3.2.4.1 Growth

Growth has many aspects. To start with, it may be helpful to clarify the term itself. It is understood that growth can be positive or negative. Zero growth is an option as well. Growth can relate to balance-sheet or off-balance-sheet transactions. Even in the case of zero growth, the structure within can change. Lending to customers in long-term maturities may be planned to increase to the extent at which short-term advances are to be curtailed, or vice versa. In this scenario, despite the volume not being changed in total, the impact on credit risk for example would differ due to an altered maturity spectrum. All the mentioned possibilities are included in the term 'growth level'.

Products and customers in many cases go hand in hand. Specific customer segments have specific needs. Or to put it in another way, certain products are not within the requirements

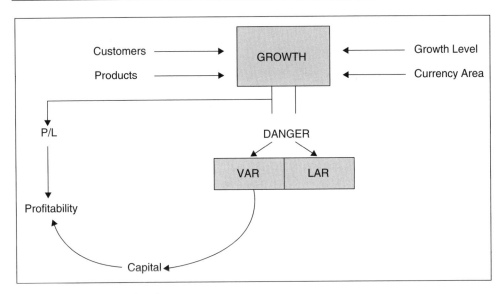

Figure 3.3   The circle of VAR

of all bank clients. The retail sector will hardly ask for standby credits in order to secure funding in case the CP market fails to provide the means. On the other hand, a corporate does not belong to the client base asking for consumer loans. This may sound trivial. Nevertheless, business plans have to be broken down into great detail. It is the specified information about the type of product, its quantity and timing factor which is required for setting up a proper product-specific base on which to compute the impact on VAR for the periods ahead. When computing the downside risk the results will differ significantly depending on whether one assesses exposures to investment grade customers or consumer credit lending, for example.

Once growth is specified with respect to customers, products, currency areas and the respective levels, we arrive at two structural components of the circle: VAR and P/L. For our further discussion we will separate the components into the two blocks of 'risk' and 'finance', the latter including capital and thus profitability as well.

3.2.4.2   *VAR: the downside risk and its effect on capital*

Credit, market and operational risk are computed based on the business plan related to growth. The three components and, within each of them, the various products and business lines are analysed with respect to the potential downside risk. For each product, product group, then business line up to the company level the potential losses are calculated and at the end shown as a total sum. The downside risk is presented under the assumptions of both the normal case and the stressed situations. It is an amount in currency value related to 1 day, but can also be calculated for a period. Sometimes it is referred to as the term 'risk potential'.

How likely it is for the losses to become effective is easier to answer when we look at a specific product or a specific product group within a portfolio and as long as we limit the question to the normal case. We arrive at the loss under normal conditions of a specific product or portfolio based on its historic behaviour in volatility and linked to the level of confidence. When, for example, applying 3σ or standard deviations as a threshold, within an annual period the statistical probability of reaching the level of the calculated loss turns out to be at 99.87%. It would be misleading to interpret the level of 99.87% as certainty. The statistical approach relates to probability and probability only. The statistical method assumes that the volatility of the period of reference continues for the next one in an unchanged manner. Whether or not it does, only the future will tell. Moreover, statistically speaking, there will be a single day in the period under consideration when this level is even surpassed. For this day the potential downside risk cannot be calculated on the basis applied for expected losses. It will be bigger, but by how much cannot be determined using this concept. We now deal with a stressed situation where scenarios based on past and extreme occurrences in the environment are considered to arrive at the unexpected losses.

When predicting the potential loss the statistical calculation is founded on further hypotheses like amounts exposed or positions taken. However, the amount involved may be smaller or bigger than anticipated and a directional position may be correct by chance and thus produce a profit of the magnitude of the potential loss. The second point does not really matter in light of the concept applied, which focuses on negative deviations. It is by chance that the positioning turns out to be financially favourable; poor chance would have actually produced the potential loss. As to the first point, a deviation in the amount involved is a different matter. It most likely plays a more important role in the process of a longer-term view as in planning, for example. However, as the VAR calculations, at least for expected losses, are also produced daily and based on actual data from the previous day, the deviations are judged as acceptable for the potential downside risk. Despite the fact that the outcome is not certain, only probable, the approach is of significant value. Indeed, there is no alternative to it.

The risk potential calculated in this way has its counterpart in shareholder capital. Capital in this context is named 'risk capacity'. The term stands for its function to act as a buffer and to absorb effective losses originating from downside risk. As capital in this respect is vital for assessing the solidity of a bank, we will look at it in more detail.

3.2.4.3   Shareholder capital as a buffer

There is more than one way to look at capital. Generally, we have used it relatively loosely and substituted it with terms like shareholder capital or own means. In the contexts applied at that time, a further distinction was not necessary to separate it from external funds in general. As soon as we discuss capital in its function as risk-taking capacity in detail, a clear understanding of what we refer to is necessary. It is a precise amount we are looking for, and not a general term. Capital can be looked at in three different ways (Figure 3.4).

The basis for risk capacity is the regulatory capital. It contains all means which are liable in case the potential downside risk materialises as actual losses which consequently have to be born by the buffer. The regulatory capital is thus also the basis for solvency. One can say that the term 'risk capacity' is based on a general understanding which applies to regulators, as well as to rating and bank internal assessments.

The regulatory requirement demands keeping risk potential supported by capital. The minimum level of the loss absorbing buffer is set at 4.0% for Tier 1 and at 8% for Tiers 1 and 2 combined. If we assume a loss potential of 1000 monetary units, the minimum required is 40 and 80 monetary units respectively. It follows that the higher-quality Tier 1

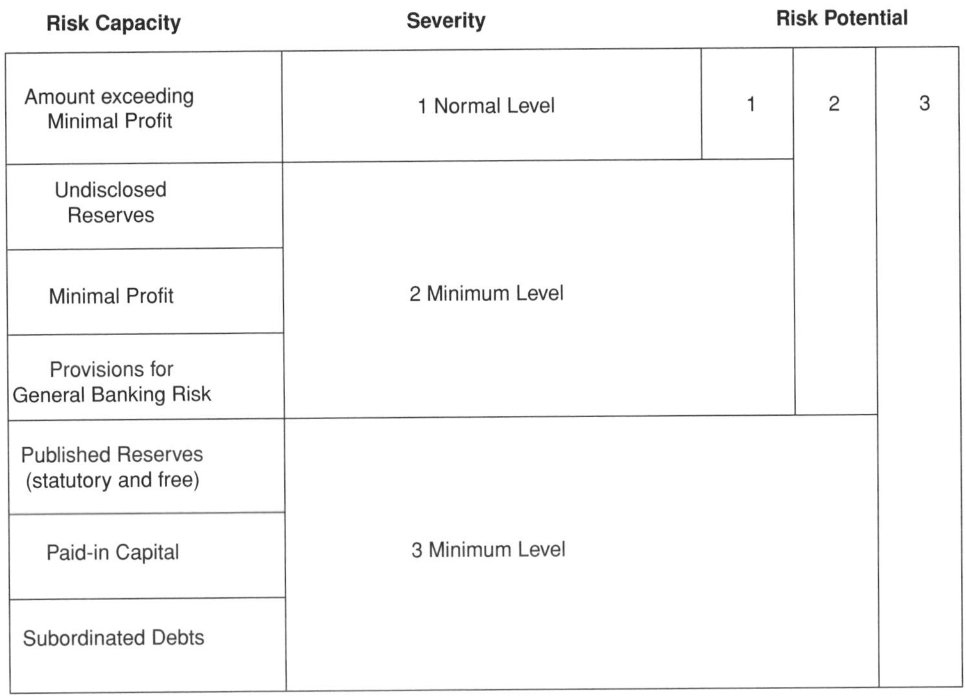

Risk Capacity	Severity	Risk Potential		
Amount exceeding Minimal Profit	1 Normal Level	1	2	3
Undisclosed Reserves				
Minimal Profit	2 Minimum Level			
Provisions for General Banking Risk				
Published Reserves (statutory and free)				
Paid-in Capital	3 Minimum Level			
Subordinated Debts				

Figure 3.4   Risk capacity, capital and risk potential
(*Source*: Adapted from Schierenbeck, 2003b, page 51f.)

can compensate for Tier 2. The reverse, however, is not possible. Tier 3 relates to trading activities.

In contrast to risk capacity, there are two different schools of thought on how to arrive at risk potential. The most obvious discrepancy has been eliminated by the Basel II Accord, which became effective in January 2008. Previously, regulators applied a simple and very rudimentary approach. Specific types of counterparties were dealt with unanimously, irrespective of differences in risk quality. For illustration, within the group of the OECD countries, sovereigns were judged as not risky at all, i.e. calculated with a factor of zero. Licensed banks got a factor of 0.2 and the risks of non-banks were assessed by a ratio of 1.0. It was an approach which assumed that portfolios were more or less equally distributed regarding the quality of the financial standing. Knowing that the assumption could be a heroic one, a new development outside the regulators started to develop: the approach of calculating the 'economic capital'. The wording is somewhat misleading at first glance. It is not the risk capital but the risk potential which is addressed. Instead of taking average factors for specific types of counterparties, as done by the regulators, the risk of each name was to be assessed based on its own financial strength. The principle taken is the one we know from our discussion of VAR.

With Basel II in force, the risk calculation is no longer different. It is now what is called the economic capital, which is taken as the risk basis and supported by Tier 1 and Tier 2 capital with 4% and 8% respectively. One difference remains, however. Regulators leave out interest rate risk from the banking book (i.e. the balance sheet) and thus treat it differently from trading books. Professionals in banks and rating agencies work with the total sum of risks, including the one on the balance sheet.

These are the legal or regulatory minimum requirements. But how is the market going to assess a name which stays just above the minimum levels? We will address this question in the context of liquidity. For now it suffices to say: it would not be a comfortable position to be in.

3.2.4.4 The financial aspect

Capital, due to its multiple function, is also part of the financial aspects, together with P/L and profitability. We have taken out all components on the flowchart not related directly to the VAR circle. The number of items we now deal with is small, which makes it easier to concentrate on the relevant subjects. The sequence of relationships is clear, easy to understand and the terms have already been explained: growth determines not only VAR but P/L as well. Net profits are the denominator of the equation, capital the numerator and the result is profitability. But what does it mean in a business sense?

To get to the answer we will start again with growth. Once growth has been set as a goal within the preliminary business plan, both expected P/L and VAR are calculated. The latter in its function as risk potential is compared with the level of capital presently available. Capital in its role as risk capacity has to fulfil the regulatory minimum requirements. This is the legal aspect; whether this minimum is sufficient for the market remains to be seen, but will be dealt with at a later stage. Irrespective of the angle from which we look at it, capital and its level is an issue.

First of all, capital as a means of financing assets is an expensive vehicle compared with any other alternative. On the other hand, when put into relation with the total size of the balance sheet in banks, the argument has to be put into perspective. Its indirect link with net earnings definitely carries more weight and this in more than one way. As much as P/L is determined by growth, so is VAR and, consequently, so is capital. The regulatory link between the last two items brings capital into the role of a limiting factor. Any expansion related to the balance sheet or off the balance sheet uses up shareholder capital. Assuming well-balanced ratios at the outset, as a given quantity at least in the short term, capital restricts the options for growth due to its function as risk capacity. Whether or not the implications on net earnings are detrimental remains to be seen. If they are, profitability will suffer. Alternatively, capital could be increased in order to allow P/L to reach the expected target. If this route is followed it depends on the deviations of both items whether profitability is in an acceptable range. It is for these reasons that Schierenbeck (2003b, page 1f.) proposes to evaluate business alternatives firstly in the light of risk capacity and then on the grounds of earning implications.

In a way we are again faced with a polygon which has to be brought into balance. As a consequence alternatives for growth will be limited for each bank. To conclude that each member of the banking industry is forced as a result to move in a uniform structure would exaggerate the point made. The industry requires specialisation and the market honours it. Moreover, the structures of the markets that single banks are covering do actually vary and allow for a differentiation in the approach – and still with good results. On the other hand, it cannot be dismissed that the introduction of VAR and the focus on profitability have reduced the spectrum within which management can sensibly choose what business routes to follow.

Up to this point we have restricted our discussion to the VAR circle. There are indeed further links originating from the respective items. As they are directed to elements outside the circle concerned we will address them in the particular circumstances. Before moving to the liquidity circle we will first remain with risk as potential and capacity and its structural components. The subject might be of relevance at a later stage.

3.3   LAR: LIQUIDITY RISK AND THE MISSING THEORETICAL CONCEPT

The downside risk, expressed as VAR, has been well developed from a theoretical as well as a practical point of view. Over time it has become a standard approach and has found its way into the frame of regulations of bank supervisors and the analysis of rating agencies alike. LAR, however, has been neglected for a long time by the academic world. For example, Schierenbeck (2003a, 2003b) in his textbooks on banking puts LAR next to VAR as one of the two main risks for banks, but does not follow up on liquidity due to lack of insufficient research. Bartetzky (2008, page 3f.) comes to the conclusion that until today textbooks have still focused on theories which were developed in the nineteenth and up to the mid-twentieth centuries. Only in recent years has research on liquidity picked up. Matz (2002) and Matz and Neu (2007a) mention it specifically and contributed significantly to the understanding of managing liquidity. In addition, numerous research papers on aspects like non-maturing deposits, contingent credit lines or prepayment options have been published. Their emphasis, however, is on liquidity management or facets of it. They hardly touch liquidity policy, or at best in an indirect way only. Yet a practitioner has to act within a framework, and this has to be wider than liquidity management itself. The framework has to consider and integrate elements by which liquidity management is impacted and which in turn it influences. Why is that?

In comparison with LAR, the principle of VAR is relatively straightforward and in several ways. Its result is largely determined by historic and external volatilities which can be generally measured, be they price fluctuations in the case of market risk, failure rates in the credit bracket or losses occurring in connection with operational risk. All three sub-risks focus primarily on one internal determinant: the actual exposure in the case of market and credit risk and the quality of processes and handling with respect to operational risk. In other words, the degree of the risk potential to a large extent is in the hands of the management itself. As all other risk elements are established externally and mostly through market forces on which a single bank has no significant impact, the size of VAR largely becomes a directly manageable financial instrument for banks. It can be enlarged or reduced by changes in exposure. Furthermore, VAR does not stand on its own. If the downside risk becomes effective, there is a buffer to absorb the losses. It is shareholder capital which takes the brunt. In this sense, VAR is neither an ultimate nor an absolute quantity but a relative one. Its magnitude and severity are to be expressed in relation to the size of capital that is available to absorb potential losses.

3.3.1   A basic understanding of LAR

LAR acts in another environment. The main differences (the following is largely based on a presentation given at the Schmalenbachgesellschaft in Frankfurt, on 5 October 2007) relate to the lack of a buffer and as a consequence to its multi-dimensional relationships. We will explain the meaning of the statement in more detail.

By adapting the definition of downside risk, liquidity risk can be described as in Box 3.2:

Box 3.2 Defining LAR under normal conditions (*Source*: Adapted from Bartetzky, 2008, page 19)

The maximum loss of liquidity which is not exceeded under the assumption of a defined probability in percentage points (the confidence level) within a defined period.

Just as noticeable, the definition relates to the normal case. The period is defined – usually 2 years. The probability of the loss in liquidity occurring is also set as a benchmark for comparison. And the database is available in-house as long as the balances of the respective accounts are kept on historic record. Based on this information, LAR under normal conditions can be calculated. The question arises, however, of why no external factor plays a part. When we did the same calculation for VAR, for example, we had to refer to the volatility in market prices and credit risk turning into loan losses. Does this mean that liquidity is not affected by external forces?

As Figure 3.5 below shows, there are external forces at work. Market conditions can change. Assets previously qualifying as marketable and thus as liquid may suddenly be difficult to turn into cash. Assets may not be sellable without price concessions. The repo market may no longer function and collateral previously judged as acceptable may not fulfil the requirements regarding quality. Furthermore, funding sources that the bank normally could rely on may suddenly reduce the amounts and tenors normally made available or dry up completely in extreme circumstances. In these cases we talk about special circumstances which occur relatively rarely. However, one cannot neglect them. Although these incidences come up usually over longer intervals and are infrequent, their impact might be severe, even fatal, for an institution. It thus makes sense to distinguish these rather rare but severe cases from the more frequent but less severe circumstances. Referring back to the concept of LAR, we separate the normal case from the stressed situation. We will not enter into technicalities at the moment, as they will be dealt with later when addressing liquidity management. For the purpose of liquidity policy, outlining the principle will suffice.

The normal case does not refer to special circumstances but actually takes experienced volatility into account. The timespan applied usually covers the previous 24 months. Based on information available at the time, an assessment about positive or negative liquidity gaps for the days to come can be made. Most transactions causing a flow of cash contain a value date of $t + 1$ or more (t being value today). The contractual part of the business done at t at the latest is available for assessing the most likely gap to be covered or invested at the payment date. *Ex post*, the forecast may turn out to be imprecise. Especially for banks, a large part of cash generating flows is determined by third parties like customers and participants in the interbank market. The control of flows is thus not fully in the hands of the institution. It also cannot be excluded that operational mistakes add to the discrepancy between forecast and actual payment liquidity gaps.

The historic data of the underlying period of 2 years will show the deviations from the forecast for each day. Once they are sorted according to size, the respective confidence level can be applied. Depending on the level chosen, one or more days are excluded – in decreasing order according to size – from the calculation. It is advisable to aim for a high level of confidence in order to incorporate large deviations compared with forecasts. Nevertheless, whatever level is applied, one will stay within the set frame of 2 years of actual experience. It is this restriction that makes it obsolete to ask for the reasons behind the result calculated.

The outcome of LAR under normal circumstances ought to be calculated by each bank based on its own data and cannot be adapted from the experiences of other institutions. The specific business structure, the behaviour of its customer base, the quality of the operational conduct, etc., of each institution does not allow relating to external data. Even when setting the level of confidence at three standard deviations and thus very high, one will not cover the very extreme cases possibly affecting the institution. This brings us to LAR under stressed conditions.

LAR, like VAR, is calculated following specific methods to get the result. For the normal case, or the expected loss, the data taken refer to a time period of usually 2 years. For the unexpected losses triggered under stressed conditions, the time restriction is taken off. In the case of VAR, volatilities were obtained from older and extremely severe occurrences, sometimes dating back several decades. Although the data used referred to times outside the 2-year frame, the principles stayed the same. For losses under stress conditions, it is the extreme market volatility applied to the same exposure as in the normal case.

For LAR the method poses serious problems when applied to stress conditions. We cannot simply extend our own experience beyond or even well beyond the 2-year frame. Even assuming we have the data from so far back, which is highly unlikely, two principal shortcomings block the way.

Firstly, we would be comparing apples with pears. Banking institutions over the years have undergone major changes in the size and structure of balance-sheet activities, off-balance-sheet activities, composition of customer base and customers' changing needs, just to mention a few. As LAR in the normal case is attributed to a bank's short-term experiences, for stress we would refer to the liquidity implications of an institute which may only have the name in common. In order to prepare for present and future potential stresses, relying on the experiences of a differently structured and exposed bank in the past would be inappropriate and dangerous.

Secondly, as a consequence of the previous shortcoming, the sources initiating the stress now count. Depending on where the pressure starts, the effects will be felt in different ways and affect different segments on the balance sheet. Basically, we can distinguish four principal

		RELATED TO CAUSES	
		Bank related	Market related
RELATED TO EFFECTS	Liabilities	Restrained attitude of investors in debt market	Market disturbances in form of 'flight to quality'
	Assets	Marketable assets of specific name no longer liquefiable	Marketable assets of one or several segments no longer liquefiable

Figure 3.5 Institution and market-related effects on assets and liabilities

constellations (Figure 3.5): the cause can be market related or institution related and in both of these cases can affect either the asset or liability side of the balance sheet. Bearing this in mind, in contrast to VAR one will not be able to come up with a single stress figure. Depending on the initiator of the stressed condition, the outcome will vary and might do so significantly.

As a consequence, the calculation of LAR under stress is based on another method. A scenario approach might be the most appropriate one to choose. It would allow an analysis of the impact of various origins and at the same time come up with institution-specific solutions.

3.3.2   The multi-dimensional character of LAR

Once LAR is calculated under normal and stressed conditions, one ends up with a sum as in the case of VAR; whatever the amount or amounts, however, there is no independent financial item serving as a buffer to absorb the shortfall. Shareholder capital cannot take over the function it plays for VAR, for two reasons. Capital plays an almost negligible role in funding when it comes to banks. Shareholder capital to total assets is mostly within a one-digit range and often at the lower end of the spectrum. But even this small portion cannot be taken as a buffer. Most likely it is already employed to finance longer-term assets. And if it is kept in the form of short-term assets that are easily liquefiable, the amount is already incorporated in the present liquidity status and cannot be used a second time.

Alternatively, one could consider asking shareholders to increase their stake. But even a relatively moderate loss of funding would require a substantial increase in shareholder capital with the well-known negative implications on profitability. Following this route means simply shifting the issue from the LAR to the VAR circle, without solving the underlying problem. Even if we assume support for the proposed capital increase and that profitability still lies within an acceptable range after the action, we would be too late to counteract the outflow in time. To sum up, we thus have to conclude that loss of liquidity can only be compensated by liquidity itself.

This leads us to the second point: the multi-dimensional relationship of LAR. As a starting point we will take the conclusion that loss of liquidity can only be compensated by liquidity itself. This means that the cause of the problem and its remedy are based on the same financial quantity. Left to itself, it is a classic vicious cycle whereby the absence of an actual liquidity shortfall keeps the equation in balance, yet once the LAR becomes effective, the elements of the network it is related to are affected and start to play their negative part on liquidity themselves. If we recall the findings in various previous sections, as long as market participants keep assuming that payment obligations can be fulfilled now and in the future, borrowing funds in the market generally is no problem for a bank. At the very moment when fulfilling the obligation is in danger, the market will react. Growing with the severity of the danger, firstly risk premiums will be added, then maturities shortened and amounts curtailed up to deleting lines altogether. Furthermore, for the market it does not matter whether the danger is real or perceived. It will respond in both cases in a similar way.

The question therefore arises of how to keep the equation in balance under difficult circumstances. Two solutions come to mind in this respect: one related to liabilities, the other to assets, or a mixture of both.

All assets could be financed congruently, thereby securing the funding till the assets mature and come off the books. We will not discuss the difficulties of issuing bonds frequently and in relative small amounts in order to cover loans as or shortly after they are granted. We will also not refer to the costs involved by keeping the liquidity profile fully matched, although both points would be heavily disputed in any bank if the proposal were forthcoming. Instead we will address a point which touches upon the future of the respective institute and thus goes to the heart of the business.

If one funds long-term assets with long-term liabilities and short-term ones with short-term funds and each asset exactly in line with the respective maturity, the liquidity gaps over all periods will be nil. All assets are securely funded till their maturity. At each day in the future receivables and outgoing payments will match, which is the equivalent of saying that payment obligations are secured till the last asset comes off the books. Concerning the liquidity aspect, the bank is safe if management decides to cease business altogether, which is the equivalent of following a policy of gone concern as in the case when a subsidiary or a portfolio is discontinued. On the other hand, management works under the assumption of going concern when related to the whole of the institution. The approach implies continuing business by keeping the customer franchise intact. Even under restrictive conditions regarding business policy, it entails serving customer needs in the future. Especially in the case of cash-management-related lending, requests from customers most probably emerge as early as the next day. If they cannot be fulfilled, the franchise will be eroded rapidly. In the case of market-related funding problems, the approach discussed will save the financial institution from illiquidity but at the expense of remaining a bank with its customer base intact. This means that it is an appropriate approach for liquidation but not for liquidity policy.

Alternatively, the liability approach could be substituted by structuring assets in an appropriate way. Instead of adjusting funding maturities to match assets, the latter could be geared towards highly liquefiable instruments. By doing so, assets to be put on the balance sheet would be chosen on the basis of their capability to reduce funding easily in case of a liquidity stress. The instruments are the ones we dealt with when discussing marketability of assets: they can be sold immediately like Bunds and US Treasuries, securitised and sold as in the case of consumer loans etc., provided as collateral or as part of a repurchase agreement. Whatever step is taken, funding needs are reduced to the extent of the volumes still achievable. The assets sold will release funding and the remaining measures turn into reality the inherent potential of the instrument to finance itself.

However, there is also the other side of the coin to be considered. Limiting business to instruments that can easily create liquidity reduces the scope for management to strive for profitability: attractive business which does not fulfil the requirement is left out and many of the instruments which fall into this range are characterised by a relatively small margin as liquidity has a value which is incorporated into the price achievable. These two negative implications hold true as soon as the respective policy is applied. Even in the period when funding is not an issue, the restrictions to be followed burdens the endeavour to achieve a high level of profitability. Yet the burden might be acceptable if one could assume that implementing the approach would solve the problem also under stressed conditions.

The assumption of keeping the assets highly liquid is based on the understanding that they can easily be turned into cash whenever necessary. It implicitly implies that assets held stay at a generally acceptable level of creditworthiness and that markets stay liquid and work smoothly. Yet the stress on liquidity may just be initiated in these sectors. Assets formerly of good quality may suffer in standing as the issuer falls below investment grade and the respective instruments thus become illiquid. As in the case of the US subprime mortgage crises in 2007–2008, uncertainty may spread over into other markets, causing a flight to quality and reducing the willingness of market participants to purchase anything below top rating. Markets then get constipated and assets previously qualified as liquid cannot be turned into cash any more, at least not in a timely fashion and without undue price concessions.

As could be demonstrated, neither assets nor liabilities can be structured in such a way that problems can be overcome in an economically and acceptable way under a stressed condition. This does not mean, however, that neither of the steps can be employed at all. It only indicates that neither of them suffices to solve the problem on its own. In combination with further measures they still may have their value. In order to establish the wider picture we will refer back to the chart in Figure 2.5.

3.3.3   LAR and the elements within the integrated circuit

Before evaluating the circuit one has to recall a basic difference between VAR and LAR. The downside risk measures implications on earnings and whether they can be borne by the bank if the potential risk becomes effective. For this reason the route follows P/L and capital. Liquidity risk does not relate to earnings but to cash, as it is cash at hand, assets easily made to cash and the future payment obligations and receivables which determine the payment status today and in the future. We are therefore looking for cash elements within the chart.

As before, we will start with the risk element: LAR or liquidity risk as it is named in the chart. Growth again is an input factor for LAR, either through on- or off-balance-sheet transactions. Simultaneously, growth determines cash flow, which in turn links up with flow of cash. Liquidity risk itself leads to the liquidity level which meets flow of cash from the opposite direction compared with cash flow.

As to the main driver, we take over the findings from discussing VAR. It is through growth that its impact on the size of the balance-sheet and the effects on off-balance-sheet activities has a strong bearing on liquidity. As we stated there, even in case of an overall zero-growth policy, the structure within the balance sheet may change sufficiently to alter markedly the liquidity status of a bank. We now set up the combined VAR and LAR circle (Figure 3.6).

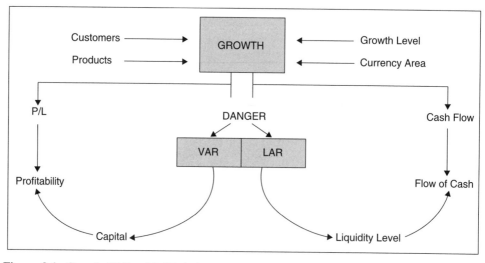

Figure 3.6   Growth, VAR and LAR circles

3.3.4   The elements within the circle and their relationship

Growth and its connected items have been dealt with previously. We will not repeat them here but move straight to the other elements of the circle. Particular issues initiated by growth will be integrated when discussing the specific item of the circle.

3.3.4.1   *LAR and the missing buffer*

LAR is calculated under the assumptions of both the normal case and stressed conditions. Based on the method underlying the model, the procedure follows the principles we learned when calculating VAR. For expected losses, i.e. in the normal case, a timeframe of the past is chosen from which the volatility is taken as a basis for most likely future aberrations. Linked to the present exposure, one arrives at the potential downside risk for each product or segment. Adding up the results of each single calculation gives the risk potential of the bank as a whole.

However, one should be aware that volatility is subject to different forces in LAR compared with VAR. Volatility for downside risk is formed externally. It is the action of innumerable participants in the market which determines the result. And each one of them acts independently and has no decisive impact on the outcome in large and liquid markets. Most importantly, the bank under consideration is a price taker and cannot influence the level of volatility. For illiquid markets the method does not apply.

In contrast to VAR, volatility of liquidity has several origins and thus is a specific determinant for a bank when it comes to the normal case. Much depends on the business structure. A large international clearer cannot be compared with a regional savings bank. Engaging in investment banking activities will produce dissimilar flows when weighed against a bank focusing on more traditional retail and corporate business. Yet, as the basis for volatility is taken from a bank's own experiences in a past period, each bank can rely on its own data. And although the disparity between banks may differ greatly, one will get the result applicable for the specific institution.

The same cannot be said when dealing with a stressed situation. As explained in the introductory section, stress can be either initiated externally or caused by the bank itself. We called it market-related or name- or institution-related stress respectively. Furthermore, the cause may be linked to the asset or the liability side of the balance sheet. Especially when taking into account a stressed situation, LAR, due to its various origins, is multi-dimensional and can thus not be expressed as a single figure. As Bartetzky (2008, page 18) mentions, it is the loss under extreme market conditions, the 'fat tail', which is difficult to assess. Referring to historic data does not necessarily solve the problem as the pattern has a tendency not to repeat itself, a point strongly stressed by Taleb (2005) and Bernstein (1996). Bearing further in mind the severe impact on the institution in case payment obligations cannot be secured, it is the stressed situation which is at the forefront of liquidity considerations producing Taleb (2007) type 'Black Swans'.

Against this background we are confronted with the lack of a buffer which could absorb any losses on liquidity. Referring to our previous findings, a shortfall in liquidity can only be compensated by liquidity itself. Thus, we have no other way than to set up a benchmark which takes over the function that capital plays in the case of VAR. It is the so-called liquidity level which we have introduced, and against which liquidity risk is going to be measured.

3.3.4.2   *From cash flow to flow of cash*

Cash flow is an earnings-related term. It contains all elements of income and cost from the commercial activities of a company and a bank. In a bank the balance sheet of the operating

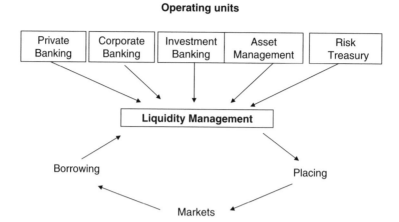

Figure 3.7   Segregating cash from operating units and liquidity management

units related to commercial activities is not in equilibrium, however, as the asset and liability sides do not match by the difference which has to be funded or can be invested (Figure 3.7). In the case of most banks, funding will be needed in order to match both sides. To get to the flow of cash we assume, in line with general practice, that gaps will be closed with the liquidity section of the treasury at market rates. Earnings-related effects out of treasury activities which are done in the course of managing the downside risk are part of the cash flow. They are judged as an integral element of commercial business and are thus separated from liquidity.

What makes cash flow relevant for the circle of LAR is its focus on the cash element of earnings. The difference from P/L can be small but relevant for our discussion. The sets of data are the same for both financial items. The angle of focus, however, differs. While the P/L shows the financial result produced by business activities within a given period, cash flow distils the cash element of it during the same timespan. And liquidity is related to cash.

In the step to follow, the information contained in cash flow is transported to the liquidity department. The organisational setup required to achieve it will be dealt with later. The emphasis here is on data information and not on the result. Liquidity with its situation-specific (actual payments to be made now) and structural (liquidity gaps over the total of the balance sheet) elements requires information covering the longest maturity that the bank is engaged in. There is no time restriction as in cash flow, but a sequence of cash gaps till the latest maturity. Although the information may be aggregated for a high-level view, it is indispensable to have it segregated at least into currencies.

When the liquidity manager takes over these flows, he or she replicates cash flow with all its gaps. Whether the sum of liabilities exceeds or turns out to be short of total assets depends on the customer and business structure of the respective bank. As stated earlier, apart from exceptions in the retail sector (which we will leave out in the further discussion), banks will usually be short of funding. Either way, they almost certainly will be faced with gaps in the time brackets. For the liquidity gap structure various terms are used with no single one having become standard yet. In order to simplify it, we introduce a term which is neutral but relates to the characteristics which are flows and the elements of cash: namely, flow of cash.

Flow of cash when replicated from cash flow is not in balance. Funding is necessary to bring liabilities up to assets, which is taken from shareholder capital or the markets. Two questions now arise: how is the composition of assets and liabilities to be structured; and what is needed in order to secure an appropriate liquidity level to withstand stressed circumstances? The liquidity level will serve as a benchmark on which liquidity management has to be founded. As liquidity can only be secured by liquid means in various forms, one inevitably will be faced with an enlargement of the balance sheet beyond the size generated commercially. In other words, what is required is a buffer within liquidity as there is no independent financial item which can take over the function that capital provides for VAR.

3.4   AN ATTEMPT AT AN INTEGRATED CONCEPT FOR LAR

In the previous sections we established the circles of both VAR and LAR. Based on our chart of the financial items of a bank, the first one follows the route related to earnings and its correlated elements. LAR, however, focuses on cash and its links. For the moment we will stay with the high-level perspective and not address the term 'liquidity level' in detail. As indicated earlier, its relevance for both LAR and flow of cash is paramount and the relationship rather complex. It thus deserves to be dealt with separately and in depth. Furthermore, not digressing into a detailed analysis and understanding of a single point, however important it may be, makes it easier to follow the high-level view of relationships.

3.4.1   The crossing of the two circles

When setting up the chart showing the relationships of the financial items of a bank, we referred to a method which is generally used to solve highly complex problems in business management. The principle it is based on requires sequences of relationships with the following restriction: no arrow must cross another arrow. It is this criterion which enhances its value compared with normal graphical presentations showing simply the multilateral links between numbers of financial terms. The restriction secures a logical sequence and names the main driver, which in our case is growth.

Why then does the arrow from cash flow to flow of cash cross the one leading from downside risk to capital? Is it because the chart is set up incorrectly or are there valid and thus acceptable explanations for the fact?

VAR and LAR are two similar concepts but refer to different aspects of risk. In our methodical approach we therefore dealt with each one separately and established the circle for each of them unrelated to the other. It meant simplifying the complexity somewhat for the benefit of clarity. It is now time to open the frame again. Earlier on, when discussing financial equilibrium (2.2.2.2), the direct and indirect relationships between growth, security, profitability and liquidity were evaluated and explained. Already the link between liquidity and profitability was a sign of a connection of some kind, although each of them belongs to a different circle. The decisive determinant, however, is represented in the cash flow.

In a way, cash flow is the link between the two circles. On the one hand, it represents earnings as does the VAR-related P/L. Its calculation is defined by the same accounting rules as the latter. The only difference lies in the restriction to cash, as it is the cash aspect of the P/L exclusively which is taken. That is why we find the term 'cash flow' in LAR as a counterpoint to P/L in VAR. Both of them relate to the same earnings but viewed under different aspects.

Cash flow as an earnings-related term and associated with the commercial activities of a bank then bridges the divide to liquidity. The data, from which cash flow and flow of cash are taken, are again equal as between the former and P/L; however, they are reviewed once more from a different angle. As stated earlier, the time restriction inherent in cash flow is removed and we get to a sequence of gaps till the last period of exposures. As cash flow bridges the divide when reviewed from the two points of view, crossing of the arrow is a necessity. It is in this way only that we segregate VAR and LAR based on the same data and the same reality.

3.4.2   The VAR circle and its external implications

We refer again to the discussion when addressing the elements of the financial equilibrium. Leaving liquidity out for the moment, growth, profitability and risk, the remaining three elements, are strongly linked with each other. Out of the three parameters, profitability is the only one not representing a stock value but a ratio resulting from P/L and capital. Taking this fact into consideration, we arrive at an extended polygon made up of the terms growth, risk, profitability and its two determinants, P/L and capital. This corresponds exactly with the terms we find in our VAR-related circle. As stated earlier, it is not a coincidence but the result of a logical sequence.

From our previous discussions we also concluded important findings in our context. A minimum level of net earnings or P/L is essential to any company and thus also to a bank. At least over a period of some years, cost and an appropriate level of dividend payments are to be secured to keep shareholder support alive. Furthermore, P/L is an integral part of capital. Any severe losses will usually not only forfeit dividend payments, but reduce the amount of capital at the same time. A strong capacity to produce earnings on the other hand permits management to add extra reserves with the effect of enlarging the capital base. We also have learned that the amount of capital is seen as a strong indicator of the financial strength of a bank, when considered in relation to the potential of downside risk. Profitability, the ratio made up of P/L against capital available, signifies whether or not the latter is employed in an efficient manner.

A sound balance in the VAR circle indeed not only affects shareholder attitude; external stakeholders respond to it as well, such as customers of the retail and wholesale segments, depositors and other providers of funding. Being risk aware if not risk averse, the financial strength of the institution that is exposed has to be in line with lenders' risk appetite. Not matching its minimum security profile turns these groups away. Any bank so affected may easily find itself burdened with falling earnings and lack of funding. In this way we get the second link from VAR to LAR: this time it is not the accounting view distinguishing P/L from cash flow, but the economic aspects of profitability and flow of cash which includes external funds.

3.4.3   The missing link

Remaining with the high-level view, we refer once more to the chart showing banking activities in a procedural form. To make it easier to follow the upcoming point of argumentation, we present it here once more (Figure 3.8) but integrate the circles of VAR and LAR as already discussed.

The circle for VAR is indicated by the ——, while that for LAR is marked in — —. Together, they cover a wide range of the graphical exhibit. Nevertheless, one part is left out. The third area, which completes the graphical coverage, is not presented as a circle. It takes the shape of a — · —, starting at profitability and ending at flow of cash.

Profitability together with its basic drivers of P/L and capital are the main financial items forming the financial strength and thus solvency of a bank. The latter nowadays is very much expressed as a category within a rating scale. Whatever the rating methodology and whether

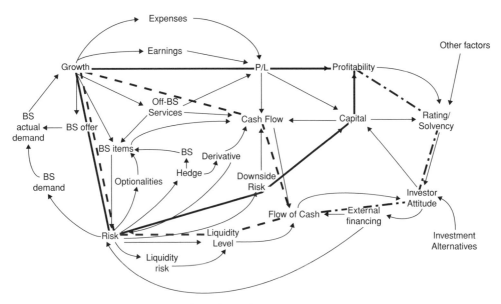

Figure 3.8   The structured business flow of a bank

the scale is shown by a ranking in letters or figures, the head end covers the absolute top quality which gradually erodes to insolvency at the bottom of the scale. On the scale a line is usually drawn. It separates what is called investment grade, which encompasses a minimum rating level up to top quality. Below the line we find high-risk exposures, also known as 'junk' (euphemistically named subprime), with insolvent addresses at the bottom.

Investors are a heterogeneous group, even when it comes to risk appetite. Expected return on the investment is weighted against the danger of insolvency of the institution in question. Conservative depositors or shareholders put security first and are ready to accept a lower return accordingly. However, the promise of premium compensation when compared with the average return within the investment grade can be tempting. For this reason, there are always investors who are ready to take the higher risk if they find it still acceptable and well compensated by the offered premium return.

Irrespective of the level of credit risk judged as acceptable or desired, investors refer to ratings when they value the financial strength of a company. At least for banks, rating debtors of any kind for credit risk is a must within the Basel II Accord. Assessments produced and published by rating agencies are one source only. Banks and some large investors have set up their own credit departments to evaluate counterparty risk. For borrowers with a rating already available from rating agencies like Moody's or Standard & Poor's, investors may rely on them if they wish to do so. Many a bank indeed prefers to base its investment decisions on an internal credit analysis. In either case, ratings play an important part when such decisions are taken by shareholders and investors, whether to start, increase, reduce or end exposures to the respective bank.

The decisions consequently relate also to external financing. As stated above, flow of cash when taken over from cash flow is not in balance, neither concerning the amount – since total assets and liabilities will not match – nor when it comes to periods. Liabilities received by the liquidity manager tend to be of a short-term nature while at least a substantial portion of assets

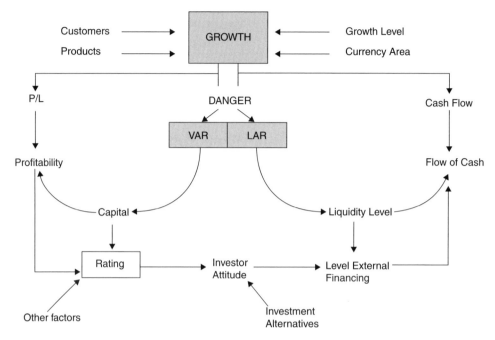

Figure 3.9   Linking together the VAR and LAR circles

relate to medium- and long-term maturities. To get the volume gap closed and to achieve the liquidity structure desired, the external markets have to be tapped.

As we have added the external items related to financing, we established the link between the VAR and LAR circles. This will allow us to complete the graph in Figure 3.9.

3.4.4   Bridging the divide

We now add the funding element to our previous graph of the VAR and LAR circles. The steps taken follow the line of argument we have just concluded. Profitability and capital, which are quantitative internal data, are taken and, in connection with further factors, a rating level is calculated for the institution under consideration.

Investors on their part will take the rating into consideration when preparing investment decisions. The attitude towards a specific investment is formed not only by the rating of the bank under consideration, but also in comparison with investment alternatives as well as the risk appetite. Leaning towards investment alternatives may have two causes, either relating to the bank concerned or that are more market specific as in the case of flight to quality. In other words, each bank is competing with not only the banking group as a whole on the basis of its comparative rating, but also alternative investments outside its own sector.

Whatever the cause, it determines the quantity, the type of lending as well as the maturity spectrum of potential investments the lender would be willing to supply. From the borrower's point of view, it signifies the level of external financing it can reasonably expect to receive from these funding segments. The circumstances are not limited to normal conditions but encompass possible stress scenarios as well.

In the next step, possible supply meets actual demand. When cash flow is transposed into flow of cash and supplemented with present funding one gets to the existing gap structure of liquidity. Whether size and structure meet the required level will become transparent once they are compared with the liquidity level. The latter is defined in such a way that payment obligations now and in the future are secured when applying possible LAR or liquidity stress scenarios. If present volume and structure of liquidity fall short of those demanded by the liquidity level, the markets have to be tapped.

3.5 SUMMARY

We have now completed our attempt to place liquidity policy within a framework which encompasses all the relevant elements related to it. Starting with our sequence of relevant banking activities accompanying liquidity, the following findings were arrived at:

- **Growth** is the initiating element for both VAR and LAR. When assessing growth, the group of customers, products, the currency areas as well as the level of growth are to be segregated in a sufficient manner. Changes in any of the determinants of growth can have significant implications for liquidity and its structural composition. It is for these reasons that detailed information is paramount for any liquidity management with a chance of succeeding.
- The **VAR circle** covers the business sector of a bank. In it, capital is a constraining factor for management when it comes to taking on risk. Rules from supervisory bodies for banks limit the risk potential expressed as VAR to 4% and 8% respectively for Tier 1 and Tier 2 capital. Since 2008 it is the economic risk which is applicable for calculating the ratios. Within the supervisory frame, the total of credit, market and operational risks is taken as a basis, but with the exception of the interest rate risk related to balance-sheet exposures. They are left out of the calculation. The latter as well as the minimum requirements for Tier 1 and Tier 2 will need further special attention, as markets may view them differently from supervisors. Growth also impacts on P/L and thus indirectly on profitability. The weight of the parameters in assessing the financial strength of a company expressed by its rating requires management to treat the VAR circle as a magic polygon. If it cannot be kept within equilibrium acceptable to the markets, it affects the format or perceived rating and thus funding capacity in a negative way.
- The **LAR circle** covers the liquidity and thus also the funding aspects. Liquidity risk technically follows the principles established for downside risk. In contrast to the latter, the origin of risks is not exclusively market related but can also be bank specific. In both cases it is markets and their participants which respond but for different reasons: once because of the liquidity constraints of whole markets or market segments; the second time due to the doubtful financial strength of the bank concerned. Liquidity risk therefore can affect assets as well as liabilities.

    Furthermore, there is no company-related tangible stock available to act as a buffer if LAR becomes effective; liquidity in itself is the ultimate buffer within a company for any liquidity problems. As the liquidity level is neither a tangible nor originally defined financial item, it has to be established within the process of business planning. Volumes in total and segregated, as well as the structure required for the policy of a going concern, are to be defined.

    Measured against the calculated liquidity structure following a stressed situation one arrives at the gaps. Ideally, the liquidity picture after such stress meets the liquidity level set by management. If it deviates from the goals, information and requirements are passed to flow of cash and the respective manager. Growth also affects the cash-related element of P/L, i.e. cash flow. Replicated without the constraints from accounting rules but shown as a sequence of liquidity gaps, cash flow leads to flow of cash. The desired structure of the latter therefore has to be created through funds from the markets to such an extent that it meets the requirements established by the liquidity level in volume and structure simultaneously.

- **Rating** or financial strength links the VAR and the LAR circles. The relationship, however, is anything but straightforward. Ratings, whether produced in-house or by agencies, are largely based on facts and figures. For these reasons they contain a relatively strong element of objectivity. At the same time and for the same reasons, the past dominates the assessment. Under normal conditions an investor will generally follow the view on this basis. Under specific conditions the investor may have a different perception compared with the present rating. Irrespective of whether the perception turns out to be better or worse than the rating, the investor will act based on his or her view and not on calculated financial strength.

  Depending on the risk appetite and the compensation for the specific level of uncertainty, the investor will decide on how to act. The investor may prefer investment grade only or allow for placing part of the amount below this level. If it is investment grade, the band is wide and numerous structures in the portfolio are possible. Even after the investment decisions are made, the funds that a specific borrower can look forward to are not based on a mechanistic process. The borrowing bank competes with investment alternatives available to the lender.

  Competition can express itself in various forms. Quality of the bank and respective compensation when compared with other borrowers are just two of them. Institution-related liquidity risk, which very much depends on the financial strength of the company in focus, is supplemented with market-related disturbances. Upheavals in large and normally well-functioning markets may turn these markets into a state of comparative or even absolute illiquidity. This can affect assets that are potentially marketable as well as new funds to be raised through the money or capital markets. In both cases, the capacity of the respective bank to produce cash via either of the two channels is constrained and may lead to serious problems in fulfilling payment obligations.

- **Flow of cash** is the triangular point where present cash structure, additional financing needs and the required liquidity level and structure come together. Any disturbances will manifest themselves in the form of negative gaps, expressed as differences between the planned and the actual liquidity structure which needs to be financed. Taleb's Black-Swan-Effects are of special concern.

  Obviously, financing will always play an important part within liquidity policy and management. Longer-term assets above the level of shareholder capital available need respective funds to get financed. Moreover, the total of assets viewed as longer term from an economic standpoint exceeds the level of assets with longer maturities. We refer to our discussion on the franchise. Some previously medium- to long-term loans may be close to final maturity. In principle, they could be judged as short term and be treated accordingly were it not for the argument of keeping the franchise intact as much as possible. Under the assumption of a going concern, at least the amount considered as due to prolongation ought to be treated as medium- to long-term obligations. This is the same principle as applied to cash-management-related customer exposure, which has already been judged to be treated as medium- to long-term assets from an economic point of view.

Over and above this, the bank will have assets on the balance sheet which potentially can create liquidity if necessary, either through selling or by a repo transaction. The field of products is relatively wide and encompasses tradable instruments with highly liquid markets up to credit portfolios which can be bundled in an SPV (Special Purpose Vehicle) and than securitised. Depending on the instrument or portfolio, the degree to which assets can be turned into cash will vary in the time and amount involved. At the highly liquid end, even larger quantities of sovereign bonds like US Treasury Bills or German Bunds can be sold immediately under normal conditions. At the other end of the spectrum, it will take time, for example, to prepare a portfolio consisting of corporate loans or consumer credits and get it ready for securitisation.

The time needed to create cash from marketable assets is just one point to consider. A second one relates to the basic capacity to do so. Accounting principles allow assets to be kept on the books even though they are no longer freely available – at least for a certain time. They may have already been employed as collateral and can thus not be sold as long as they are not released from the service they provide. Other assets may by now have been used for repo transactions. In this way, the capacity to create liquidity has already been used up. Through the repo transaction the former external financing has been replaced with self-financing. Even when selling the assets, the overall liquidity position does not change. We can therefore conclude that not all potentially marketable assets can be taken as liquidity for future purposes, but for the share which has been financed externally on an uncovered or unencumbered basis, to use the technical term.

4

A Policy Framework for Liquidity

At this point we should have established a fair understanding of liquidity as part of banking risk. Due to the lack of a generally accepted theoretical approach concerning liquidity and its risk elements, we addressed the question from the point of view of a practitioner. However, a practitioner cannot work in a conceptual vacuum. Without a concept in mind and adjusted to the realities of his or her specific bank, the practitioner is at risk of looking like the tail wagging the dog, as the saying goes. What does this mean?

4.1 SOME THOUGHTS AND CONSIDERATIONS

As stated before on various occasions, liquidity is not an ultimate goal for any company or bank. In fact, it is not even an intermediary goal comparable with growth, net income, profitability, etc. Like downside risk, liquidity is an element of danger which plays its full part only under adverse circumstances of a greater magnitude. Mostly, it could extend over several years, the level of liquidity risk stays low and can easily be managed. There are relatively rare occurrences which bring liquidity risk up to high and extremely high intensities what Taleb calls the Black-Swan. While showing up at infrequent intervals, their impact is usually severe and in some cases leads to total illiquidity and to the failure of the respective institution. It is for these reasons that liquidity and the proper management of it are challenging.

Without a theoretical and generally accepted frame such as the one available for VAR, liquidity managers have nothing but the experience they have gained themselves. Experience indeed is still a fundamental element when assessing the quantitative implications of liquidity risk in the normal case. As we learned while discussing the principles of LAR, the calculation for the normal case is based on internal data which are specific to the institution under consideration. It is experience in its purest form.

As soon as we move to implications initiated by stressed conditions, the rules change. We can no longer rely on our own data but have to refer to externally determined elements: that is, the behaviour of market participants vis-à-vis our own institution when confronted with various conditions. Whether or not these conditions are related to our specific institution or to general market conditions, and whether or not they affect the asset or liability side of our balance sheet, they are indeed relevant for steering the own ship through stormy waters and avoiding any rocks. The fundamental problems that liquidity managers face in their endeavours to reach a safe haven at the end are twofold: lack of predictability as well as lack of deterministic behaviour.

It would be helpful if upheavals relevant for liquidity management were to announce themselves in some way. With hindsight it becomes obvious that a problem was looming – but only with hindsight. Before the event the world may not have looked perfect at all, but it was still stable in an acceptable way – stable enough for the risk to be assessed as manageable and the compensation for taking it appropriate. We have experienced it again and again. No market watchers and rating agencies ring the alarm bell before the event. The adjustments follow after the incident. We will not enter into the reasoning behind this conduct but take as a basic understanding that stressed conditions will generally occur without prior warning and are thus not predictable.

Moreover, the behaviour of customers and market participants does not follow any deterministic pattern. That is, one cannot attach an amount receivable from the market for each notch in the rating scale. And the same change in rating may have insignificant effects for one bank while another institute may simultaneously experience remarkable positive or negative responses from lenders and investors. A general observation, e.g. when ratings are lowered the portion of long-term funds available will decline and funding spreads will widen, is helpful for a general understanding of market attitudes. But forecasting actual behaviour under specific circumstances and related to a specific bank is not possible. When it comes to market-related impacts, the experience is hardly different from the one just described. Events tend not to announce themselves. A specific economic and financial constellation may indicate a higher probability for such an event. Such critical phases may last and even accelerate, but they may also evaporate. Should these critical conditions actually turn into a real event, forecasting the timing will be highly unlikely and assessing the concrete implications of the stressed circumstances most improbable.

We can therefore conclude that liquidity managers deal with probabilities. The latter can refer to unexpected high losses or any other encumbrance affecting the externally perceived financial standing of a bank. There is also the probability of a market-related stress to be dealt with – the probability that the stress is initiated through funding difficulties, drawn optionalities or a less liquid environment for marketable assets, just to mention the most common sources of potential liquidity problems.

In order to deal with these types of danger one could try to quantify them and select the most appropriate mathematical method to arrive at quantitative results. In the end, however, it would mean overcoming the weakness of any particular assessment based on probability by calculating the probability of the probabilities. On the other hand, liquidity aspects develop their full capacity in the small region beyond the level of confidence, where one walks on uncharted territory. It is in this small area where a bank faces its most serious risk of grave harm, namely illiquidity. Following the route of pure probability is thus not advisable.

Taking experience as an approach does not help either. In our previous discussions we learned about its positive value for the normal case. When it comes to the stressed situation, however, we are left without a sound database for assessing such circumstances. A specific bank may have experienced one or two cases of stressed situations, but rarely the most severe ones. But how should a liquidity manager act if both the mathematical and the historic approaches, i.e. the experience, do not lead to acceptable solutions?

The lack of a full coverage of the subject by a generally accepted theoretical approach makes it advisable to advance in a practical manner. Practical in our understanding and the corresponding application relate to concepts. Concepts should not be confused with plain experience, although the latter plays a significant part when formulating them. The knowledge gained in the course of managing liquidity for decades needs to be collected in a logical frame. The graph in Figure 3.9 is one result of this endeavour. It distinguishes between financial and liquidity-related determinants and the relationships within the respective circles (which we called VAR and LAR); at the same time it shows how both of them are linked together and state the elements which influence the intensity of the link. At Commerzbank, for instance, constructing these types of concepts has become vital since the turn of the millennium as a basis for formulating the elements of liquidity policy and management. The following discussion is thus largely based on experiences at and concepts adapted by Commerzbank.

4.2   AN OVERVIEW OF ELEMENTS REGARDING LIQUIDITY POLICY

We start with an overview, with the aim of showing the most important elements of liquidity policy (Box 4.1). At this point the focus is on principal items that are indispensable for any coherent and complete frame.

Box 4.1 Liquidity policy and its elements

- Policy scope and frame
- Defining terms
- Authorities and responsibilities
- Methods and tools
- Scenarios and concepts employed
- Limits and limit structures
- Reports and reporting frequency
- Contingency planning

Any liquidity policy needs to include all the above elements as a minimum. The headings sometimes cover a wider range of subjects related to them. In the overview, the optical segregation of 'contingency planning' has been done on purpose. Although it is an indispensable part of liquidity policy, it should be dealt with separately and this for two reasons: firstly, all prior elements are regarded as essential under normal conditions; secondly, contingency planning is the specific preparation for stressed circumstances, at the same time depending heavily on the prior items.

4.3   THE ELEMENTS OF A LIQUIDITY POLICY IN DETAIL

The purpose of any liquidity policy is to help a bank fulfil its payment obligations now and in the future. Achieving the goals is done on the basis of a going concern related to and securing the lowest possible burden for the institution. Liquidity policy therefore addresses all measures necessary to achieve the respective goals.

4.3.1   Policy scope and frame

The statement that liquidity policy is to be based on a going concern and securing the lowest possible burden for the institution sets the ground rule. Managing liquidity just to be safe from liquidation would be below the scope. On the other hand, how much business should be securely covered? All of the present business? Or should it be restricted to the present core business or include newly developed lines envisaged to become core later on? These questions ought to be answered expressively, otherwise liquidity management may not comply with the business policy envisaged.

Whatever level is to be secured, it will combine long- and short-term assets as well as contingent liabilities, which were discussed under the term 'optionalities'. Applying going concern implies upholding at least a minimum amount of short-term assets for potential outflows from optionalities. Partly, the question was already referred to in the previous paragraph.

What is needed is an expressive reference on behalf of the liquidity manager. The timespan should be stated. In the case of backup lines, for example, in the short term the bank may be legally bound to fulfil ongoing contracts. Yet, an expressive statement about the potential prolongations of maturing contracts is necessary.

A further circle encompasses questions related to the principal organisational approach. One can opt for a group-wide policy framework only, with respective limits allocated and responsibilities assigned to various units and subsidiaries. A central body then coordinates activities and reviews adherence to the limits and rules. Alternatively, the proposals related to and execution of liquidity policy can be put into one function with responsibility and authority for the whole group. In such a case, the central body then also carries the responsibility as internal lender of last resort.

4.3.2   Defining terms

In order to keep the possibilities for misunderstanding and misinterpretation as low as possible, a common language with respect to the use of terms is important. This is especially true because of a lack of clearly defined and generally accepted terms in the area of liquidity, be it on a national or international level. The contents which must be defined are:

- Liquidity: The definition of the term 'liquidity' used within the bank may already possess a wide spectrum. Even if one were limited to one interpretation of the term for in-house use, it most certainly would not remain the only one. Regulators require adherence to the liquidity rules set by them. It is highly unlikely that their definition will coincide with the internal understanding of liquidity. Banks in different countries and reporting to several regulatory authorities may find as many diverse interpretations of liquidity as institutions.

    But even in-house one needs to distinguish several aspects. Liquidity can be related to markets, to products, to ratios, etc. In order to keep potential misunderstandings under control, the terms ought to be clearly defined concerning their meaning and numbers reduced to an essential minimum.
- Liquidity risk: Firstly, the term 'risk' needs to be defined before it can be used in various combinations. The term may only be used for circumstances and implications which are quantifiable. The meaning can be extended and become more generic, including general 'danger' as well. Once defined, the term can be linked to all relevant liquidity elements such as market liquidity, funding liquidity, available net liquidity, etc.
- Gaps: In many cases risk is not assessed as such in the initial phase but as gaps. As gaps can present themselves not only negatively but also positively, they represent a neutral statement of reality without judgement. In many cases gaps are the forerunner of and the basis of risk assessment. Examples include flow of cash gap, intra-day payment gap or long-term funding gap.
- Others: These include any further terms used in the liquidity policy paper and not already mentioned above. A policy paper of a large bank will inevitably cover a fair number of pages. It may thus not be felt appropriate to define all terms at the beginning. Sometimes, the level of understanding may be enhanced when the respective term is defined and explained in the context of the subject to which it relates. Although terms must be defined in any circumstances, there is some leeway on when and where to do so.

4.3.3 Authorities and responsibilities

This section needs special care when being drafted. The concept presents an extension of the earlier decision on whether one wishes to follow a centralised or decentralised approach. The structure and wording have to make clear for any reader the line taken. Thus it should not be phrased in general terms which are subject to interpretation. The requirements not only relate to the authority given, but also include the responsibilities demanded. Furthermore, it is advisable to widen the scope as far as possible to show the link to other functions and departments within the bank. Liquidity policy is embedded in a general framework of risk policy which in turn is part of business policy. The interrelationship and the structure envisaged by management are to become visible. The following methodical structure may serve as an indication of how the section could be composed.

4.3.3.1 *Matrix, functions and relationships*

It is advisable to start with a specific organisational chart including all relevant functions and indicate the flow of command and relationships (Figure 4.1). In this way, it becomes obvious at a glance what functions are involved, who is a driving force, what elements of decision making are related to a specific function and what type of feedback reporting the function requires and from whom.

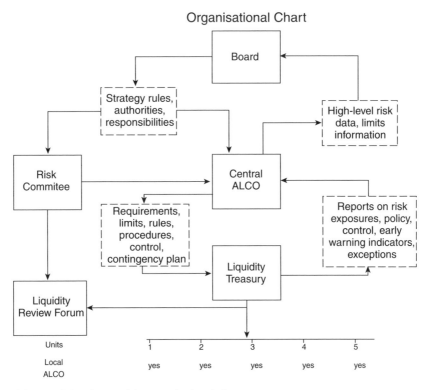

Figure 4.1   Possible scheme of the organisational chart

(Reproduced by permission of Commerzbank AG)

The structure relates to own experience and as such can only serve as an illustration. Banks do differ in size, complexity as well as line of command and therefore should adapt the structure accordingly. Three topics are at the forefront:

- For banks that have a wide geographical reach and/or larger specialised units managed by their own board, establishing a local ALCO (Asset/Liability Committee) is a must. When we deal with separate legal units it is a requirement from bank supervision as the management of the legal entity is not permitted to delegate (even upwards) a vital control function. The responsibility always stays with the local management, irrespective of whether it is located in the home country of the bank or abroad. Legally speaking, branches are a different matter. However, if due to their location they report to another banking authority than the central unit, setting up a local ALCO is very much recommended. Although the ultimate responsibility remains with headquarter, there are local requirements to be observed and the required speed to act needs consideration, such as for clearing in the local currency. Recognising the fact that liquidity and the risk related to it are embedded in the frame of general banking business, involving local management has great benefits. In some cases, local banking supervision may even demand it on the basis of best practice.
- The second topic relates to the ALCO as a separate body. When talking about larger banks, segregation from the risk committee is highly recommended. Liquidity, as one of the major banking risks, will not escape the responsibility of the latter. In particular, in the light of the basic rule to segregate management and control in order to ensure impartial calculations of risks and adherence to limits and guidelines, the risk committee is always involved. The ALCO does not have the technical infrastructure to perform these tasks; and the treasury as an acting body cannot control itself. For smaller banks and in particular for those with a limited geographical reach, the structure shown in Figure 4.1 may be exaggerated for the size of the tasks to be performed. In their cases, the business is rather local and does not require setting up local ALCOs, which reduces the level of complexity. The variety and structure of the business might also be less difficult. Integrating the ALCO into the risk committee can therefore be an acceptable measure in these circumstances.
- Whenever the geographical reach is extended, local ALCOs are established as a means of best practice or as a result of supervisory requirements. The management of the bank now has two options: to follow either a centralised or a decentralised approach. In the organisational chart the two are expressed by a solid line (direct control) or a dashed one (delegated authority). Traditionally, management tended to lean towards decentralisation, based on the understanding that local management has a better understanding of its markets and customers. Recent experience, however, clearly indicates that stressed situations often occur all of a sudden and without advanced knowledge to local market watchers. Moreover, when the stress is initiated in their own regional territory, they rely on support from the group, represented by the Group Treasury. The latter thus has to take over the function of internal lender of last resort. If it does so, the Group Treasurer must manage liquidity directly and on a group level (i.e. along a solid line).

Once the structure has been decided and clearly transposed to the organisational chart, the functions of each body have to be defined. The task includes authorities, responsibilities and line relationships equally. At this stage, all the relevant aspects should be pointed out. It is sufficient if the description answers the following questions: what is required from each organisational part and who is the recipient? A general indication is given in the organisational chart in Figure 4.1. This is not the time to go into technical details such as specific limits, frequency of reporting, how to treat limit breaches, etc. The aim can be summarised as follows: the organisational chart and the description of the functions on it allow a qualified reader to understand the concept applied (centralised versus decentralised), the structure chosen (who performs what function) and the general tasks to be fulfilled by each group. If done in this way and fulfilling the conditions stated, one arrives at a coherent picture which serves as a basis for the more detailed elements to come.

4.3.3.2 Policies and guidelines

When setting policy in detail some basic principles should first be defined before referring to each function in the organisational chart. There is more than one way to achieve a coherent policy, yet, based on experience over many years, we can conclude that some of the principles related to authorities and responsibilities are essential for the policy to function properly, even under stressed conditions. Especially under stress, the mechanism in relationships between functions should not additionally bear lack of clarity and overlap the policy defined. It is a request which applies also to normal circumstances, but which aggravates working conditions under stress in an undue and unnecessary manner. The following basic principles have proven to be helpful under normal circumstances and have retained their value under different actual stresses as well.

Board of directors

- Being responsible for the bank's strategy, assuring compatible business and risk policies. The latter includes downside as well as liquidity risk.
- Deciding policy-related principles at the highest management level, i.e. the board of directors. This applies as well to policy changes, adjustments and granting exceptions.
- Clearly defining and segregating liquidity management from control and consequently allocating the respective duties to the units concerned. In our case: the risk committee and controlling department on the one hand, and the central ALCO and Group Treasury on the other hand.
- Defining whether liquidity policy will be based on the business concept of going concern. If it is, defining the period necessary for management to readjust to normal business conditions. Liquidity policy cannot solve business-related problems. However, it can buy time for the board to adjust business policy without undue constraints from liquidity. Further, the part of the present business that has to be secured at all costs is to be defined, e.g. core, future core or all present businesses.
- Assessing and monitoring business-policy-related risk potential against available risk bearing capacity at a strategic level. This contains downside as well as liquidity risk and considers rating related implications on funding capacity. Defining the acceptable risk appetite considering the implications discussed in the VAR and LAR circles as well as rating implications and their links to investor attitudes.
- Assuring liquidity policy and corresponding liquidity management to be appropriate and specific for the bank. This requires a proper analyses of the specific management, assets/liability and risk structure of the institution, including contingency planning.
- Delegating duties which require expert knowledge to the respective committees and their expert departments, i.e. the central ALCO and risk committee. This includes limit proposals,

developing procedures/guidelines and assumptions. All of them are subject to approval by the board.

- Deciding whether to follow a centralised or decentralised approach in liquidity policy.
- Establishing principles for reviewing the organisational setup, policies, limits, procedures/ guidelines and assumptions. An annual interval is usually appropriate. In case of any liquidity-related disturbances, the review should be conducted shortly after the event and not left till the next ordinary assessment date. The experience is still relevant and potentially needed adjustments or improvements can be realised without delay.
- Defining stressed circumstances and assuring procedures for these cases are in place. This includes stress scenarios, the function or committee which declares the stress and starts the respective procedures, the function in the lead as well as reporting and decision procedures. As a housekeeping provision, the function declaring the end of the stressed situation and return to normal business.
- Receiving high-level information for assessment of adhering to limits and procedures and deciding about measures to be taken in the case of overstepping.

Central ALCO

- This is a high-level committee and ideally the board is represented by the CEO, the member in charge of the treasury and the CFO. The CRO can be present at this level but it is not essential, as all risk-relevant aspects go through the risk committee of which the CRO is the chairperson. At the next management level the treasury, financial controlling, risk controlling and strategic controlling functions (in lieu of 5–10 operational managers) should be represented. Experience shows clear benefits of having finance integrated in addition. If felt necessary, more functions can be called to join on a 'when needed' or permanent basis. The former approach has the advantage of keeping the group small and thus, generally speaking, more efficient. The boundaries set by the board decide the competence delegated to the committee.
- Reporting to the board and receiving from it the parameters for its own activities, authorities and duties. Providing standing and exception reports on limit adherence, measures taken and proposals.
- Forecasting capital ratios, proposing respective measures to be taken and implementing those according to board decisions.
- Formulating requirements and instructing the treasury to develop proposals concerning limits, rules and procedures. Proposals received are decided on if within the frame of delegated authority; otherwise, and if validity of the proposal is confirmed, the latter is presented to the board for decision/approval.
- Formulating requirements with reference to contingency and funding plans to be produced by the treasury. They will cover normal as well as stressed conditions, encompassing various scenarios with an assessment of probability of occurrence and degree of severity related to assets and liabilities.
- Requiring proposals from the treasury regarding minimum liquidity reserves and minimum cash flow coverage ratios for situation-specific and structural liquidity frames. Deciding on the proposals and controlling adherence once implemented.
- Requiring from the treasury proposals on liquidity limit concept and allocation. The latter refers to subsidiaries, foreign branches, as well as 'virtual' branches. The last group covers large banking sectors like private banking, corporate banking or investment banking. Especially in the home country of the bank, the consumption and creation of liquidity

is to be segregated according to sources. Costs and benefits ought to be properly allocated. The limits are also to include currency exposures and their limitation. The ALCO, after assessing the proposals as valid, will propose them to the board. Once accepted and implemented, the limit utilisation is periodically reviewed and corrective steps taken if necessary.

- Formulating for itself a board-approved concept for responses to breaches of limits. Three basic constellations are to be covered:
  - The limit stays, but the excess is acceptable on a temporary basis.
  - Proposal to the board to adjust the limit and accept a temporary excess.
  - Excess is unacceptable. Ordering to rectify and start escalation process if deemed appropriate.
- Requiring from the treasury a funding concept aimed at retail and corporate customers to strengthen the more stable funding element. Periodically reviewing amounts and time structure in order to assess progress made and using the findings as an early indicator of investor attitude towards the bank.
- Formulating a policy for local ALCOs, including locations, members and chairperson, direct reporting line (to the treasurer or ALCO), authorities and responsibilities.
- Defining a policy for optionalities to limit unexpected drawings on liquidity.
- Qualitative discussions.
- Together with the chairperson of the risk committee, defining policy rules and procedures – subject to board approval – covering the following elements:
  - Securing all risks and exposures with limits controlled independently.
  - Delineating management and control functions. It is worthwhile putting some thought into this point. On the one hand it is important to review and decide on correct and independently controlled data and procedures. On the other hand the treasury is using basic data for management purposes like scenario analysis, assessment of future developments, etc. This is to ensure that the treasury is managing within a frame of controlled data and procedures, but equally it is to ascertain that control keeps a healthy distance from the management process – hence the following point.
  - Agreeing on setting up a 'Liquidity Review Forum' with the aim of taking an intermediary role in defining (new) risk, measurements and procedures within the scope of controlling liquidity-related activities. Bringing together the aspects of managing (treasury) and control (risk controlling) in the process of preparing proposals for decision will speed up the process and improve the quality of the decision.
  - Defining the scope and frequency of independently produced risk reports presented to the ALCO. The agreement will cover normal and exceptional circumstances and include escalation procedures.

Treasury

- Fulfilling requirements from the ALCO related to concepts and procedures to be established, 'what if' analyses to be calculated and proposals to be made.
- Proposing and setting quantitative restriction on the basis of limits or guidelines. Limits have the benefit of being clear concerning 'wrong' or 'right'. Guidelines allow for leeway within a band and thus for flexibility. In some cases limits may be too strict in a financial sense without adding greater value to security. For example, one may wish the total of the net liquidity gap beyond 1 year to be closed and the annual gaps to be limited. If the rule is set as a limit, the treasury has to act as soon as the threshold is exceeded; it may even

concern the period 9–10 years and the total net gap being zero to positive. If the rule is set as a guideline, the treasury has time. It can take advantage of better market conditions or develop other forms of financing than going straight to issuing in the capital market.

- Defining policies, procedures and limits for each local ALCO. Regulations from local supervision/central banks are to be integrated, although this could mean having to fulfil the requirements from two national controllers i.e. the tighter gets precedence.
- Setting up dedicated teams servicing wholesale customers and depositors. The aim is to establish personal relationships with the benefit of increasing funding potential and greater stability in their lending behaviour by building up trust. The latter is particularly important in case of institution- or market-related uncertainties.
- In the function as internal lender of last resort:
  - Allocating guidelines on maximum exposures overall and composition of basic structure on assets and liabilities, including contingent liabilities/optionalities. Giving total flexibility to subunits undermines preparing for stressed circumstances as the composition could change fast.
  - Aiming to finance all units of the group directly. Keeping exceptions at a minimum. Otherwise funding policy will be cannibalised with higher funding cost and reduced knowledge about lenders' behaviour. Investors assess the credit risk from a group perspective but opt for better returns offered given the same risk.
  - In case exceptions are granted, assessing the risk (circumstances and amounts) of the self-financing unit losing funding capability. Putting up reserves to be in a position to finance the gap if necessary.
  - Assessing the risk and its implications of rating-related asset and liability as well as contracts covered under optionalities. Integrating them into the stress analyses.
- Taking all possible measures to perform liquidity policy and management at the level of best practice at least. The term 'best practice' signifies the subject to be implemented and experience gained by a (larger) number of banks already. The most advanced at this point are ahead of best practice, so it should be seen as a minimum.
- Assessing and monitoring the insured deposits with the bank (in Germany, *Einlagensicherungsfond*). There is no guarantee that these deposits will not be withdrawn in a severe institution-related stress situation. Yet they are as stable as any external short-term funds can be.
- Defining rules and regulations based on what potentially marketable assets can be segregated into immediate liquid, liquid within specified timeframes and illiquid.
- Participating together with risk controlling in the Liquidity Review Forum with the view of achieving results in good time and soundly balanced; that is, adhering to risk aspects as well as considering practical aspects of handling.
- Reviewing policies, procedures and limits annually or after an event. Reporting on the findings to the ALCO and proposing adjustments if necessary.
- Communicating with front line managers on an open and proactive basis. The treasury, due to its risk management function, can easily be perceived as the one which limits business opportunities. While this is true in a way, the treasury can also advise on how to act best and to the benefit of the operating units within constraints set by regulators and the board. It is beneficial to have regular meetings at shorter intervals on an individual basis with board members responsible for business segments. At the same time, the treasury will get a better understanding of how business works and can consider the knowledge in its policies, procedures and managing liquidity.

- Reporting on market behaviour, special events and specific observations. This includes spread development of own bond issues in the primary or secondary markets on the one hand, compared with the developments of spreads from a selected peer group on the other hand; changes in the willingness of market participants to provide funds; changes in money market spreads; absorptive capacity of markets regarding marketable assets, etc.
- Adhering to requirements from regulators wherever applicable and taking a proactive attitude towards them. The treasurers of banks with locations abroad and in different currency areas should keep in contact with them on a regular basis. This not only enhances own knowledge, but for regulators also puts a face on the bank. Updating and periodic presentations with respect to liquidity policy and present status also give them a better insight into the bank. This is a vital part of preparatory work which cannot be compensated for in any way once disturbances have started.

Risk committee and Liquidity Review Forum   We will not enter into a detailed discussion on the two functions. The risk committee is the risk controller with a range well beyond liquidity. Accordingly, our subject is but one part of it, although at times with severe implications. Its integration into the organisational frame is, however, paramount for its function as independent controller. However prominently the central ALCO is staffed, it is a managing body and one which is not allowed to control itself. As all relevant points related to our subject have been addressed within the sections above we will not go deeper into the subject for fear of repetition.

The same goes for the Liquidity Review Forum (LRF). It is not general practice to have that function set up. Yet experience has shown it to be very useful, especially in rather complex organisations and with large, specialised banking subsidiaries attached. Within the small group the learning curve on both sides is steep and consequently appropriate solutions fulfilling risk as well as practical requirements are found speedier.

4.3.4   Methods and tools

The methods available to an institution largely depend on its level of information systems. Some years back, the necessary technical infrastructure often lacked the sophistication required to get all data on contracts concluded and relevant to liquidity. The growing complexity of the banking business has added to it. In the meantime, banks that are advanced in this matter have built the appropriate information systems. Whether even advanced banks cover all entities and products of a group without exception is in the light of the subprime crisis, an open question. Setting up the technical infrastructure and, most probably even more, defining the appropriate parameters for complex financial instruments is time consuming. The priority list within the projected plan understandably will attach time-wise a higher emphasis on covering areas and products incorporating the large volumes. Following this approach allows a relatively high percentage of the work to be done within a shorter period. Yet a low share outstanding may not give reason for comfort. The uncovered pieces may be part of the most volatile sector and thus affect the liquidity structure to an overproportionate extent in a stressed situation. Hence, analysing the potential effects and weighing the volumes covered against implications to be expected is advisable when setting up the project.

As a reminder, during the phase of building up, the required infrastructure cannot serve as an excuse to neglect uncovered fields. The duty of a liquidity manager did not start a couple of years ago, just after methods and information systems had been developed. Performing the duty with more sophisticated means is valuable support for any manager, but it is not a *conditio sine qua non*. Admittedly, the alternative in the form of an 'expert assessment' and based on best knowledge is a second-best solution only and requires a larger buffer to cover the higher level of uncertainty. On the other hand, neglecting the subject is the worst possible approach with no indication of what disturbances could bring about.

Any calculation of probable gaps in the future has to integrate on- as well as off-balance-sheet transactions. The term 'probable gaps' also demands the attachment of a level of confidence and probability. For the 'normal case' of LAR, the result serves as a forecast and thus as the basis against which the actual gap at payment date is measured. The degree of missing reality against forecast is taken as deviation. It determines the level of the liquidity buffer necessary to secure fulfilling payment obligations under normal circumstances.

For stressed conditions, future liquidity status is calculated by applying different scenarios. The respective results are taken as the basis for contingency planning. The measures aim at supporting liquidity management in its endeavours to take the most appropriate measures in relation to the stage and nature of a potential liquidity crisis involving the bank.

There is no unanimous way of achieving the goals. The banking sector consists of a wide and diversified range of participants with different balance-sheet structures. We will restrict ourselves to some basic tools for illustration. All of them could be called essentials in today's liquidity measurement.

The four components we look at are: expected liquidity exposure (ELE), dynamic liquidity exposure (DLE), balance-sheet liquidity (BSL) and available net liquidity (ANL).

- Expected liquidity exposure (ELE): This is based on contractually and therefore legally agreed transactions. For this reason it is sometimes referred to as 'legal flow of cash gap'. The method covers on- and off-balance-sheet contracts. Any legally binding contract has two parts which are at the disposition of the parties involved: namely, amount and date of payment. The expected flows of cash can be of a deterministic or stochastic nature.
- Dynamic liquidity exposure (DLE): ELE, which was described above, is a good basis to start with. The restriction of relating exclusively to contractual clauses has its shortcomings. It is a static view and does not take into consideration the dynamic element of banking business, which is an element we stressed in the summary of Chapter 1. As mentioned earlier, a part of the loans to customers will not be repaid finally but indirectly extended through new borrowing. Equally, not all of the deposits will be withdrawn at maturity but prolonged, just to mention two examples.

  In order to achieve forecast flows closer to reality, the specific behaviour needs to be considered. The tool employed is sometimes called dynamic trade strategies (DTS) and incorporates behavioural effects on positions like sight, savings and time deposits or committed lines, for example. Expected cash exposure adjusted for effects from the DTS tool produces the DLE.
- Balance-sheet liquidity (BSL): The third tool consists of a concept to determine balance-sheet liquidity. BSL indicates to what extent the bank is able to cover a potential liquidity shortfall by making use of its liquidity reserves. One refers to marketable assets which can either be liquidated or serve as instruments for repo transactions etc., like bonds, equities and loans eligible for securitisation. In Germany, for example, if loans conform to strict conditions they are also eligible with the Bundesbank.

  The BSL concept restricts the potentially liquid stock in two ways. Firstly, only 'unencumbered' assets are accepted. Those which presently are subject to a repo or a collateral transaction are excluded until they are free for use again. In addition, assets potentially available for BSL are grouped into different buckets reflecting the level of market liquidity of the specific instrument. The range covers various stages from immediately liquefiable in large amounts until totally illiquid. Based on the classification, one arrives at a projected amount of secondary liquidity per period.

- Available net liquidity (ANL): This is determined from the sum of the previous tools taken together. We started with ELE and adjusted the contractual and static views. By employing DTS we integrated the economic relevant element of customer behaviour and got to DLE. The gaps in DLE are then compared with BSL and its time structure. The combined result serves as a basis for the funding policy and liquidity management of the bank.

Within the frame of these tools, segregation of the time horizon and the level of detail are elements which need to be determined. The published proposals related to the time horizon cover a wide range of possibilities. Where they differ is the duration of the daily, weekly and monthly buckets. Daily ones for 1 week only have been mentioned as a minimum in the light of the particular severity in the first few days of a stressed situation. From experience, 1 week is too short a period of time. Whatever range per time bucket is chosen, one would be well advised to ensure that the technical capability does not impede flexibility. Requirements may change over time or under specific circumstances and ask for a higher level of granularity as used at the time. Again from experience, a granularity of daily buckets for the current and the following 2 months; monthly ones for the following 18 calendar months; annual buckets up to and including year 10; and 5-year periods beyond have all served well, even under stressed conditions.

The level of detail not least concerns currencies. All tools should be applied first to the respective currencies that the bank is engaged in as the payment obligations have to be fulfilled in each legal tender. The monitoring and steering of it demands a clear segregation. Only for high-level information should one use home currency equivalents as in the case of group reporting. Furthermore, up to the level of DLE, with its sub-elements ELE and DTS, data should also be segregated down to product level or even down to book level where appropriate. Such a high granularity allows for specific insight through aggregation/disaggregation by product, business line, location and currency.

4.3.5   Scenarios and concepts employed

When addressing scenarios we firstly distinguish between the normal case and stressed condition. Secondly, implications of stressed conditions are to be assessed under predefined actual events of the past. It is also vital to add at least one 'virtual' scenario, one which has not happened yet but could happen in the future.

For the normal case most of the policy-related risk parameters are already defined by the method. Two subjects are left open and are to be decided at this level. The first item concerns the level of confidence. We dealt with this point in detail when dealing with LAR and will therefore abstain from discussing it here again. The second point refers to the level of the buffer seen as appropriate within the policy framework. For the normal case, using the tools mentioned in the previous section will provide a forecast of the liquidity gap. The forecast will be compared with actual gaps to arrive at the deviation. When taking all deviations over the base period of 1 year and putting the amounts in descending order of size, we arrive at the maximum loss to be expected as soon as the level of confidence is attached to it. That is for the normal case. The calculated loss has to be covered by a liquidity buffer. To define the size of the buffer or, to put it in another way, to define the percentage that the maximum calculated loss is allowed to consume from the buffer is a policy decision.

For stressed situations, policy decisions cover a wider range of items. There is no uniform stress. Its source may be induced through markets or the institution itself; the implications can affect assets or liabilities. Related to policy, three items are at the forefront:

- Firstly, the type of stressed situations experienced in the past are chosen. It is not necessary for an institution to have been affected by them in the past. Bank structure, policies and markets, which make up the environment of a specific bank, change over time. Liquidity management concerns today and the time ahead, and is not about the past. The following principle can be taken as a basic rule: choose at least one historic severe event for each product and market segment that the bank is engaged in today and select geographical areas in which the bank is present or affected by today. Examples could include an equity crash, a credit crunch with its implications on interest rates and market liquidity, severe turbulence in the foreign exchange market, regional crises as seen in Asia. As a short reminder, any of the events chosen most likely will not repeat themselves. Selecting events that the banking industry came across sometime in the past just improves the understanding of what might happen. With this in mind, one should abstain from qualifying extreme stresses experienced in the past as so-called worst-case scenarios. The next one could be worse than anything experienced so far. We just do not know how the next Black Swan acts.
- The second item relates to the scope of securing the business activities in case of liquidity stress. Is it sufficient to secure shareholder capital in case of a severe stress? In other words, is the policy order given to the liquidity manager for this case to secure proper liquidation of the firm, with the condition that all bills have to be paid and capital returned to the shareholders? Or is the intention to continue banking business with its franchise on a 'going concern' basis? Depending on the policy stated, liquidity management will follow different routes, and they are not easy to reverse, especially when the timeframe given is short or a crisis already looming. If the 'going concern' option is chosen, the range has to be further defined. The decision may limit the activities to be secured to core business, extended to include future core business or encompass all activities performed today. The answers to these questions derive from the bank's strategy and the corresponding business policy formulated.
- The third point relates to the one just discussed. Yet it emphasises an aspect of it which is sufficiently important to be dealt with separately: the level of security to be bought. We started by selecting the stress scenarios and subsequently chose the scope of business which ought to be secured under stress. Unfortunately, there is still one variable that is undetermined. For the benefit of clarity, we will approach the subject within a wider frame. Security and thus securing liquidity does not come free, but has a cost label attached to it. Furthermore, the higher the level of security bought, the costlier it will be. If securing liquidity follows the cost pattern of any other insurance, and there is no reason to believe it does not, the costs will not rise in proportion to the level of security bought but in an exponential manner. On the other hand, the likelihood of an extremely severe event is very small; also, we do not know the implications with certainty but deal with probabilities. Therefore we are faced with a trade-off which needs to be clarified. The choice is between high cost with a better chance (no certainty) of securing the business intended to be covered

and somewhat lower cost with a higher risk that not all of the businesses aimed to be covered is secured in the case of an extreme event. In any trade-off there needs to be a buffer to take the brunt. Here it is the probability of business activity secured, which brings us back to business strategy and policy. Each time one lowers the probability of having the chosen activities secured under extreme circumstances, the chances grow of having part of it not financed if push comes to shove. Consequently, we have to enlarge the business elements of core, future core and opportunistic businesses and add one more item: business at disposal and disposable within a defined timeframe in case of necessity.

4.3.6 Limits and limit structures

Setting limits serves two purposes. For lower levels, the frame given allows the local liquidity manager to act in accordance with the general policy of the bank. For the liquidity manager of the group, working with limits is the necessary basis to enable a general policy to be set up and followed. Especially in banks with a decentralised business, it is the only way to get a framework which can be taken as a basis for managing liquidity under normal and also stressed conditions. The management in charge knows the maximum exposure overall, per currency, location and business unit. Limits set on individual currencies should correspond to the portfolio structure and volume of the respective business or location, provided market conditions allow for it. Limits are set by location and currency, whereby a location may use several currencies in addition to the local one. Limits are segregated according to levels. The distinction to be made is twofold: external versus internal level is one and vertical authority the other.

Supervisory authorities demand at least information about liquidity status and the concept in place to assure that liquidity is managed at all levels up to the group as a whole. Apart from the more procedural requirements, bank supervisors set actual limits which have to be adhered to. In Germany, for example, this is the 'Liquidity Requirement' (*Liquiditätsverordnung*). In short, it says that over the coming month the sum of maturing assets is to exceed the sum of maturing liabilities, thereby securing more liquidity flowing in than out in this period. To get a realistic picture, for marketable assets and saving deposits for example, assumptions have been built into the concept related to economic instead of legal maturities. The highly aggregated figure expressed in the home currency is primarily for external use to supervisors, rating agencies and analysts. Supervisory limits are set not only for the group, but for each legal entity of the group irrespective of whether or not they belong to the same supervisory jurisdiction.

For practical purposes the level of aggregation is too high. Gaps in individual currencies, business segments and locations need to be limited in order to secure that immediate and future payment obligations are fulfilled (what we called situation-specific and structural liquidity respectively). Especially for larger banks with a wider geographical reach, supervisory rules ought to be seen as minimum requirements which have to be supplemented by a more detailed internal limit scheme.

We now address the vertical element. It contains the authority for setting limits as well as the ultimate authority level to which a breach of limits is to be escalated. The principle of management states that the same authority level should be chosen both for setting limits and being informed about a breach of them. It is the one who sets the original frame who also should decide how to act in case it is overstepped, e.g. accepting on a temporary basis,

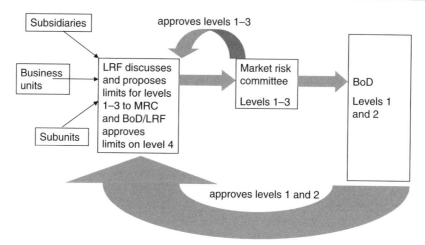

Figure 4.2 Overview of a possible limit concept
(Reproduced by permission of Commerzbank AG)

adjusting the limit or ordering the rectification of the excess within a specific timeframe. It is also understood that the respective committee may not have sufficient technical knowledge and experience. In these cases the committee will refer to experts to provide a professional assessment as a basis for decision making.

In Figure 4.2 limits are segregated into four levels. The latter not only serve as a medium for sub-allocation, but form a basis on which escalation processes are defined. Figure 4.3 presents a possible solution.

When defining the limit concept, it makes sense to apply principles which also relate to management in general. Levels of authority should be brought into line with the severity of implications and the specific professional knowledge required. Furthermore, responsibility for 'doing' must be separated from responsibility for 'controlling'. It follows that the highest-level limits, which include all externally provided data, are to stay with the board of directors (BoD).

Level	Organisational unit	Escalation committee
1	Group level	Board of directors
2	Large subsidiaries/ units of large areas	Board of directors
3	Business units	Risk committee
4	Subunits	Liquidity Review Forum

Figure 4.3 Limit setup and escalation
(Reproduced by permission of Commerzbank AG)

The overall limit is then broken down into business levels of which there should only be a few. Large, legally independent units are one, since they report the data externally. Further horizontal segregation depends on the policy with regard to a centralised or decentralised approach, which was discussed above in the section entitled 'Authorities and responsibilities'. Even for level 2, decisions should stay with the board.

How to progress further down depends on the business philosophy and the size and complexity of the institution. Experience indicates delegation. Since level 1 and level 2 are in the hands of the board, the strategic allocations have been determined. The sub-allocation should be done by functions closer to business activities. Following these arguments, there are good reasons to delegate further levels to the risk committee. But how many further levels will be appropriate?

A smaller and regionally orientated bank might be well served by two levels. Larger banks may prefer three levels in order to cover separate locations. The point is especially valid if different currencies are involved, which demand several clearing centres for the bank as a whole. For a large and internationally present bank four levels are much more appropriate but hardly exceeded either.

While discussing limit structure and authorities for various levels, a vital point has been left out: managing liquidity and its relation to the internal 'customer base'. As stated above, limits should be in line with the business concept if circumstances permit liquidity management to secure payments under normal circumstances and stressed situations. Setting limits is thus the result of a partnership consisting of the business segments, liquidity management, risk controlling and the authority in charge of the limit level. We are back to our magic polygon. Maximising any of the elements of growth, income and profitability on one hand and risk avoidance on the other hand is not possible without negative ramifications for the other side of the equation. Defining the rules in such a way that each partner can and does play its part properly is therefore vital. It means maximising the overall result without taking undue risks.

4.3.7   Reports and reporting frequency

Liquidity reports cover liquidity elements which change daily or even during the day (for which there exists an intra-day market) up to the ones which show greater stability, like the available net liquidity (ANL).

Reports follow the limit structure discussed in the previous section. Whenever a limit is defined, the actual utilisation and hence also a potential breach of it have to be computed and reported. Computing and reporting limit utilisation is to be done by risk controlling.

Reports are distributed on a 'who has to know' basis. Therefore, they follow a bottom-up approach. The person in charge of managing the lowest level receives reports about his or her utilisation of the limit. The level above should receive reports on all the limits of its area of responsibility, thus moving from the lowest level to the top – the group. Responsibility encompasses three groups, as in Box 4.2.

As for the frequency of reporting, one usually distinguishes reports at daily, weekly and monthly intervals. Limit utilisation on the currency and location/business unit level is generally presented on a daily basis. Information related to balance-sheet liquidity and similar concepts are produced at weekly intervals. Consolidated higher-level reporting tends to be on a monthly basis. However, it is understood that if disturbances are expected or already ongoing, intervals should be shortened.

Box 4.2 Addressees of limit reports

- The liquidity manager in charge of a specific liquidity segment up to the group treasurer or group liquidity manager, if liquidity is not part of the treasury.
- The authorities who have defined and allocated the limits, e.g. the board, the risk committee and the central ALCO. For practical reasons each committee selects representatives who receive daily reports while information is provided to all members at regular sessions.
- Supervisors outside the home country often require local management to assume responsibility for all activities within their unit. This applies not only for subsidiaries but equally for branches. Branch management does not actually need to be involved in the 'doing' but has to be part of the information scheme.

4.4   CONTINGENCY PLANNING

4.4.1   Introduction

Having personally experienced several market-related and an extremely severe bank-related stress towards the end of 2002 when in charge of group treasury, the author can confirm a key assumption of contingency planning: neither is it possible to predict well in advance the timing, type, severity or duration of a stressed situation, nor is one in a position to catch up with time-consuming issues missed during preparation. With this in mind, we will commence by explaining what contingency planning is not about.

Contingency planning is *not* about:

- Setting the scope and the frame for liquidity policy which includes all details with respect to business to be secured.
- Defining terms to be used throughout the bank in order to have a common language which is a basic requirement for normal communication.
- Setting up the liquidity-related matrix structure and defining the functions within the structure and their relationships to each other.
- Evaluating and deciding on appropriate methods and tools to manage liquidity in normal circumstances and under stressed conditions.
- Choosing and implementing the scenarios to be employed, which are necessary to obtain the most likely implications in severe circumstances.
- Taking all monetary steps to prepare for the potential events.
- Deciding on a limit frame for the elements of location, business units, currencies, etc., and the respective granulation.
- Deciding and stating where to use guidelines or set fixed limits and setting the amounts on the required level of granulation.
- Deciding which reports to produce, by what function within the bank, the frequency of reporting, the respective level of aggregation and the addressees of the different reports.

All these elements *are* essential and form the basis of contingency planning, but they relate to the liquidity policy which is to be formulated and implemented. Without the essentials in place in case of a stressed situation, the chance of surviving a severe liquidity crisis at best is greatly reduced but could drop to an insignificant level. Ideally, the components of liquidity policy were in place long before the testing event and have become routine in the meantime. Routine in this understanding does not mean simply following the formal procedures. For us, routine describes a state when the teething troubles in the early stage of implementation have been overcome: people involved have familiarised themselves with the relevant duties; bugs have been removed from the programs; reports and reporting structure have been adjusted to correct any misunderstandings experienced; internal tests have been successfully concluded; and the processes of communication as well as decision making have been activated several times in the actual course of business.

Let us compare a contingency plan with the aide-memoire of a military commander entrusted with the protection and defence of a specific territory. The organisational structure is in place, the everyday routine works without friction. Potential dangers in whatever form have been analysed and quantified. The requirements on specialised staff and equipment have been fulfilled. Units have been deployed in the best way to defend against any form of potential danger. And regular tests in the form of military drills and manoeuvres have been used to familiarise everybody, irrespective of rank, with the potential risk conditions. Unfortunately, the commander is still not ready to counter stressed events in a professional way. The potential danger has many faces, not just one. Consequently, our military commander prepares the units in an optimal way but on the understanding that there is more than one form of risk which they have to be ready for. Yet, for the actual case, whatever it might be, the preparations are suboptimal because quantitative constraints have had to give way to concessions when preparing for all eventualities. This is the time when the aide-memoire comes into play.

In the case of an actual event the commander will have to adjust the units for the specific case. Military history over several thousand years has told our military commander to plan for these constellations in advance in a considered way, evaluating all aspects and with time to spare. Once the battle starts there will be no more time for planning, only for acting. The individual plan for each case obviously cannot be done in a very detailed manner. None of the scenarios is completely predictable. Our commander needs flexibility to respond, but within a well-thought-through framework. It is adjustments that must be dealt with and not fundamental questions. But where is the relevance to liquidity contingency planning?

In the discussion of the VAR and the LAR circles we referred to liquidity being multi-dimensional, in stark contrast to VAR. The latter has a single dimension only: whatever risk may become effective, it turns into a financial loss for which there is a buffer established in the form of shareholder capital. In the terms of our military commander, downside risk has only a single face of danger and preparations can be made to meet this very specific case exclusively. Yet liquidity is without an external buffer and has to take the brunt itself. As we concluded, it is liquidity that has to compensate for loss of liquidity when risk turns into reality. The specific danger can show its face in various places and the remedy must be appropriate irrespective of whether the cause relates to an institution or is a market-specific one or affects assets and liabilities. The conditions that liquidity managers work in are thus very similar to the experience of our military commander: Preparing an optimal structure and setup to cover the possible dangers envisaged in total, but also being aware that in the event of a specific stress, an adjustment has to made for the explicit realities. It also follows that the concrete alternatives ought to be clearly defined in principle while the responses are to be kept loosely formulated in order to allow for flexibility in the concrete circumstances. Sound preparation is paramount since stresses can occur unexpectedly, through routes not necessarily predicted and with a speed that makes surviving the first few days the critical period. A liquidity manager may be lucky if the stress builds up gradually and gives time to respond in stages and time to develop respective strategies. However, the potential implications are too severe to work on the basis of luck.

4.4.2 The frame of contingency planning

In principle, contingency planning is an extension of liquidity policy. It is for this view that it is taken as part of policy and not addressed in the coming chapter dealing with liquidity management. Technical and even more economic considerations do not permit a bank to structure its balance sheet in such a way that liquidity risk is avoided in all circumstances. As we have discussed, neither keeping all liabilities in line with maturities of assets nor adjusting the economic maturity of all assets, which considers the possibility to sell and to enter into a repo transaction, are feasible alternatives. Liquidity gaps are thus in a way an inevitable element of banking. Weighing the likelihood against the severity of an extreme event and combined with the risk appetite of the institution determines at the end the gap profile which is assessed as still appropriate. The subject has been dealt with when examining the liquidity level within the LAR circle.

An extension of policy implies a setup which principally stays unchanged but for the adjustments, of which there should be few. Especially under stressed conditions, the technical setup should not be altered under any circumstances. The risk of malfunctions is too high. Key functions at all levels should be handled by experienced personnel, which is only possible if they have been part of the routine. Otherwise, new functions have to follow a learning curve which will result in lengthy discussions to get an understanding of the principles and methods. As a result, most probably new discussions on how to deal with a liquidity crisis will emerge. As time elapses, and the window open with the chance to succeed is short, the possibility arises that management will be forced into a corner out of which it can merely react, while what is needed are proactive, decisive resolutions. What then are the adjustments to be considered for a contingency plan?

4.4.3 Defining a stressed condition

Up to this point the terms 'normal conditions' and 'stressed conditions' have been used in a clearly defined manner but more in the form of an *ex post* conclusion. Yet contingency planning is not about establishing the fact that one is in the midst of a most severe liquidity crisis. Surely, an event may occur without any warning signals, like 9/11. There are cases, however, where pressure builds up gradually and manifests itself in early warning signals – but spotted after the event has taken place. A solid liquidity policy is forward looking and has to watch for signals that may lead to a crisis. The following list of potential causes can be taken as examples. For further insight we refer again to Figure 3.9.

- **Growth**: An extensive programme of growth includes risk if liquidity is not already secured. Planning an acquisition is another form of potential risk. It is advisable not to limit the assessment to the present and future liquidity conditions and the available capacity to absorb new needs when preparing the acquisition. It is equally important to assess the present liquidity policy applied by the firm to be acquired. Its liquidity management may be based on a sound policy or may turn out to be critical. The acquisition may trigger a downgrading of the parent company or the new affiliate. In any case, pre-empting measures have to be taken. Both alternatives of growth will increase limit utilisation in the name of the parent company. In the case of an acquisition it is even more pronounced. Lenders may judge it as an undue concentration of risk in a single counterparty and shorten the new overall limit compared with the one given to both of them on an individual basis.

- **The VAR circle**: Both P/L and capital are decisive elements in the external assessment of a firm's solvency and risk level. Any change to the worse can cause a reduction in the funding available. Forward looking does not stop here, however. A severe economic downturn will affect future earning possibilities. The impact of the economic environment has many aspects which can and should be assessed separately. A slow or slower level of growth is usually followed by a reduced demand for banking products. A sharper downturn (it does not necessarily have to be a recession) will increase the fallout rate in lending. Economic forecasts, whether internal or external ones, showing falling macroeconomic indices, can be used as an instrument of forewarning. Overheating in sectors of the economy or markets can be followed by sharp and fast corrections when the bubble bursts. Any of these items have to be reviewed periodically, not only for tangible changes but for perception as well.
- **Rating/investor attitude**: Rating by and large is no early indicator but rather the stamp after reality has shown its face. That is, as far as the external rating from agencies is concerned. Internally, the level of information is sufficient to foresee an increased likelihood for one's own potential downgrading. The problem lies deeper. Hope will often persist till the external verdict is given.

Investor attitude covers a wide range whereby it is advisable to look not only at the immediate actions, but also at the factors which will impact later on the attitude. The directly measurable items consist of several elements. As stated on various occasions earlier, the responses of lenders to a decline in the actual or perceived credit quality of an institution in exceptional circumstances can take the form of an immediate cut-off. Very often, however, the responses escalate gradually. Widening spreads in unsecured funding compared with the overall market is a clear first sign that lending risk to the institution is perceived to be increasing. It will be more visible in the secondary market of unsecured bonds than in short-term funding like CD or CP instruments. One point to consider: wider spreads do not necessarily reflect a lack of trust compared with peers. Analysing our position in foreign markets revealed that higher-rated peers in some cases could only borrow on higher spreads than us, as they were hardly visible in these foreign markets. Access to markets in volume and rating-related spreads requires keeping the name in the market to assure recognition and limits available.

A higher grade of escalation includes shortening maturities and reducing short-term un-committed lines. The unwillingness of a counterparty to continue granting longer maturities is easy to detect. A silent reduction in uncommitted unsecured lines – and it will be a silent one – needs action to find out. For this kind of threat the level of availability has to be tested at intervals to be defined. The cause of a response may not be triggered by one's own bank at all. A national or international peer may have lost market confidence. Experience has shown that under these circumstances general hesitancy prevails – at least at an early stage – and can affect one's own institution, as happened to our peers when we at Commerzbank suffered a severe stress in late 2002.

Investor attitudes are also affected by elements beyond the banking sector defined in a narrower sense. We refer to policy decisions of the state authorities and state-related institutions. Any change in law, regulations and policy of government, the central bank or bank supervisor related to banking must be analysed with respect to direct and indirect consequences for the bank. With indirect consequences we relate to the potential effect in the behaviour of market participants. As their specific assessment implies also to shares held, a drop in the share price compared with the market segment qualifies as an early indicator. One can distinguish between one's own shares compared with the banking sector and shares of the banking sector vis-à-vis the whole market. In the first case it is an institution-related signal; in the latter one it signifies mistrust with the banking sector as a whole.

- **The LAR circle**: As we have dealt with the external items to watch in the context of investor attitude, we can limit ourselves now to internal points of early warning indicators. The quality of any policy depends not least on the quality of adherence to the rules and regulations set up. Breach of limits is just one way of expressing what it means. In the context of a funding policy, for example, one will segregate funding sources into retail, wholesale corporate, wholesale unsecured interbank, wholesale unsecured capital market and wholesale secured. Based on a view about the 'ideal portfolio structure', amounts are allocated to each type of funding. Dealing with each sector can be very subtle.

Box 4.3 Defining limit-related terms

Limit: Stands for a restriction which is not allowed to be surpassed. It can be set as a floor, as a ceiling or a combination of both. Any violation of it triggers (predefined) penalties.

Guideline: Represents a restriction which is aimed for. If the objective is not reached, reasons are analysed and measures taken, but no penalty is applied.

Alert: An item put on (higher) alert, indicates an increased awareness with respect to potential breaches of limits or guidelines as well as looming dangerous developments. It is a preventative measure to avoid an undesirable status.

For interbank borrowing in total one usually sets a limit (Box 4.3), and exceeding it is an act that is not seen as acceptable. For retail or funding from the corporate sector one might put in a floor. Falling below the floor may not be acceptable for the equilibrium within the ideal portfolio envisaged. It is no limit breach, however, as limiting means putting a level not violated by the bank. In the specific case, the amounts fall below a level aimed for due to the lenders' changing attitude. We should therefore call it breach of guidelines. On a lower level of aggregation, one may sensibly wish to see the composition of the 20 biggest lenders from each corporate and financial sector by name, amount, tenor and developments of funds given to us. A continuous lender in the past may have reduced the amount drastically or the composition may be such that too few lenders cover too much of the total funds. Faced with such occurrences, we cannot talk about breach of limits or guidelines as the amount will still stay within the parameters aimed for.

Furthermore, when dealing with customers the franchise is at stake. Not accepting deposits because of a structural imbalance is seen by the customer as a severe breach of reliability. Cash available at the hands of any firm's treasurer tends to fluctuate and most probably is biggest shortly before dividend payments are due. Changes in the composition may have reasonable causes, but we do not know before we investigate them. Therefore, one has to put such items on higher alert. The group of higher alerts also includes conditions where amounts are close to limits or guidelines. There is no breach at the time, but room for manoeuvre gets tight and the subject should be discussed in order to counteract a potentially undesirable development. Higher alert also covers marketable assets. Assets may technically qualify as marketable given that the instrument is traded in a market. Actual marketability requires more: instruments or portfolios should be turned into cash in a short timespan, at larger amounts and with no undue price concessions. Whether or not assets that are potentially marketable still fulfil the requirements can only be evaluated through testing the behaviour of the markets.

In conclusion, the sum of early indicators is rather large; in fact 18 such indicators were mentioned. Clearly, not all of them are equally significant, so one has to be selective. Matz (2007a, page 129) proposes as 'best practice' to specify a number of early indicators that define when the liquidity environment is no longer normal. As early indicators do signify various degrees of severity, we will come forward with a proposal of how to allocate and deal with them. It is a personal assessment based on own experience and should thus be adjusted to take into considerations the specific circumstances of a bank.

The indicators have been grouped into medium, high and concern in respect of severity (Figure 4.4). Concern contains indicators which ring the alarm bell. Potential danger for the bank is imminent. Each of the items has a potential if not actual bearing on funding capacity. Time to act is at a premium. Evaluating and deciding on the steps necessary to be taken should not be postponed till the next ordinary ALCO meeting but addressed instantly. Pre-emptive measures provide the opportunity to take a coordinated stance in action as well as communication and increase the chance of avoiding an uncontrollable escalation. Not every deviation from normal conditions in the 'concern' section will automatically trigger the status of 'bank under stress'. An isolated incident should be dealt with without delay but still under normal conditions, while an accumulation of two or three occurrences will most likely exceed the threshold to stress. Yet the rule should not apply for the four events marked with a star. The severity of each one of them is of a degree to justify if not necessitate an immediate declaration of stress.

High severity is of a different category. Although it needs to be addressed in detail, an extraordinary general meeting is not called for. Neither a single nor a combination of two to three incidents will qualify for saying the bank is under stress. In case of a larger accumulation, effects on the items under 'concern' would be unavoidable and thus dealt through that channel. In a way, they are the true early warning indicators; the acute danger has not yet emerged while the warning signals for potential developments towards detrimental responses listed

Medium	High	Concern
Economic downturn	Drop in AA rating level	*Name-related 'in trouble' rumours
Asset or liability	Drop in stock price	*Drop within A rating
concentration	Correspondents decrease	*Correspondents eliminate lines
	line	*Business partners refuse longer
Reduction in earnings	Size per funding	dates or unsecured lending
Generally wider spreads	transaction reduced	Customers ask for information
in secondary markets	Growing early withdrawals	concerning the bank's status
Generally higher	Significant reduction in	Brokers/dealers reluctant to show
funding cost	earnings	name
	Rapid asset growth	Sharp widening of bank's
	funded as non-stable	secondary market spread
	Frequent downturns in	Bank-specific higher markets
	markets	funding cost
		Exceptional demand for collateral
	Rating-sensitive providers	Significant loss to be announced
	retreat unexpectedly	Sharp increase of early
	Decline in asset quality	withdrawals
	Customer base reducing	
	deposit volume/tenor	

Figure 4.4 Severity of early indicators

under 'concern' have become virulent. The upcoming item(s) should be analysed, discussed and decided on in an ordinary ALCO meeting, based on thoroughly prepared documentation and proposals for action.

Items at the 'medium' level of severity usually do not pose great danger in the short to medium term if in isolation. In combination with points of a higher degree of severity, the impact can turn out to be of a dangerous nature. Putting them on the ordinary agenda is thus highly advisable.

Putting all indicators on the ordinary agenda is prudent management in all circumstances. It gives the managers and committees responsible the equivalent of traffic light signals of green (in line), yellow (watch) and red (not acceptable). To utilise the instrument successfully as well as efficiently the periodic sequence and the benchmark against which the traffic light signals are compared need to be predefined.

4.4.4 Policy scope and frame

The two main subjects under this heading refer to: which elements of present business should be covered and what is the choice for a centralised or decentralised approach regarding liquidity policy?

From the previous discussions we can conclude that it is almost impossible to tighten any previous stand in the above points. It would be a lengthy process, for which there is no time under stress. Furthermore, covering a wider range of present business means finding additional funding, which is the actual commodity one is short of by the very definition of a stress. The only practical alternative at hand is to reduce the level of present business to be covered. If one elects to be faced with a longer-lasting liquidity problem, it is advisable to reduce the size of the balance sheet and shed business at disposal and disposable at this time. Otherwise, the problem tends to be aggravated or become a terminal one because of hesitating to take a painful cut at an early stage.

4.4.5 Authorities and responsibilities

As stated on several occasions, the original setup ought to cover normal and stressed conditions. Especially in difficult circumstances, experience is essential. On the other hand, liquidity stress is a state of crisis and needs crisis management. The respective committee calls for a setup in membership with experience in matters of liquidity, being capable of drawing conclusions fast and entrusted with the authority to speak on behalf of the board.

For efficiency reasons the committee has to be kept small. To engage the board for key decisions the CEO, CFO and treasury officer must be members. Considering the heightened importance of managing the overall risk of the bank, it is advisable to include the CRO in this phase. What about board members of important business lines? While it seems sensible at first sight to involve all affected parties, a closer look will reveal the setting up an enlarged board.

At the senior management level the group needs to be part of the ALCO. The technical knowledge and the experience gained in the various functions are indispensable. Some other functions may be invited on a 'when needed' basis. This refers in particular, but not exclusively, to the senior manager responsible for communication. Internal and external information cannot be neglected and needs special attention in a crisis.

Keeping the special team small does not exclude wider parts of the bank. Senior managers in the team will set up predefined working group, dealing with specific issues. There is no need, however, to have all special issues debated within the crisis team: it is the conclusions and proposals which are to be put forward, and which can be used as basic information to reach decisions, that are important.

The degree of adjustment depends on the structure of the present 'Liquidity Committee'. The closer it comes to the requirements just listed, the smaller the adjustments will be. Personally, the author prefers an experienced body like the ALCO, with the key functions more or less in place and with the necessary experience to deal with a stressed situation. After all, a stressed liquidity situation is an infrequent state in liquidity management, but still part of it. Thus, with the ALCO there is an existing body for decision making with the required expertise. Obviously, the actual 'doing' happens outside the committee but the frame of actions is clearly defined.

The impression may have gained ground that the board is to hand over management of the bank to the crisis team. Although the CEO and other members are part of the team, the ultimate responsibility stays and has to stay with the full board. This starts with the approval of the contingency plan. Related to the power of decision making, the contingency plan has to state clearly which elements of authority are delegated to the crisis team and under which circumstances. Any ruling of the team beyond this frame demands a respective proposal to and approval by the board.

4.4.6   Methods, tools and scenarios

If methods and tools have been selected professionally, conforming to existing best practice and appropriate to the business of the bank, general changes will not be required. However, as the stress is now a concrete occurrence and no longer a single element with many possibilities, one may wish to get further details of the actual circumstances. New specific scenarios may be added in order to conform to the reality now visible. It is unrealistic to believe that all types of stress combinations can be forecast. Reality more often than not exceeds the imagination of human beings.

4.4.7   Limits and limit structure

Faithful to the principle of not changing functioning structures and technical systems when entering a crisis, setting limits, including their structure and granulation, is an element of liquidity policy. It is a prerequisite at that time also to consider stresses. In the cause of managing a stressed situation limits may need quantitative adjustments in order to direct behaviour onto the path seen as most appropriate. It most probably will affect limits related to asset components in order to avoid undue lending. Especially if the assessment reveals a possibly prolonged crisis, business policy will have to be redefined and limits adjusted accordingly.

4.4.8   Communication/Reporting

We consider these two elements together, as both of them are forms of information. Information is an important necessity all the time. Almost all points stated in 'Authorities and responsibilities' and all elements listed under 'Reports and reporting frequency' within the policy framework for liquidity belong to it in the true sense. Information, especially structured information, is a vital management tool even under normal conditions. When the firm is under stress, it becomes paramount.

Box 4.4 Requirements regarding communication

- Naming the function or group – including deputies in case of absence – which is entrusted with contacting the respective party.
- Defining the level of frequency and addressees regarding presentations and contacts.
- Formulating the content and frame of messages to be brought to the attention of the respective group of recipients.
- The function to be contacted and the respective deputy.
- Establishing visiting and call reports.
- Deciding which functions/committees to be informed about visits/calls.
- Establishing policy to follow up points of special interest or concern.
- Formulating an in-house information concept, including information channels and medium.

The state of the matter and actions to be taken or already taken are communicated in messages to all stakeholders concerned, since their absence can give rise to guessing and thus rumours. To quash the latter once they have spread is extremely difficult. Recall the proverb 'There is no smoke without fire' and it will be remembered for certain. Credibility is a key aspect in communication and has to be earned over time. It implies a coherent and stable information policy towards regulators, central banks, depositors, lenders, issuers and rating agencies, and not the least directed to shareholders and the bank's own staff. The points listed in Box 4.4 should be considered in this context.

In this way, information policy in normal circumstances establishes the groundwork for dealing with a crisis: contacts are established with a face attached to the institution, which works both ways. Both sides have used the time to increase their learning curve. The partners get an understanding of the bank's (liquidity) policy while the bank will learn to focus on the relevant information the partner requires. The requirements differ depending on the group addressed and may easily deviate from our perception regarding their need.

Information is an obligation to be fulfilled by the bank in question. While it is advisable to keep it in mind and act accordingly all the time, it is essential to give it the highest priority level in case of a crisis. This means no delay in contacting and informing, verbally first, followed by presentations. Honesty in the assessment presented helps not to rock the trust established over years. Trust is the biggest asset in the present circumstances – and the crisis may turn out to last longer than just a few days. Information entails a special focus on the media. Under normal circumstances, liquidity is not of interest to them. The communication is established on banking subjects more relevant to them in the normal course of business, like strategic focus, net earnings, dividend payments, etc. Yet journalists have to respond immediately to new circumstances – it is the essence of their job. If the bank is not providing information they will get it from somewhere else or start to think in 'what if' terms. The effects are similar to rumours discussed earlier.

Information also relates to the internal recipients: management and employee briefing is vital and this for two reasons. The staff have to know what is going on. Uncertainty hampers the performance of their daily activities as they are lost for direction. 'Go on as usual' is not appropriate advice; it is not the usual business environment of the bank. Furthermore, employees do not live in a vacuum. They have external contacts, be they customers, counterparts, friends or other contacts of any kind. Even if members of the board and senior management are well prepared for the event and plans are finalised and in the process of implementation, if this is not communicated to the group as a whole, uncertainty will prevail in the major part of the bank. It will be recognisable to any external party, who will conclude that the problem is beyond the top management of the bank.

Reporting the second item is less problematic. Under the condition that reporting has been set up properly within liquidity policy, the key information is already available. Detecting and preparing for a potential liquidity crisis is an ongoing process, which requires having the necessary programmes in place. Yet the focus will be more specific and the frequency at which reports have to be produced will be shortened. Changes in the asset and in particular in the liability segments can alter drastically daily, although relative stability has been observed in the pre-crisis situation. It is important to know whether or not the changes are within the expected range and if the plan has to be altered – hence the shorter frequency. Depending on the actual stress, special reports are required, focusing particularly on determinants typical of the specific type of liquidity crisis.

To round off this section, a few words on central banks are in order. They provide several functions for a bank. Clearing is one of them. To secure a smooth process, the bank will keep accepted securities with the central bank, ready to be pledged in case of need. The need will primarily manifest during the day when payment orders are not covered by incoming funds. Related to this function, but nevertheless to be differentiated, is the function of lender of last resort. In times of crisis it is more than payment flows within the day which have to be smoothed out. The total balance will be negative till the end of the day, as creating inflow through borrowing or turning assets into cash is reduced. The amount pledged with the central bank is the fastest available liquidity buffer and with absolute certainty. It is a phone call away and based on assets judged by the central bank as eligible in advance. Very short term, they build the nucleus of liquidity management. Not even call money is as reliable in the very short term. The exceptional position of (clearing) central banks demands that the relationship be established and kept at a high level, and keeps them especially informed. Furthermore, the types of assets qualifying as eligible are not cast in stone in all circumstances. There is room for exceptions in times of crisis, as long as the solvency of the bank is not in question and pledged assets match the quality standard demanded.

4.5 A TECHNICAL FRAMEWORK SUPPORTING LIQUIDITY POLICY

4.5.1 Introduction

Any business policy derives from the particular strategy and sets the framework for the managing part, in our case liquidity management.

The three circles of VAR, LAR and investor attitude are elements of policy. In the end, they cumulate in flow of cash, expressed as a specific gap structure. The result may be according to the goals formulated in advance or present an undesirable structure. In the latter case, liquidity management is obliged to take the necessary steps to rectify the missing balance. If market conditions do not allow for it, reverse implications on growth are unavoidable. In other words, we are back to our magic polygon, but this time at the overall level.

Liquidity level and flow of cash are the decisive terms we now will take a closer look at. We dealt with them before but from a different point of view: the centre of attention within the LAR circle was on the relationship to the other elements. This time, the technical aspects will be at the focus. We will start with the liquidity level, as it precedes and impacts on the flow of cash.

4.5.2   The liquidity level (LL)

The liquidity level is a quantity to be defined by management. Like capital for VAR, it defines the risk capacity for LAR. Despite the comparable function in this respect, liquidity level differs significantly when it comes to technical aspects. It may be helpful to recall the facts before entering deeper into the subject.

Capital is an exogenous factor which takes over the function of a buffer for losses, if potential downside risk turns into reality. Exogenous in this context signifies that capital is determined by a function outside the particular circle, namely the management. The size of a buffer thus determines the quantity of potential losses it can absorb if they become effective. It follows therefore that capital is a limiting factor for taking downside risk. Both capital and downside risk are quantifiable. It is these facts which allow supervisors and analysts to apply capital ratios on this basis, and which are taken as indicators for the financial stability of a bank. How does liquidity level compare with it?

We will start with the last point mentioned above. For liquidity buffers covering stresses official ratios are neither given nor recommended in any of the directives or proposals from major regulators and international institution. There is no defined buffer to compensate for LAR effects under stress. The introduction of a management-set liquidity level is not standard. It is an endogenous element we believe it is necessary to introduce. Endogenous in this respect means: it is an act of decision made by management and defines the liquidity structure demanded to secure the level of business activities intended even under a severe stress. The decision relates to business strategy and policy.

From experience, it is unrealistic to assume that business will continue as usual when faced with an extremely stressed condition, and this will be more pronounced if it is a prolonged one. The implications on costs, when securing present business fully, have to be compared with the probability of such an event. When computing the effects, it would be misleading to compare average hedging cost with average returns secured. As concluded earlier, marginal hedging costs tend to increase while business earnings decline when viewed as marginal income. Unfortunately, there exists no general formula to arrive at the level where marginal costs balance marginal loss of income. Banks differ too much to allow for such an equation. The assessment has to be done on a bank-specific basis.

As stated above, any setting of a liquidity level impacts on business strategy and policy. Whatever level of security is chosen, it has to find its way into the business plan. The statement is a plausible conclusion when the level secured does not match present business activities. It means that some parts are disposable in case of necessity. However, it reaches beyond this point. Liquidity policy and management are not about today: they are forward looking, anticipating future developments. The business plan and the respective preparations may go beyond present business concluded and recorded in the accounts. Planned growth will also be affected. This leads us back to a principal question regarding liquidity: what will its function be? If it is to protect the bank against all detrimental effects possible and without any adjustments, we are going to maximise it and allocate to it the function of a driving force. On the other hand, the assessment may decide to place it at the level of capital in the context of VAR: as a protector against adverse events, but not available to an unlimited extent. Sandwiched between the two extreme alternatives is the level of costs that the bank is ready and available to bear.

4.5.3 Liquidity level and the impact on flow of cash

As we stated earlier, flow of cash derives all information which forms the basis for calculating cash flow. Yet restrictions on period under consideration are lifted. As a result, flow of cash presents itself as a sequence of flows, both from assets and from liabilities which allow computing the gaps. For a better overview and thus a better understanding, it is placed into buckets, combining daily results in each of them. The number of days contained in a bucket lengthens as we depart more and more from the starting point. The scale applied may start with daily balances and extend to annual ones, or even combine to exceeding 10 years in a single number.

Flow of cash represents flows from assets and liabilities irrespective of whether created by balance-sheet or off-balance-sheet transactions. If liquidity management had only to deal with normal conditions, it would be sufficient to take the gaps as an indicator for the present and future squaring of balances. The main challenges of the job were reduced to performing it in the most cost saving way, as the availability had not to be questioned. The real test of liquidity management occurs when the bank faces stressed circumstances, which are rare occasions but severe up to potentially fatal ones. Under stress, the capability of getting new funds and turning assets easily into cash is no longer granted. Calculating LAR under stressed conditions takes the particular behaviour into account and comes up with the effects to be expected. What, however, is the significance for the liquidity level (LL) and in which way does the latter impact on flow of cash?

If a new bank were established, the organisational and technical structure for liquidity management would be set up. The technical frame would assure electronic links for all cash-related activities of the bank, including treasury risk management, to the liquidity management department of the bank. For most banks, the business-related part would produce a negative balance in flow of cash, and this in two ways: the volume of assets would exceed liabilities; and, in addition, funding from customers would be short term while a larger part of lending would be medium to long term. In the initial phase, the imbalances would be more or less corrected through capital paid in, which principally can be taken as long term. Simultaneously, risk controlling would evaluate the stability of the various sources to create new liquid means, on the basis of which the liquidity manager would set up an appropriate concept and choose the additional funding sources accordingly. But this is not the way it happens in most cases.

More realistically, the bank was founded a long time ago. Liquidity management has been done in the traditional manner, i.e. based on the 'Golden Banking Rule'. Predominantly, having access to funding all the time has been perceived as a given fact. Some more forward-looking liquidity managers have gone further, challenging the assumption of permanent access to funding sources, and have acted accordingly. Around the turn of the millennium, either from deep inside or pushed by supervisors at a later stage, banks started to apply an advanced approach. Research on market behaviour in particular segments has picked up. Although a comprehensive theoretical structure is still missing, the concept of LAR has brought a quantitative aspect into play. It replaces in part the so-called 'professional assessment' which in many cases has been a euphemism for 'best guess': the emphasis is on 'many cases', which excludes all the ones where it does not apply. We will not enter into details at this point, but deal with the subject in the chapter covering liquidity management.

For our purposes it suffices to acknowledge that LAR stands for a concept (but not yet a method) which allows the most likely effects on the liquidity position of the bank to be assessed under various conditions. LAR and its multi-dimensional character will not allow for

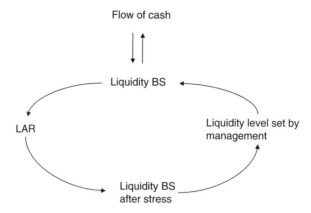

Figure 4.5 Securing against liquidity risk and the impact on flow of cash

a single scenario. The multi-dimensional character demands multiple scenarios, at least for stressed situations. For the time being, we assume that LAR indicates to us the most likely effect on the liquidity status of a bank. The following scheme may support the explanations (Figure 4.5).

Step 1. When introducing scenario analysis, the liquidity management will start with a specific flow of cash (FoC). It contains all cash-relevant transactions and positions from business and other departments of the bank. Moreover, it includes all transactions which liquidity management has concluded till now in order to close gaps and fulfil regulatory as well as internal requirements. In other words, the liquidity manager has most probably already augmented the size of the balance sheet in order to conform to the rules.

Step 2. FoC is segregated into the appropriate structure necessary to cover the different behaviour of markets and market participants: for example, retail market; local and foreign corporate markets; other wholesale markets subdivided into money and capital markets on a secured or unsecured basis; secondary markets for sale and repo transactions of secured and unsecured assets. As all of these groups react differently to changing circumstances, their behaviour is modelled or assessed. At the end of the process one arrives at the liquidity balance sheet, i.e. a structured statement of flows according to the inherent liquidity status of instruments and portfolios. Applying the concept of LAR for the various scenarios, one arrives at the implications on the liquidity balance sheet, which will result in altered structures of it, after the modelled specific event. We call it the liquidity balance sheet after stress.

Step 3. Management of the bank has made its business decisions related to liquidity management: business policy is defined; the business plans are forward looking and the types of growth including phases are included; and bank management has decided on the level of business which has to be secured and therefore has concluded which part it is ready to let go in case of necessity. From these parameters, a qualified liquidity manager is capable of formulating the structure required, which after approval becomes the liquidity level set by management.

Step 4. When computing the respective liquidity balance sheets after various stresses with the liquidity level set by management, one will usually spot gaps. Positive ones are not critical for the aspect of security; nevertheless, they should not be neglected. It gives the opportunity to cross-check whether liquidity is too plentiful and the financial burden on the bank too high compared with the duty assigned. The liquidity manager has to act on it. Negative gaps are critical. They tell in no uncertain terms that the bank is not secured at the level determined by management to be appropriate. The respective gaps are to be closed and liquidity management needs to take the necessary steps to achieve it. As a result, the liquidity balance sheet and hence FoC are adjusted accordingly.

Step 5. FoC, and through it the liquidity balance sheet, again are the starting points and the revaluation is repeated in line with the rules set up. As the activity of banking is subject to numerous external factors like business cycle, customer preference, etc., plan and reality will easily deviate over time. Adjustments are thus a necessary occurrence. Moreover, one cannot exclude that market conditions have turned in such a detrimental way that they lead to the assessment that some of the growth proposed in the planning period can no longer be financed. In such circumstances, the growth policy has to be adjusted to match availability.

4.6   THE LINK TO LIQUIDITY MANAGEMENT

As already expressed, liquidity is not an aim in itself; as a protector it cannot be an ultimate goal. It is because of the potentially severe implications when neglecting it that its ranking is lifted so high as to become part of the magic polygon. In the last few paragraphs above, liquidity management was introduced rather frequently, although the topic related to policy. This is not at all surprising: policy needs execution, which is management; the latter requires a framework or policy within which it can work in a coordinated manner. In isolation, both policy and management are rather lost.

Liquidity policy in the banking literature has the status of an orphan. It exists, but it is widely neglected at the same time. On the other hand, if management means combining and directing key elements in a purposeful manner to achieve goals, liquidity has to be part of it. The benefits have become obvious in the course of this chapter:

- Liquidity is embedded in the planning process and can play its part in optimising the framework of business and financial policy.
- Management of the bank explicitly decides its liquidity risk appetite. The risk taken relates to the business opportunities it is ready to forgo in an extreme stress.
- In this way, it is aware of potential consequences of its business approach.
- Giving clear directions as to the extent of securing business, the relation to costs becomes transparent and can be judged against the benefits. (Hedging costs are always perceived to be too expensive.)
- It provides a framework for liquidity management within which it can act. Otherwise, there is the danger that liquidity management is not in accordance with business policy.
- Liquidity policy is the transformation channel through which business policy is transposed to liquidity management.

Does this mean that liquidity policy is reduced to a simple executioner of business policy decisions? It should not be seen that way. It serves a purpose: securing fulfilment of the payment obligations of the bank, even under stressed conditions. In case difficulties are of a prolonged nature, liquidity management gives business management the opportunity to take appropriate measures to keep the firm on a 'going concern' basis, i.e. securing the franchise, however defined. In other words, sound liquidity management buys time for management. Furthermore, policy is about the goals to be achieved and not about the methods and activities necessary to achieve them. The latter belong to liquidity management, which has the technical and market knowledge to assess also the framework within which potential alternatives of policy are feasible. Both policy and management therefore necessitate each other. We will now turn to the aspects of liquidity management.

5
Conceptual Considerations on Liquidity Management

5.1 INTRODUCTION

To address liquidity management we now focus on market-related issues. As we have learned, liquidity management does not stay in isolation but interrelates with liquidity policy in both directions.

Liquidity management is embedded in liquidity policy, which provides the framework within which to act. The level at which the present business is secured cannot be decided by liquidity managers. Cost implications when buying security as well as the impact on unsecured present activities under stressed conditions necessitate involving the board of directors in the process of setting the framework. The board ought to be aware of and decide on the level of protection it assesses as feasible. Or to put it in another way, the board needs to know and choose the degree of risk appetite it is willing to accept for the benefit of lower costs.

The majority of the members of the board are neither specialists in liquidity matters nor do they have the necessary infrastructure within their area of control to rely on. The liquidity management department thus fulfils an external and an internal duty simultaneously. Externally, it brings in the expertise in the form of alternative proposals to allow top management to make informed decisions when setting up the framework. In this respect it is paramount to taking the advisory function seriously and not be tempted to influence the decision into a direction favoured by the liquidity manager personally. The price would be too high as it is the company which is potentially at stake. However, in case the discussions are leading up to decisions which are not supported by the facts, it is equally paramount for the expert to present his or her case firmly. Finding a sound balance between the two elements is what we mean when we talk about taking the advisory function seriously.

The internal duty relates actually to managing the bank's liquidity on a 'doing' level. Market expertise, although of great importance, simply is a precondition which has to be taken for granted. A first question centres on the business to be protected. The answer is given within the policy framework but has to be translated into a structure which is easy to understand and does not need expanded explanations. Furthermore, it requires catching future planned business developments as well as allowing the integration of changing market conditions to be envisaged potentially. In a second stage the concept is enlarged, permitting us to link changes in flows triggered by altered market circumstances. Components on assets and liabilities will change their degree of being liquefiable under different market conditions. The overall liquidity status of the bank will be affected accordingly and thus has to be captured. The extent by which the changes most probably will occur under various conditions will be dealt with in the third stage. In this context, alternative methods will be analysed and evaluated for the level of being appropriate to assess best the implications under normal and stressed circumstances. By following this route, we will arrive at a concept required to define the liquidity level to be determined within the framework of liquidity policy.

5.2   FROM ACCOUNTING PRESENTATION TO DEFINING THE LIQUIDITY BALANCE SHEET

We start with the traditional accounting presentation and gradually add the elements which will lead to the liquidity balance sheet on a 'going concern' basis. This means adding all the adjustments necessary to arrive at a forward-looking structure, whereby customer franchise, investment models and changing market conditions can be integrated.

5.2.1   Accounting and flow of cash presentations

The official balance sheet set up by accounting follows specific rules and aims which do not focus specifically on liquidity aspects. The centre of attention is the type of grouping on the asset side and provider of funds. Maturities attached are only shown partly and in a rudimentary manner and do not fulfil the requirements of liquidity management. The example in Figure 5.1 may illustrate the point.

For liquidity management purposes a sequence of cash relevant flows is required. At the start, we neglect the characteristics of counterparties and portfolios on both the asset and the liability side. We will focus exclusively on the maturity structure. In this way we are going to establish the formation which we named flow of cash.

In the example we present an overview of the most important elements. Refined differences are thus neglected.

When comparing the two presentations there is no divergence in the volume of the balance sheets. The difference lies in the composition chosen for assets and liabilities. Flow of cash neglects anything but pure cash aspects. The elements it contains are currency, amount and value date. In a way it represents the extreme opposite of the accounting balance sheet: a prime focus on type of counterparts on the one side and almost exclusive concentration on

Accounting BS			Flow of cash view			
Assets	Liabilities		A (Inflow)		L (Outflow)	
1 Cash	Due to banks	31	28	Days	Days	22
32 Due from banks	Due to cust.	32		1–30	1–30	
42 Due from cust.	Sec. liab.	28	37	Months	Months	52
20 Securities	Provisions	1		1–12	1–12	
1 Fixed assets	Capital	4	35	Years	Years	26
4 Other assets	Other liab.	4		1–10	1–10	
100 Total A	Total L	100	100	Total A	Total L	100

Figure 5.1   Accounting presentation of liquidity view

cash-related maturities on the other side. Unfortunately, neither of the extremes can be taken as the final solution. The shortcomings of the accounting presentation have already been explained. Flow of cash poses other difficulties. It is a static view and tries to forecast the future based on present data. Moreover, it does not incorporate discretionary and behavioural attitudes. What does it mean?

Setting up any liquidity structure at the start has to be based on accounting figures. One cannot begin without accepting the economic reality expressed by the accounting data. The specifications of all these transactions have gone through a comprehensive control process and thus are as reliable as any data can be. Founding the liquidity structure on any other sources poses the risk of relying on deal specifications of a lower quality or even hardly checked. The strength of accounting at the same time is its weakness when it comes to liquidity management. The applied principle to accept only booked transactions explains future liquidity gaps based on present account entries. Even for the day before a large acquisition it would not indicate any structural change in flows or in the size of the balance sheet. The implications of policy decisions, even smaller ones than the acquisition taken as an example, are neglected and thus have to be added separately.

Flow of cash is based on contractual specifications. Although large parts of the portfolios within the balance sheet may have fixed maturities, there are exceptions with significant impact. Put options for early repayment may have been sold or granted; the latest possible maturity date has been fixed, but the actual repayment may be made earlier. Call options may have been written (the right of the customer to draw a committed loan). We do not know whether or not the right will be claimed and to what extent. However, if it had been done the gap forecast would not be correct. Also securities might have a long-term underlying maturity date. Taking the latter as final is correct if the securities are illiquid, and may be sensible in cases where they represent strategic portfolios. Outside these exceptions, they are most probably sold before or even well before maturity.

Behavioural attitudes are another example where legal and actual maturities deviate. Legally speaking, savings deposits are usually of a short-term nature and could be withdrawn at short notice. Factually, however, to a large degree they are tacitly prolonged and even stay relatively stably invested in stormy market circumstances. Customer borrowings for general cash management purposes tend to behave in a similar way. The maturity spectrum of the funds required by the customers is from short term down to overnight. The funds are paid back at each maturity. Nevertheless, the total volume of lending for cash management purposes stays relatively stable irrespective of the short maturity level. In both cases, legally short maturities turn out to transform into longer engagements – on both sides of the balance sheet.

It is obvious from the examples that none of the two concepts can be taken as a final basis for liquidity management. It also has transpired that both forms of arrangement are needed: accounting collects the contractual information and transports them to flow of cash (FoC), which presents them in a timely order based on legal maturity dates. For assessing the actual dates (economic behaviour) one has to rely on the accounting structure again, as the latter provides information about the characteristics and behaviour of specific portfolios. Based on these conclusions we will now set up an appropriate frame.

5.2.2 The basic frame of a liquidity balance sheet

The liquidity balance sheet is to be seen as an instrument. Its function can be defined as follows: presenting the liquidity structure of a bank based on an 'economic' view; that is, integrating realities induced by business decisions, characteristics of instruments, market conditions and behavioural effects.

5.2.2.1   The components on the asset side

Assets play a vital role in liquidity management, and in several respects. The length of time they can stay on the books with high certainty differs significantly. For instance, 10-year corporate loans with no amortisation, no early payback option attached and no default by the borrower will stay on the books for the next 10 years. Securities traded professionally on the equity or bond market on the other hand will be kept very short term, although the underlying instrument may be a 30-year US Treasury bond or shares, which by definition have no defined maturity profile at all. Other examples made previously illustrate the point further.

For the purpose of securing a liquid condition in order to fulfil payment obligations, an allocation to time band on a realistic basis is indispensable. Even under normal conditions, assessing the most likely gaps in the days and weeks to come is necessary to take the correct action in advance. When preparing for stressed circumstances, a proper classification is a *conditio sine qua non*. Mistakes in the correct allocation will lead to preparatory measures based on wrong assumptions and may jeopardise the existence of the bank unnecessarily.

A stressed condition in liquidity may be of a short- or longer-term nature. Experience shows that the first 5 days are the most critical period irrespective of the stress scenario, as it takes time until further cash is received through market transactions. The condition very often lasts longer but rarely exceeds 1 year, by which time the verdict is given one way or the other: the bank has either survived or failed. For the reasons mentioned, we will apply a three-stage time approach to assets.

Liquid assets (up to 5 days)   The items consist of cash and any assets which turn or can be turned into cash within the following five working days:

- Cash in hand and cash created through repayments of maturing assets within the period are part of liquid assets.
- Assets immediately sellable or qualifying for repo transactions are another group. In this context two points are to be considered specifically. Firstly, they must not already be employed as collateral or otherwise; that is, they have to be of an unencumbered nature. To assess the quantity qualifying within this group, the markets for the respective instruments are to be liquid and the absorbing capacity within the time period needs to be evaluated. Secondly, minor liquidity constraints do occur rather frequently, either under normal conditions or in case of very short-term stresses. In all these cases, liquidity management should not interfere with business activities. For this reason it is advisable not to include portfolios belonging to operating units at this stage and thus limit the amount to portfolios in the hands of liquidity management built up for liquidity purposes.
- Any shortage of cash will first affect the capacity to fulfil payment obligations. This immediate danger is counteracted by keeping high-quality assets as collateral at the respective central banks. There is no uniform understanding among central banks of instruments qualifying as collateral. Policies differ and the impact has to be evaluated for each case. On the other hand, these amounts are available immediately and just a phone call away. It is thus advisable to show them separately under the heading 'of which available intra-day'.
- Further assets with the same qualifications.

Less liquid assets (1 week to 1 year) The segment contains assets falling due or qualifying for being turned into cash in the respective period. As we consider a longer period, segregation into at least monthly time buckets is required. It is significant to know whether cash can be created already at the early stage or rather towards the end of the period. The time bracket contains:

- Deposits or longer-term engagements with banks and other financial institutions falling due in the period and as a result providing cash inflow.
- The assets exceeding the amount which is judged necessary to keep the required customer franchise regarding corporate and private customers and falling due before the end of 1 year.
- Reverse repo transactions maturing within the timespan.
- Assets qualifying for sale and repo agreements for which the transaction cannot be executed within the first 5 days but still in the period up to 1 year.
- A portion of contingent liabilities (optionalities) not yet drawn and with a total maturity profile of less than 1 year.
- Assets eligible for securitisation within the time under consideration: the necessary preparations for securitisation are cumbersome and time consuming. In addition, markets are not very receptive to names not seen before in the respective segment, and respective limits may not be in place. It is therefore advisable to consider only assets for securitisation if certain requirements are fulfilled. For example, two placements within the last 3 years successfully executed. In addition, the receptiveness of markets needs to be considered. In many banks, the amount qualifying in principle will outweigh the effective timely market capacity.
- Cash creating trading portfolios. In case of a longer-lasting liquidity squeeze, interference in business activities can no longer be excluded and one may need to resort to business portfolios. Important conditions have to be observed, however. The assets should not already be employed for self-financing or as collateral. The amount available needs to be agreed beforehand and approved by the board of directors as the commitment impinges continuously on the way that the trading business is structured and conducted. We will refer to them later as 'assets as risk'.
- Further assets with the same qualifications.

Assets not liquid within 1 year Any asset is liquid, given time. Even so-called 'illiquid' long-term engagements are maturing or can be sold some day in the future. For liquidity management, the timeframe is shorter: assets with maturities beyond 1 year are technically not providers of liquidity within the time horizon considered by liquidity management – hence the label 'illiquid'. Here again, because of the extremely long timespan, cash effects are to be segregated into annual buckets:

- Tangible fixed assets. Based on a 'going concern' assumption, these are not available for sale. Yet, in case of a sale of tangible assets and combined with a lease-back transaction, the respective part can be booked under liquid assets. The same procedure applies to planned sales, provided the timeframe is realistic and within the 12-month period.
- Due from banks and other financial institutions with a remaining maturity profile exceeding 1 year.
- A portion of contingent liabilities (optionalities) not yet drawn and with a total maturity profile of more than 1 year.
- A portion of conduit volumes financed directly in the market and not through the internal liquidity desk. The portion covers the amount which under certain stressed conditions has

to be financed by the liquidity department of the bank in its function as internal lender of last resort.

- The level of the franchise as defined by bank management regarding corporate and private customers, with assets to be financed on an unsecured basis. The maturity structure is not relevant in this respect, as the customer franchise is to be seen as a long-term item.
- The level judged necessary to keep the franchise regarding wholesale and retail customers, with the assets to be financed on a secured basis. The separation becomes necessary due to the different funding markets to be tapped. Problems in one market segment do not automatically extend into other funding sectors.
- The assets exceeding the amount which is judged necessary to keep the required customer franchise regarding corporate and private customers and not falling due within 1 year.
- Further assets with the same qualification.

In order to set up the frame, liquidity management needs input from the board.

Earlier on we distinguished core business, capacity expansion (business which will become core business at a later stage) and attractive investments. The degree to which present business activities are to be secured even under stressed conditions must be defined by the highest authority within the bank and cannot be left to liquidity management. The choice made consequently will affect the allocation to the various liquidity buckets. If the board decides for example to protect all business activities presently conducted, there will hardly be any cash generating items in the buckets named 'liquid assets' and 'less liquid assets'. The same is true if all present trading activities are judged as indispensable, irrespective of liquidity-related circumstances.

On the other hand, liquidity management is required when it comes to assessing the marketability of assets. It requires professional knowledge and a close involvement with the markets. To gauge the extent of market liquidity and absorbing capacity within the different timescales is highly relevant when it comes to specific assets types as the subprime crisis has once again demonstrated. Therefore, it is advisable to follow a rather conservative approach and not become too confident. As market conditions change, so does the marketability of assets. It relates to products, volumes as well as respective haircuts. Allocating marketable assets to the specific liquidity bucket is therefore not a 'once and for all' decision. It should be done periodically and additionally after each market disturbance.

We now will address the funding side.

5.2.2.2   The components on the liability or funding side

We now have the structure on the asset side of the liquidity balance sheet. The corresponding liabilities are the items which fund the assets. By definition, the sums on both sides are equal. The structure differs, however.

The scheme of the liquidity balance sheet   For the sake of better understanding, the relationship between assets and liabilities of the liquidity balance sheet are presented graphically. In contrast to assets, liabilities are grouped into two segments: sources of funding and stability of funding (Figure 5.2).

Despite some overlap, the two sides of the liquidity balance sheet do not respond to the same forces. For the largest part, the type, structure and volume of assets are a result of the policy defined by the bank itself. It is the management of the bank which determines growth,

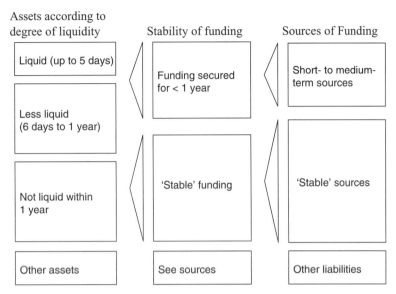

Figure 5.2 The general frame of the liquidity balance sheet

(Reproduced by permission of Commerzbank AG)

with its implications regarding the on- and off-balance-sheet activities of different categories. (For details see 2.3.4.1.) Management equally decides on the level that present businesses will be secured against detrimental liquidity scenarios. The only subject where management cannot decide on its own refers to market liquidity for marketable assets. On the other hand, the quantity, type and diversification of such assets are again determined by the bank.

For funding, which is the other side of the coin, decision making does not lie with the management of the respective bank but is executed by the market. The present level of shareholder capital can be taken as an exception, but it is too small a portion of all funding needs to be relevant in this context. Subordinated debts and other forms of funding belonging to the bank's own means are again externally determined, however.

Funding sources state the type of financing which most likely stays for less or longer than 1 year. In some cases, contractual specifications or the nature of the fund, like shareholder capital, make it easy to allocate the portfolio to either of the two groups. Yet behavioural attitudes often play a significant part. A share of contractually short-term liabilities may be continuously prolonged and thus 'stable' while only some part will be withdrawn, i.e. a quota is 'sticky' even under market uncertainty. Or the assessment reveals that some share of longer-term funds presently qualifying for 'stable' will not be rolled over under specific market circumstances. The fact is expressed visually in the above figure. When transforming 'stable sources' into 'stable funding' the volume shrinks for the benefit of 'funding secured < 1 year' which exceeds the amount of 'short- to medium-term sources'. The technicalities applied to arrive at funding on the basis of sources and behavioural attitudes will be dealt with later. At this point it is sufficient to assign portfolios to the respective group of sources.

Short- to medium-term sources (up to 1 year) The group contains portfolios which by their very nature are volatile. The depositors' attitude is such that under normal conditions a prolongation is most likely. In cases of stressed circumstances, a share of these funds is expected not to be prolonged at maturity as many counterparties to the transactions entered into them on an opportunistic basis. The focus, however, is not on individual names but on the portfolio as a whole. The latter contains the following items for instance:

- Bank deposits with a remaining maturity of less than 1 year. Within the period relevant for this time bucket the lender has a choice of whether or not to prolong its engagement. From the lender's viewpoint, interbank activities are not an element of customer franchise. The depositor thus will not see any need to protect a business relationship under more difficult circumstances. Because of the uncertain outcome of the lender's decision, the portfolio does not qualify as 'stable'.
- CDs and CPs issued and still on the books. Again, investors do not judge their engagement in these instruments as part of a relationship business. They look at it as opportunistic instruments to employ their overflow of short-term cash as long as they seem to be 'risk free'.
- Liabilities related to trading transactions and falling due within 1 year. A prolongation is uncertain.
- Repo transactions maturing within 1 year.
- Bonds issued and falling due within 1 year.
- Further liabilities with the same qualifications.

'Stable' sources (exceeding 1 year)   These sources are marked by two characteristics: Either they stay on the books for certain, as in the case of contractual obligations; or at least part of short-term funding is most likely to last, due to the investors' behavioural attitude. Examples include:

- Senior debts issued and with a remaining tenor of 1 year or more.
- Other funds with a remaining maturity of more than 1 year.
- Deposits from retail customers. Experience indicates a relatively high level of stability of this source; also in the case where the bank concerned is burdened with a reduced financial strength. Whenever the funds are secured through a national deposit insurance scheme, the stability of the source is even more pronounced although not guaranteed.
- Deposits from non-bank wholesale customers. The group responses are more volatile to changes in bank-related and market circumstances than retail funds. The business contact is on a relationship basis and, even more important, the hedging effects generated through borrowings from the bank concerned provide a cushion for their exposure. For these reasons, some part of the funds can be assessed as stable. One exception needs to be considered. Some institutions deposit exclusively with borrowers of a minimum financial standing. If the rating were to fall below the minimum standard applied, funds would be withdrawn at the respective maturities for certain.
- Subordinated debts and other forms of own means with a value date of more than 1 year away.
- Shareholder capital and capital-related reserves as long as they are officially declared as capital reserves and represent cash. One point of special consideration should be mentioned: own means may be reduced through a share buy-back programme or unexpectedly high level of losses.

- Undeclared reserves. The item necessitates careful handling. The reserves can easily evaporate if they are subject to changing market conditions. Assuming they are stable, the question arises of whether a conversion into declared reserves will be accompanied by an increase in cash.
- Further liabilities with the same qualifications.

We have now concluded the groundwork for setting up the liquidity balance sheet on the assumption of behavioural attitudes and the bank's intention to secure the defined degree of customer franchise under liquidity-related stresses. Assets are defined as called for under the assumptions integrated into the policy framework, except for concrete numbers. Funding sources are segregated into short to medium term and stable, also called 'unstable'. What remains is quantifying the extent to which funding sources convert into 'stability of funding'. The latter actually represents the real level of funds available to finance assets.

Before starting to quantify the effects on both sides, we will first complete the scheme of the liquidity balance sheet and its role under stressed conditions. As stated earlier, the liquidity balance sheet is an instrument that incorporates both liquidity policy and management. As such, it relates to the liquidity level and the funding structure required in order to withstand undue consequences caused by adverse conditions. The structures on assets and liabilities have to match in such a way that the management-defined status of liquidity is sufficient to secure the level of 'securing the franchise' under various forms of adverse conditions. The scheme requires linking the liquidity balance sheet with outgoing flows under stressed circumstances.

5.3   THE LIQUIDITY BALANCE SHEET AND LIQUIDITY FLOWS

5.3.1   An analogy as introduction

The technicalities are not dissimilar to the ones encountered in normal accounting presentations. Accounting starts with the balance sheet at a specific point in time, e.g. at the end of year X, books all transaction during the coming year on the basis of double accounting on the balance sheet and onto the profit and loss account. At the end of the period one arrives at the new balance sheet of the year X + 1, with the sum of profit or loss for the period under consideration included. For our purposes, we begin with the liquidity balance sheet of date X, book all transactions related to the period concerned and arrive at the new liquidity balance sheet of the date X + 1. Admittedly, the explanation of the process is simplified but explicates the principle.

5.3.2   Setting up the liquidity balance sheet

For our purposes, two specifications should be mentioned which need to be added on this high-level view.

Preparation for potential difficulties related to liquidity demands a forward-looking approach. Any problems shown up until yesterday will have been mastered, otherwise concerns about liquidity problems would be obsolete. Unfortunately, future events are not predictable with certainty but probability only, and this in two ways: the roots for pressure on liquidity may be induced through institution- or market-related causes and can concern assets or liabilities. It follows that the preparations need to include not only one but several possible cases. The degree of the impact for each case is another element which can be assessed on the basis of probability only. The distinction between losses under normal and stressed conditions is helpful but does not solve the dilemma that a liquidity manager is faced with. Analysing past experiences tells a specific story: causes of stressed situations tend not to repeat themselves and implications are rather growing than floating within a band determined from past experiences. Future events may thus be more severe than anything encountered before. As a result, flows cannot be taken in an accounting manner to arrive at the new liquidity balance sheet but ought to be forecast in order to assess the most likely outcome under various stressed conditions. This leads to the second requirement.

As potential liquidity problems can be triggered by various causes, one cannot limit considerations to a high-level view. Different causes will be accompanied by diverse implications on the liquidity status of the bank's balance sheet. To consider them properly, the specific elements concerned need to be isolated when forecasting the potential impact. We distinguish three basic types of origins:

- Market-related and affecting assets: A partial or full amount of asset portfolios held for liquidity purposes may no longer qualify as marketable within band 1 (up to 5 days) or band 2 (6 days up to 1 year); or, although available abundantly, marketable assets may not qualify as 'eligible' with central banks and thus are not employable as collateral for fulfilling payment obligations.
- Institution-related and affecting liabilities: Due to severe losses, for example, the financial standing of the bank may have deteriorated to a level where lenders refuse to invest amounts and tenors up to a level previously judged as acceptable. Furthermore, rating-related funds may cease to be prolonged, with the financial standing still well within investment grade after the downgrading.
- Market-related and affecting liabilities: Markets may be characterised by a flight to quality with funding capacity reduced without any deterioration in the bank's financial standing.

In order to cover the various cases of stress, the effects ought to be forecast individually and specifically, which requires segmenting the flows and the respective part of the accounting balance sheet. That should not pose any undue problem for the financial department. Unlike anticipating future flows in the ledgers, segmental presentations are not uncommon in accounting, if not for external purposes then at least for internal use.

In the next step we will bring together the basic structure and the specific items of the liquidity balance sheet (Figure 5.3), for which the groundwork has been laid above. Working with actual figures is still delayed. In order to reach that stage we need to detect the mechanism which permits 'sources of funding' to be transformed into 'stability of funding'. As the subject is rather complicated it makes sense not to complicate unnecessarily the point under consideration. Funding thus is to be understood as 'stability of funding' which is set against assets of the three liquidity levels.

The liquidity balance sheet is a high-level instrument which incorporates all elements derived from liquidity policy and necessary in the context of proper liquidity management. In relation to the asset side we should mention in particular the following policy issues:

- It incorporates future developments in the form of data which are based on business plans.
- The part of business which is judged as essential to protect the franchise is stated expressly and thus made visible.
- The franchise is segregated into assets eligible to be funded on a secured as well as on an unsecured basis. The distinction takes inherent differences of behaviour into consideration;

Liquid assets (up to 5 days)	Short- and medium-term liabilities (maturities up to 1 year)
Intra-day: Cash and collateral at central banks Further: Assets at banks and similar groups, available in 5 days Marketable assets within 5 days and unencumbered	Deposits from banks and similar groups Short-term securities like CD and CP Maturing long-term securities Maturing trading-related liabilities Repo transactions falling due

Less liquid assets (6 days up to 1 year)
 	
Assets with banks and similar groups
Maturing reverse repo transactions
Marketable assets within 1 year and unencumbered:
  for repo transactions
  for sales
  for securitisation
Portion contingent liabilities with maturities up to 1 year
Customer assets falling due within 1 year and exceeding customer franchise.
Trading portfolios reducible within 1 year
Tangible fixed assets close to sale
	Subordinated debts and comparable instruments falling due < 1 year
	
	Senior debts falling due < 1 year
	
	Retail deposits not stable
	
	Wholesale deposits not stable

Assets not liquid (within 1 year) Tangible assets to be kept or planned Due from banks and similar groups with maturities longer than 1 year Portion of contingent liabilities > 1 year Portion conduits or other units externally financed Level of franchise on secured basis Level of franchise on unsecured basis Customer assets which exceed franchise with maturity longer than 1 year Reserves in hand of liquidity management	Stable funding (to stay > 1 year) Shareholder capital and reserves assessed stable for > 1 year Subordinated debts and comparable instruments maturing > 1 year Senior debts due longer than 1 year; of which secured respectively unsecured Other funds maturing > 1 year Deposits from retail regarded as stable > 1 year Wholesale deposits assessed stable longer than 1 year

Figure 5.3   The liquidity balance sheet in detail

(Reproduced by permission of Commerzbank AG)

for example, in case of an institution-related stressed condition, unsecured funding will normally be more strongly affected than secured funding.

- The potential effects from off-balance-sheet commitments are integrated and thus made visible. Conduits and contingent liabilities are easily 'forgotten' otherwise.
- Assets with fixed maturities but falling due within the next 12 months are segregated from longer-term tradable assets which can be turned into cash given some time. There is a need to differentiate as the calculation of 'time to cash' in portfolios of a non-deterministic nature requires special assessment.

- The portion of primary liquidity is stated and, even more importantly, the share of immediately available funds (cash and collateral at central banks) is segregated. Cash available from central banks belongs to the first level of defence in case of stressed circumstances and is especially important when the latter occurs without warning.

In contrast to the asset structure, the liability or funding side is not so much determined by the business and financial policy of the bank's management than by market and other third-party behaviour. Again, the structure takes into consideration that policy issues are segregated and easily recognisable. For example:

- Maturity periods are broken down into 'available up to 1 year' and 'longer than 1 year'. The segregation permits one to review that the asset level defined so as to be protected from adverse circumstances is actually covered by 'stable funding'.
- The volumes of short-term funds regarded as stable are segregated into the portfolios of 'retail' and 'wholesale' deposits. Capital market funding is grouped into secured and unsecured issues, in line with requests related to the asset structure.
- Own means are segregated into shareholder capital and reserves as one item and subordinated debts as another. The distinction takes into account legal as well as maturity considerations.
- Short-term funds from wholesale markets are segregated into bank deposits and securities outstanding, like CPs and CDs. Each of the three products will get a different market reception under various business conditions. The desire for geographical and segmental distribution as well as limitation of volumes requires a separate listing.

5.3.3 Defining appropriate risk levels

What is important at this stage, however, is the necessity to define the level of risk appetite. There are two elements related to this point: the allocation to and the degree of covering 'assets not liquid within 1 year'.

The concept works on the basis that all portfolios are assigned to one of the three asset classes when related to liquidity. Any allocation which tries to anticipate future developments naturally contains an element of uncertainty. The actual outcome may deviate from the underlying business plan. Markets may be such that drawings under 'contingent liabilities' can exceed or fall short of the amounts reserved, or the sum of drawdown of the latter may have been forecast correctly, but the segregation into 'up to 1 year' and 'over 1 year' turns out to be inaccurate, just to mention two examples:

- The concept works also on the basis that all vital business portfolios, which are deemed necessary to keep the customer franchise, have been included in the lowest liquidity category, i.e. 'not liquid within 1 year'. Here again, there is no deterministic method available to come to a conclusion. For some of the portfolios the grouping is obvious, as neither the remaining maturity nor the lack of securitising it leave any option open. Defining the franchise, however, is challenging. How much of the present short-term core, future core or opportunistic business should be insured? Looking at the likelihood of an extreme stress occurring, management can easily be tempted to accept a riskier approach. However, as soon as the severity of such a case is considered, only the most secure stand seems to be the appropriate attitude. Management therefore is faced with two types of requirements.
- Irrespective of the way in which the allocation to the three liquidity groups has been decided, one deals with an assessment of future developments – with an approximation of the most

likely outcome based on present data and the best judgement possible at the time. Reality will most likely deviate from business and financial plans. The uncertainty will relate less to the question of whether or not deviations will show up; they will, and with very high probability. More important is the uncertainty about the degree and the direction of such a development. Knowing that assessments and forecasts for a specific date drop in quality the further one moves from the starting point, it is advisable to review business and financial plans at shorter intervals than necessary for the annual budget. For liquidity purposes it is not sufficient to evaluate and explain, for example, quarterly deviations on an *ex post* basis; this would be backward looking and similar to driving a car by using the rear mirror only. The need is for a new assessment of the most likely development over the next 3 to 12 months, but based on updated actual experience.

- The second requirement relates to the allocation to the liquidity segments directly. Which part should be stably financed and to what extent? The question refers to risk appetite. The term itself leaves a wide range of alternatives open and is therefore not defined in a quantitative manner. How then is risk appetite expressed and what consequences are to be expected when choosing different levels? All portfolios which are entered into the section 'not liquid within 1 year' will be stably financed. Management could decide in principle to allocate all business, from core activities up to opportunistic transactions, into this liquidity segment. As a consequence, almost all assets would be financed securely for 1 year at least. In other words, this asset portion would not be at any funding risk for at least 1 year in case of any type and severity of liquidity stress. For the assets with a higher liquidity grade, namely 'liquid' and 'less liquid', the picture is different. They are funded by liabilities of maturities less than 1 year. Furthermore, it is the assessment that in specific stress scenarios management is willing to forgo prolongation of the maturing assets if funds no longer come in. The speed and degree at which the balance-sheet volume decreases depends on the type and severity of the stress as well as the maturity structure of the funds available up to 1 year.

Risk appetite already manifests itself in the allocation. The sum of assets relying on non-stable funds will gradually fall in line with the reduction in the corresponding liabilities. In an extremely severe and long-lasting event, all assets not financed with 'stable funds' could potentially disappear, leaving only the stably financed portion on the balance sheet. All business related to the former group and affected in the specific case will gradually be terminated. The relationship with customers will suffer or be terminated. Considering these implications, a conservative risk approach should protect all franchise business and define franchise not too narrow-mindedly. The wide range which is covered in this way will reflect on costs for insuring against such events, however. A less risk-averse management may wish to save on insurance costs. Reducing the latter would require keeping some part of the franchise not securely financed and thus at risk. Given the low probability of an extremely severe stress, one may make a case for this approach. However, in order to eliminate any misunderstanding within the bank, this part of the franchise has to be officially and expressly declared as 'assets at risk', which have to be given up under severe circumstances.

The actual question for management centres on how to bring cost and potential reward into balance. To calculate the cost aspect already poses some difficulty. Interest rates for short-term money are subject to fluctuations at each prolongation date while assets originally funded long term are still based on rates applicable when deals were concluded. Techniques to forecast short-term rate developments exist, but are not sufficiently accurate for the results to be taken without adding a margin for inherent errors. This means that calculating the cost differential between long-term and forecast short-term funding does not produce a firm result but a figure based on best assessment. The calculated financial reward can only be of a potential nature, however, as in the absence of any serious liquidity stresses, there would be no need to pay the premium in the form of the cost differential.

Protection of income is one element which impacts on the potential reward. The level of the likelihood of such events occurring is the second one. The protection relates to income in two ways. On one hand, it secures the flow of income even under stressed conditions. If these businesses were to be discontinued, income would drop. To revive relationships again at a later stage takes time, energy and resources, all of which should be taken against the expenses for insurance. On the other hand, fixed costs like salaries, upkeep of the infrastructure, etc., would stay unchanged for at least some time. The effect on net income and profitability would be detrimental. As both of them are parts which make up the financial strength of an institution, a declining level of income might increase the risk perception of investors and lenders. How perception would turn into action depends on various other elements. Nevertheless, one can certainly assume that a declining income would not add comfort to third parties in the case of general liquidity problems. If the institution were already classified as somewhat doubtful, the negative news on earnings could act as a trigger for lenders to reduce their willingness to commit themselves.

In a business sense, the potential reward needs to be evaluated against the probability of severe events actually occurring. If the past is any indicator, this happens rather frequently. Over the last 20 years or so we know of about 14 severe market-related occasions of international or internationally stretched dimensions (Figure 5.4). For institution-related stresses we cannot apply general statistics. The samples are too small and the result insignificant for a specific institution. We have learned, however, that severe business problems potentially affecting the capacity to borrow can rise up unexpectedly and suddenly. The year 2008 demonstrated once more that even banks with a prime standing and a recent accolade as bank/banker of the year are not immune to an institution-related severe event.

Risk appetite contains many elements. The complexity faced is high when defining an appropriate risk level. It is caused not least by the need to work primarily with probabilities: when comparing costs for short-term with long-term funding; when assessing the frequency and severity of potential events; when evaluating the impact on customer relationships. Given

1987	US stock market crash
1990	Collapse of US junk bond market
1991	Oil price surge
1992	UK pound leaves the ERM
1994	US bond market crash
1995	Mexican crisis
1997	Asian crisis
1998	Russian rouble collapse
	Long-term capital management collapse
1999	Gold and metal price volatility
2000	Collapse in telecom and media sector
2001	9/11 payment disruption
2002	Argentine crisis
2007	US subprime mortgage collapse

Figure 5.4   Cases of severe liquidity stress in the last 20 years

(*Source*: Adapted from Matz, 2007a, page 39)

all the imponderables it seems advisable to cover as much as possible, but at least the core and future core business. In order to keep costs at an acceptable level, emphasis should be put on an appropriate and cost-efficient funding structure within 'stable funding'. In this respect, it is the liquidity manager who will be asked to come up with solutions.

In all the discussions we draw the borderline for 'stable' funds at a remaining maturity level of 12 months and longer. As stated above, the decision to do so is somewhat arbitrary and could be replaced with a shorter period of 6 months, for example. In most stress-related circumstances the 'time to normal business' can be counted in days, weeks, or a few months if the condition is longer lasting. This is especially true if a bank is faced with severe disturbances which originate in and are triggered by markets; however, there are exceptions to the rule as well. Yet when the source of the distress lies in the institution itself, it is often because of its deteriorating financial strength. To bring the company back to cruising level again will take time. Setting the threshold at 12 months gives senior management time to breathe. That is, for at least 1 year all assets declared as vital are fully financed and management can redirect bank policy without additional pressure caused by the need to sell part of the franchise due to liquidity constraints – at least not during the period insured.

5.3.4   The link between liquidity balance and flows

The structure which we have set up above equals the presentation of the liquidity balance sheet at the end of year X, as explained in the introductory paragraph. Assets are assigned and reflect the actual maturity spectrum of such instruments and portfolios with deterministic behaviour, the time to turn tradable assets into cash as well as business considerations related to the franchise to be secured. Liabilities are segregated into two portfolios on the basis of a single characteristic: if one can assume for funding purposes that present levels of the various portfolios will be kept on the balance sheet for at least 1 year, the liability portfolio is grouped under 'stable funding', otherwise it is declared as short to medium term and thus 'non-stable' funding.

5.3.4.1   Basic consideration

The allocation to either the asset or liability groups is done according to the potential behaviour under specific circumstances. Specific in this context signifies that the status of uninterrupted supply of liquidity is disturbed. The disturbance can originate in one of the following ways:

- The net amount of outgoing payments is larger than forecast and prepared for. As a consequence, the bank is short of immediately available funds necessary to execute payment orders.
- Marketable assets previously qualifying for immediate sale, for repo transactions or as collateral may have their liquid status reduced. The condition can be of a quantitative or time-related nature. Quantitative in this sense means that only part of the original portfolio qualifies as liquid within the period allocated; time-related refers to a lengthening of the period necessary to turn the instruments into cash, e.g. from liquid to less liquid.
- Conditions in the funding market may be such that depositing with and investing in debt certificates from banks in general may be seen as inappropriate under the circumstances. What is recognised is a flight to quality, i.e. lower but still solid investment grade addresses are substituted by top-rated (mostly sovereign) names.

- The institution may be faced with a marked drop in its financial health whereby the risk profile needs to be negatively adjusted by investors. Alternatively, the reduction in the financial strength may be relatively minor; however, levels of threshold (e.g. the divide between investment and non-investment grade) may be approached or passed.

Whatever the cause, the original structure of the liquidity balance sheet will not stay the same. It will be altered in one way or another, depending on the cause of the disruption and its severity. These are the alterations which are referred to when using the term 'liquidity flow'. In line with the intention to give senior management a secured period of 1 year, we will analyse the adjustments over a period of 12 months. We will therefore start with year X, add the changes in the flow and arrive at the new structure of the liquidity balance sheet for the date year X + 12 months. If the liquidity composition at the beginning is correct in types of instruments and maturities, the bank will be in a position to fulfil its payment obligations up to and until 1 year from then, and this is required for each single day and under any scenario outlined above.

   In the next step, the effects caused by the basic scenarios stated above will be explained in more detail and, where possible, supported with a graphical display.

5.3.4.2   The change in asset liquidity

Concentrating on assets, we assume for the time being that liabilities are unchanged in volume and structure. We recognise two cases related to assets: unexpected cash outflow triggered by net payments larger than anticipated on the one hand; and congestion in one or several market segments which turns marketable assets from a higher level of liquidity into a lower one on the other hand. We will start with the payment issue and assume all contracts on the basis of a going concern.

Payment issues   Assuming that liabilities remain unchanged, the total of assets cannot change either. That is not to say that the structure of liquidity is appropriate by definition. Ongoing transactions affecting payments may turn out to consume more cash than anticipated and prepared for today. Cash immediately available is thus short of payment obligations. Even if there are other assets qualifying to create cash on the basis of normal value dates, the receivables will not be in the accounts today. As a result, cash in hand is insufficient to honour all payment obligations in time. If the basic assumption of no increase in liabilities remains and tradable assets cannot be turned into cash within hours, the bank will be in a state of temporary illiquidity. The above condition may be caused by congestion in secondary markets for tradable assets, which coincides with our second example.

Congestions in markets for tradable assets   We again assume that liabilities remain unchanged in volume and structure. On the basis of accounting principles, assets will have to match liabilities, at least in terms of volume. Assets have been allocated to the respective liquidity buckets in line with business intentions (defined franchise), maturity structure of non-tradable instruments and, where applicable, the volume and degree to which specific instruments and portfolios are liquefiable under present market conditions. If market conditions for securities change, the following will happen.

   Any congestion in these markets will lead to a lower degree in the liquidity status of the instruments affected. For our illustration we assume that parts of securities which belong to

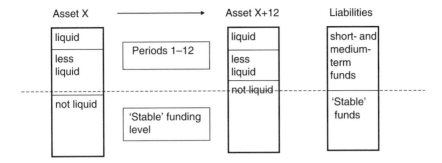

Result: Non-liquid funds increased and no longer
           secured with 'stable' liabilities

Figure 5.5   Change in asset liquidity

the 'liquid' groups and which are listed under 'less liquid' will have their status lowered. As a result, the volume of assets qualifying as 'liquid' shrinks. Depending on the severity of the downgrading, they will fall into the category of either 'less liquid' or 'not liquid within 1 year'. Part of the securities in the second block will also suffer and will be listed in the third group. The consequences of the shifts over a period of 12 months are presented graphically in Figure 5.5.

Since we assumed that liabilities remain unaltered in volume, the shift within the asset categories leads to diminished amounts in the first two groups and an increase in assets 'not liquid within 1 year'. More importantly, 'stable funds' originally covered assets 'not liquid within 1 year'; in fact, slightly more so. After the event, there is a shortage in the respective funding segment.

Interim conclusions   Due to the fact that we decided to keep liabilities unchanged, the conclusions can only be provisional. The decision to follow this route was taken in order to find out the specific effects on assets by applying one variable element only. Keeping the volume of liabilities unchanged can principally be achieved in two ways. Firstly, no liabilities are maturing in the period under consideration, as the minimum remaining maturities are of a longer-term nature. Considering the character of banking business, one cannot assume having no liabilities maturing in the short term. Especially the bank's function as a partner for corporate customers' cash management does not permit it. Secondly, the volume is kept constant by replacing maturing liabilities with new borrowings. The latter is the condition on which we base our case, i.e. compensating funding for maturing liabilities is not disrupted but limited to original volumes.

Having continuous access to replace liabilities falling due will keep assets at an unchanged level. And if funding capacity is not yet exhausted, there will even be room for asset growth within the range of additional availability. In other words, assets are always financed under the conditions that funding markets allow maturing liabilities to be replaced (minimum) and anticipated asset growth does not exceed the unused funding capacity (maximum). Within these conditions, not even the types of instruments and the structure of maturities matter. As in our example, part of assets 'not liquid within 1 year' may be funded short to medium term instead of 'stable'. However they are financed, and as long as the volume of liabilities holds, this can go on without any adverse effects. What then is the relevance of asset liquidity?

Its foremost concern is securing the fulfilment of payment obligations when they fall due and in the currency they fall due. Nothing else other than cash available immediately and in the legal tender required allows potential negative gaps to be closed with the clearer. Whether the clearer is a national lender of last resort or a private institution is not relevant; cash has to be available and usually placed with the clearer in the form of a current account deposit or as eligible collateral. To prepare for any contingency, reserves have to be held at a level which allows the closing of any negative balances which may occur on and within a specific day. Failing to do so will cause a state of at least temporary illiquidity. In this context, asset liquidity is not necessarily a risk factor because of the declining funds coming in; it is a stand-alone issue, even if funding is abundantly available.

Liquidity portfolios not related to secure payment obligations are a different matter. In many instances, out of all the underlying security portfolios there will be no more than a small share of them qualifying as liquidity reserves, even though this time we include both the 'liquid' and the 'less liquid' segments. The reasoning is as follows. Some of the securities will not be liquid, considering the required timeframe, and a significant share will be used up in repo transactions or as collateral and thus no longer be unencumbered. The remaining portfolios qualifying as liquidity are held for three purposes. Firstly, only that part of optionalities likely to become effective has been covered stably; any drawings on and above are a burden to liabilities. Secondly, in its function as lender of last resort, liquidity management needs to support externally financed conduits and independently acting units of the group in case of necessity. Thirdly, business opportunities may be better than anticipated; assets as well as earning potential therefore could increase and liquidity should not become a bottleneck. From the examples mentioned, we can conclude a striking difference between the two types of asset buffers.

In case of payments, it is the wrong maturity-related allocation of assets which poses a severe risk irrespective of the quantity available. In our additional examples it is the quantitative lack of free liquidity which can pose the problem.

Yet the quantitative lack of free liquidity in our second set of examples does not pose any difficulties to liquidity per se. As long as the sum of liabilities stays unchanged, a shift from higher to lower liquidity levels will destroy the balance in liquidity structure. Yet, all assets are financed, although on a fragile basis. Even if additional funding is restrained and cannot keep up with the additional demand, it is not necessarily liquidity which is at stake. Why is that? Being short of funds can be compensated by assets which could be discontinued. And these short-term assets do exist and are available in the form of franchise elements with short maturities and technically can be discontinued. As a consequence, however, management will be forced to forgo its policy intentions and reduce its amount of short-term assets originally declared as franchise with respective implications for its business concept. Thus, we do have to distinguish clearly between business and liquidity-related issues. A threat to liquidity would only come into play once this source is used up. If the corresponding price is seen as being too high, and in order to avoid negative ramifications on the business concept, one needs reserves which are to be kept at the appropriate level.

5.3.4.3 The change in liability liquidity

In order to isolate external effects on asset liquidity, funding has been kept stable. And where it was necessary for illustrative purposes, funding has been expressly changed. Now, we are going to enlarge the concept. When dealing with liability liquidity the restriction on funding is to be abolished. Even more, altered conditions on funding will become the focal point.

Originating powers   From our overview we know that liability liquidity can be affected by two circumstances. The capacity to fund the required amounts can be restrained by either institution- or market-related causes.

Institution-related occurrences refer to the declining financial health of the respective bank. It can deteriorate gradually or within a very short period of time. The assessment may be based on actual data and information provided directly by the bank concerned, or simply perceived by the market. In either of these cases, market participants respond to them and will curtail their exposure with the respective institution. Depending on the starting level of the risk profile and the degree of the risk increase, responses can occur in the form of shortening maturities, reducing amounts, or both. As a result, the borrowing institution is faced with a smaller capacity to fund itself. In the extreme case, the funding capability may cease entirely.

Market-related occurrences are very often a by-product of severe market disturbances like an equity crash or the subprime mortgage crises experienced recently. Uncertainty about the full implications in general and specific effects on individual banks often leads to a behaviour which is known as 'flight to quality'. To compound matters, banks themselves seem not to be in a position to assess easily the implications on their own institution. In the aftermath of such a state, market participants will not be willing to deal with nuances but tend to go for what they see as the most secure addresses and which are not engaged in the segment concerned. Thus, more often than not, the whole banking industry is affected. The degree of the impact may vary for the various groups of banking, depending on whether or not the crisis is geographically limited or related to specific banking areas. Yet the consequences for the affected banks are the same, apart from the severity: fewer funds will come their way, and the capacity of funding will be curtailed.

Despite the different reasons for the institution- and market-related occurrences, they result in a decline of funds available to finance the present level of assets. In a milder version of declining capacity to finance itself, shrinking from overcapacity to maximal funds actually needed to keep assets at the present level, the impact will nevertheless be felt. Spreads to compensate the lender for accepting higher risk will increase. In the case of more severe instances, the capacity available will not be sufficient to cover the gap of financing and assets will have to be reduced.

The implications on assets   In contrast to asset liquidity, we are now faced with forces leading in the same direction. Although the underlying reasons differ, the results in both cases are similar: the inflow of funds is reduced. For our purposes, we can combine them when analysing the effects on assets. However, we may separate them again when dealing with aspects of how to prepare for such liquidity conditions. Not to do so now will, however, not impinge on our ability to come to relevant conclusions at this point.

This time we start with liabilities at the date X (Figure 5.6). The structure is unchanged from our previous example. Liabilities are grouped into short and medium term on the one hand and 'stable' funds on the other hand. 'Stable' funds again cover slightly more than assets 'not liquid longer than 1 year', as the asset structure has been kept unaltered from the original setup at the date X. Short- and medium-term funds cover the remaining part of 'liquid' and 'less liquid' assets.

In a severe case, where the inflow of deposits and related short- and medium-term means are no longer fully prolonged and new financing is too small to compensate the shortfall, the total of liabilities will decrease. The extent to which the reduction takes place depends on the type and thus on the severity of stress. In the extreme, over time the bank may lose all its

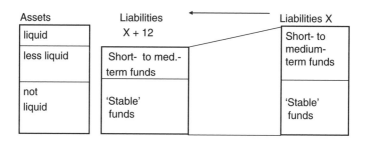

Result: The 'not liquid' part is secured, but 'liquid' and
'less liquid' assets are to be reduced. It
might affect core business relations

Figure 5.6   Change in liability liquidity

short- and medium-term funds. The only part which is secured for the coming 12 months is
the share of 'stable' funds.

Interim conclusions   In a funding-related stress, not all of the present assets can be financed
any longer externally on an unsecured basis. The non-marketable portion affected cannot be
prolonged at the next maturity date. Marketable and unencumbered assets are to be sold,
employed in a repo transaction or used as collateral. Seen from an accounting point of view,
there are slight differences depending on the action taken. Although they do not contradict the
general statement just made, it may be worthwhile to address them in somewhat more detail.
We start with a tradable asset on the books which is financed on either a secured or unsecured
basis.

Marketable asset financed on unsecured and secured basis:

- In the initial stage, the instrument is booked as security under assets. The unsecured funding
  part is shown in short-term liabilities (assuming no congruent financing).
- If sold beforehand or discontinued at maturity, the cash received can pay back the amount
  borrowed to fund the security. Thus, both sides of the balance sheet are reduced to the
  amount of the transaction completed.
- If used in a repo transaction or as collateral, the entry on assets stays unchanged. The
  cash received can be used to pay back unsecured borrowings. Unsecured funding is now
  substituted by secured funding, also booked under liabilities. The size of the balance sheet
  is not affected.
- At maturity of the repo and collateral arrangements, but still within the lifespan of the
  underlying instrument, secured funding ceases and needs to be replaced by an unsecured
  funding. Alternatively, the repo and collateral arrangements can be prolonged or renewed
  with another party, with secured funding remaining in place for another period.

What can we deduce from the above?

It is highly unlikely that short- and medium-term funds drop to nil, even in the most severe
stress. At least the amount borrowed on a secured basis will stay, as will the corresponding
assets. But more importantly, what type of assets will stay? What is their significance within
a policy framework?

At least a bank focused on wholesale customers will provide the whole range of on- and off-balance-sheet products, including the ones related to sales trading and sophisticated financing. The management of the respective risks remains with what is generally called 'investment banking'. Being asset driven, due to the lack of a natural depositor base, wholesale banks' need for funds is substantial and saving funding cost is an issue for them. Under normal market conditions, secured funding is advantageous to borrowing on an unsecured basis. Hence, investment banking will stretch the use of this vehicle to the limit in order to save costs. For the liquidity manager, these encumbered assets are not available in a crisis. Even worse, should the repo markets for these instruments become congested, there will be a need to finance them by liquidity management at the next rollover date, if they are not maturing or sellable. And congestion in a market is usually not limited to a part only, but spreads through all segments of it, i.e. the capacity to sell as well as to fund on a secured basis. As a consequence, unintentionally and at the expense of short-term franchise portfolios, 'stable' funds have to be redirected to finance assets perceived to be liquid. Retail-oriented banks might be acting in a more stable environment, provided the dependency from wholesale funds can be kept at a low level. Otherwise, the effects under stress will not be dissimilar from wholesale-focused institutions.

Unexpected negative implications are not limited to tradable assets. In specific circumstances, assets defined as disposable can also pose problems under severe market liquidity conditions. At the time when the allocation in 'potentially disposable' and 'franchise' is concluded, all portfolios of the first group have been declared as not subject to legal or moral commitments to continue after the maturity date. However, there are two main vagaries of business which can impact on the original intention.

Repayment in cash at the maturity date may not be effected. The borrower may be willing but not capable of fulfilling its obligation timely or at all. Within the planning process, the expected volume of failures within the customer base will have been assessed and reserves will have been defined and taken into consideration in the budget. Yet the assessment related to the amount necessary to cover the expected shortfalls is usually based on an average, drawn from statistical evidence in the past. Depending on the view of the economic cycles, the reserves will be adjusted. If reality then turns out to be worse than the prognosis, shortfalls will exceed the amount considered in the budget. With funding markets functioning, liquidity can be arranged. In our assumption of scarce and declining means, the gap will have to be bridged by the short-term franchise, if no special measures have been taken.

The second vagary we wish to mention results from the level of liquidity risk being taken. Risk appetite has been defined as 'the allocation to and the degree of covering assets not liquid within 1 year with stable funds' (see 5.3.3). In the present context, we do not relate to the examples discussed above but refer to some common dangers in any assessment. Assessing risk and defining risk appetite are taken in a conscientious process. When comparing risk coverage on the one hand and cost for insurance on the other hand, leaving a part of the franchise that is not stably financed has been decided deliberately. Based on a diligent judgement regarding the allocation to stable and short- and medium-term financing, as well as to defining the appropriate risk appetite, the later change for the worse in liquidity status has not been deliberately neglected at the start. The outcome has been judged as highly unlikely and taking the risk as acceptable. The effects now experienced were caused by market conditions which turned out to be worse than reasonably expected. As long as stressed conditions are market related, average in severity and short term in duration, there is a chance that the underlying expectations may hold. Yet, in a severe liquidity crisis, previous savings on insurance premiums do not balance against the hazard of losing non-covered elements of the franchise. If the severe stress materialises, it will lead to reduced income or may even jeopardise the economic status as a bank with an intact customer base. By severe circumstances we mean an institution-related crisis, longer-lasting market-related disturbances or a mixture of both. In the last case, none of the elements needs to be extremely severe, the combination of both of them might be sufficient to produce the undesirable result.

5.3.5 Policy implications

Within the framework of liquidity policy, three issues came up requiring input from liquidity management (Box 5.1).

Box 5.1 Open points to be answered by liquidity management

- Assessing business-policy-related risk potential against available risk-bearing capacity.
- Defining stressed circumstances and their implications for the liquidity status of the bank, including methods to achieve it.
- Proposing the appropriate structure, type and size of limits and developing as well as suggesting suitable procedures/guidelines and assumptions for them.

The answers to the three points above are rather complex and need careful evaluation and consideration. Furthermore, they cannot be of a standardised nature. Because their underlying elements are to a large extent decided by the bank's management, the recommendations are bank specific, not general, and partly related to each other. As the liquidity balance sheet addresses the capacity and potential of liquidity risk, we will now attend to the first point. The remaining points require some quantitative groundwork and will thus be dealt with in Chapter 6.

Earlier on, we concluded that risk potential can affect either assets or liabilities. And in both cases, it can be induced by institution- or market related conditions. Figure 5.7 lists them accordingly

This figure relates to our discussion of asset and liability liquidity. Market- and institution-related causes were introduced at an early stage. Dealing with asset liquidity in detail revealed the two causes not covering all relevant aspects. Although asset liquidity in the form of marketable assets may be abundantly available to secure a healthy structural liquidity status, fulfilling payment obligations may still not be secured, and with it the liquidity and solvency of the bank. We will thus add payment obligations as a further item to be analysed and integrated in detail.

Assets	Liabilities
Payment obligation	Institution related
Market related	Market related

Figure 5.7 Types of risk potential

5.3.5.1 Payment obligation risk

The risk associated with payment obligations is the primary focus of any liquidity management. Accounting principles ensure that assets and liabilities are in balance, whatever the conditions encountered by the bank. Yet the maturity structure of the balance sheet does not unconditionally imply that payment flows per day and per currency are balanced or positive. In order to avoid temporary illiquidity and the potentially severe consequences, days with negative gaps ought to be bridged. To determine the risk potential, expressed in amounts of the gaps to be envisaged, we need to calculate the LAR effects. Although the computation will we be done in the next chapter, we already know the important qualitative elements of the relevant risk capacity.

Based on the previous conclusion that lack of liquidity can only be compensated by liquidity again, dedicated reserves need to be built up. If not taken care of, amounts to be covered could be excessive. Technically speaking we refer to structural liquidity, in contrast to payments, which are known as situation specific. To keep the future gaps within an acceptable band, it is advisable to structure the balance sheet in such a way that the potential volatility of negative balances is limited. Two remedies can be employed to achieve the desired effect. Firstly, implications are considered in the course of business planning, whereby the chosen alternative supports the endeavour to get an acceptable business-induced structural liquidity. Realistically, actual business opportunities will hardly fit the requirement, at least not fully. Although it is advisable to use this instrument to the highest possible extent, the following remedy will always have to be employed as well. Secondly, acceptable gaps in future brackets will be defined and the liquidity manager entrusted to take the necessary steps to bring them into line if necessary. In this way, foreseeable negative balances can be kept within a defined band and limit the uncertainty to unplanned circumstances.

The remaining two qualitative elements refer to the level at which the reserves are liquefiable and the funding conditions for them. The assets need to be resilient against any vagaries of the markets. First and foremost, it would not be appropriate to risk them becoming ineligible for turning into cash. The reserves to secure payments are needed without delay, in fact even during the day. Liquidity managers should sensibly hold them with the respective clearers, which also define the instruments they qualify as eligible. The other potential threat derives from potential funding problems. Illiquidity has to be avoided under any circumstance and ranks even higher than protecting the franchise. While the latter may be lost partly or only insignificantly, liquidity is of a dichotomous nature: the bank is liquid or it is not liquid. Payment obligations can be fulfilled or they cannot. The reserves to secure a liquid status thus have to be available whatever the funding conditions. To be unencumbered is one request. Not to be jeopardised by funding restrictions is another. The latter condition demands financing with 'stable' funds, as only this route permits the portfolio to be upheld in the state of available reserves.

5.3.5.2 Market-related assets risk

Market-related risk refers to all marketable assets. From the point of view of allocation, the portfolios can be divided into four groups. Two of them belong to the operating units, the remaining two to liquidity management. In line with the above explanation, marketable assets related to the fulfilment of payment obligations have been added as a separate instrument in the hands of liquidity management.

Marketable Assets	
Liquidity management	**Operating units**
Payment related	Not 'stable' financed
Security related	'Stable' financed

Figure 5.8 Marketable assets segregated according to ownership

We will start with the assets belonging to the operating units (Figure 5.8). It would be a grave misunderstanding to assume that all tradable assets are at the disposal of liquidity management. Part of the activities of operating units includes marketable assets. The degree will vary from unit to unit and most probably be most pronounced in investment banking. In many instances, the assets form part of the franchise of the respective operating unit and are thus a vital source of continuing income. It is one of the key duties of liquidity management to help to preserve this income, in addition to securing payments each day and in any currency. Especially when setting up the contingency plan, segregation into 'theirs' and 'ours' is paramount. Any misunderstanding or misinterpretation by liquidity management could produce severe implications regarding the perception of the bank as a reliable partner and thus on future income. Assets that are part of the franchise are financed with 'stable' funds; the remaining part is done on a short- and medium-term basis.

Marketable assets in the hands of liquidity management can be payment or security related. As we have already dealt with payments, we will now focus on the latter. The portfolio serves as a buffer for expected drawings with a short-term horizon of up to 1 year and unexpected utilisation of optionalities irrespective of the underlying maturities. The eventualities can result from committed lines not (fully) utilised or connected with the function as internal lender of last resort and determine the risk potential not yet covered. From the total outstanding, potential drawings expected have already been allocated to the securely financed part, i.e. the part not liquid within 1 year. They include portions of reserves held to finance conduits and other units in case their external funding ceases to be available. Yet a substantial share of the total exposure may still be uncovered, and the potential will turn into reality in the case of severe market conditions. Irrespective of the amounts computed, which we will perform in the next chapter, we already know the effects. If no or insufficient reserves have been built up and additional or compensating funding is not available, we eat into the franchise. Short-term obligations, assessed as vital from a business policy point of view, cannot be prolonged or committed to another customer at the next maturity date. The extent to which the open part should be covered is a difficult question. Experience tells us it is not the full amount. Market-related modelling according to statistical evidence is one way of doing it. However, it cannot take into consideration the risk appetite of a specific bank. The considerations as outlined in 5.3.3 above can be taken as a guideline.

For the qualitative elements of risk capacity we can be more precise. They are not dissimilar from the ones discussed for payments. Assets need to be resilient to market disturbances in the form of congestions. The reserve portfolio represents the buffer to absorb the risk potential in liquidity, as does shareholder capital for downside risk. Large parts of the security segment do not qualify in this respect, either because of a rating below the top level or due to a lack in depth and volume. However, German Bunds, US Treasuries and comparable instruments can be taken as quite safe in this respect. Concerning the quality of funds, one has to bear in mind that the reserve portfolio is securely financed. It cannot perform its function if it is subject to potential funding problems. It will thus be covered by 'stable' funds.

5.3.5.3 Institution- and market-related liability risk

There is a significant difference between asset and liability risk, which should not be underestimated. At the end, any structure of assets on the balance sheet is determined by the bank and its management. Of course, the volume of assets depends on actual demand. And, of course, actual demand may increase overall or in areas not desired. Nevertheless, if felt inappropriate, supply can be kept at any lower level and in any desired structure irrespective of actual demand. Management can easily adjust price conditions to distract the surplus that it is not willing or able to provide. Failing to do so without an equivalent liquidity backing could endanger the existence of the firm.

On liabilities, management cannot rely on such a degree of control. This time the freedom of action lies with the third parties, the ones who decide on the volume and tenor up to which they are willing to provide funds in whatever form. The causes for the reduction in funds coming the bank's way can be institution or market related. The characteristics of both of them have been explained before in detail. Thus we will not repeat them, but focus on additional important qualities of liabilities in Figure 5.7.

- The direction of the impact regarding both types of stressed situations is comparable: the capacity to fund the bank is declining. What can and most probably will differ is the degree of severity. Which of the two events will turn out to produce a sterner impact on the funding capability cannot be known without a detailed quantitative analysis, which will follow in the next chapter. To illustrate the point made, let us look at two sets of comparisons and start with an institution-specific event.
- For calculating respective stress implications, it is generally recommended to apply a downgrading by two notches. It may happen in real terms within a short period of time, or it may take the form of one-notch downgrading accompanied by a 'negative outlook', whereby the market perceives the negative outlook as a further decline in financial health, and expected with a high level of probability. If we compare two banks, one with a rating at the high AA level and the other graded at the low A, the difference in the potential impact is obvious. The first bank will still stay comfortably within the investment grade segment. The second bank will come close to or even cross the line to non-investment grade, a segment which is qualified as being extremely risky to invest in and often named 'junk'.
- There is a further and often neglected bank-related event. Risk-sensitive investors may link their willingness to expose themselves to a specific rating of the bank concerned (Comptroller of the Currency, 2001). The focus is not the previously mentioned divide between investment and non-investment grade, but a level within investment grade. Some lenders decide to end any relationship with a bank with a long-term rating below AA. The US CP market for example is subdivided into different categories. The top rating segment like A1/P1 contains the vast majority of the total CP volume. In all these cases, tapping the market is no longer possible if the bank's rating falls below the respective threshold. Depending on the funding volumes involved, it can pose a serious problem if not considered in risk planning.
- Alternatively, we observe a market-related event affecting funding. We again start with our two banks and the original ratings of high AA and low A, but with no expected downgrading.

The first bank is highly dependent on the wholesale market, while the second bank gets a significant share of funds from the retail sector. In a market-related event like a bond or an equity crash, the entire banking sector is observed with caution, due to its participation in the disturbed market segment. Under these conditions, the A rated bank will benefit from its funding strength in the less sensitive retail market. Conversely, the AA bank will have a higher proportion of its external funding exposed to the risk-sensitive wholesale market and suffer more in degree.

- For both events and market segments, the intensity of the response is not independent of the 'area' (Comptroller of the Currency, 2001). In its home market, where the bank may have had a long presence and be well known and appreciated, wholesale and retail customers may act differently from the ones where the presence is less well established. Our own experience supports this view. While responses in the home market may be recognisable in quantity and/or in maturity, in less penetrated areas they may become severe or even absolute, i.e. flows may shrink to an almost negligible share of the previous volume.

5.3.6 Policy recommendations

In the previous sections, the liquidity balance sheet, the link between it and flows as well as their implications on liquidity policy have been evaluated and discussed in detail. The findings answering the first open point in Box 5.1 will now be presented in a concise form of policy recommendations for the respective item.

Policies applied should distinguish between asset and liability events. Volumes, structures and qualities of asset portfolios can largely be determined by the bank and its management. The same is not valid for liabilities: there, the power of action lies with the lenders and investors. The recommendations in detail are as follows.

For assets:

- Asset portfolios are to be allocated by management to 'franchise' and 'non-franchise', i.e. subject to sale or discontinuation in the case of necessity. The latter, also called 'assets at risk', preferably has a ranking order attached.
- For each operating unit the balance-sheet volume is defined, at least in form of a guideline.
- Optionalities which may lead to sudden funding are to be limited by type, maturity and quality of borrower.
- Securing that conduit and other independently financing units are treated like optionalities. Treat them as rare exceptions but they should never be dismissed.
- Marketable assets available for liquidity management in a crisis need to fulfil the following requirements. They must: not be dedicated to operating units; have an unencumbered nature; and actually be exchangeable into cash at negligible price concessions.
- For payment purposes, a specified reserve portfolio needs to be established and held, which is sufficient to cover daily negative gaps with the clearers. The instruments within the portfolio are chosen to qualify as eligible by the clearers.
- For security reasons the reserve portfolio is set up for the purpose of protecting the franchise against unexpected and uncovered potential drawings, especially from optionalities and related items. The quality of the main share should be comparable with the one for payments, as in extreme cases the central bank may be the only source to turn tradable assets into cash. The reserve volume depends on the underlying exposure as well as the risk appetite seen as appropriate.

- For all financially related proposals, the amounts need to be segregated into currencies.

For liabilities, funding cannot be controlled and directed by the borrowing bank. Thus, the recommendations refer to a set of measures with the aim of reducing the probability of a severe condition occurring, and, if not avoidable, aiming to keep its impact within acceptable levels. The underlying intention is not only to avoid illiquidity but to keep the strategic customer base intact even during a severe stress:

- Management should endeavour to reach a high level of financial health, as too low a rating, or a sharp decline in it, poses the risk of an institution-related liquidity stress.
- The defined franchise and further engagements with a maturity of longer than 1 year are to be financed with 'stable' funds, i.e. with a remaining tenor of at least 1 year.
- Reserve portfolios for payments and security are financed with stable funds.
- A high level of retail funds should be promoted. They are comparatively durable to disturbances, if covered by a national insurance scheme but consider exceptions.
- A policy of well-distributed funding sources should be followed, avoiding concentration and thus dependency on an individual, a segmental group or a geographical area.
- Tapping funding segments with a rating trigger within the investment grade spectrum should be specifically limited. The closer the own rating gets to the trigger, the more restrictive the principle should be applied.
- Specifically limit the amount of funds borrowed in the so-called 'out of area' regions. Integrate their needs into the group-wide funding policy.
- For all financially related proposals, the amounts need to be segregated into currencies.

With the above summary of recommendations we have come to the end of this chapter and will now progress to the quantitative part.

6
Quantitative Aspects of Liquidity Management

When we addressed policy implications in Chapter 5, three key issues were brought up and expressively stated in Box 5.1. The first point was discussed immediately. It dealt with the qualitative aspect of risk potential and risk-bearing capacity in the context of business policy. When establishing the frame for liquidity policy, one of the conclusions led to the setting up of the liquidity balance sheet as a practical way of combining policy aspects of business and liquidity within a single tool. It was thus appropriate to examine this point then, although it meant spreading the three points over two chapters.

The remaining two points in Box 5.1, i.e. defining stressed circumstances and their implications for the liquidity status of a bank on the one hand and defining the appropriate structure, type and size of limits on the other hand, are quantitative elements in the real sense. Traditionally, the quantification of the respective impacts on the liquidity status caused by external or bank-specific changes in circumstances is done in the following manner. Assets and liabilities are grouped into buckets with similar behaviour. Depending on the type and severity of the internal or external disturbances, the effects on the liquidity status are simulated. As long as the respective results do not produce appropriate conditions for securing payment obligations for the period assessed, corrective action needs to be taken. For examples related to this approach see Matz (2002, page 177f.), Matz (2007a, page 37f.), Frauendorfer and Schürle (2007, page 327f.), Sauerbier, Thomas and Wehn (2008, page 77f.) and Schröter and Schwarz, (2008, page 247f.). Taking policy as a point of departure, our approach differs somewhat, although we also do not and cannot neglect the factual behaviour of the respective groups of assets and liabilities under given and defined circumstances.

The concept employed in this book takes a specific liquidity balance sheet as the centre of focus – specific in the sense that some preconditions are already built in. From the basic analysis, we have learned not to be satisfied with securing payment obligations as the only target of liquidity management. This goal could be achieved when preparing the institution for an undisturbed process of liquidation. Yet business policy demands a higher level of security: the bank asks the liquidity manager to protect its status of 'going concern'; that is, the franchise, however defined, should be made safe for a period to be decided by the top management of the bank. Through this route, the board buys time to take and implement the necessary measures which are aimed at bridging the crisis until normal conditions prevail again. Although unanimous in their endeavour to protect the business against liquidity-related pressure, banks will differ in their view about the exact degree of protection, given the relatively rare occurrence of severe stresses and the cost for insuring against them. Thus, flexibility and the capability to integrate specific levels of risk appetite are further requirements that the concept has to perform.

The liquidity balance sheet already incorporates a scenario by allocating portfolios into a specific structure. Generally speaking, the underlying scenario will hardly be of an extremely severe nature. Consequently, potential negative surprises up to 'black swans' are built into the concept. Since pressure on and loss of liquidity can only be counteracted by (surplus) liquidity, the upcoming question relates to buffers. They now need to be quantified.

When we speak about quantifying the liquidity risk, we do not relate primarily to computing numbers. Again, it is concepts which we will tackle, analyse and qualify. In the course of newer developments in liquidity risk measurement, mathematically orientated methods have emerged. Although they are still very much at an infant stage, we will not neglect them and instead we will evaluate their contribution to our subject.

6.1   GENERAL CONSIDERATION

The quantification related to liquidity contains four aspects: the behaviour of the balance-sheet structure under various circumstances; the basic conditions required when applying a dynamic business point of view; forecasting the most likely gaps; and linking the findings to liquidity policy. We will start with a basic overview, followed by more specific and detailed analyses necessary to arrive at recommendations for liquidity policy.

6.1.1   The liquidity balance sheet and its behavioural changes

The size and structure of a balance sheet is subject to alteration as soon as one brings a time aspect into play. It not only applies for its presentation according to accounting rules, but is equally true when focusing on the liquidity dimension.

Internally, the strongest force for possible changes in the structure is business policy. Derived from it, growth can express itself as positive, negative or neutral. In all three cases, even if the volume is kept unchanged, the effects can relate to on- and off-balance-sheet transactions as well as to the maturity structure of assets and liabilities. One can thus conclude a strong and direct link between business policy and basic liquidity structure, even if other circumstances, like markets, remain stable. Business policy contains a second element as well. Derived from business strategy, it states the relative importance that specific types of businesses are given: core, future core or opportunistic activities. Once management has decided which part of the total range to qualify as franchise, the elements which need to be secured against any disturbances are defined.

Externally, it is the market condition and behaviour which we recognised as vital determinants. Irrespective of whether participants – in their function as lender, investor or trader – do respond to name- or market-related circumstances, the effects will be felt in a similar way: the funding capacity is reduced. We can distinguish between two basic occurrences: all or some of the assets characterised as marketable lose their quality and thus their status; or the market segment for the respective security is congested. For both conditions, the total of easily liquefiable means will decline in (undesired) favour of a lesser availability to turn into cash. The second occurrence is funding driven, or, to be more precise, a result of shrinking funding potential. The impact depends on the degree of the decline. Is it excess potential or actual funding needs which cease to be available? How deep does the process eat into funding the present level of assets? By how much does the balance sheet need to be reduced?

From the frame outlined we can conclude some indispensable requirements which have to be incorporated into the quantitative process:

• With business policy as a force impacting directly on liquidity, the quantitative concept needs a dynamic dimension; planned and expected future developments ought to be integrated.

- Disturbances of any larger severity to a specific bank are the exception and not the norm, although the intervals can be counted in a small number of years and not in decades as can be deduced from Figure 5.4. Thus, one has to distinguish between normal conditions and stressed situations. 'Normal' has to be defined in such a way that minor but frequent upheavals are covered.
- Stressed circumstances do not produce a unanimous moulding; they can differ in character and show degrees in severity. This adds complexity but must still be taken into consideration when choosing the scenarios to be analysed.
- The same specific stress will not produce unanimous effects on all banks. The implications need to be assessed individually for each institute.
- Possible liquidity constraints are risks in the future, including the immediate future, but definitely do not refer to the past. The concept has thus to assess and incorporate adverse developments potentially lying ahead.

6.1.2 Formulating the basic conditions and relations

Any mathematical view of conditions and relations is founded on a language of its own. Up to the present stage, we have applied a descriptive analysis. In a first step, the most relevant findings will be transformed into the appropriate idiom, on the basis of which we will conduct our further debate on the subject. In our discussions we will primarily analyse the views of Fiedler (2007), Heidorn and Schmaltz (2008) and Reitz (2008). Given the early stage of the new development, the assessment regarding their value of contribution to our questions inevitably needs to be a very personal one.

In order to establish a sound basis we will first define the principal terms to be used. Due to the infant stage of the mathematical approach, no coherent terminology exists. In the absence of any clear definitions we will rely primarily on Fiedler (2007), but will adjust the terminology, where necessary, to stay in line with the descriptive terms used in our previous discussions. This is justifiable for two reasons: our dealing with the subject enters deeper into it and in more detail. Besides, the terms used will be familiar and not necessitate permanent translation in order to link to the subject described and discussed previously.

If we define, as we have done, being liquid as the capacity to fulfil all payment obligations as and when they fall due and in the respective currency, then it applies for each currency and each period:

$$\text{ELE}_t - \text{LaR}_t + \text{CBC}_t > 0$$

defined as follows:

ELE_t: The Expected Liquidity Exposure in the period t, which is made up of the difference between the negative and positive expected flow of cash:

$$\text{EFC}_t^+ (\text{inflow in } t) - \text{EFC}_t^- (\text{outflow in } t).$$

LaR_t: The Liquidity at Risk, which stands for deviations of in- and outflows in specific circumstances in a defined period. As in VaR, risk is usually defined as danger while opportunities are excluded, the focus being on lower inflows and larger outflows. (Note that LaR is used very specifically, while the terms LAR and VAR stand for expressing liquidity and downside risk in general.)

Box 6.1 Definitions and abbreviations of terms (*Source*: Adapted from Fiedler, 2007, page 182)

ELE_t = Expected Liquidity Exposure
FC^+_t = Inflow of cash
FC^-_t = Outflow of cash
t = Period

ELE = $ELE_D + ELE_{ND}$
ELE_D = Deterministic
ELE_{ND} = Non-deterministic

ELE_{ND} = $ELE_F + ELE_V + ELE_H$
ELE_F = Floating
ELE_V = Virtual
ELE_H = Hypothetical

FLE = Forward Liquidity Exposure (cumulated)
FLE_t = $FLE_{t-1} + ELE_t$
FLE_0 = Nostro balance

LaR^α = Liquidity at Risk
$\ldots^\alpha\ldots$ = Confidence level α

$FCaR^\alpha$ = Flow of Cash at Risk
$ELaR^\alpha$ = Expected Liquidity at Risk (flow of cash risk)
$VLaR^\alpha$ = Value Liquidity at Risk (NPV risk)

MCO = Maximum cash outflow: $FCE_t < MCO_t$
$AMCO$= Adjusted MCO: $FCE_t + CBC_t < AMCO_t$

CBC = Counter-Balancing Capacity
CBC = $A + S + R$
A = Asset liquidity
S = Sale liquidity
R = Repo liquidity
$S + R$ = Balance-sheet liquidity

CBC_t: The Counter-Balancing Capacity. It contains asset buffers which can be turned into liquidity through sale, repo, collateralisation, etc. Equally, it includes the capability to get the required funds through the renewal of maturing contracts or new funds from other third parties. CBC can comprise: F = funding liquidity; S = sale liquidity and R = repo liquidity; $S + R$ = balance-sheet liquidity.

If the equation holds, i.e. if the calculated liquidity exposure for each specified period, adjusted for detrimental changes of in- and outflows, is covered by the capacity to get cash, payment obligations can be fulfilled.

If we ask for the capacity required to secure payments in line with the equation and in a specific time period, we arrive at

$$CBC_t > -(ELE_t - LaR_t).$$

That is, the counter-balancing capacity, be it as asset reserves or funding not fully utilised, needs to exceed the sum of future exposures. Exposures are measured as net expected flow per period and adjusted for potential negative deviations, the LaR.

Nostro accounts kept for payment purposes will usually end the day with either a positive or negative balance. The differences are then invested or borrowed on an overnight basis. The transactions are reversed the following day, thus establishing the prior nostro balance again. In order to take the cumulative effects into consideration the formula is adjusted to

$$CBC_t > -(FLE_t - LaR_t).$$

FLE stands for Forward Liquidity Exposure. It is defined as

$$FLE_t = FLE_{t-1} + ELE_t.$$

This formula, although reflecting the condition correctly, is based on too static a view. Thus, further elements need to be added. We will call them adjustments to reality.

6.1.3 Adding dynamic elements

Dynamic in this context relates to specific characteristics of a behavioural or situation-specific nature. We distinguish three elements which are to be added for adjustments to reality.

6.1.3.1 The first adjustment to reality relates to ELE in general

As a precondition for calculating the ELE, one needs to analyse the behaviour of instruments or respective portfolios as to amount and time when cash will actually flow. Although in many cases both amount and time of payment flows are clearly determined, the condition is not fulfilled for all instruments initiating flows of cash. For instruments with a so-called stochastic flow pattern the most likely amounts, timing or even both of them need to be evaluated. Deterministic and stochastic behaviour of instruments related to amount and timing can produce four combinations and are segregated into the categories shown in Figure 6.1.

Category	Specifications	Examples
I	Time determined Amount determined	Interest payment and capital repayment of fixed rate loans and deposits
II	Amount not determined Time determined	Dividend payments; swap-related interest payments for periods not yet fixed
III	Amount determined Time not determined	Loan contracts with a flexible payment structure
IV	Amount not determined. Time not determined	Sight and saving deposits; cash exposure from own account trading; clearing for third parties.

Figure 6.1   Deterministic and stochastic behaviour of instruments
(*Source*: Derived from Reitz, 2008, page 125)

Cash implications from instruments in the first category are not hard to assess, given computerised support. Both parameters are known and the behaviour is of a deterministic nature. The remaining categories differ in this respect. At least one element is not determined. The most likely behaviour of the non-deterministic parameters needs to be assessed on the basis of stochastic models or experience.

6.1.3.2   The second adjustment to reality relates to the flows within ELE

Derived from the knowledge gained, the ELE is made up of instruments which are either of a deterministic or a non-deterministic (stochastic) behaviour. The condition can be expressed within our terminology as

$$ELE = ELE_D + ELE_{ND}$$

where ELE_D stands for deterministic and ELE_{ND} for non-deterministic or stochastic.

While the deterministic behaviour is clearly defined with both parameters fixed, stochastic attitudes can present themselves in three different forms. That is:

$$ELE_{ND} = ELE_F + ELE_V + ELE_H.$$

The indices F, V and H name the characteristic of the stochastic flows generated by the respective instrument (Box 6.2).

Box 6.2 Characteristic of non-deterministic flows (*Source*: Adapted from Fiedler, 2007, page 182f.)

Floating: The (stochastic) flows are directly linked to market prices, e.g. swap-related interest payments.

Virtual: The behaviour of the (stochastic) flows cannot be related to market prices or any other observable factor, e.g. saving deposits, non-contractual early repayments.

Hypothetical: This group relates to deterministic as well as stochastic flows generated by new business and prolongations. Furthermore, it can include liquidity effects stemming from credit or operational risk.

Floating and virtual elements reflect a behaviour which, firstly, one could call 'externally triggered' and, secondly, is related to present business. However, referring back to the concept of the liquidity balance sheet, we also need to consider aspects of growth and franchise, just to mention two important pillars which are 'internally triggered'. It is the group (hypothetical) which provides a necessary platform to integrate the liquidity aspects of business and financial policies.

6.1.3.3   The third adjustment to reality defines liquidity at risk (LaR)

Once the amount and time elements are established for deterministic and stochastic transactions and portfolios, we arrive at the ELE. When taking a sequence of periods till the last transaction is covered, i.e. t_1, t_2, t_3 till t_n, and this both for in- and outflows of cash, we arrive at the equivalent to our 'flow of cash balance'; the term used in German is *Liquiditätsablaufbilanz*. In an *ex post* or retrospective view, the calculated balances will turn out to be incorrect. The forecast in the form of ELE or FLE is based on assumptions and incomplete information. In other words, even if liquidity management were to close all forecasted gaps in advance, there would still be a balance remaining when the future date becomes payment day.

The methodical principles of LaR endeavour to determine the potential deviations in advance. The calculation of LaR is supported by mathematical models, based on historic balances. In contrast to VaR, all underlying data refer to the specific bank. Equal to VaR, however, positive results are neglected; the focus is on smaller inflows and larger outflows. In a further step, the level of confidence, signified as α (alpha), will be attached. Based on historic data, the amount covered by the level of confidence expresses the maximum value by which LaR is calculated to deviate negatively. In technical terms it is expressed as LaR_α, whereby α stands for the level of confidence applied.

As a basis of our further discussion we again take

$$\text{CBC}_t > -(\text{ELE}_t - \text{LaR}_t).$$

In detail,

$$\text{CBC}_t > (\text{ELE}_t + (-\text{LaR}_t)) + (\text{ELE}_t - (+\text{LaR}_t)),$$

i.e. +LaR means the inflow is reduced and –LaR means the outflow is increased.

If the probability of this occurring is α (alpha, the level of confidence), it will result in

$$\text{CBC}_{\alpha(t)} > \text{ELE}_{\alpha(t)} = \text{ELE}_{\alpha(t)^+} + \text{ELE}_{\alpha(t)^-}.$$

And if we take a dynamic view, with integrating overnight exposures, we arrive at

$$\text{CBC}_{\alpha(t)} > \text{FLE}_{\alpha(t-1)} + \text{ELE}_{\alpha(t)}.$$

CBC is then determined by

$$\text{CBC}_t = F_t + S_t + R_t$$

in which F is the additional funding capacity on an unsecured basis; S the sale or decline in prolongation of assets against funds not needed to protect franchise or financing assets > 1 year; and R the use of unencumbered marketable assets to replace uncovered by covered funding for the period of the contract.

The deviation of LaR may turn out to be positive or negative. As the focus is on danger, however, potentially positive effects are neglected. That is,

$$\text{LaR plus negative deviation} = \text{(expected) ELaR.}$$

ELaR is calculated for each period (t). To apply LaR in a meaningful way, the respective probability α (level of confidence) needs to be attached.

Any change in the liquidity status can also be followed by financial implications which relate to downside risk or VAR. Any change in the expected flow of cash (EFC) will trigger adjustments in borrowing, placing, etc. As time elapses between assessing the expected flow and its adjustment, prevailing prices applicable now may have changed in the meantime. The cases producing negative effects are covered by the term '(expected) flow of cash at risk'. Mismatched positions in liquidity, even if kept on purpose, fall into the same category. The potential losses out of adjusting or squaring non-congruent liquidity positions are expressed as

$$\text{VLaR} = \text{Value Liquidity at Risk.}$$

VLaR is thus a 'downside risk' element, but stemming from liquidity. And if attached with a level of confidence, it says that with a probability of α the cost for the adjustments will not exceed an amount X.

We will not enter into a detailed mathematical discussion of the strength and weakness of the various models to calculate ELE, FLE, CBC, LaR, ELaR and VLaR, including the effects when applying a probability factor. From the growing list of recent publications we will simply refer to a few additional authors, e.g. Bardenhewer (2007), Elkenbracht and Nauta (2006), Frauendorfer and Schürle (2007), Gruber (2005), Kalkbrener and Willing (2004) and Zeranski (2005).

For our purposes it is sufficient to understand the principles applied. We have also been able to integrate the vital liquidity-related elements of our previous discussions into the mathematical concept. In the next step we will address the considerations required to define the buffers and bring in our personal assessment.

6.2   LIQUIDITY AT RISK AS ONE DETERMINANT OF THE BUFFERS

To start with, we will introduce some assumptions and evaluate their implications. They are not necessarily realistic. Nevertheless, they will help us to get a better understanding of the mechanism.

6.2.1   The interdependences within the equation

As a basis for our discussion we take the following formula presented previously:

$$\text{CBC}_t > -(\text{FLE}_t - \text{LaR}_t).$$

The formula signifies that the buffer CBC for the period t needs to be at least equal to the sum of the expected forward exposure FLE and adjusted for LaR. The latter is the most likely negative deviation from expectations. It is obvious that the size of the buffer is determined by FLE as well as LaR.

FLE is made up of the balance of the previous day and the ELE of the day under consideration. The latter consists of three types of flow-generating sources: bank internal operating units, third-party decisions and corrective measures by the bank's liquidity management. As we have seen before, the respective composition of present as well as potential assets and liabilities generated by these groups is not immaterial for liquidity management. But is it also relevant for specific elements of the equation?

- Operating units of the bank: Quantity of transactions done and planned is just one group of items. Yet the envisaged credit quality is an aspect which decides about the potential level of non-performing loans in the future and impacts on FLE. Increased business activities in optionalities (potential drawings) increase LaR, as does a decline in retail funding, which then has to be compensated by less stable sources. Focusing on fee business produces lower flows. Activities in marketable assets which can be securitised or used for covered funding will require less unsecured funding through liquidity management, hence also fewer reserves for stressed periods.
- Third parties: In many instances, third parties act for operating units in the function as counterparts to deals and transactions. Nevertheless, they comprise some qualities not covered

under operating units. Their behaviours can diverge in somewhat more difficult circumstances of the bank concerned. A higher aptitude to retreat from depositing increases LaR,
as does a tendency towards very short-term lending. The basic business concept of private
or corporate third parties tends towards borrowing longer term and lending shorter term, and
borrowing from more than placing with the respective bank. Their genuine business thus
produces a negative FLE; that is, over longer periods, the overall outflows exceed inflows
from the point of view of the bank.

• Liquidity management of the bank: Given the character of banking business, every liquidity management is faced with a liquidity structure of longer-term assets and shorter-term
liabilities. Many, if not most of them, have to deal with an additional specific imbalance:
operating activities bring about a significant surplus of assets against liabilities. Although it
is understood that a single and specific ELE_t may still be positive, the cumulative effect of
say $FLE_{t + 10}$ will produce a negative balance. The gaps need to be financed. The shorter the
periods chosen and the less stable the sources being tapped, the greater will be the negative
impact on LaR. There is a further implication. Even if all the gaps of FLE were covered, the
protection against detrimental impacts from LaR would stay. The respective buffer is built
in the form of marketable assets. The quality and inherent risk of them is again reflected in
a changing LaR.

6.2.2 The missing aspects

We will concentrate our discussion on two major aspects, one of which is implicit and the
other explicit in nature. We will start with the implicit aspect.

Assessing the most likely ELE and LaR effects is done through modelling. For each portfolio, parameters have to be chosen. But which parameter should be selected? The funding
capacity in the wholesale markets may vary between increasing and drying up at high speed.
Marketable assets qualifying as highly liquid may keep their status, lose the required quality,
or the absorptive capacity may decline despite an unchanged level in asset quality but due
to congestions in the markets. When it comes to non-performing loans, the result may be
better than budgeted, e.g. based on the average of the last 10 years, or supersede anything
experienced in recent history.

The answer is in the above formulations. Firstly, only negative results are taken. The focus is
on danger and not on opportunities. Secondly, the potential negative implications are calculated
with a probability attached, indicated as α. The latter, also known as level of confidence, does
not include all eventualities. It refers to a database covering a defined timespan and relates to
the experience of a specific bank. 'Timespan' and 'specific bank' are the key words in this
respect. That is, neither all negative deviations of the timespan are taken into consideration,
nor is experience of the more distant past, i.e. before the beginning of the timespan considered.
Yet working with these restrictions makes sense in a way, as banks and the environment they
act in do change over time. Experiences from other institutes are left out as well, although
they may have been affected much more severely than the bank under consideration. This is
understandable as well. The data are not published, which leads to the lack of a sound database
to which a level of confidence can be applied. And even if they were, the structure of the two
banks would not necessarily be comparable. As a result, introducing a level of confidence
implies that some potential effects are not covered, the fat tail – where illiquidity looms.

The aspect of an explicit nature refers to payment clearing accounts. The period t can be
defined at need and according to preference. Yet it contains at least one full day. By doing

so, it frames a daily concern of liquidity managers: the functioning of the payment process. Assuming we expect in- and outflows to be in balance, according to the equation there would be no need to keep any reserve cash. Yet clearers will not execute payment orders without a positive balance in the account of the ordering bank or collateral in their hands. Due to time differentials and other reasons, part of the receivables will arrive later in the day. Without sufficient means to bridge the intra-day time gap, the execution of payment orders comes to a standstill.

6.2.3 Conclusions

The outcome of our discussion by and large confirms the statements made before. Yet we believe the mathematical presentation gives a deeper and more precise insight into the matter:

- The earlier view has confirmed that a mathematically based assessment of liquidity risk means separating the cases into 'normal' and 'stress', as the database does not allow both conditions to be covered. The need to apply a different method for each of the two conditions also became obvious. In this respect, it is not unlike VAR.
- Modelling future liquidity risk based on historic data has its limitation, which relates to two circumstances. Firstly, data actually at hand are the ones collectable in-house. This is unlike VAR, which collects volatility data from markets. Secondly, if the respective bank has not just gone through a crisis itself, extreme and thus rare circumstances will not be reflected in the database.
- The models work with a level of probability named α or level of confidence. Within the frame covered by the database, which leaves out extreme conditions, we arrive at an amount which does not fully cover actual and 'normal' experiences. Even with α at 99.9% and 99.95% of a 1-year basis, according to statistical evidence the maximum amounts calculated would be exceeded at least every 4 and 8 years respectively.
- Market experiences not covered by the in-house database, like stressed circumstances not experienced within the timeframe that the database is taken from, are not included in the model.
- The amounts at risk below the threshold defined by α on the one hand and the amounts involved beyond the threshold in the fat tail on the other cannot be derived from the same models.
- Related to liquidity risk, we need a buffer which covers the amount defined by α under normal conditions and an additional one for the excesses represented by the fat tail. Simultaneously, securing the proper functioning of payment execution during the day needs to be incorporated into the buffer as well.
- Financing relates not only to LaR but also to balances in ELE or, more appropriately, FLE. Three parties relate to it, of which two belong to the bank: operating units and liquidity management. Parties have influence on structures by conducting business in a specific way.
- Business policies may take into consideration effects on gaps and ease the pressure. For example, underlying maturities of assets can be shortened if they are structured as marketable. Payment flows could be chosen to fit into the cash composition. In this way, natural hedges will be established.
- Liquidity management could let the size of the gap of FLE_t be determined by chance, i.e. balances are closed just before payment day. When applying gap limits for periods ahead and well ahead, funding requirements at short term can be defined and kept in a controlled manner.

Having laid the groundwork for the quantitative part, we can now progress further. The discussion will continue to be based on the liquidity balance sheet and will take the above conclusions into consideration. The focus will be on the buffers required to safeguard management's intention to protect the defined level of 'going concern', i.e. the franchise and including the risk appetite seen as appropriate for the respective institute.

6.3 DEFINING AND QUANTIFYING THE BUFFERS

In line with the intention expressed previously, quantification does not relate to computing but refers to the concept to be applied.

6.3.1 Principal considerations

Following our approach outlined above, a vital part of present business is already secured. Whatever activities management assesses as franchise is funded on a stable basis, i.e. with funds of a remaining maturity of 1 year at least. The segregation into stable and other funding is derived from the bank-specific business policy. Depending on the management view, the former can be restricted exclusively to core business or could encompass all present and planned activities. Yet the latter alternative is unlikely to be chosen given the implied cost of 'insuring' funding for a minimum period of 1 year, especially when compared with the declining return of marginal business. By separating assets into two categories, management expressly states that it is willing to discontinue part of its present activities and forgo a share or all of new activities planned in case of necessity. Moreover, the businesses potentially affected are defined and named.

What still stays at risk are realities beyond the assumed probabilities. In the areas not stably financed, inflows may be below outflows, exceeding the amounts calculated under the assumption of a specific probability. Higher than expected drawings on contingent liabilities, or forced prolongation of maturing assets (due to the financial difficulties of borrowers or other events mentioned before), may be originating sources leading to the circumstances. Furthermore, shares of marketable assets belonging to operating units may become less liquid or cease to be liquid at all within the defined timeframe. As a result, either the balance sheet tends to grow, as the volume of assets increases, or the proper structure envisaged becomes upset, as liquefiable assets have lost their status. In isolation, neither of these events is of serious concern, as long as funding is not interrupted. Corrective actions will be taken speedily and the appropriate structure re-established.

Yet the picture changes as soon as further funding is limited. Even if we were able to keep funding as well as the maturity structure at present levels, the balance sheet could not grow and there would be no means for the corrective actions available. At best, we would be faced with only a declining liquidity status of marketable assets, i.e. a shift from more liquid to 'not liquid within 1 year'. As long as the present funding level holds, the franchise will be endangered but not eaten into it. The liquidity structure will be out of line for protecting the franchise in severe conditions, but without actually producing detrimental effects at the moment. However, if assets that are not stably funded were to grow and not just shift into the 'non-liquid' segment, we would actually eat into the franchise. The prolongation of policy-related essentials would have to be brought to an end until the negative effects were compensated for. Yet, should funding even decline in more severe circumstances, the franchise would be negatively affected irrespective of whether the bank is additionally facing a negative shift in liquid assets or growth in not stably funded ones. If no special measures were taken, if the asset level were to adjust downwards to the new liability volume and once all non-franchise elements financed over the medium to short term were used up, the brunt would be on short-term assets declared as franchise.

Summarising the knowledge gained indicates that banks have some instruments at hand which allow them to determine a fair part of their destiny concerning liquidity risk. With a proper liquidity approach, the franchise, however defined, can be secured with a high probability, if one is willing to do so. Funding it securely for a minimum period involves some cost. But if this is done in the normal course of business and not just when a crisis is looming, the costs are not excessive. Related to assets, there are only two critical points left open: defining the franchise and the vagaries of probabilities. Choosing the elements which will be included in the franchise and thus protected is fully in the hands of the bank's management. It can thus be controlled. Uncertainties about the right selection are not unlike any other management decision and are not liquidity specific. Yet, in the context of probabilities, the risk of a deviating result from expectation is inherent in the concept. Consequently, the amount by which the negative divergence is likely to occur under specific circumstances needs to be assessed and taken care of by establishing compensating buffers.

What then is the significance of liabilities, their structure and the related funding sources? They definitely are the weakest point in the equation. In the final analysis, they are determined by the lenders and investors. Management of the bank has an indirect impact only: a high level of financial health, expressed in the rating, increases the chance to tap these markets successfully. Conditions like flight to quality may, however, reduce the amount coming the bank's way without any deterioration in its external stability. A well-diversified funding concept and focusing on more stable sources such as retail funds and avoiding 'out of area' concentration improve the chances but are still fragile elements under the condition of severe stresses. As a consequence, the focal point cannot be on liabilities as one has to concentrate on assets.

Asset volume, structure and quality are the three major drivers when it comes to structural liquidity. They derive from business policy, expressed in the form of growth, with all its facets. Funding, including its appropriate level and structure, both of which are only achievable with the consent of third parties, cannot take over that function. Most banks are asset driven and require funding to close the gap. The latter thus acts as a limiting force, of which we need enough to secure at least payments and protect our franchise. As in the actual condition of a stress when funding is scarce at best and declining rapidly under more severe circumstances, one has to prepare for the event in advance by building up reserves.

6.3.2   The possibility to apply modelling

We base our discussion on Fiedler (2007) and the further developed approaches described by Reitz (2008) and Heidorn and Schmaltz (2008). At this point we will not elaborate on specific techniques but concentrate on the inherent principles applied. Furthermore, we will evaluate whether or not the approach is able to integrate our concept of franchise.

We again start with the basic equation

$$\mathrm{CBC}_t = -(\mathrm{ELE}_t - \mathrm{LaR}_t).$$

The equation is not dissimilar to that for VaR. In comparison, the buffer CBC stands for capital, ELE for the profit and loss in the period under consideration and LaR for VaR. In this context it is assumed that P/L of the period is shown separately and not already integrated into capital.

According to our concept, we distinguish assets and liabilities in the following manner:

- Assets:
  - Franchise irrespective of remaining maturity and commitments longer then 1 year.
  - Buffers for securing payments and protecting the franchise in case of unexpected problems in cash inflow: because of forced prolongations, higher than expected outflows from optionalities or a decline in the liquidity status of assets belonging to the operating units.
  - Assets the bank is willing to discontinue in case of necessity.
- Liabilities:
  - Whatever needs to stay on the balance sheet for at least 1 year is stably financed, i.e. with funds which due to contractual agreements or their 'stickiness' can reasonably be assumed to stay for the respective period at least.
  - In the segment 'short- to medium-term funding', all borrowings which most probably will not be replaced at maturity are combined. The degree of the decline will depend on the severity as well as the length of the stressed circumstances.

The parameter ELE consists of expected inflows and outflows in the period under consideration. This is expressed as

$$ELE_t = EFC_t^+ + EFC_t^-.$$

According to its characteristic, EFC can be expressed as:

- EFC_D = deterministic
- EFC_{ND} = non-deterministic or stochastic

where EFC_{ND} is subdivided into:

- EFC_F = floating: related to market indices not yet known but assessed as precisely as possible.
- EFC_V = virtual: estimated deviation, given certain changes in market- or name-related circumstances.
- EFC_H = hypothetical: like expected non-performing loans, effects from business policy decisions.

Following the method defined in this way, we should be able to integrate our conceptual elements. On the liability side, funding sources are transformed into stable and less 'sticky' components. Regarding assets, we should be able expressly to name and consider elements defined by business policy. One concern stays, however: CBC, the Counter-Balancing Capacity. The following questions arise: Should we include all assets qualifying? And what about the minimum standard required for qualifying as a buffer?

The first point we have touched upon already and indicated a preference. Principally one could include all potentially liquid assets on the balance sheet, irrespective of ownership. Unencumbered liquid assets held by operating units would therefore be included. Technically speaking, this makes sense. On the other hand, operating units have business at the forefront of their thinking and not liquidity. Consequently, if appropriate, they will sell liquid assets or employ them for self-financing. Having control over the vital liquidity portfolios is still indispensable for the manager in charge of securing payments and protecting the franchise even under severe conditions. One way to achieve the requirement could be through internal deals: liquidity management acts as the internal counterpart for repo transactions. In this way, it borrows liquid assets under clearly defined conditions, keeps control over them and at the same time provides the respective funding to the owner. From the point of view of the whole bank, liquidity is only transferred from one sector to another, provided the portfolio is funded externally.

The second point relates to the quality of the assets. According to the equation, the CBC compensates for the funding gap. The latter exists for an expected balance (ELE) and the implied risk that expectations will not be fulfilled at the point in time in the future (LaR):

$$CBC = ELE + LaR.$$

We mentioned previously that, for liquidity risk, CBC has some similarities with capital in its relation to downside risk. Similar it may be, but not equal. Capital as a buffer is a parameter which stands on its own. It may be bigger or smaller, but it is tangible and unchanged in amount to face different degrees of losses derived from downside risk. CBC does not match these qualities. It represents a variable component. In cases where LaR is affected by congestions in the repo or secondary market for marketable assets, for example, CBC may be affected as well. As pressure on liquidity can only be counteracted by liquidity again, our buffer should not be subject to possible deterioration by the same forces which cause the pressure at the start. Otherwise, *in extremis*, the buffer can evaporate before it is supposed to counter-balance the gaps. The first signs of the specific interrelationship were detected when we dealt with asset and liability liquidity in the previous chapter. Analysing the equation has deepened the conception, however. Managing liquidity with the aim of securing payment obligations and protecting the franchise will have to consider the specific conditions that the elements of the buffer are subject to.

6.3.3 Securing payments

The determinants for securing payments are ELE and LaR. ELE represents our term 'flow of cash'. The instruments and portfolios can relate to one of the characteristics which we described in the four categories. As ELE is composed of deterministic as well as stochastic payment flows, they are to be determined by using appropriate methods. Although the calculation will be performed for each day, for practical reasons a clustering into daily, weekly, monthly and annual periods has become the norm. The further away the payment dates are, the more the balance is subject to changes through new transactions. Thus the period taken into one cluster will lengthen with the decline in quality information.

LaR then can be expressed as the difference between expected and actual balance at payment day. A widely used practical approach takes these daily deviations from a base period of 1 or 2 years and collected in-house. Negative peak days are analysed, followed by adjustments. The latter may consist of three elements. Should peaks turn out to relate to relatively eventless circumstances, the most likely impact of turbulences is assessed and added. Collateral necessary to secure the execution of payment orders intra-day is also considered. And, last but not least, an amount for unexpected events (e.g. related to contingent liabilities) is added. The total buffer is then calculated from the three sources of potential deviation and the expected balance.

However, special attention must be paid again to the formula. The buffer CBC is determined by ELE and LaR. ELE is the expected balance and under the control of liquidity management.

If not managed at all, and the open amount left to chance, the gaps at payment day could be immense and extremely volatile. Buffers on the other hand are rather strategic instruments and their volume should not be changed on a daily or weekly basis. Stability is very much required. Furthermore, keeping buffers implies costs and they in turn suggest keeping the volumes as low as possible. Against this background, ELE needs to be limited, with the volume granted to stay open and declining as the maturity date approaches the actual payment date. Ideally, at the opening of the latter, all expected gaps are already closed if not slightly overfunded.

As we stated, the presently used method outlined above requires several personal assessments. The mathematical approach outlined in Fiedler (2007) aims to quantify the deviation on a model basis. A more detailed insight is given for example in Heidorn and Schmaltz (2008), Reitz (2008) or Zeranski (2005). The starting point is again in-house collected negative net outflows in the past, after deduction of the expected flows. As before, we will not enter into a detailed mathematical battle with formulae, but again concentrate on the basics. We thus arrive again at LaR, which in this case should not be assessed but calculated using mathematical models. LaR then estimates the liquidity risk in the form of unexpected outflows under normal market conditions, i.e. required balances can be borrowed at any time and at normal market conditions (Zeranski, 2005, page 236f.). From the in-house database for the last 1 or 2 years, a probability level α, the level of confidence, is chosen. It determines from past experiences the level of unexpected negative deviations from the expected sum.

The question of which method to use is still open, however. They can be subdivided into non-parametric (e.g. historic simulation), parametric (e.g. Monte Carlo simulation) and semi-parametric (e.g. peak-over-threshold) methods. Historic simulation, although often used because it is easy to implement, is not seen as appropriate: changes in customer behaviour can lead to outflows exceeding experiences made in the past. Parametric methods assume a standard distribution of events. Various studies have revealed. however, that the assumption is not carried by empirical evidence in the case of liquidity. Peak-over-threshold (POT) takes as a basis the 'Generalised Pareto Distribution' (GPD). Although it refers to the same data sample as the parametric and non-parametric methods, it is less dependent on historic data for an approximation of the actual distribution in extreme zones. Furthermore, the POT method has more clarity in the area of the fat tail. Although it cannot eliminate it, POT allows an evaluation of whether the distribution is heavy, medium or short tailed. It is for these reasons that POT is favoured today when assessing the implications of LaR, as analysed by Zeranski (2005, page 114f.) and supported by Heidorn and Schmaltz (2008) and Reitz (2008), for example.

Although POT is advanced compared with the other methods, its result cannot be taken as final. As in the old-fashioned, widely applied way of calculating the most likely unexpected effect, adjustments are still necessary. Certainly the amounts shown come closer to reality than the ones achieved by using other methods. By penetrating deeper into the fat tail, POT can clarify more the dangerous area in the extreme, where the bank is at peril. Yet more clarity must be distinguished from full clarity.

The only empirical analysis using POT is referred to in Zeranski (2005, page 194f.) where the validity of the hypotheses was confirmed. The institution studied was a smaller retail bank in the federal state of Bavaria, which later became insolvent. That is, the bank was certainly under pressure. However, being regional and retail orientated helped to dampen volatile changes in flows: retail funds are more stable; and there is no 'out of area' wholesale funding to speak of. Furthermore, the depositor insurance scheme in Germany must be one of the most generous ones: single deposits up to 30% of the 'liable' shareholder capital are insured. Even given the somewhat special circumstances of the tested institution, POT has its value and can replace taking the peak days, analysing and adjusting them. There are still two remaining adjustments, but they are not covered by using POT: keeping the payment system functioning during the day and covering for special events like an unexpected level of drawings under committed lines not specially prepared for.

The two adjustments may not be so relevant for smaller, regional and retail-oriented banks, with no developed clearing function for third parties and a business concept where optionalities play a moderate part. For large and international banks with a wide geographical and product reach, they are indispensable. We will not repeat in detail the reasons we have discussed before. Yet it is generally accepted that business concepts and especially customer behaviour can differ widely from bank to bank and thus have to be assessed in the light of the bank's own experience and likely deviations from it. Modelling sub-elements may be helpful, and where necessary it should be done. On the other hand, many a behaviour cannot be predicted with a sufficiently high probability.

As an example we will take the likelihood to be drawn under contingent liabilities in order to finance a CP issue. The latter is part of a general funding programme. Funds are needed for certain; the question is whether to do it through the market or by utilising the line with the bank established for this purpose. One way of assessing the likelihood to be drawn means developing a link to the interest rate payable to the market and the one agreed in the contract with the bank. Assuming a logical business attitude, the customer will always choose the more financially advantageous route. If the bank manages to predict interest rates relatively precisely, the likelihood to be drawn can be assessed with a high level of probability, and the closer one gets to the actual value date of the borrowing decision, the lower the uncertainty will be. But what if the bank becomes the ultimate lender, because the market is unwilling to finance the issue, for whatever reason? The trigger now is not the market rate but market conditions like the availability of funds in general or a (surprising) decline in the financial health of the borrower. Predicting these two triggers is much more difficult and, as banks have experienced many times, these triggers can change rapidly and drastically.

During all the discussions about choosing the most appropriate model and the necessity for adjustment, we should not forget the basic underlying principle: 'financing' to the extent needed is possible. The models as well as the adjustments cover only the 'unexpected' part of flows but not a decline in or a lack of new funds. Furthermore, regarding assets, expected drawings of optionalities are included for example, while the share not catered for and any deterioration in the liquidity status of marketable portfolios are left out. In the understanding of the LaR concept, these occurrences are part of a stressed situation and are not an element of 'normal' conditions.

Although we have already gone deep into the matter of securing payments, we cannot finalise it yet. Stressed conditions, or at least some of them, may have a further impact on payment flows, beyond what we concluded at this stage. We will therefore come back to the subject after having evaluated the buffer for protecting the franchise.

6.3.4 Protecting the franchise

We now leave the 'normal' case and move to stressed conditions. Referring to the generally used terminology, we will focus our discussion on 'structural' liquidity after dealing with the 'situation-specific' one.

6.3.4.1   In search of an approach

In the previous section, when quantifying the buffer for securing daily payments, we worked under the assumption of 'normal' conditions. That means being able to rely on bank internal data to which an appropriate model is applied. In a first step, the ELE is calculated. Where both parameters (amount and time) are known, the necessary parameters are set. For instruments and portfolios which behave in a stochastic manner, the expected item not yet determined has to be assessed. This can be done by using appropriate models. If this is not possible, one has to refer to experience.

The stochastic elements of the expected flows of cash (FoC) related to assets and liabilities are assessed as a first approximation of reality. In a second step LaR is calculated. The aim is to quantify the difference between *ex ante* expected flows and *ex post* experienced actual flows. According to present research, as described above, POT seems to be the most appropriate mathematical model for achieving the goal. It brings more clarity into the fat tails than any other model or method known today. But what about the remaining part of the fat tail?

To answer this question, we refer back to our discussion about the concept of VAR and LAR in Chapter 3. VAR under 'normal' circumstances takes as a basis market movements over a specific time period. After applying a level of confidence, depending on the size and the direction of exposures held, the respective potential maximum potential loss under the given restrictions is calculated. For the non-covered part of the fat tail, special analyses are performed, called stress scenarios. The data are again taken from market movements. Yet this time one refers to extreme events, not included in the present database for the 'normal' case. Fitting events sometimes may date back 20 years or more. After calculating the (negative) financial impact of each event applied on present exposures, the biggest loss is taken as the worst-case scenario. The respective risk potential is put against the risk capacity in the form of capital, which serves as the absorbing buffer. The ratio between risk potential and risk capacity is one of several elements taken to assess the rating level and financial health respectively.

Liquidity risk under 'normal' circumstances is arrived at in a similar way, although one does not use market information but refers to in-house data, i.e. name-specific data. The key difference between VAR and LAR is in the data collected, but it does not alter the concept. Similarities come to an end, however, as soon as we enter the stressed condition. For liquidity stresses we can refer to neither external nor in-house data. According to our findings, they either do not exist or refer to business and market circumstances which no longer prevail. Consequently, we have to establish them according to bank-specific circumstances and under consideration of the most likely stresses and stress combinations that the banking industry has faced in the recent and distant past.

A mathematically based model to calculate the impact of stressed conditions is presently not available, according to Reitz (2008, page 140). Nevertheless, the formula (CBC ≥ ELE + LaR) is also applicable to stressed circumstances. ELE is not unknown in the concept of the liquidity balance sheet; in fact the latter in its basic form represents the ELE. For this reason we take the liquidity balance sheet as a basis and add to it LaR to arrive at the buffer to secure the franchise. However, this will not be possible without further developing the former and adjusting the presentation of it.

6.3.4.2   The liquidity balance sheet adjusted

When calculating the effects on the liquidity structure of the balance sheet, it is quite common to start by choosing portfolios and specific instruments with similar behaviour in terms of liquidity. When applying the chosen scenarios to them, the implications will be measured and one thus arrives at an altered liquidity structure specific for each situation. In case the outcome is not compatible with the requirements set by banking supervision and/or management, adjustments and corresponding actions become necessary. We have chosen a different route. By taking liquidity policy as a starting point, some important parameters are already set at an early stage. Furthermore, the structural changes to the liquidity balance sheet observed when discussing some basic assumptions have given a deeper insight into the mechanics of connections between assets and liabilities and within each of them separately. We now make use of the additional knowledge gained and integrate it into the adjusted liquidity balance sheet.

The scheme with respect to liabilities has not changed, apart from covering a wider range than the franchise and longer-term assets. It is the concept behind assets which has to be restructured following our previous analysis. It has much to do with the meaning of liquidity on the one hand and with its conceptual application on the other. Listing assets according to the timing of cash flowing back, either because of maturing or its degree of marketability, is a necessity when the most likely flow of cash for payment purposes and its steering is calculated. If in need, marketable assets can be put to use as a buffer, although only as long as their funding does not cease. In order to perform the function as protector, being able to create liquidity at need is a necessary condition for instruments within the buffer, but needs to be supplemented with the independent financing secured. That is why portfolios and instruments making up buffers are now shown as segregated. For which period should financing then be secured? As defined within liquidity policy, the aim of buffers is to uphold goals related to payment obligations and business protection, even under difficult circumstances. Management in this way buys time to implement counteracting measures and to bridge the period until normal conditions roughly again prevail. The purpose behind this exceeds the proper management of liquidation and includes protection of a predefined level of going concern. It is thus advisable to apply the same minimum funding period as for the franchise.

Any adjustments in structures and concepts usually lead to changes in the meaning and its interpretation (Figure 6.2). It also applies here. On the other hand, we believe that readability and ease of interpretation have been enhanced. The changes relate solely to assets. The segregation into two liability groups is unaltered, as are the portfolios within each one of them.

Assets	Liabilities
Assets at risk	Short- to medium-term funds (non-stable)
Buffers: payments franchise	Stable funds
Franchise	

Figure 6.2   Liquidity balance sheet adjusted

Previously, assets were grouped into liquid, less liquid and not liquid, whereby each level related to a specific timeframe. As long as we focused on 'time needed to receive cash', the approach was appropriate, as well as a precondition for forecasting the structure of the liquidity position over the maturity spectrum. The moment we add policy requirements, the level of liquidity inherent in an instrument or portfolio needs to be judged in the light of the purpose it is supposed to perform. We did this with assets with a maturity longer than 1 year. In addition to the actual and expected contractual obligations fitting into the category, we added all franchise elements with a shorter maturity spectrum. Only by attaching a specific purpose did we allocate them to the least liquid section, and through this measure we could link it to stable funds.

The actual change now refers to the first two segments, whose names we changed from 'liquid' and 'less liquid' to 'assets at risk' and 'buffers'. The renaming became necessary after the introduction of the purposes to be performed. It is the result of segregating the assets to be given up in case of necessity, which are named 'assets at risk' on the one hand, from the marketable assets qualifying and dedicated to secure the fulfilment of payment obligations and protecting the franchise, on the other hand. Instruments and portfolios have to fulfil three basic requirements in order to qualify as elements of any buffer: They require a high degree of marketability, need to be unencumbered and call for safe financing over the remaining period to maturity of 1 year at least. As a positive side effect, the part that management has decided to be willing to forgo is expressly presented; in many of the generally known stress presentations, the business affected by the declining flows is not easy to detect.

All assets with the required parameters for buffers intact could be taken in principle, even if they belong to and are in the hands of operating units. As stated before, however, it is advisable to adapt a more restrictive stance. To retain control over the actual amounts and the actual degree to which one is able to turn them into cash, the qualifying assets should be in the hands of liquidity management. The quantitative part technically could be done via repurchase agreements, with the benefit of knowing the amounts transferred and secured for the contractual period. A further filter to be applied needs to cover the qualitative elements: Have the related markets sufficient depth and breadth to cover the full amount available immediately or at least in a short period of time? When the bank acts as the issuer, liquidity management has to evaluate market acceptance: is our name known in this segment? Will potential buyers have set limits for us and what is the still unused capacity? To illustrate the point with an example, a portfolio of corporate loans can be securitised. But what is its liquidity status? If this type of securitisation has not yet been done, the 'time to cash' is too long to consider it within the buffer. A rule of thumb applied personally by the author is: leave marketable assets in the operating unit if the type of transaction is not regularly done in the respective segment as well as currency, and requires lengthy preparation.

Following the concept of the adjusted liquidity balance sheet, we now have the practical frame for liquidity management. The key elements can be summarised as follows:

- The period of grace that bank management wishes to buy in order to counteract name- or market-induced negative effects on liquidity has been defined.
- Business-policy-related goals have been formulated and found their equivalent in the portfolio allocation into 'assets at risk', 'buffers' and 'franchise'.
- The length of the period of grace, in combination with the protective and protected asset groups, define the optimum level of 'stable funding'.
- As the liquidity balance sheet is derived from business policy and goals, it contains a dynamic element.

- All three asset groups are explicitly named, defined and can be presented in detail. Potential misunderstandings about the implications of severe disturbances, resulting from the liquidity policy chosen, are reduced if not minimised.
- The level at which the buffer and franchise are covered through 'stable' funds is subject to choice and reflects the risk appetite of bank management.
- Equally, the size of buffers protecting unexpected and thus unplanned negative changes in the forecast and expected liquidity structure are also chosen by bank management and do reflect its risk appetite. (Risk appetite is limited by supervisory requirements.)
- 'Non-stable' funding is expected to decline in difficult market conditions. Its extent depends on the degree of severity regarding the stressed situation.

6.3.4.3   The interrelationships within the liquidity balance sheet

Using the adjusted liquidity balance sheet as an instrument provides a simple and illustrative overview of the basic liquidity structure chosen by the bank management. It also allows the testing of management decisions taken with respect to consistency and achieving goals. Furthermore, it paves the way to simulate alternative routes to achieve the goals and allows for integrating the various levels of risk appetite that management can choose from. Although stressed situations can impinge on both sides, we will start with liabilities, and this for obvious reasons. In 5.3.4, when dealing with changes in asset and liability liquidity, we came to the following conclusion: assets affected by changes in market conditions can produce an unwanted liquidity structure. This in itself does not give way to any immediate problems, as long as funding can be kept at present levels. Still having access to funding sources permits liquidity management to rectify the unwanted imbalance compared with the structure it is aiming for.

The focus now is on the portion which is not characterised as 'stable' funding. These short- to medium-term liabilities are falling due within the next 12 months and would, as well as could, normally be prolonged or replaced by borrowing from alternative investors. In case the bank is now faced with a liability-related stress, the capacity for new funding will be reduced. The severity and the duration of the decline in further funding are dependent on the type of stress. When analysing appropriate scenarios, we arrive at a selection of severity levels, each with a specific pattern. It is the pattern which determines the structural gaps between 'non-stable' funds and 'assets at risk' and over the period under consideration.

The reduction in funds available has to be born by 'assets at risk', in both speed and degree. Assets in this group need to fall off the balance sheet according to the speed and degree of funds declining. Reviewing the impact of the respective severity levels on assets at risk gives the first chance to evaluate previous policy decisions: Do we actually have sufficient assets at risk falling due in the timespan required? Do we actually still agree to shed all of them from the balance sheet if required? If both of the questions can be answered positively according to the best of our knowledge at the time, and if stable funds cover obligations over 1 year, the short-term franchise as well as the payment-related buffer, there would be no need for any further buffer. Moreover, any marketable assets produced in the normal course of business could be kept in 'assets at risk' and employed to cover financing or alternatively taken over by liquidity management to stock up the payment buffer. That is, if we view the expected flows under the different and selected stress scenarios.

Expected flows are the starting point, with LaR still to be determined. This is not dissimilar from the technique utilised when determining the payment buffer, i.e. LaR under normal circumstances. The difference lies in the method available: for 'normal' conditions we refer to the deviation between expected and actual gaps based on in-house experience gained in the past. For any 'stressed' conditions this route is closed, as we explained previously. Neither are data of severe disturbances far back in the past available, nor would we have sufficiently broad samples of data as required for any mathematical modelling, leaving aside the fact that the structure of the bank today is most likely not comparable with the one during previous occurrences.

Since we cannot fall back on any mathematical formula, we will first recall the sources of potential deviations between expected and actually possible liquidity structure. They are:

- Assets at risk cannot be turned into cash as expected.
- The level of contingent liabilities to be drawn has been underestimated.

Related to the first instance, we can easily imagine three underlying reasons:

- An 'asset at risk' falling due cannot be paid back in time, but still remains within the status of going concern; technically, it could be called a forced prolongation.
- The fallout rate of loans can exceed the budgeted amount.
- The quality status of marketable assets in the operating units may have been overestimated; it takes longer to turn them into cash than originally expected.

Concerning contingent liabilities, the degree of uncertainty is most probably even more pronounced. Backup lines for CP issue, for example, in most cases have not been utilised for very long periods. Now, all of a sudden, one of the issuers is faced with a lower financial standing, which does not permit it to access the markets further. The company will then make use of its contract with the bank. The impact is even stronger if the market conditions relate to a general liquidity squeeze; in this case, not one but several lines may be drawn on within a very short period of time. Even worse, under these circumstances the bank itself may be faced with difficulties in the funding markets and liquidity management may be asked to step in as lender of last resort.

Three assumptions are shown in Figure 6.3. Drawings under optionalities turn out to be larger than anticipated and assets at risk cannot be kept at the level planned due to forced prolongation (increase in franchise). Under normal circumstances, funding would be increased accordingly to cater for the larger asset balances. We assume, however, that conditions do not permit an increase in the funding level. As additional funds are not available, the asset structure needs to be adjusted. Without any special provisions established beforehand, bank management can choose between giving way with respect to the payment buffer on the one hand and the portion of the franchise with shorter maturities on the other hand. Or, to put it in another way, the choice is between risking illiquidity and endangering the business substance of the bank. To avoid both of these undesirable alternatives a further buffer is demanded.

The quantity of buffer for securing the franchise is not easy to determine. In fact, it could range from no buffer at all to substantial amounts required to be judged as appropriate, depending on the level of optionalities and the share of assets at risk not being reliable for creating liquidity. In their chapter 'View from the Mountaintop', Matz and Neu (2007c, page 382f.) refer to liquid assets in relation to the likelihood of a bank failing:

> US banks that failed in the period Q1 2000-Q2 2005 held, on average, unencumbered securities equal to 9.7% of total assets about four or five months before they failed. That is roughly equal to the average holdings of unencumbered securities for all US banks during that period.

Expected Asset Behaviour	Actual Asset Behaviour	Liabilities unchanged
Asset at risk	Asset at risk	Non-stable funds
Franchise < 1 year	Franchise < 1 year	Stable funds
	Payment buffer	
Payment buffer	Actual drawings	
Expected drawings		
Franchise / Obligations > 1 year	Franchise / Obligations > 1 year	

Figure 6.3 Unexpected effects: assuming some forced prolongation and optionalities larger than expected

Later on they concluded that 'the holdings of unencumbered securities are probably a very poor indication of strong or weak liquidity risk management'. Indeed they are; and by now we also know why they are a very poor indication, and this in four ways. If at all, unencumbered securities ought to be related to the magnitude of declining liabilities under stress; the timespan within which they can serve as protector depends on the maturity of funding related to them and which is not expressed in the ratio; the quality of securities is also not defined within the ratio and the amount employable in a crisis is thus subject to market conditions; and, last but not least, whether the buffer is designed to secure a proper liquidation of the bank or to protect the franchise cannot be concluded from the ratio either.

6.3.4.4   The elements combined

It has become quite obvious that managing liquidity means dealing with many a variable element. This also reflects on liquidity policy. Unfortunately, the easiest way out of the complexity is closed. Even if we were to match-fund all assets, leaving aside the headaches caused by optionalities and other vagaries, at best we would prepare for a proper liquidation of the bank. Steering the bank through severely troubled waters and keeping an essence of its purpose, i.e. serving a customer base reliably, would be beyond reasonable expectations. Considering further financial and other implications of such a way, building a 'Liquidity Fortress', as phrased and dismissed by Matz (2002, page 376), is of no avail either. What consequently is required is optimising and not maximising. Optimisation is reached through individual decisions on all relevant items on a scale between acceptable and maximal, and in a well-balanced mix. That is, what we called risk appetite plays its role as well.

Having been aware of the complexity at an early stage of our analysis means that many of the items have already been defined, such as: segregation between franchise and assets at risk; stable and non-stable funding; the way to define the volume of the payment buffer. What is still subject to clearer specification is some levels. The graphic illustration below (Figure 6.4)

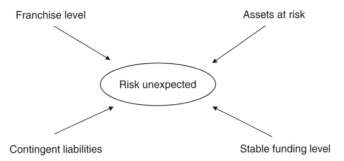

Figure 6.4   The elements combined: their impact on risk

shows the elements where management has room to decide on a more restrictive or a rather lenient attitude.

As was mentioned in the detailed discussions related to each specific item, management still has a certain range of choice when defining the expected flows and staying within the liquidity frame. Depending on the degree of expected flows (anticipated behaviour), the amount to be added (unexpected behaviour) in order to arrive at the possible flows will vary. The amount is smaller, or may be negligible in the case of a very conservative assumption as to the most likely behaviour. However, it will widen in line with a more relaxed supposition. The deviations of expected and possible flows are transmitted to the centre point which in total represents the unexpected risk in the worst case. In a first step the degrees open for decision are explained for each item:

- Franchise level: The franchise can cover a wide range of own activities, starting with 'core', moving to 'future core' and encompassing all opportunistic businesses as well. Drawing the line between franchise and non-franchise is a sensitive task. Cost implications due to longer-term funding needs are just one point to consider. Equally important are earning consideration, and this from two angles. If the franchise is defined too restrictively, severe stresses will most probably be accompanied by a visible reduction in income, which in itself may aggravate the condition the bank is in already. Earning considerations extend also to the stress-free period. Only the franchise is financed stably and thus longer term. Highly liquid assets tend to earn a lesser earning spread. And the portion shifted to 'Assets at risk' requires a relatively high grade of liquidity. Yet the parameters needed to come to a conclusion with a high degree of certainty are available in-house. One could assume that unexpected implications would be moderate.
- Assets at risk: This group contains assets which are supposed to be turned into cash within the defined timeframe, if needed. Either they actually mature within the period and will not be re-established, or they are kept with the operating units and marketable, which allows cash to be created even during their lifespan. Three fragments are to be watched, as we learned from the previous analysis: what we called 'forced prolongation; higher than expected credit losses; and a decline in the liquidity status of marketable assets. As the first and the last points have some common characteristics we will first address credit losses.

   The amount of loss taken into the budget does not necessarily mirror the worst case resulting from respective stress tests. The figures are rather based on an expected outcome for the planning period and thus lower than the calculated maximum based on the worst case. For this reason, it is advisable to take also a somewhat more pessimistic view to arrive at the unexpected quantity.

Unwanted prolongation most probably does not play too big a part. If the franchise is defined in a not too restrictive manner, most transactions potentially subject to forced prolongation are covered by it. Nevertheless, it is worthwhile to focus on large single exposures and assess their repayment at due date under a more pessimistic view. Smaller amounts need only reviewing if whole business segments or geographical areas start tending towards economic or business weakening.

Getting the liquidity status of marketable assets in the hands of operating units correct is much more challenging. Evidently, the degree of liquidity should have been properly assessed beforehand and a portion of marketable assets allocated to the third category. The same would have been done with trading positions, including structured products and portfolios. The tripartite of liquidity management, risk controlling and investment banking will have come to an agreement on how to define the liquidity status of the respective transactions and portfolios. Most probably, the outcome will be based on critical but not really severe market conditions. To cater for unexpected shifts, more conservative scenarios are to be included.

- Contingent liabilities: The expected scenario for contingent liabilities usually works with a percentage share for each segment. In the preparation for Y2K (when computer programs had to be adapted to switch the first digit of the year from 1 to 2), the Federal Reserve Bank of New York, for example, indicated for CP backup lines a level of 10% and 20% related to top rating and lower ones respectively. When choosing the level, it is desirable to include elements like geographical distribution and name concentration within the portfolio. Experience shows that the expected amount in most years is not reached. Nevertheless, the precaution is necessary as circumstances can change fast and often are not predictable. The figure can increase significantly, however, if a credit crunch or a similar event needs to be anticipated. Any deviation from the anticipated flow under stress has to be declared as unexpected, whereby elements of distribution and concentration have again to be taken into consideration.

When related to the function as lender of last resort, predicting the flows is challenging as they are by nature dichotomous. For years, independent operations, conduits and similar vehicles have had no problem in financing themselves directly in the markets. Once problems occur, however, they tend to spread over all of them. What threshold should be taken as appropriate: a quarter, a half or all unsecured funding? Whatever is done will probably turn out to be too much and too little at the same time – excessive in normal circumstances and not sufficient in seriously troubled markets. It is important to recognise that any concept of protection has its limits. In cases like the one mentioned, the liquidity portfolio has to be managed within the context of the whole group; that is, the larger units must be integrated into the overall daily liquidity regime and not just into the concept. For smaller SPVs it is possible to grant the right for self-financing, as long as, when combined, they do not take up a substantial portion of the reserve required. Also a specific share of potential funding is already considered under expected drawing; for extreme cases a further, not yet considered portion is required.

Based on practical experience, there is an overriding question about independent funding anyway. There may be legal restrictions on funding from the parent company. But if such restrictions exist, this would affect funding in a crisis and management would be faced with a different and probably more severe obstacle. But what if independent financing is done for cost reasons because of superior asset classes in their books? The advantage can still be employed to a large extent within the group's funding scheme. Yet, in the end, holding protection has a price to be paid, which goes against the benefit of independent financing. Moreover, within a liquidity regime all opportunities also need to be explored and exploited within an overall frame and its context of security. Thus, if calculated properly, the price advantage may not cover the increase in risk.

- Stable funding level: Although the stable funding level has been defined, there is still some room for deciding on the degree to which it should cover franchise, long-term obligations and buffers. In our discussions up to now we indicated coverage of 100%. The reality might deviate from that assumption. In our case at Commerzbank, we have always applied a range from 95% to 110% of the assets to be covered. The actual level has been dependent on the assessment of the future market climate with regard to liquidity aspects. Within the frame and as long as felt acceptable, cost considerations have been allowed to play their part. Low-spread periods have been chosen for alimentation, especially in the long end where spread volatility is more pronounced. As from the concept full coverage is expected, any positive or negative deviation from the level needs to be declared as unexpected. A conservative attitude compared with 'full' coverage will therefore reduce the unexpected risk.

6.3.4.5 Determining the buffer

After having assessed the potential underestimation of stress-related changes, expressed as unexpected deviation, we now move on to the next step and account for the balance. The previous section dealt with the subject in an illustrative way. For each of the four items the major sources for the unexpected deviations were presented and considerations discussed. While the principle will apply to all types of banks, the outcome will certainly differ, given the divergent structures and environments that financial institutes are acting in.

In Figure 6.5 we will enter each effect in an accounting-related T-bar. Depending on the outcome of the calculations, the effect either creates (indicated with +) or eats up (indicated with −) liquidity. The balance of all items gives the liquidity status based on the difference between expected and worst-case scenarios and represents the unexpected part respectively. In order to get a feel for the different outcomes, the case is exemplified for two types of banks: one is a regional savings bank, the other an international bank with a strong wholesale customer orientation, including a developed investment banking sector.

In the figure we have made possible assumptions which could be characteristic of the two houses. The numbers 1 to 4 refer to the following items:

Savings Bank			BS size in 1000s		International Bank	
+	−				+	−
	10	1	Asset at risk	1		20
	10	2	Franchise level	2		100
Nil	Nil	3	Contingent liabilities	3		100
	50	4	Stable funding level	4	50	
	70		Balance			**170**

Figure 6.5   Unexpected most severe effects on two banking types

Savings Bank	International Bank
1. Regional economic downturn would produce higher fallout rate	1. Not considered; few large fallouts and more forced prolongations
2. Almost all assets had already been declared as franchise	2. Operating units assess franchise at too low a level to protect business concept fully
3. Only real estate financing which is predictable	3. Apart from real estate also backup financing. Considered amount not for extreme stress
4. Level covered at 95%, as very stable funding assumed	4. Level covered at 105%

The results show that both banks have a potential further risk in the extreme of 70 and 170 units respectively. These balances represent the buffer needed to protect the franchise under the most severe conditions. Taken at face value, liquidity management would have to establish a portfolio of this amount in high quality, principally central-bank-accepted assets and financed for 1 year at least. However, taking it at face value may not be the intention of management. One could argue that taking the extreme deviation from expectations for each single item replicates the equivalent of the biblical Flood, and building a wall of protection against it mirrors the liquidity fortress which was dismissed. There is some truth in the argument, as would be confirmed by our military commander we consulted earlier.

Human and technical resources available are limited. The first task is to set up the basic structure, allocate the resources in the most appropriate way and keep an element (in our case the buffers) for immediate disposal. What elements are set and which are kept to hand depend on the scenarios to be faced and their severity. Liquidity managers face a similar task. The basic structure and the rules have been set. We presently know the gap for what one could call the 'worst-case scenario', i.e. the uncovered part in case each single variable element was to turn against the bank. Although such a scenario cannot be dismissed, it is one of several only, represents the most extreme case and is thus a very rare occurrence even within stressed conditions, which themselves are infrequent by character and definition. If the board of directors decides on the level at which it is ready to accept liquidity-related risk, the cost involved related to the decision as well as the remaining threat to the business concept and policy, then top management needs a more subtle analysis than 'worst case' only.

'Subtle' in this context has two dimensions: type of stress and severity level of stress. Paul Sharma of the FSA in London in an interview (5 March 2008) segregates 'shock' events and 'chronic' adverse developments at more than one severity level (Figure 6.6).

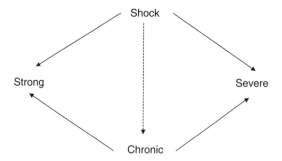

Figure 6.6   Types and severity levels of stressed conditions

(*Source*: Based on Paul Sharma's terminology)

The type of stress is easy to distinguish, at least *ex post*. Shock in this context signifies a short but hefty deviation from normal conditions. The limited time dimension leaves out stresses linked to name-related causes accompanied with lack of confidence. Although confidence in some cases may be shattered in an instant, getting it back takes time, as it has to be re-established and cannot be turned on like a switch. In the case of shocks, building up confidence is not an issue as the latter has not been broken. That is, payment flows are negatively affected due to 'technical' difficulties and not because of changes in attitudes, towards either financial institutions or market segments. Malfunctions of payment systems at the bank or national clearer level are typical examples of shocks. The breakdown of the system is instantaneous, usually lasts for hours or a few days at the utmost and does not impinge on confidence in institutions and markets. From a liquidity perspective, once triggered, shock-related stresses do not allow for planning and preparations. Being able to act immediately and adequately in quantity of cash in the required currencies is asked for. The focus is on the first few hours, followed by the next 1–5 days.

A chronic stress is a different matter, but not unknown to market participants. At the start, the pressure may either be immediate or build up gradually, but the end of it is not hours or days away. It can be weeks or months before normal conditions return. As mentioned earlier, there have been cases lasting up to 1 year before a positive or negative verdict was given. In cases of chronic stress, the pressure drags on. And if no special measures are taken, the bank is in danger of drifting into a vicious downward spiral. A decline in new funds to keep the present level of assets financed forces management to sell marketable assets, or discontinue the prolongation of maturing ones. The longer a chronic stress lasts, the more selling and discontinuing prolongations of assets will eat into the franchise. In such a process, the position that the bank is in can easily be aggravated further, through both customers and lenders: lack of reliability will drive customers away beyond the level caused by the shortage of funds; the deterioration in income and reputation to follow reduces lenders' willingness to expose themselves even from present lower levels. To counteract chronic stress, stamina is required, in addition to the capacity to survive the initial stage.

As we stated earlier, it is not difficult to distinguish the two types of stress – *ex post*, i.e. after the even. To make the correct assessment *ex ante* cannot be taken for granted. In some cases it is easier: name-related stresses are chronic, almost without exception. As confidence is questioned it will take time to regain it, and this is not done within a few days. But how many experts correctly predicted the prolonged and geographically widespread impact of the US subprime mortgage crisis starting in mid-2007? Five years earlier, it would probably have been contained within the United States. This time, its effects were felt well into the following year and well beyond the originating boundaries. When referring to shocks, the stress known as 9/11 (the terrorist attacks on the twin towers of the World Trade Center in New York and the Pentagon in Washington, DC, on 11 September 2001) is taken as a prime example of a shock–stress. After initial mounting pressure on the actual day, the strain subsided within 2 days to normal market conditions, not the least due to the Federal Reserve Bank and other major central banks worldwide handling the crisis in a most profound, professional and admirable manner. So with hindsight it was a clear shock type of stress. What, however, if confidence had been eroded? How much time would it have taken to rebuild it? Certainly more than acceptable to qualify as a shock.

Both shock and chronic are terms already familiar to us. The latter is the underlying condition we based our concept of the liquidity balance sheet on. And in the adjusted liquidity balance sheet, with payment and security buffers, we prepared the floor for integrating shock effects. This has not happened by chance, but it is inherent in the concept to put (liquidity) policy before management of liquidity. By following this route, key elements which need to be protected are defined at the start, and the basic ways open to achieve protection are relatively easy to analyse; and we have done so.

Business is not about security at all costs, whether financially or in the form of suffocation within too strict a frame. Thus, shielding the bank against the sum of all segmental worst-case scenarios is a possibility, but should not be defined as the norm. Liquidity is only one of the risks any company faces. It has to be kept within a sound balance of general risk management. Therefore, still open questions relate to the remaining quantitative assessment in the light of shock as well chronic conditions and applying different levels of severity.

The question then arises about the degree of segregation into severity levels. Specialists tend to go for what could be called a 'scenario battle', believing that more detailed information enhances knowledge. Our own experience does not confirm the inherent assumptions of this view as to precision and clarity. In liquidity management, precision regarding raw data is already a challenge, and the banking industry does not have all structured products reflected correctly with respect to their liquidity dimension. A further serious threat to precision is caused by non-deterministic instruments. As soon as we enter this field and thus require modelling, it is probabilities that one works with, not certainty. Furthermore, many of the modelled results require input which is based on personal assessments made by the model builders and users. As a consequence, the result is clearly stated in firm figures but needs to be interpreted as the middle of a band with a possibly wide deviation to both sides. With too fine a granulation of scenarios, the outer ends of the bands would come closer and each scenario less distinct from its neighbouring ones. Such a state impinges on clarity. The situation will be intensified as soon as one adds scenarios to severity levels.

Actually, two stress scenarios are already available, namely the extremes on both sides. If all four sub-elements behave in a moderate manner under stress, the outcome is comparable to the 'expected' liquidity balance sheet. In other words, no additional buffer is required. Assets at risk, franchise level, contingent liabilities and stable funding level will not be affected more intensely than anticipated and catered for under 'expected'. At the other end of the spectrum is the 'worst-case' scenario. In this case we assumed that each of the four sub-elements behaved in an extreme manner, which in combination lead to the 'worst-case' scenario which was quantified in Figure 6.5.

It is now up to liquidity managers to define further possible and realistic stress scenarios within the extremes. At least one strong shock is a must. To cover chronic stresses, a strong as well as a severe name-related event needs to be incorporated as well as single market-related scenarios for assets and liabilities on the 'strong' level Although rare when confined to infrequent occurrences, it is advisable to select one scenario of a market-related event in which asset and liability effects are combined. To distinguish it from the worst case, a strong rather than a severe level should be chosen.

Now we have answered the second question of Box 5.1. To get a better understanding of the mechanism in place, however, we will pick two further scenarios for the purpose of illustration and related to the International Bank: namely, a severe shock and a strong chronic scenario. We start with the first one, the severe shock.

A shock scenario has been defined as being triggered by an externally induced cause and producing a short-term but hefty impact on liquidity status. As an example we mentioned the event known as 9/11 in 2001. Shocks are not name related, otherwise confidence would be hampered and need to be re-established, which is contradictory to the short-term nature of the

Example 1			BS size in 1000s		Example 2	
+	–				+	–
	20	1	Asset at risk	1		20
		2	Franchise level	2		70
		3	Contingent liabilities	3		
50		4	Stable funding level	4	50	
30			Balance			**40**

Figure 6.7 Two more examples for the 'International Bank'

shock event. However, in what form does the impact on liquidity status present itself? Basically, the respective bank is faced with an unexpected and unanticipated worsening balance between expected inflows and outflows of cash: that is, LaR now exceeds the level calculated under 'normal' conditions. The impact is without warning and felt immediately, i.e. today and during the next few days, and can be caused by a larger outflow (e.g. drawings on contingent liabilities) or a smaller inflow of cash (e.g. disruption of expected incoming payments) compared with expectations. If the resources in the form of cash, including capacity to borrow in time, do not suffice to secure the fulfilment of payment obligations, the bank risks illiquidity and hence insolvency.

What level of resources do we have to hold to avoid the risk of insolvency? To get the answer we will refer to the basic structure of Figure 6.5. There we assumed a worst-case scenario for each of the four items: that is, for each item we calculated the deviation from the basic underlying assumptions that we chose when setting up the liquidity balance sheet. The sum turned out to be an amount of 170 units needed to cover all eventualities over a period of 12 months to the full extent for the International Bank. In case of a shock, only specific items are affected and, moreover, for a very limited period only.

In example 1 in Figure 6.7 we choose an amount of 20 units for forced prolongations due to technical disturbances. All other items stay within the expected magnitude integrated into the basic liquidity balance sheet. As can be deduced from the example, assets at risk stay at 20 in debit and stable funding level at 50 in credit, as the latter still exceeds the minimum coverage of 'assets not liquid within 1 year'. The result shows a net credit of 30 units. Does this mean we are safe in case if the above stress event occurs? When assessed from a structural point of view, the bank is in fact even over-liquid in this scenario, since it has built up a reserve cushion bigger than the potential loss of cash through this event. Structural in our concept relates, however, to the timeframe of 1 year, yet what we are faced with are risks over the next 72 hours or so, and the cash element of 20 units is required in this short timeframe in order to fulfil its purpose and avoid illiquidity.

Now is the time to finalise the discussion about securing payments in 6.3.3 and especially the question at the end: is the result achieved through models like POT equal to the size of the buffer required for securing payment obligations? We do not know without computing the immediate effects on cash caused by specific stressed conditions for an individual bank. However, we can conclude that the payment buffer needs at least to cover the bigger amounts. And it is most probably safe to say that the effect on cash under specific stressed conditions for most, if not all banks, will (sometimes significantly) exceed the value computed by applying POT or similar methods. One small detail remains: where do we allocate the additional amounts for securing payments which are triggered by stressed conditions? Because of the stress-related background, one could link it to the buffer reserved for securing the 'franchise'. Personally, the author prefers to augment the 'payment' buffer to distinguish better between situation-specific and structural liquidity components.

For the second example we choose a strong chronic scenario which is specified as follows. Chronic already signifies the longer-term character of an event. In our case, we assume a name-related stress following a critical downgrading in the bank's official rating. In these circumstances, we no longer talk about days but months, maybe up to 1 year to overcome the problem. Over such periods it is the structural element of liquidity which will come into play. We further assume the downgrading to come as a surprise to the market and causing an initial shock, followed by a longer-term hesitation to establish new and stable levels of engagement in tenor and amount.

When assessing and forecasting the implications of the scenario in the second example, the following alterations may be felt to be appropriate and are thus added to the effects of the basic case. In the normal or basic case, operating units are too optimistic when judging the volume of securitisation of bank assets still in the pipeline by the amount of 20 units in assets at risk. (The amount could be even bigger if the bank were faced with an additional congestion in third-party marketable assets, a condition which does not apply, however, for present assumptions.) The expert assessment comes to the conclusion that in the base case the level of franchise is too low and cannot be upheld in case of a name-related stress without severe implications on the business concept. The deviation on franchise level is judged to be in the region of 70 units. Contingent liabilities are not expected to be affected as in this name-related stress, market-related disturbances do not come into play. And lastly, the stable funding level stays at 50 units above the required amount necessary to finance all the allocated assets in the bracket 'not liquid within 1 year'. The total thus turns out to be 40 units in debit. Therefore, in order to be fully secured for this specific event, the buffer needs to be alimented accordingly.

The same assessments and calculations are performed for all scenarios defined according to the liquidity policy. As has been shown in Figure 6.5 and 6.7, the outcome will change and the maximum spread between 'best' and 'worst' case will probably differ substantially. Two further questions arise in this context: What level do we prepare for? And how do we allocate the total sum between the two buffers securing payment and franchise respectively?

The answer to the question about the appropriate level is a very bank-specific one. The extremes, which are the equivalent of the absolutely worst case which can be imagined (Figure 6.5) on the one hand and the basic (normal) scenario with no need for further measures on the other hand, would be dismissed by most managers. And rightly so, either on the grounds of cost in relation to protecting against the biblical flood or reverse stresses at relatively high probability. Over the last 20 years or so the banking sector has experienced about 14 liquidity crises of different types and magnitude but with an international reach.

To strike the right balance between probability and severity of stressed events as well as cost, the level of securing the franchise cannot be based on mathematical models but is subject to management decisions based not least on risk appetite, which has been dealt with in detail in 5.3.3. Risk appetite does manifest itself in the chosen degree of allocating assets and liabilities into the four groups named 'asset at risk', 'franchise level', 'contingent liabilities' and 'stable funding level'. The first choice is made when setting up the basic liquidity balance sheet. Which assets to classify as 'franchise' and thus indirectly define assets that are dispensable in case of need, assessing the level of 'contingent liabilities' to be financed already and the degree at which 'assets not liquid within 1 year' are covered by 'stable' funds are all elements giving a first indication of risk appetite. The attitude towards it is expressed in the deviation between 'basic' and 'worst-case' scenario, as presented in Figure 6.5. An extremely cautious and conservative basic approach would lead to an almost insignificant balance when calculating the 'worst-case' scenario, and immense reserves in the contrary case. Achieving a proper balance is not easy and requires a deep understanding of the business goals to be achieved and thus protected.

As mentioned earlier, we suggest abstaining from fighting a 'scenario battle'. Nevertheless, applying a minimum number of scenarios as suggested above is to be seen as a must. Scenarios related to a specific institution will, however, differ regarding the needs for the volume of the buffers. Protection against more severe negative changes in the liquidity structure covers lesser ones as well. For this reason, it may be advisable to work with an 'artificial' scenario covering all the effects required to be protected. At Commerzbank we call it the 'virtual' scenario: it has proven to be effective for the various types of stressed conditions experienced, and with the benefit of simplifying communications with the members of the ALCO and the board of directors alike.

One last point before we finalise this specific subject: the potential scenarios are proposed and calculated by the technical experts in the bank. Deciding on the level of risk appetite for the bank is the prerogative of top management. Consequently, meaningful discussions are vital to assess the level of elements where risk appetite can sensibly be expressed. There is some truth in the saying 'garbage in, garbage out!' The elements within which the risk appetite can be filtered also depend on the assessed likelihood of the specific circumstances of markets and the specific structure that the bank is working in, and they will change over time. The question relates not least to the level of 'stable funding'. As mentioned earlier, at Commerzbank we keep it in a band of 95% and 110% of 'assets not liquid within 1 year', with the focus on 100% and above. Lower levels are acceptable if conditions are assessed as smooth for some months to come, while expecting funding spreads to decline in the future, giving the possibility to stock up the gaps at a lower cost at a later date.

6.4 LIMIT-RELATED INPUT FOR LIQUIDITY POLICY

The principles to be applied to limits have already been dealt with in the context of contingency planning. Benefits of diversification, proposals on how to structure them, controlling aspects as well as the escalation processes, and not least the proper use of guidelines as a softer and sometimes more flexible form of limitation, have all been presented. Nevertheless, some specific points needing experience and thus specialist input from liquidity management could not be dealt with at that stage, as acknowledged in the third point of Box 5.1, and will be addressed now.

6.4.1 Limiting risk through segregation

As we have learned, financial risk in banking is subdivided into downside and liquidity risk as the two key elements. The former, consisting of credit, market and operational risk, can be aggregated to a total sum of downside risk of the institution and is compared against capital, the latter serving as the buffer in case risk materialises into actual losses. The condition familiar to us states that risk capacity needs to be in (sufficient) excess compared with risk potential in order to secure solvency of the bank. Sufficient in the sense of being able not only to absorb the losses, but to be still in a position to fulfil capital requirements, the basis for keeping the banking licence. Since downside risk in its different forms can be aggregated into one sum of risk potential, it also can be segregated. And by taking risk capacity as a starting point for defining the maximum risk potential acceptable, the latter can be segregated into its components of credit, market and operational and allocated to business operations, locations, etc. By applying respective limits to each product group and location, the limit system works as a management and controlling instrument from the bottom to the top level of the bank. (For examples see Heuter, Schäffler and Gruber, 2008, page 219f.). Is there any similar instrument at hand when it comes to liquidity risk?

When using the term 'liquidity risk' from a policy point of view, for reasons of simplicity we concentrated on fulfilling payment obligations under the condition that the franchise is secured as well. Under the realistic assumption of not having all assets congruently financed, an element called 'liquidity transformation risk' remains. In order to measure the effects from closing open gaps, actual and altered funding levels are compared and the changes expressed as costs or earnings over all positions and currencies produce an earnings-related result from which one arrives at 'liquidity value at risk', or LVaR for short. The focus is on a potential negative deviation in NPV (Net Present Value) and as such it adds to the risk potential and needs to be covered by capital – which allows this specific element of liquidity risk to be allocated and segregated as any other VaR element (Bartetzky, 2008, page 17f.).

Liquidity risk in its character as payment risk is a different matter. Although the role of capital via indirect channels should not be underestimated, it cannot serve as the buffer in case of liquidity crises. Furthermore, the concern related to liquidity risk does not centre on the outcome under levels of probability but deals with extreme events beyond it. This, in combination with insufficient and often inappropriate data, does not allow for an aggregation in one single defined figure, a precondition to segregate into different segments and setting limits accordingly. Consequently, using an all-bank covering limit system cannot be the answer to control the liquidity risk of an institution.

6.4.2 Limiting risk through general ratios/metrics

If an overall integrated limit system does not serve the purpose, ratios and gap limitations may do so. In the context of evaluating optimal processes for the management of liquidity risk, Schröter and Schwarz (2008, page 263f.) list the most commonly used metrics at present. We will not enter into a detailed discussion encompassing all the pros and cons of each item but assess the value for limiting liquidity risk on an institutional basis or at least for relevant segments of it:

• Liquidity ratio: From a practitioner's point of view, such liquidity ratios have merely some limited value, and not just because the time horizon in the actual formula spans a rather long period. Without doubt, setting these types of ratios allows the total gap from in- and outflows to be kept within the period under consideration at a level which is assessed as acceptable; that is, forcing the managers in charge to secure continuously a positive balance in tradable and central bank eligible assets in case assets falling due are short of liabilities maturing. The liquidity ratio for the next 12 months is given by

$$\frac{\sum_{i}^{12\ months} Funding\ need}{\sum_{i}^{n} Assets\ not\ eligible\ at\ central\ banks} \leq 100\%$$

(following Schröter and Schwarz, 2008, page 264f.).

The question of forecasting actual movements over the coming period and not provided through booked transactions as required in a dynamic view, or the focus on proper and undisturbed liquidation instead securing a status of 'going concern', are just two points which put the ratio in a state of relative value. The unease relates, however, to the significance of the calculated result and its meaning for fulfilling payment obligations. Being liquid, i.e. ending up with a surplus after having added up all positive and negative balances over a full period, does not necessarily imply being able to fulfil payment obligations every single day within the timeframe. And liquidity is about fulfilling the obligation every single day. Elements and figures, once established and in practical use, do tend to have independent lives. In other words, data may no longer be looked at in detail and their possible ambivalence may not be recognised after some time. It is thus one thing to use data which need further explanation within the group of specialists, but grading it up to a relevant indicator on a policy level is not recommended.

- Liquidity at risk (LaR): Applying the method of LaR permits us to assess the most likely negative deviation in liquidity status, on the basis of a specifically selected level of confidence and assuming 'normal' conditions. The benefit of using LaR and limiting it is linked to defining the appropriate level of reserves not only on the grounds of risk, but also on cost considerations.

  Due to the restriction to 'normal' conditions, LaR cannot determine the buffers in case of actual necessity; that is, under severe stress. Limiting the item may still be of value, provided some quantifiable relationship exists between effects stemming from LaR on the one hand and stressed conditions on the other. Unfortunately, simulating effects from various stresses have not shown any stable relationship to the underlying LaR result, however loose it may be. The type of stress, structure of the balance sheet and differing commitments in optionalities, just to mention the most significant determinants, produce non-homogeneous results for a bank.

- Funding ratios: These are seen as a helpful instrument to express long-term funds as an appropriate ratio to long-term assets. That is,

$$\frac{\sum_{i}^{n} \text{Long-term liabilities}}{\sum_{i}^{n} \text{Long-term assets}}$$

(following Schröter and Schwarz, 2008, page 266). The period suggested exceeds 1 year.

To start with, we will ask a few questions for clarification: Which elements on the balance sheet belong to long-term liabilities? How are they defined and do some of them fall into a different category under specific conditions of stress, for example? On long-term assets, are they based on contractual or where necessary on modelled maturities and thus leave out policy-induced franchise assets of a basically short-term character? Does the equation contain assets and liabilities of on- as well as off-balance-sheet transactions contractually concluded, but leave optionalities out? If any of the questions can be answered 'yes', then the ratio does not fulfil our requirements of needing to be dynamic, consider behavioural attitudes and integrate policy requirements for protecting the franchise. Integrating all these elements would be a challenge and, even if done, because of differing implications depending on the actual stress applicable one would end up with more than one funding ratio – notwithstanding that ratios give a view over the full period only and neglect deviations within it. With a result needing interpretation, we would not recommend using the instrument as a relevant indicator on a policy level.

Whether the level of covering assets by funds within the same time category, and to the extent seemingly applied, can be called fitting is difficult to say and would require detailed analysis. It might, if one or more questions above contained a confirmatory answer as to the request but with the disadvantage of not accomplishing the set requirements.

6.4.3   Limiting risk through gap controlling

Flow of cash is the main gap systematic we have been working with. Whether it is funding, liquidity or any other related ratio, they all ultimately rely on FoC. In the reality of liquidity management, there is a significant difference of whether we look at FoC under the aspect of ratios or gaps. Ratios structure elements of the underlying data in desired combinations in order to attain pictures of relativity from which conclusions can be drawn. Gaps do not aim that high; they simply present the result of a pair of variables, in our case the difference between in- and outflows of cash. As we have seen before, getting to size ratios is not so easy and often not very satisfactory when applied to liquidity with its multi-dimensional character. We may therefore decide not to aim that high and instead use a less complex instrument, such as gap analysis.

Gap analysis, by its very nature, can only capture isolated and clearly distinct elements within the complex of liquidity, but has the capability to present it in a sequential form. There are two main areas where this particular restriction can be used: firstly, when defining the buffers and, secondly, when reviewing the liquidity structure. By coincidence, they are two areas where ratios have proven to be too complex, as discussed above.

For the payment buffer we refer to the basic formula

$$CBC \geq -(ELE - LaR).$$

Questions about calculating LaR have been dealt with in detail already in 6.3.3. The focus now is on ELE. If one aims to keep the buffer (CBC) within a predictable range, both determinants need to be assessed. For liquidity management, ELE has the benefit of being a determinant which can be steered to a large extent. Even if the flows generated in and through the operating units produce a growing shortage of inflows over outflows, liquidity management under normal conditions is in a position to square the balances. The open question is whether it is done at payment date or before.

Without any corrective measures, balances in ELE can be extremely volatile from day to day (Figure 6.8). This is of not much concern as long as access to funding is not hampered in quantity and speed. Yet, in case of disturbances, negative balances ought to be covered by the buffer. For cost reasons, buffers should not be inflated unnecessarily. Hence, the negative balances per single day require limitation, and the gaps permitted should be reduced along the maturity line towards payment day. There is no general rule about the size of the limits to be applied, since banks differ with respect to customer segment, business concept and the market environment they are acting in. What can be concluded is that the stricter and tighter the limit of any negative ELE deviation, the smaller the buffer necessary to secure payment obligations. And for many a bank, the uncontrolled swings in ELE would easily exceed the LaR effects most of the time.

The second application of gap analysis refers to the liquidity structure in the medium to long term, i.e. in the periods exceeding 1 year. The payment-related effects are in the distant

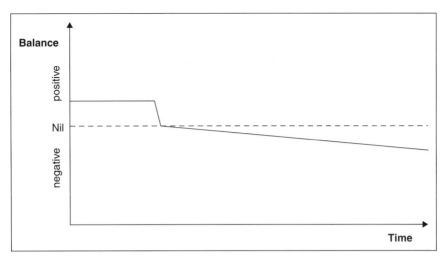

Figure 6.8   A limit frame for ELE: schematic presentation

future; that is, beyond the period we have defined to buy time for senior management with the franchise being protected. Applying the respective ratio to the structural condition of liquidity present in this period does not add any insight: the ratio would simply reflect the degree to which 'stable' funds cover 'assets not liquid within 1 year' at best, or give an indication about the status of preparation for untroubled 'liquidation' in case franchise-related elements are not included. The structure of liquidity is subject to dynamic processes, including the passage of time. A liquidity profile which is in line with policy decisions now may not be appropriate in 1 or 3 months, by which time funding conditions may have deteriorated in price, quantity available or a combination of both of them. Being aware of the gap evaluation within the period under consideration is thus as vital as knowing the ratio and level of coverage. With maturities sufficiently far away, there is no pressure to act immediately as the timing of the action can be chosen within a time band. Figure 6.9 shows a possible graphical presentation for easy reference.

The graphs divide the whole period into 1-year buckets, with the flows beyond 10 years summarised in a single one. The zero-gap path is shown as a straight line from 1 year up to 10 years and beyond. Horizontally, assets are entered according to remaining maturity, while liabilities are integrated into the vertical structure and also in line with tenor. From this a type of grid is established, reflecting the net position per period in comparison to the zero-gap path. As the process chosen is on a cumulative basis, the position of the balance indicates excess coverage (below the zero-gap line) or a shortage (above the zero-gap line) for the period concerned. The position within the grid at the shortest date is equal to the gap in the liquidity balance sheet ('stable' funds against 'not liquid within 1 year').

If by chance or design the net cumulative position in each period stays below the zero-gap line, the structural liquidity position of the bank is positive over the whole long-term range. Even so, some years may produce a shortage; the overall result does not become negative as long as the previous year's surplus is not exceeded. On the other hand, some individual or a series of periods may be negative on a cumulative basis, although the position within the grid on the shortest date may not differ at all from the example before, where there are no shortages

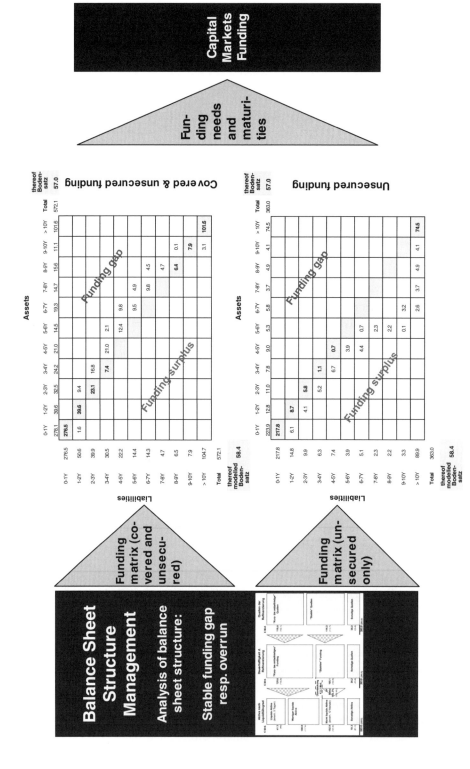

Figure 6.9 From 'stable' funding concept to funding plan – exemplary data (Reproduced by permission of Commerzbank AG)

at all. The graph at this point only presents a picture of the facts. No conclusion can be drawn as to the quality, or, more precisely, to the intended quality of the liquidity structure. It is nothing more than an instrument to work with, and that is when liquidity policy comes into it.

The question policy has to answer is: what is the intended quality of the liquidity structure? Or, moving one step down the ladder: How is risk appetite and cost bearing willingness brought into balance? Should negative gaps beyond 2 years be left open as long as the net balance at 1 year fulfils the set requirements? Or should the bank take advantage in times of low long-term spreads and close negative or even create positive balances, considering that conditions with respect to volumes available and prices to be paid may be detrimental at the later date when funding becomes unavoidable? Cost considerations suggest waiting as long as possible and not acting before forecasts indicate the time to act, thus saving funding insurance costs. On the other hand, without proving it, long experience shows that the banking and related sectors, such as rating agencies, have not shown much evidence of being overly successful in their forecasting capability. And if the unforeseen future stress turns out to be a strong and chronic one, the former savings will probably turn out to bear no relation to the cost then occurring, either through the wider spreads to be paid or by not being able to exploit business opportunities to the full.

The two examples on short- and long-term liquidity aspects illustrate clearly the differences between applying ratios or gap analysis. For ratios, irrespective of how in- and outflows are distributed within the underlying timespan, as long as the sums of in- and outflows do not change, the ratio will remain unaltered. For liquidity management, the structure of liquidity and how it presents itself within any timespan is essential for steering it in a qualitative and professional manner – hence the preference for gap analysis over ratios.

We therefore prefer to link the liquidity balance sheet to a balance of flows (Figure 6.10).

The concept is not dissimilar to the well-established accounting segregation into balance sheet and profit/loss statement: the first one represents a stock view, the second one a con-templation of flows. In fact, it is where we got the inspiration from. One starts with the actual balance at a specific point in time. While the frame can be taken as a general basis, it has to be

	Balance O/N 7D 14D 1M 3M 6M 1Y 2Y 5Y $\geq$ 10Y
Assets at risk Optionalities Franchise < 1Y Franchise/obligations > 1Y Payment buffer **Net Assets**	
Non-stable funds Stable funds **Net Liabilities**	
Net commercial gap Franchise security buffer **Protection of franchise (%)**	

Figure 6.10   Liquidity balance sheet and balance of flows

applied to each single scenario defined within liquidity policy and the contingency plan. The presented segregation into time buckets is for illustrative purposes only. For shock scenarios one may sensibly emphasise the short terms and consequently use daily time buckets for the first 2 weeks, for example. Asset as well as liability items not only will change in degree depending on the severity of a stress, but may also change direction, as will be explained in the following commentary.

Assets at risk   Management is prepared to discontinue commercial assets within this group, if stressed conditions require doing so. Maturity dates can be taken as a starting point which may need adjustments. For example, the bank may be faced with forced prolongations or a fallout rate exceeding planned amounts. Depending on the type of stress, the latter two points will produce dissimilar effects.

Optionalities   The portfolio can change not only in degree but in direction as well. Specific scenarios will reveal drawings to exceed the standard expectation and use up more liquidity than planned for in the standard scenario. Reverse impacts can also not be excluded: customers may make use of early payback or management may decide not to prolong granted optionalities at the maturity date of the contractual obligation.

Franchise < 1 year   Within a given framework of business policy the franchise up to 1 year might not be altered at all. Yet, if business policy is altered it may affect the amount either way, with the restriction that enlarging assets requires funding to perform better than expected.

Franchise/obligations > 1 year   Referring to the franchise element, there is no visible difference from the remarks made for the group up to 1 year. Obligations with an originally remaining maturity beyond 1 year and not qualifying for franchise are a different matter. Depending on their remaining lifespan, they may fall out of this portfolio within the time sequence of a chronic stress and become allocated to assets at risk.

Payment buffer   The amount required to secure payments has been assessed as discussed in 6.3.3 above. Short term, the amount is fixed. Should management decide to reduce high-volume transactions within a chronic stress and thus smooth daily gap volatility, for example, the volumes kept for this purpose could be reduced in more distant maturity buckets.

On another subject, allocating the payment buffer separately and not within the buffer for securing the franchise relates to a personal preference. For reasons of clarity, the two buffers should not be mixed. Preparing to fulfil payments in all circumstances is a supervisory obligation; securing the franchise is a decision made by bank management. One may view it differently, however.

Net assets   This item represents the net result of the assets above at each time chosen. As long as management abstains from declaring a larger part of medium-term lending-related transactions as assets at risk, the amount will decline from day 1. The degree and the speed at which it occurs depend mainly on the amount allocated to the portfolio and the remaining maturity spectrum.

Non-stable funds   In the end, funds available cannot be controlled by the bank's management but depend on the decisions made by market participants. As explained in various instances, management can prepare the ground for a favourable attitude but the decision lies with the markets. In principle, it applies for non-stable and stable funds.

The level of the fund's 'stickiness' depends very much on the stress scenario under consideration. Non-stable and stable funds are thus strongly interweaved. Due to the dissimilar behaviour of alternative investor groups, calculations have to be performed at a granulated level and for each single investor segment. However, management is not fully at the mercy of markets: fostering more 'sticky' sources and keeping the amounts of non-stable funds at appropriate levels as well as fittingly diversified are measures supporting the endeavour towards reduced volatility.

Stable funds   When it comes to stable funds the freedom of action for management is much enhanced, provided it is done in advance. Borrowed funds with a remaining maturity beyond 1 year can be assumed to stay at the full level of the contractual amount, provided no optionalities are embedded. For capital, taking a haircut is advisable. Serving as the buffer in case downside risk becomes effective, capital can shrink given specific scenarios.

Net liabilities   These represent the sum of both stable and non-stable funds. Depending on the volatility of the latter, the amount will fall by various degrees.

Net commercial gap   The term 'commercial' signifies the underlying purpose of the portfolios considered: keeping the business of the bank running at the level defined by business policy, even under stressed liquidity conditions. If the balance were to stay in surplus under the most severe scenario, no additional buffer would be needed. Apart from rare and thus negligible exceptions, the balance will be negative, however, indicating a threat to maintaining the desired level of the franchise.

Franchise securing buffer   This represents the counter-balancing asset to compensate the gaps produced in the most severe case. Qualifying assets for this purpose need to be marketable, unencumbered and require a market which is liquid and able to absorb the quantity envisaged in time and volume.

Protection of franchise in per cent   As long as the buffer exceeds the negative gap, the franchise is fully secured and at a level of or above 100%. This is when the risk appetite of management comes into play. One may opt for less than full coverage out of cost considerations, but with the danger of damage or even loss of vital parts of the franchise in very severe circumstances.

Liquidity balance sheet and balance of flows are two sides of the same coin. The former refers to a stock approach and permits management visually to recognise liquidity implications stemming from business decisions taken, as well as comparing them with policy intentions. Taking the business decision as a basis, liquidity management will employ the latter concept, assess and define the appropriate steps to be proposed to the ALCO and finally implement the sanctioned scheme. Applying the suitable time buckets for the respective scenarios and fulfilling the requirement, however defined, are paramount. Spotting negative gaps within the time sequence is the prime purpose of this instrument, coupled with limiting deviations seen as undue.

6.5   TRANSFER PRICING AND AN ALTERNATIVE CONCEPT

Funding under 'normal' conditions is assumed to be available at the time and in the volume required without limitation. Under specific stressed conditions, the latter will not be available to an unlimited extent. Keeping funding requirements controlled has thus been named as one of the goals within liquidity policy and 'contingency planning' in particular. The question is still open: how should it be done and on what basis? And this question leads beyond the choice between applying limits or guidelines. Although indispensable elements of any funding policy, the recommendations made for a diversified funding policy, minimising 'out of area' borrowing or promoting deposits from the more stable retail sector, do not fit the full picture when it comes to policy. To get to the point we will start with some principal considerations.

6.5.1   The generally applied approach

The allocation of liquidity costs has a high priority within the frame of supervision:

> A bank should incorporate liquidity costs, benefits and risks in the product pricing, performance measurement and new product approval process for all significant business activities (both on- and off-balance sheet), thereby aligning the risk-taking incentives of individual business lines with the liquidity risk exposures their activities create for the bank as a whole. (BCBS, 2008, principle 4)

The Committee of European Bank Supervision also gives the subject a high priority (see CEBS, 2008, Recommendation 2).

Within the business concept of allocating cost and earnings to the respective initiators, funding costs are passed from the liquidity management to the borrowing operating units via transfer pricing. According to Leistenschneider (2008, page 172f.), advanced and generally accepted principles suggest applying market-related prices and tailoring them to each trans- action and transaction type. Vice versa, operating units are compensated for non-bank funds transferred to liquidity management on the same principles. We will not enter into detailed considerations about best methods and techniques to be used, but relate exclusively to the principles as mentioned above. (For technical considerations refer to Leistenschneider, 2008, page 171f, and Neu *et al.*, 2007, page 146f.).

The generally applied approach calculates the liquidity-relevant dimensions for each prod- uct and usually adds the cost or earning element to each single transaction, depending on whether the unit is taking or providing liquidity to the treasury. The actual transfer price is thus generally made up of market rates for the underlying transaction and cost/benefits of the market-related liquidity price. To take an example of the mechanism at work, we assume tightening tendencies in the wholesale funding sector, with liquidity spreads to be paid grad- ually increasing. Through the transfer systematic the rise in cost is built into the pricing of borrowings. Gross margins in operating units will shrink accordingly, leading business with marginal return to be discontinued, if set ROI standards cannot be upheld, for example.

The looked-for mechanism will work, but is it also compatible with policy considerations? We will look at it from various angles to get a better understanding of the questions arising and implicit effects:

- Due to a funding policy orientated on diversification, not all sectors may be affected equally; some of them may even experience no cost pressure at all. Which segment is then taken as the basis for the new liquidity spread? Or should one apply a benchmark rate?

- Whenever a benchmark is chosen, a deviation to actually received and paid amounts is most likely. Who has to bear it, whether positive or negative?
- Liquidity is made up of three components: funding the actual asset, holding a buffer of highly liquid assets for securing the payment process and an additional reserve to protect the franchise against stressed conditions. How should their costs be allocated to each single transaction in a fair and transparent way?
- If liquidity costs are allocated to each single transaction, which route should be followed? Should the bank technically and visibly segregate the transfer price for funding and liquidity, or should there be a single price including both elements? In the latter case, transparency is at peril; borrowers have no way to check easily whether the funding price applied is consistent with market rates.
- Liquidity initiated by operating units and transferred to liquidity management generates income to the former, as they are compensated in relation to market prices and in accordance with the maturities of the funds. Due to increased funding costs, the operating unit with the biggest part of initiated customer funds may also need to reduce asset lending and shed customers who are the main contributors to funding.
- The business sectors within the operating units administering funds coming to the institution probably belong to the most successful groups in the bank in many terms: whatever the spread, there is no credit risk to be deducted, no capital to be employed and the administrative work is minimal. Their twin partners, the lenders who establish and maintain the customer base, need to consider credit risk, finance a substantial administrative workload and require capital to perform their business.

One therefore has to conclude that following a policy of adding liquidity cost on an individual contract basis can pose some conflicting results from a policy point of view: transparency is not granted; general liquidity costs are difficult to break down to individual transactions in a manner easily understood; a business concept can be broken up into artificial segments between lending and funding, based on the same customer group. Faced with the conflicting results of the policy as explained above, at Commerzbank we developed an alternative concept with the aim of minimising the undesired effects.

6.5.2 An alternative concept

Key to the new structure was the decision to switch from a transaction-related to a business-unit-connected approach. For each single bank segment, funds needed and provided to liquidity management are taken as a portfolio. It starts in the course of the budgeting process when input is given for the anticipated structure. In this way liquidity management is provided with a relatively firm frame at an early stage which allows total funding requirements to be assessed against funding capacity. It is 'growth' that we are addressing here, as described in 2.3.4.2 and in Figure 2.7, and further presented in Figure 3.9 in a wider context.

Figure 6.11 shows the consolidated book from the liquidity manager's point of view after all transactions have gone through the transfer process from operating units to treasury. Transfer pricing was performed under the following rules: up to 1 year, the rates paid to the market are applied. For capital market transactions, the interbank swap rate price for the respective period is taken as the transfer price, and these for assets and liabilities. As the latter will deviate from actual cost, an allocation systematic comes into play.

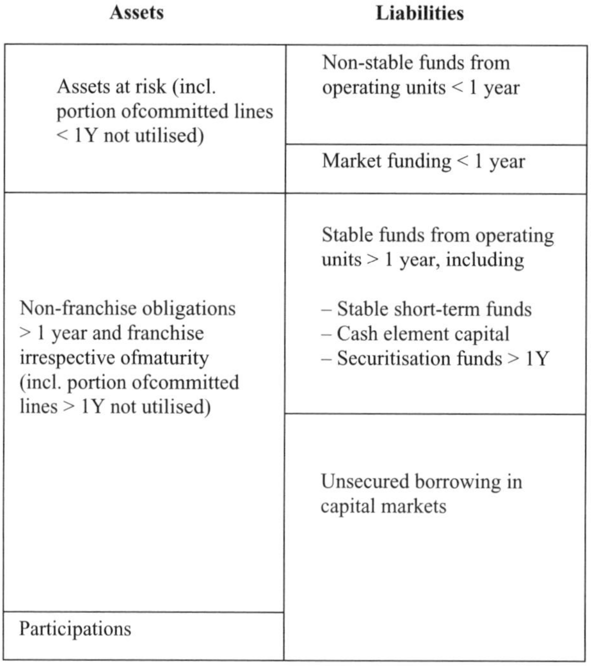

Assets	Liabilities
Assets at risk (incl. portion ofcommitted lines < 1Y not utilised)	Non-stable funds from operating units < 1 year
	Market funding < 1 year
Non-franchise obligations > 1 year and franchise irrespective ofmaturity (incl. portion ofcommitted lines > 1Y not utilised)	Stable funds from operating units > 1 year, including – Stable short-term funds – Cash element capital – Securitisation funds > 1Y
	Unsecured borrowing in capital markets
Participations	

Figure 6.11   An alternative structure to allocate liquidity cost (consolidated view)

The structure is based on an 'economic' view and not on the legal maturity spectrum. In other words, capital-market-related liquidity costs for funding assets defined as long term (i.e. non-franchise obligations > 1Y, franchise irrespective of maturity, participations as well as the two buffers) are considered. Figure 6.11 presents an overview of the setup.

A deconsolidated scheme is set up for each unit, based on which the liquidity cost for each of them is determined. Transactions leading to short-term balances have been executed at market prices and need no further consideration. What remains are cost allocations related to liquidity spreads paid in the capital market. Three elements are now distinguished:

1. Balances from the stable funding gap, expressed above as unsecured borrowing in the capital markets, is debited (credited) depending on whether the unit is a net borrower or net lender.
2. Then the respective allocation for the buffer set up to protect the franchise is calculated. To assess the cost share on this buffer we take the balance of unsecured borrowing and add stable short-term funds; as the buffer covers any type of unexpected deviations, all such elements need to be incorporated
3. What remains is the allocation of cost related to secure fulfilment of payment obligations. If possible, it is done according to the share in payment turnover. Otherwise, the unit's portion of total assets can be taken as an approximation.

From the three balances, the net amount is calculated. Then each unit contributes its share to the total cost of capital market liquidity spreads paid by the bank. Since it is the full board which in the end decides on the degree of covering liquidity risk of the bank, the autonomy of the operating units is limited to creating stable funds and emphasising assets to be securitised.

The change introduced does not mean that the 'conflicts' within a unit have vanished. They still remain, but the unit is no longer divided artificially through general rules applied for the sake of transfer pricing. The conflict from this moment is put into the hands of one person, the respective executive. And this executive now has the freedom to find and implement an appropriate solution fitting the business and management concepts.

Transparency is the second issue needing attention. The requirement stretches over three components of liquidity cost expressed in a wider sense: the benchmark rate for funding; the liquidity spread applicable for transactions concluded; and the cost for keeping buffers, as follows:

- Benchmark rate: As a benchmark the prevailing interbank rate in the respective currency and with the applicable tenor is taken. No liquidity spreads whatsoever are added when the transfer price is entered for the internal deal between liquidity management and the respective unit. In this way, there is continuous and full transparency regarding the market rate applied. The principles work as well for funds initiated by the units and transferred to liquidity management.
- Transactions concluded: Based on the specific funding-related balance sheet per unit, funding needs and the structure of them are assessed. This is done on a net basis, i.e. flows from and to liquidity management are taken and netted. The total cost of funding for this purpose is calculated and allocated to the respective units. There are cases where a unit is a net provider of liquidity and thus earns out of liquidity.
- Buffer-related costs: Buffers, whether to secure payment obligations or the franchise, are strategic items and consequently decided by the board of directors. Transparency with respect to volumes and structure is thus given. The allocation of costs can be done on predefined objective parameters, which also provide the level of transparency required.

The alternative approach has not solved all of the problems stated above. However, transparency has been greatly improved. Furthermore, moving to net balances for each unit gave executive management room to take business decisions encompassing all aspects, i.e. bridging the segregation between lending and initiated funding within the same customer segment, thus defining a coherent policy. Even after experience over several years, the concept is still favoured against the former, single-transaction-related approach.

We have now answered the third and last open question in Box 5.1. We will not enter deeper into detailed aspects of liquidity management. Two recent publications on liquidity management already cover it in detail (see Matz and Neu, 2007a, and Bartetzky, Gruber and Wehn, 2008). And starting with policy, its implications for liquidity management and the later feedback on liquidity policy have now been established.

Concepts can be logical, convincing or at least interesting, but they still have to prove valuable in reality. The following chapter will deal with preparations for potential events based on the concepts presented above and their validity under actual stress.

7

The Concept in Practice

7.1 INTRODUCTION

Any concept in the end has to prove its validity when being tested in reality. To arrive at a concept requires a process to be gone through. This was especially true when we started in the mid-1990s and liquidity management at that time was not so much in focus as it is today. Of course, bank supervisors formulated requirements which had to be adhered to. However, they concentrated on keeping a certain amount of tradable assets, with the view of being able to turn them immediately into cash if fulfilment of payment obligations called for doing so, or asked for a ratio between incoming and outgoing flows of cash. Banks themselves were rather confident that funding would not be a serious problem as long as solvency was not at peril. As a result, for the latter, liquidity risk too often was seen as a subsequent risk, neglecting the possibility of being solvent and illiquid at the same time, whether due to flight to quality or congestions in the markets for tradable assets. The centre of concern was related less to the quantity of cash being receivable but more on the price to be paid in order to get it. This view is now gradually changing, also hesitantly. Even nowadays, the literature too often still stresses in detail the cost impact and only remarks on the quantitative aspect incidentally, although it is primarily the second facet which can turn out to be fatal.

The organisational setup reflected the part liquidity played in the understanding of bank management: managing the daily payment flows. The duty was mostly allocated to the money market desk as a sub-function to interest risk management, whereby liquidity management as understood today was not part of it. The attitude also was mirrored in the publications of that time such as those edited by Weisweiller (1991a, 1991b). However, some advanced thinking was indicated when a balance sheet was segregated into interest rate and liquidity aspects, e.g. in Duttweiler and Jamal (1991).

Management of liquidity cannot start as and when sophisticated technical processes and methods become available or are in place; it has been and will be a duty which has to be performed irrespective of technical standards achieved at the time. In the 1990s, knowledge hardly surpassed some basic principles, several of them dating back to the previous century. Going forward and tackling the subject resembled an expedition into uncharted territory. Applying 'best practice' would have been the equivalent of accepting an extremely low level of sophistication and waiting for progress to be made by others, and having the findings published. It happened, but after a long delay, and the credit goes very much to Leonard Matz, who, to the best of the author's knowledge, brought out the first fully encompassing book on liquidity risk management in 2002. Like many other colleagues, we had to follow the path towards a better understanding and develop a framework which we thought appropriate for the bank and circumstances we were working in.

According to Bartetzky (2008, page 17), measuring liquidity risk has not reached yet the level achieved by market risk, where risk-orientated limits have become a generally accepted standard; regarding liquidity, a sound data quality and a properly set up flow-of-cash balance sheet for many a (local and national) bank would already be a milestone towards a standard. It is for these reasons that we also cover the process of setting up the structural elements, although in a very concentrated form. It may be of some help. The chapter will be divided into five sections, which are:

- Establishing the base
- A shock event
- A name-related stress
- The subprime crisis
- Conclusions.

The development of any concept, unfortunately, does not follow a straight line of progress. It evolves over time, and with detours as an integral part of it. As much as possible we endeavour to follow the structure shown above. Nevertheless, for the sake of clarity, sometimes it may be necessary to bring in elements from another section. We will deal with them as rare exceptions, however.

7.2   ESTABLISHING THE BASE

The conceptual base was established in the mid-1990s and gradually implemented in the following years. At the beginning, only rudimentary elements were defined, but were enhanced with growing knowledge gained over time.

7.2.1   Introduction

It was about the mid-1990s when we at Commerzbank recognised the need to bring liquidity into focus and put the task of managing it at an equal level to interest risk management. There was no obvious pressure to do so, quite the contrary. The market-related stresses in the previous 10 years or so originated for the most part in US markets, and the brunt had to be borne primarily by the banks in the United States. Moreover, the US bond market crash in 1994 provided European banks with opportunities for extremely cheap funding, as investors had lost trust in US banks and shifted substantial amounts to Europe; these applied to short- and long-term maturities. The funds available were therefore plentiful and cheap.

However, there was no guarantee that Europe would not be the epicentre of future upheavals. Just a few years earlier, turmoil in the foreign exchange markets had spilled over to the interest markets when the UK pound was forced to leave the European Monetary System in 1992. Although the implication on funding for our bank was minimal, it underlined the point made before. Having followed a very decentralised approach in respect of managing liquidity in Commerzbank, a group-related analysis showed shortcomings in our technical, organisational and methodological approaches for dealing with a severe stress affecting us directly.

The analysis allowed us to draw some fundamental conclusions. To define and even more to implement an appropriate concept to deal with liquidity risk is a major task, taking years to set up. And it had to be a concept, as time and cost considerations would not allow for changing policy decisions. It also emerged that the technical part would use up most time to be implemented. Although not at a level assessed as suitable for the future, we had sufficient information regarding liquidity status at that time to bridge the time gap required to develop new concepts and programmes. The analysis further revealed the need to integrate the liquidity concept into the framework of business and financial policy.

7.2.2 Policy aspects

Starting with policy aspects, even considering them at all, was triggered by a simple observation over years as practitioners responsible for liquidity management: even in smoothly running markets, the liquidity structure of the bank could change significantly, based on policy decisions regarding growth in all its facets. We did not know at the time about all the links to and from the other financial parameters as shown in Figure 3.9; the potentially significant impact of growth was assessed as given, however. It became obvious that we could not neglect growth and even had to make it a cornerstone of any liquidity policy. From it, and over time, a planning process emerged: consider all the foreseen business intentions of the operating units, compare them with the funding capacity evaluated and take the result as a basis for situation-specific and structural liquidity management.

A further policy item centred on the interpretation of 'securing liquidity for the bank'. It clearly transpired that bank supervision was focusing on enabling the banks to fulfil payment obligation and no more. In the extreme, it could lead to what we called 'preparing for smooth liquidation'. While it may suffice for regulators, shareholders and thus the senior management of banks can and will not be satisfied with such an outlook. From their point of view, a liquidity crisis is just one part of business risk like a recession, credit default rates or crashes in market segments. Thus, the aim has to surpass 'smooth liquidation' and protect the essence of the bank as well. What is now termed as 'franchise' was originally phrased as 'even after a serious liquidity stress we want to remain a bank with the core customer base intact'. Through a lengthy process, including many detours, we arrived in the end at a similar structure to the 'liquidity balance sheet adjusted' as presented in Figure 6.2. By applying this instrument, liquidity management had a base for acting within the confines of top-management-approved rules; moreover, it turned out to be a form of presenting the key elements in an understandable manner for liquidity professionals and bank management alike.

Through the 1990s and even till today, all CEOs of the bank insisted on being personally informed and involved in liquidity and balance-sheet risk matters of the bank. Things started with weekly meetings in a small circle, including the CEO, the board member for the treasury and a market analyst, in addition to the treasurer and the manager responsible for liquidity within the treasury. Soon, it transpired that having the treasury prepare its own data on liquidity and thus control itself was contrary to newly formulated corporate governance. It was decided by management to alter the policy and segregate 'doing' and 'controlling', by setting up the latter function within the risk controlling department. As progress was made in implementing formulated goals, the foundation was laid for a process leading over time to the setting up of the organisational structure shown in Figure 4.1.

A further and intensely discussed policy issue related to whether to go for a centralised or decentralised approach regarding liquidity management. The question did not relate so much to the bank itself but to separate legal entities like subsidiaries and conduits. Since developing a technical infrastructure and integrating the multitude of corporate centres and locations is a lengthy process, we had some time to decide on the subject – and we needed it. In the end, the decision went clearly in favour of a centralised approach, with the treasurer as the functional head and responsible to the central ALCO at head office.

On the basis of the principal policy decisions on liquidity, the operative part was readjusted and gradually implemented according to progress made.

7.2.3   Adjusting to the new concept

This section deals with the steps taken by the treasurer with respect to liquidity, based on the policy formulated. The issues relate to technical infrastructure, organisation and securing payment even in stressed conditions. We will not follow up in detail any measures taken by risk controlling but refer to them whenever necessary.

7.2.3.1   Technical infrastructure

Technical infrastructure relates to data collecting and the mechanism of transfer pricing. The set and quality of data, even for Germany, were not up to the new standard sought. Above all, a group-wide online overview per segment, location and in total was not available, due to the decentralised approach applicable to liquidity, and some of the data still had to be extracted from accounting figures. After evaluating several alternatives, we opted for a total overhaul and started from scratch. The new system, covering all transactions performed by the units in the bank (except trading positions, of which the liquidity aspect is transferred to our department in a consolidated form) and thus producing a 'liquidity ledger', allowed the so-called flow of cash to be established. It was built by an external software house and provides extremely granulated information, down to individual deals and their specific characteristics. We started with Germany and subsequently added other regions and legally independent units. Although not easy to handle, structured products were not the major concern; the real challenge turned out to be in a different quarter: to synchronise the bank's data for the purpose of accounting, controlling, risk and liquidity management. We recognised it to be paramount to work on the basis of common data, although the needs of users differed. As risk controlling had all data available from accounting, we transferred our additional information to its system in order to achieve a common database. Risk controlling since then has provided liquidity management with complete and independent information and has performed the task as independent controller and provider of risk parameters under special scenarios.

7.2.3.2   Organisational measures

Setting new goals for liquidity policy inevitably had repercussions on the organisational setup related to it. Managing liquidity and its risk could no longer stay as a sub-element of interest rate risk management. The former had to be given direct responsibility and thus status on its own. It was the beginning of segregating liquidity from the interest rate risk treasury. After going through a learning curve, we arrived in two steps at a structure consisting of three sections, each dealing with a specific element of liquidity (Figure 7.1).

The transfer pricing section is the link to the bank and the various entities in it. Its tool is the specially developed system which allows them to take over all liquidity and interest rate risk components from the operating units, with the exception of trading-related interest rate risk managed by the respective departments. The tasks consist of three duties. The interest rate risk is filtered out and transferred to the respective unit, the interest risk management. The remaining two tasks deal with liquidity aspects. The granulation in the context of transfer pricing has to permit the setting up of the liquidity balance sheet on an economic basis, i.e.

Figure 7.1   The segregation of liquidity management into sections

taking into consideration deterministic and stochastic flows and their implications on actual as against contractual maturities. The information is then passed to risk management liquidity.

The last section actually manages the liquidity risk of the bank. It is done within the confines set by the liquidity policy for normal and stressed conditions. This includes evaluating and formulating proposals to the central ALCO and the board with respect to feedback on the issues presented in Box 5.1, a task which is performed in close coordination with risk controlling. In addition, the section is in charge of preparing the relevant documentation and proposals for the monthly central ALCO meeting as well as implementing tasks resulting from the latter's decisions.

Setting up a dedicated (corporate) customer desk serves several purposes. This type of customer is usually a borrower and depositor at the same time. As the former normally supersedes the latter, it has a natural hedge vis-à-vis the bank. Leaving aside very special circumstances, the funds are relatively stable compared with interbank borrowing, although less than retail deposits. Personal contact is, however, the decisive factor under stressed conditions; people need to be informed, but not on the basis of a 'cold call'. Personal contact also allows the reason for large swings in deposited volumes to be assessed and can thus serve as an early indicator of a declining trust towards the bank. Furthermore, open communication with the customer base and closeness to risk management help to define the pricing level; under normal conditions, an adjustment by one basis point can attract or turn away funds.

7.2.3.3   *Preventive actions*

The findings in our analysis did not only disclose shortcomings of a technical and organisational nature compared with aims; the liquidity structure was also not appropriate in the case of severe and especially for long-lasting stresses. Very long periods of rather untroubled funding capability had left its mark, as was probably the case in most banks at that time. Despite lacking precise information and without the underlying concepts developed to get it, it became obvious that in case of a severe, and more so in a long-lasting stress, we would need to shed core business at a relatively early stage. And it also became noticeable that we could not wait till precise data were available, as it might take years to get to that point. Applying a rough rule of thumb, the funding structure was lengthened in maturity. Money market funding with a term between 6 months and 1 year was significantly increased to the detriment of short-term deposits. In addition, as funding in the capital market was cheap for us, not least because of the US bond market crash, issuance in the capital markets was taken up vigorously; in a specific quarter we were the biggest issuer, surpassing even the World Bank, and giving rise to the headline coming over the ticker 'Commerzbank again, moans the market'. Could we have waited till more precise figures were available? We could have waited, with hindsight. On the other hand, we increased our protection against marked impacts in case a severe stress occurred; furthermore, grasping the opportunity to secure cheap long-term funds turned out to be a saving in later years, when protection became more expensive and would have been unavoidable, due to further stresses to come.

7.2.4   In search of a policy-related liquidity concept

As the technical and, in its flow, the organisational adjustments progressed, work intensified on developing a systematic and an instrument enabling us to quantify liquidity-relevant determinants and effects. If the discussions at the meetings of the European Bank Treasurer Group, of which Commerzbank is a founding member, can be taken as an indicator, liquidity, and the best ways to manage it, have become a general market issue. In line with best practice at that time, we started by grouping assets and liabilities with similar behaviour under stress, applied stress scenarios and evaluated whether or not payment obligations could still be fulfilled. In those cases necessary, we assessed the indispensable steps to be taken in order to secure their fulfilment, i.e. not to become illiquid. In following this route, two serious problems soon emerged. On one side, what is the time period that we have to secure payments for? One month, as many regulators demanded, or for the full length of the balance sheet? And if anything between, on what criteria should the decision be based? On the other side, if behavioural attitudes with respect to portfolios are taken without reference to business policy, do we achieve the required result, or might we prepare for 'smooth liquidation', although unwillingly?

The second issues had to be answered first, as it presupposes the initial one to a large extent. It cannot be denied that taking behavioural attitudes without reference to business policy can lead to a process of liquidation in severe and longer-lasting circumstances. Accepting the conclusion leads to defining the element to be protected, what we called the franchise. It sounds trivial but it is not. It goes against the general management attitude to expand, to improve and to increase performance. Tackling liquidity problems cannot be solved by attacking the difficulty head on; all of a sudden it may require retreating, possibly even on a broad front. Thus, the process is painful and delicate at the same time, because drawing the line between costs and protecting income cannot be done using approved and established methods – it requires a policy decision. In our case, there were several attempts at an answer to the question, until we decided on the one presented in 5.2.2.

As for the length of the period protected, it meant buying time for the senior management of the bank. Although many stresses lasted less than 1 month, name-related ones, being triggered by loss of confidence, would take longer to overcome. As a consequence, we felt a need to distinguish between short- and longer-term effects, or, as Paul Sharma calls them, shock and chronic. The first buffer needs to compensate the immediate effects, and thus cover a large part of stresses at the same time; the second buffer serves as a backup, in case of longer-lasting adverse conditions, as in the case of name-related stresses, for example. But which period of protection to choose was still not answered. As trust cannot be re-established in a short period of time, we felt it needed somewhere between 6 months and 1 year. Going for the latter was not based on any meticulous analysis. Internal discussions simply led to the view; problems not solved within a year, being less of a liquidity nature but relating to a fundamental business problem, cannot be tackled by management and at least largely rectified within that period. The timeframe chosen by us was not carved in stone as a general principle. Management at other banks might come to different conclusions, after having analysed the circumstances they were living in.

Securing the security is the other side of the coin. Or, to phrase it differently, if the buffers are chosen in quantity and structure, how do we ascertain their stability in quality and time? Tradable assets may drop in quality, or congestion and decline in trust may reduce the quantity that the market is willing to absorb. Then the buffer melts like butter in the sun, even before it can be employed for its actual purpose. Quality was the remedy we found, and best quality is required to be eligible with central banks. Consequently, the portfolios need to be held in this category. Smaller portions may be kept in non-eligible but still high-quality assets, in case the respective central bank acts extremely restrictively. (There is no unanimous treatment of eligibility among central banks and it took even the European Central Bank many years to achieve it within its own system.) However, a buffer lasts only as long as its financing is secured. Any stress markedly reducing funding capacity is going to jeopardise upholding the buffers. For this reason, we decided to fund them for the period defined as 'buying time' for the bank.

The elements which have been addressed in detail in Chapter 5 have become an integral part of the liquidity balance sheet. Around the millennium, the basic structure was established, after having worked on it for about half a decade, not in the detail discussed in the previous chapters, but the essence of it was laid down and implemented. And through preventative actions on the one hand and the policy to adjust mentally and conceptionally in the course of progress made on the other hand, security was always given on a high and growing level.

The concept is a connecting link between liquidity policy and management. In case of stressed conditions, the task of surviving and overcoming them cannot be delegated to liquidity management, although it plays a key role because of its expertise and closeness to the market. Especially in longer-lasting events, a combined effort is required, encompassing the liquidity policy, management and controlling bodies. It is the mechanics of the interrelationship which will be at the forefront of the coming discussions, supplemented with specific issues requiring analysis, decisions and actions by the liquidity manager. For illustrative purposes, we have selected three stress events:

- A shock event: 11 September 2001 (known as 9/11)
- A name-related stress: Commerzbank in autumn 2002
- The subprime crisis

By the very restriction to a particular bank, describing personal experiences made in specific circumstances cannot assume the status of general validity. Effects on banks are only loosely comparable: market-related impacts differ depending on the type, the location and the business approach of the bank; name-related stresses produce dissimilar behavioural attitudes of lenders and investors according to cause, severity as well as time; and, last but not least, historic events do not repeat themselves necessarily, just to mention some topics. At best, the examples may provide some insight into the issues arising and the way we addressed them.

To avoid falling into the trap of becoming a 'story teller', we will keep to the facts related to liquidity and connected policy questions. We also assume it is not necessary to explain actions and activities in detail if they belong to the 'trade skills' common in liquidity management.

7.3   CASE 1: A SHOCK EVENT (9/11)

On 11 September 2001, at 08:45 EST, the North Tower of the World Trade Center in New York was struck by a passenger jet aircraft, hijacked by Al Qaeda members. Some 18 minutes later, another hijacked passenger jet was flown into the South Tower of the WTC. Both buildings went up in flames immediately and collapsed about an hour and a quarter after the onslaught. Further targeted buildings included the Pentagon in Washington, DC, attacked at 09:43, and the US Capitol Building in Washington, DC. The aircraft targeting the latter crashed in Shanksville, Pennsylvania, as courageous passengers fought with the hijackers to prevent it from reaching its target. About 3000 people died and 6300 were injured in New York alone. The attacks and their implications were deeply shocking to any civilised person.

7.3.1   The preparatory setup

A technical contingency plan had been in place for some time. For each treasury location worldwide an off-site emergency dealing room had been established and kept at a level of maintenance, which allowed it to be brought up to full functionality within 3–4 hours. Related support was assured, as the location was chosen for the whole branch. The site is about 30 miles (50 km) north of New York. The system for data communication of the treasury locations worldwide had been built with flexibility integrated. In addition to linking local treasuries with the central treasury, it was assured that one of them could take over the central function in case Frankfurt could not.

As mentioned in the introduction, a liquidity contingency plan had been set up, including scenario analysis. Calculating the effects of the previously defined scenarios revealed a name-related stress to be the most dangerous event, encompassing almost all other effects. From an overall policy point of view, we believed it was sensible to work with a 'virtual' scenario, based on name stress and adjusted for the minor missing elements. It has been turned into a guiding principle to keep policy-relevant issues as transparent as possible, not to burden them with details significant only for liquidity management, as long as the high-level picture is not distorted.

On a managerial level, the liquidity buffers had been quantified and allocated correspondingly, covering 'shock' and 'chronic' scenarios. Out of the total volume, at least 60% of the combined buffers qualified as 'eligible' with central banks. The major part was already put as collateral at the central banks we were clearing with and thus available immediately, or as we phrased it, 'a phone call away'. For the New York branch, being the group's centre for dollars, the collateral was with the Federal Reserve of New York. The remaining share of reserves in the hands of liquidity management were of a quality easily employable for repo transactions, collateralisation, etc., yet not 'eligible' due to policies applied by our main central bank, the Bundesbank.

7.3.2   Dealing with the stress

Any dealing with a stressed situation has at least three facets (Box 7.1), but not all of them may play a full part in concrete events.

Box 7.1 The three facets of stressed conditions

- Policy considerations
- Technical handling
- Behavioural attitude.

The first two elements apply in any case. Policy starts with the first and foremost question of whether or not present volatile circumstances still fall under the term 'normal' conditions or have exceeded the threshold to stress. In case of doubt, one should opt for the latter. Depending on the type of stress concluded, further policy measures will have to be decided during the process; unfortunately, they do not follow a predictable pattern. Technical handling has to be based on preparations as stated in the contingency plan, whereby flexibility in responding to actual circumstances is paramount. Mechanistic responses should be avoided. What is required are actions embedded in a wider understanding of the aims to be achieved; otherwise, an action judged sensible when looked at in isolation may contradict the overall goal. Especially in cases of chronic stress, where negative behavioural attitudes have time to develop, dealing with markets and people making them in an appropriate manner is paramount. Human counterparts have to take decisions, and under uncertainty they tend to retreat from continuing to expose themselves on past levels. The reduction of their risk is the reverse of the bank's power of creating liquidity, however. Taking measures to improve their confidence in the bank can turn out to be a decisive element, provided it is done on the proverbial understanding: (visible) actions speak louder than words.

7.3.2.1 Policy considerations

When we were informed about the attack, minutes after the first aircraft crashed into one of the towers, our first thoughts were of the treasury team and our colleagues in the New York branch, situated in the World Financial Centre and just a stone's throw away. The liquidity team linked up with them while the head of the central ALCO was informed. It was a brief conversation, as no detailed information was available. Nevertheless, it was concluded that the event was serious enough to make use of the predefined authority declaring the bank as being in a stressed situation. According to procedures, the head of the central ALCO informed the CEO, further members of the board of directors and took steps to arrange for a meeting of the central ALCO. In parallel, the liquidity department was to collect further information, analyse the most likely implications and take any necessary steps as and when required.

In the meantime the second aircraft crashed into the other tower. The information from our colleagues in New York was supplemented by TV news and pictures. To our great relief they were unharmed, although deeply shocked. Being familiar with the banking district of Manhattan, we thought that the communication lines for executing payments was most probably damaged, triggering an order to analyse expected dollar in- and outflows of that day and the ones to follow. Ongoing communication with our people in New York confirmed our preliminary assessment and enhanced it with some more specific details. As both of the towers had collapsed by then, it was decided to vacate the building until permission for re-entry was granted, turning out to be about 1 year later. According to our New York colleagues, the emergency dealing room was being activated and the departmental staff would make their way to it. It was agreed that Frankfurt would take over until they became operational again and all the books were handed over to us through the global network.

The arranged meeting took place the next morning in Frankfurt, by which time we had gathered sufficient information to draw an almost complete picture of the key issues:

- Some of our counterparts had their technical infrastructure damaged and could not execute payments to the Fed in favour of us. In some cases the shortfall amounted to several billion dollars.

- The quality of these banks was assessed to be beyond doubt; thus it was judged as a technical but not a credit risk.
- The previous day, the Fed had kept its window open till after midnight, and had worked energetically to reduce the problems to manageable levels.
- The Bundesbank and the Fed coordinated strongly.
- We had been keeping close contacts with the Bundesbank, which offered to provide dollars against collateral in euros, in case of need (a departure from the rules).
- The off-site emergency dealing room of New York had become operational in the meantime.
- To be on the safe side, Frankfurt borrowed dollars in the Euromarkets in favour of the bank's account with the Fed.
- By noon their time, treasury New York will most probably be in a position to take back the books and responsibilities, Frankfurt remaining in standby mode and providing dollar funding in case of necessity.

After detailed discussions, the status of stress was confirmed, the state of the matters noted and the analysis accepted. Looking forward, three issues were in the limelight: type and severity of the stress; cash reserves; impact on market behaviour.

We concluded the stress to be of the type defined as 'severe shock' and limited to technical damage for the time being. If the stress were containable within 'shock', we would suffer further shortfalls on the dollar account with the Fed, until debtor banks were able to solve their problem. Based on our information, this status could be reached within the next 24 to 48 hours.

To bridge the gap was judged as not a critical point. If the Euromarkets kept functioning as the day before, Frankfurt could borrow and transfer the cash to the Fed. Alternatively, we would have to employ our reserve buffers. Having followed a policy of keeping all assets for securing payments and the larger part of reserves for protecting the franchise in instruments 'eligible' with central banks, quantity of cash was not the problem; however, the currency that the cash was kept in could have become a potential issue. If markets were still to function, we would use the foreign exchange market and enter into an overnight transaction. In the unlikely event of serious disturbances in this segment, we would take up the offer from the Bundesbank and borrow dollars against euro collateral.

As dealing with the scenario of shock turned out to be fully covered by the contingency plan and our conceptual approach based on the liquidity balance sheet, the view turned to the most likely future behaviour of markets and their participants. A scenario of shock may be an end in itself, but it could also signal the beginning of a longer-term 'chronic' condition, if participants were to lose confidence in the functioning of markets and institutions. Since there were no indications in this respect, it was decided to watch the markets and present the findings and likely implications at the next meeting. In the meantime, responsibility was delegated to the board member responsible for the treasury, with the understanding of keeping the CEO and other members informed and to call for an emergency meeting in case matters turned for the worse.

In the following 2 days, due to the combined efforts of the Fed, other central banks and systems specialists, the technical part of the problem was solved, and in the days to come it became obvious that trust in the functioning of the Fed, other institutions and markets could be kept up, so a possible glide into a 'chronic' scenario was avoided. About a week after the attack we signalled 'end of stress'.

7.3.2.2 Technical handling

The task lay primarily with the New York Treasury and its head John Reilly, from whom we also received an account of events, as follows. After the first plane hit the North Tower and recognising the severity of the event, we immediately sent four people to leave the bank in downtown Manhattan and get up to the Disaster Recovery Site in Rye, about 30 miles north of New York. The precaution was triggered by the experience dating back to 1993 when the World Trade Center was attacked by means of a car bomb. Reaching Rye would normally take about an hour; in given circumstances it took about 4 hours, however. It wasn't until 18 minutes later, when the second plane crashed into the South Tower, we realised it was not an accident. At this point we proceeded to get everyone out of the building and to relocate the 'emergency group' to the Disaster Recovery Site. Staff not belonging to the group were sent home and to wait for further instructions. After the first attack Head Office Treasury was immediately informed about the state of the event and the contact was continuously kept open. Measures to be taken were agreed: vacating the building and moving to Rye; handing over the books to Frankfurt until further notice; making the Contingency Dealing Room operational and Frankfurt securing funding in their markets. For precautionary reasons we took printouts of all our liquidity and trading positions before we left. At that time we did expect to return to the site within days or weeks but not having to wait for about one full year.

The Head of Foreign Exchange had a day off but heard about the disaster and went immediately to the Recovery Site. So within 3 hours five treasury staff members started work in Rye. Within a couple of hours more all emergency staff had arrived, finding already a fully operational infrastructure in place and functioning. Benefiting from regular (at least once a year) tests on the site, apart from technical checks done monthly, Treasury staff were familiar with the technical infrastructure and could start operational activities without delay. For reasons of precaution the number of transactions permitted was curtailed initially; but with the technical infrastructure proving to be sound and functioning it was soon lifted.

One of our main concerns was the status of liquidity, not per se but in the light of technical disruptions preventing counterparts from fulfilling their payment obligations. Although we kept a substantial amount of collateral at the Federal Reserve, it was agreed with Head Office to secure funding the balance in their markets. At that time cell phone towers could not handle all the traffic and communication was often interrupted and not possible at all. Collateral with the central bank served as a fallback in case any communication breakdown would prevent Group Treasury from allocating the dollar funds raised to the account with the Fed. As it turned out Head Office took care of all our needs and we never lost our operating ability for a single second. For reasons of precaution on September 12 the books were still managed by Frankfurt in close coordination with us, but taken over by New York again as from the following day.

High-level communications with the authorities and members of the executive board of the bank had been secured by the branch management based on information gathered and decisions made during the early morning and late afternoon meetings with the departmental heads. The latter communicated directly with their levels at the Fed and Frankfurt.

Any disaster recovery site is designed to bridge a relatively short period of time. Treasury New York had prepared space and dealing desks for half of the staff. Yet it gradually emerged that an early return to the old location was not given, due to the necessary overhaul of the building complex of the World Trade Center. In order to re-establish full capacity, new locations had to be found.

With hindsight it turned out to be paramount to set up the Disaster Recovery Site well away from the endangered area and having regularly performed checks and tests involving the users as well. Furthermore, without a group-wide integrated system we would not have been in a state to hand over positions in detail easily and swiftly and take them back according to need and suitability.

7.3.2.3 *Behaviour attitude*

One may be tempted to assume no special considerations being needed in this respect, when faced with a shock scenario. The time under stress is short and the event is likely to be of a technical nature. By its very definition, a shock event is not accompanied with loss of trust, otherwise it could not be of a short-term nature. Yet, Figure 6.6 indicates the possibility of a shock being the beginning of a slide into a 'chronic' scenario. Policy considerations need to assess both prospects at the very beginning, as behavioural attitudes in case of the latter play a part not to be underestimated. In case of an isolated shock, acting firm and in a professional manner is the best one can ask for. That is what we attempted to do in this specific case.

7.3.3 Conclusions

Experience evolves with doing, acting under specific circumstances; analysing actual against expected and anticipated situation-specific problems; drawing conclusions and turning them into adjustments of the concept. Since we did not face any unexpected problems, it was concluded that the preparations for shock, even a severe one, were at a satisfactory level. Yet the analysis revealed a point of weakness which did not materialise in this case but may become relevant in other circumstances: creating liquidity in the currency required.

In the case experienced, four sources were available for creating liquidity:

- Collateral with the Fed New York.
- Access to a functioning Eurodollar market.
- The foreign exchange swap market.
- Assistance from the Bundesbank to receive dollars against euro collateral.

The picture could present itself differently for local currencies, and we were engaged in East European and Asian ones. Given a serious crisis with disturbances in the money and the foreign exchange markets, we may have to rely solely on the collateral kept with the central bank. It may last for a while, but not indefinitely. The point was addressed at each location and an understanding of how to act in such circumstances was reached with each central bank.

Admittedly, the severity of the problem for our bank, with neither dominant commercial nor external clearing obligations in dollars, was not comparable with US and some other dollar-focused banks. Concerning concepts and procedures, there is no difference, however. When reviewing their appropriateness sometime after the event, only minor adjustments were judged necessary. Having got the respective confirmation, and, even more, having got through an actual stress with the confirmation that concepts and procedures were appropriate, turned out to be essential. The next stress, and one of a much higher level of severity and complexity, was looming just around the corner, without us being aware of it.

7.4   CASE 2: A NAME-RELATED STRESS (COMMERZBANK IN AUTUMN 2002)

In a name-related stress the main pressure is not caused by general market circumstances affecting all banks; it is the trust in a specific institution which is undermined. Whether it is caused by internal or external circumstances, by factual or perceived conditions, or a combination of them is not the fundamental point, although it impacts on decisions about how to handle the crisis from a policy, technical and behavioural point of view. The fact is: the bank is facing a liquidity stress. The case presented here contains several of the above-mentioned elements. Thus, it will represent less an understanding of a scenario in isolation but will give an insight into the complexity of reality.

7.4.1   Evolution of a stress

The stress that Commerzbank was facing could be called an 'add-on'. After a long period of enthusiastic assessment of 'dot-com' companies, accompanied by soaring share markets, the bubble burst, a phenomenon that spread almost all over the world. In the aftermath, share prices crashed over a broad front and the danger of recession began to loom. Banks suffered in particular. Within this scenario, Commerzbank's solvency and thus liquidity were challenged.

7.4.1.1   The bursting of the bubble

Based on the enthusiastic view of 'dot-com' companies, their share prices had ballooned to P/E ratios (price/earnings ratios) of up to 50 in some cases, well above the level in more normal circumstances. When investors changed their assessment of the business segment, stock markets started to tumble (Figure 7.2). The collapse of such big companies like Enron around the turn of 2001–2002 fed anxiety even more.

The picture on the economic front presented itself rather gloomily as well. Growth and the present level of employment were at peril and in many a country recession was looming or had become an actual occurrence already (Figure 7.3).

Referring to policy considerations in this period, Alan Greenspan, the FED Chairman at that time, stated: 'The Fed's response to all this uncertainty was to maintain our program of aggressively lowering short-term interest rates' (Greenspan, 2007, page 228). For the reason 'to mitigate the impact of the dot-com bust and the general stock-market decline'. He concludes: 'By October of that year [2002], the Fed funds rate stood at 1.25 percent, a figure most of us would have considered unfathomably low a decade before.'

Not all central banks acted as sharply as the FED did. Conditions in the various currency zones and, even more, approaches with respect to monetary policy did and still do differ among central banks. Nevertheless, the trend towards lowering interest rates was a common response by all of them (Figure 7.4).

In the aftermath of the turbulence, pressure on the banks grew from various corners like a Hydra. Insolvency in the corporate sector grew sharply and so did credit-related losses; the recession reduced earning potential in balance-sheet and off-balance-sheet businesses; the value of participations declined in line with tumbling share prices and as a result of all the occurrences, their own market capitalisation shrank in extreme cases close to or even below the level of capitalisation. Rating agencies responded to the changed circumstances by reducing the level of the financial 'health label' by one or even two notches in one step. Although differences

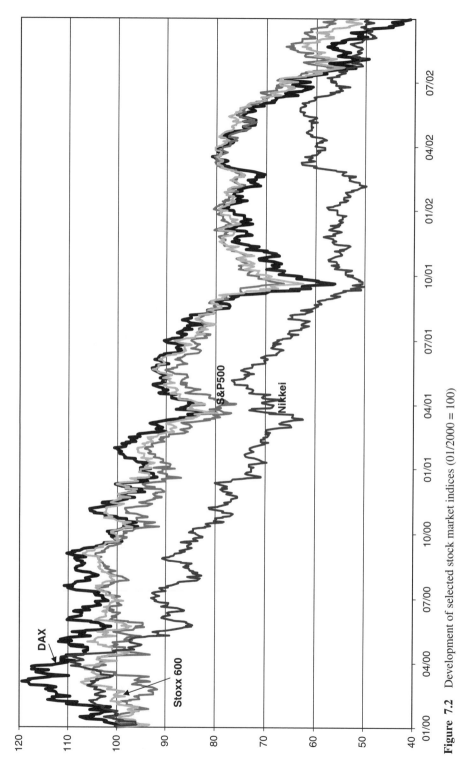

Figure 7.2 Development of selected stock market indices (01/2000 = 100)
(Reproduced by permission of Commerzbank AG)

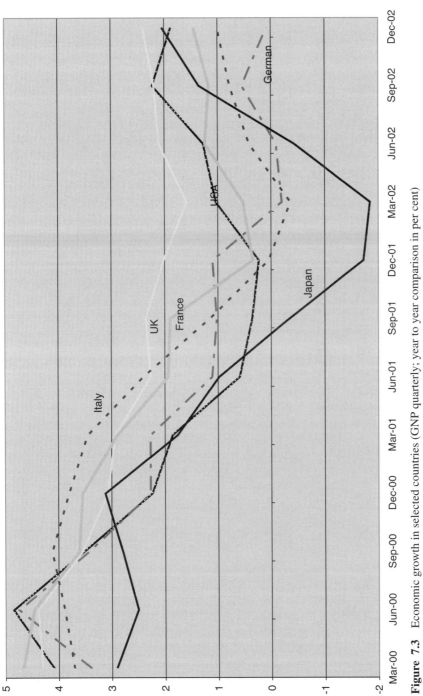

Figure 7.3 Economic growth in selected countries (GNP quarterly; year to year comparison in per cent)
(Reproduced by permission of Commerzbank AG)

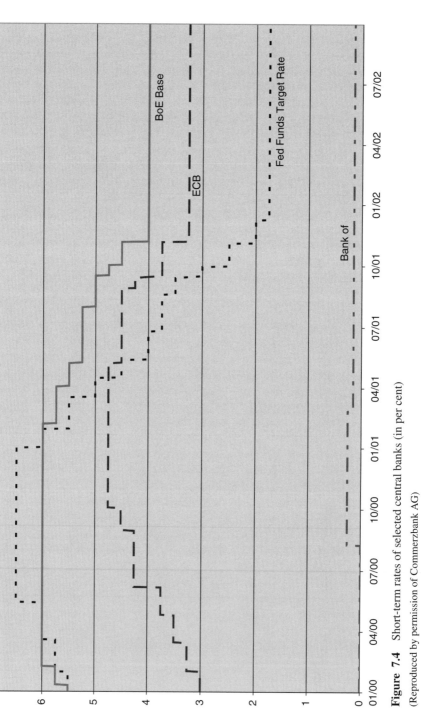

Figure 7.4 Short-term rates of selected central banks (in per cent)

(Reproduced by permission of Commerzbank AG)

with respect to regions and single banks were still observable within the general trend, the German banking industry was perceived to be particularly vulnerable.

7.4.1.2 German banks in focus

The widely spread perception among analysts at that time is mirrored for example in a publication from Merrill Lynch ('German Banks: Turning Japanese', 23 September 2002) in which Stuart Graham states: 'The German banks are in the least attractive segment of our sectoral investment clock.' The reasoning behind this statement was made up of four arguments:

- Pre-tax ROE in the banking industry had declined between 1998 and 2001 from 19.3% to 6.2%, with prognoses to experience a further reduction in 2002 due to bad debts.
- Rating outlook and recent actual downgrading by some agencies would increase funding cost with its detrimental effect on net earnings.
- Declining equity markets had savaged the unrealised gains in the banks' equity portfolios.
- Tier 1 capital ratio in most German banks was relatively low compared with the European average, although well over the minimum level of 4%.

Concern also developed about whether the German banking industry would turn Japanese, i.e. go through a prolonged period of depression. Comparing common themes, in seven items out of seven, the author observed parallels between the two industries:

- Stock market bubble
- Property market bubble
- Weak banking system
- Web of corporate cross-holdings
- Reliance on banks as big lenders in the economy
- Tough and pro active regulatory environment
- Social barriers to change and aging population.

This is not the place to discuss the validity of the arguments and conclusions, either with the benefit of hindsight or from insider knowledge at that time. Whether one likes it or not, when it comes to market behaviour, perception is what counts, whatever it is based on. And the perception was not at all favourable for German banks at that time.

7.4.1.3 Commerzbank under name-related stress

When it comes to assessing the business and financial strengths of an institution, the views of the management of the respective bank on the one hand and market participants on the other hand often differ greatly. This is not because hope prevails till the very end, but because access to internal data permits the bank's management to distinguish between false rumours and hard facts. Although management can and does put false rumours right, the market is not always in a position to differentiate between the facts and statements born out of hope. (We too have often been on the other side and faced with the task, thus experiencing the dilemma the market is in.) For this reason, markets tend to act on the following basis: prepare for the worst but hope for the best. As perception is the key word when it comes to market behaviour, we will abstain from any in-house view at this stage and consult the publications of the time. The facts available to us will play their part when addressing our considerations and responses.

On 3 September 2002, which is before the report on German banks turning Japanese, Merrill Lynch published an in-depth report entitled 'Commerzbank: Shaken and Stirred'. The outcome of the analysis was: long-term credit view NEUTRAL. The outlook was based on the following facts and considerations:

- Poor profitability of the franchise:
  – 2.Q 2002 slightly above breakeven.
- Good cost-cutting:
  – Estimate €5.2 bn against €5.5 bn targeted by the bank.
- A stretched balance sheet:
  – Negative implications for a BS of about €400 bn, in case of a downgrading.
  – An assessed Tier 1 ratio of 6.3% per end year, coupled with unrealised losses of estimated €1.17 bn on the bank's equity holdings, constrains management's room for strategic manoeuvre.
  – Asset quality has proven relatively resilient under difficult circumstances.
  – For our part, we remain unconvinced on Commerzbank's asset quality.
- Our 8% RoNAV forecast for 2004 needs kinder markets:
  – Base case assumes less difficult markets in 2003 and 2004.
  – No improvements in the markets; Commerzbank is heading, with a lot of effort, for an estimated 4% RoNAV.
- Risk of our valuation:
  – Risk provisions and capital markets are the key swing factors in our earnings and valuation.

Between 3 and 29 September 2002, the assessment took a turn for the worse. The focus was on Commerzbank and HVB (Hypo-Vereinsbank) as they were missing:

- the (relative) financial strength of Deutsche Bank (forecast earnings per share for the next year of €1.61 compared with −€0.04 and −€0.34 for Commerzbank and HVB respectively);
- Dresdner's backing by a large insurance company (Allianz); and
- state guarantees for Landesbanken as well as saving banks.

Further falling equity markets and outlook downgrading with implications on the value of participations and higher funding cost seemed to be the main forces behind the change in attitude.

The days to come brought a series of news, opinions and rumours with reference to Commerzbank, putting it into the glare of publicity.

1 October 2002 *Die Welt*. The article states, 'uncertain times being a fertile soil for rumours'. It continues: 'That must have been the thought of market participants who attributed liquidity problems to Commerzbank'. And concludes: 'They might have reached their goal since the share price responded negatively to the rumours.' (Referring to an article in the *Guardian* a few days before.) Translated by the author.

1 October 2002 *Financial Times*: 'Commerzbank raises risk provision again': from originally €1.0 bn, €1.1 bn in July to €1.3 bn.

2 October 2002 *Handelsblatt*:

Rumours in London do not exclude potential capital problems for Commerzbank. As a result, secondary market funding spreads for CB increased by 60 bp (basis points or 0.6%) to 110 bp; other German banks were affected by an increase between 10 and 20 bp.

5 October 2002 Weekend edition of the *Financial Times*, The Lex Column:

> Havoc on bank share prices this week: They dropped this week: Deutsche Bank 15%; Commerzbank 20%; BNP Paribas 22%; and Credit Suisse 29%. Credit default swaps for Deutsche relatively modest 50–60 bp, Credit Suisse ones ballooned to about 150 bp and Commerzbank ones to above 200 bp.
>
> Commerzbank faces no immediate liquidity problem. It has been over-funding itself.... But the capital base is weak.

5 October 2002 Weekend edition of the *Financial Times*, 'Merrill e-mail casts doubt on strength of Commerzbank':

> A damaging seven-line e-mail from Merrill Lynch to Standard Poor's yesterday stoked fears of financial difficulties at Commerzbank. The e-mail text according to FT:
>
> *Subject: Rumours of large Trading losses at Commerzbank*
>
> *Importance: High*
>
> *Gentleman, again the market is flooded with rumours that Commerzbank, amongst all its other problems, has sustained large trading losses in Credit derivatives.*
>
> *Apparently a number of banks have begun to shut down credit lines.*

Merrill Lynch asked for comments 'as to the validity of this and the likely impact to the bank's health'.

It seems that details of the e-mail, in mysterious ways (the author's view), filtered through the London and Frankfurt markets, bringing the share price down by about an additional 6%.

8 October 2002 *Financial Times*, 'Bad loans fears hit European bank shares':

> Commerzbank's stock fell to a 10-year low (€5.70), 'despite (the bank) denying that it faces a liquidity crisis'.
>
> At a London conference hosted by Merrill Lynch, 'Market anxiety was exacerbated by Douglas Flint, HSBC's finance director, who said: 'We do worry about systemic risk.'

8 October 2002 Standard & Poor's reduced the long-term rating from A negative to A- negative outlook, and the short-term one was lowered from A1 to A2 (within nine days 11 negative changes in rating or outlook were announced by agencies for US and European banks).

According to the *Financial Times* of 9 October 2002, 'the international rating agency insisted its action did not relate to recent markets' concern about the bank's capital ratios or liquidity, which it said to be unfounded'.

9 October 2002 In a press release, the BaFin (the German supervisor) states (excerpt translated by the author):

> The BaFin routinely examines the earnings and risk situation of German banks. Equal to their international competitors they are suffering from a fall in share prices. 'However, there is no reason to assume the respective banks might fail to meet international capital adequacy requirements by the end of the year. The current exaggeration in the markets, in particular the prevailing doubt about the liquidity of German institutes, is entirely beyond my comprehension', echoed by K.B. Caspari, the Vice President of BaFin.

11 October 2002 *Sueddeutsche Zeitung*, 'Anxiety about liquidity shortage at Commerzbank fades away' (author's translation of excerpt):

> The article states that explanations as to the liquidity standing of the bank by the CEO (Klaus-Peter Mueller) have calmed markets and analysts starting to express cautiously optimistic views about the liquidity status of the bank.

14 October 2002 Merrill Lynch report on German banks states as first point in the highlights:

> Recent market fears of liquidity problems at German banks have been very much overdone, in our view. Our own concern remains focused on the weak profitability outlook for the German banking industry.

Now 11 October was not the end of the liquidity threat, but at least, adapting a phrase from Winston Churchill, the end of the beginning and (hopefully) the beginning of the end. A trusting perception as to liquidity was not re-established; this process takes much longer, and the emerging fragile positive attitude needed to be nursed. At that time, nerves were fraught across the whole industry. One wrong move and the Hydra would rear its heads again.

Having painted the overall picture of the market mood at the time, we will now enter into detailed aspects of handling the crisis. Furthermore, we will continue with the segregation into policy considerations, technical handling and behavioural attitudes. For a better understanding of the issues, we find it more appropriate than to present the issues in sequential form dealing with the subjects across the full range.

We start with general preparations according to the contingency planning and policy decisions for handling liquidity in the period after the bursting of the 'dot-com' bubble up to the name-related stress. For the latter we take the end of September 2002 as the starting point.

The dominant use of English newspapers and analyses has much to do with the language as well as the penetration and thus the impact on forming perception across borders.

7.4.2   Preparations within the contingency plan

As stated in the previous case, working with a contingency plan based on the concept of the liquidity balance sheet had been mostly well developed. Admittedly, not to the extent explained in the previous chapters, but nevertheless the principles were established and applied. Risk control provided basic but independent information on flows, permitting us to establish the buffer for securing payments under 'normal' conditions. On the other hand, measuring the effects under stressed conditions was a hurdle still to be overcome. Based on the understanding that the duty of risk management is not dependent on the progress made in developing systems and methods but a task to be performed in any circumstances, stress scenarios were defined and their most likely effects calculated directly by liquidity management. The feasibility of assumptions was checked with risk control, yet the outcome was fully within our responsibility. Not having access to sophisticated data gathering and modelling, we depended on departmental and balance-sheet information. Retrospectively, taking a conservative stance in the assessment of each key item turned out to be astonishingly close to the reality shortly to be faced – not in each single item, but in total. Preparation for stress scenarios and measures to be taken were reviewed on a quarterly basis and presented ultimately to the board of directors for assessment and approval. One copy was locked in the safe, ready to be used as the principal guideline in case of necessity (not unlike the aide-memoire of our military commander.). Limits and guidelines to be observed were handed over to the head of liquidity management and the adherence supervised.

The particular composition of the bank's business and structure at that time showed a name-related stress to be the most severe form of any stress and, except for some minor deviations, covering all other stress-related effects. Against this background we decided to work with a 'virtual' case, encompassing the effects from all scenarios. The key elements can be summarised as follows:

- Not all of present business activities were declared as 'core'. While closing of basic business segments was not considered as a viable strategy under stress, reducing the level in specific sectors and regions was accepted and quantified.
- The 'buying time' period was set at 1 year.
- As a result, what we now call 'core' business, irrespective of maturity, and assets with a maturity of longer than 1 year, was financed with 'stable' funds.
- Measures were taken to have funding diversified. Borrowing in regions where the bank was not actively present and using non-related funding vehicles were kept at extremely low levels.
- Dedicated teams were in place to serve non-bank customers personally, in order to establish a relationship.
- Buffers were kept in the region of €30 bn combined. Out of the total, between €20 and €25 bn were kept in instruments 'eligible' with central banks, of which the bigger part was already in our account with them. The 'non-eligible' difference consisted of high-quality assets, easily convertible into cash.

In the aftermath of the 'dot-com' bubble bursting, times became more difficult. Despite equity markets being relatively stable in the first half of 2002, the financial climate started to become overcast. Indications arose from volatility in the capital market spreads for the corporate sector (Figure 7.5).

We neither foresaw nor expected the volatility that the banking industry was going to face, Commerzbank in particular. The period did entail an element of uncertainty but this did not qualify as stress in the sense of liquidity, although we were on alert. In our understanding of risk potential and risk capacity in the business and not the regulatory sense, a bank can carry a certain burden of uncertainty which differs from institution to institution. There is no accepted method to calculate it that the author knows of. Yet, we know that risk potential is composed of downside and liquidity risk. If one side of the equation increases, the other side is reduced if it is intended to keep the previous level. Consequently, we decided to keep liquidity risk low and forgo an easier stance within the band we had allowed ourselves in principle. Replenishing deviations from a conservatively defined goal with respect to liquidity status was thus executed without delay. That we did it at a still reasonable spread level turned out to be a benefit in cost, but it was the principle that was at the forefront of our thinking because we did not know about the market developments about to come. This was the status before the stress, in about September 2002.

7.4.3   Policy considerations

The stress hitting Commerzbank can be precisely dated as 5 October 2002.

The economic as well as the market environment had been clouded for some time. Share prices of banks had suffered markedly already and rating agencies had reduced and indicated to reduce further many a bank's health label. These were difficult times for everyone in the industry, but for a long time nobody was singled out. Direct pressure on Commerzbank started to mount in late September when rumours about liquidity problems circulated and continued to do so despite firm and repeated denials, culminating in an extremely sharp response by market participants following the article in the *Financial Times* and the e-mail it referred to.

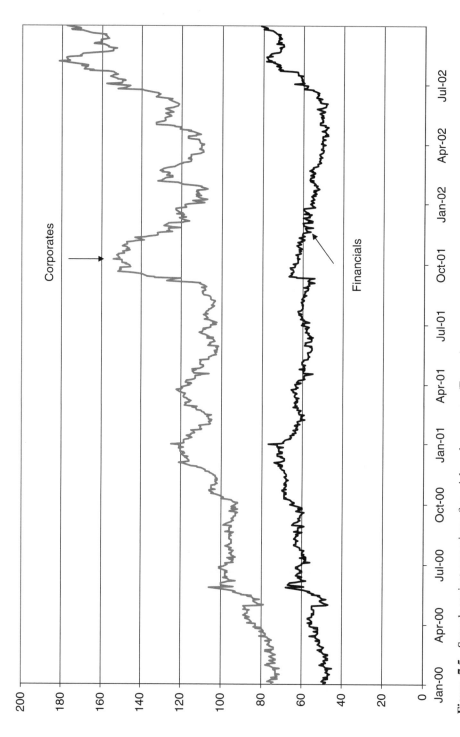

Figure 7.5 Spreads against sovereigns: financials and corporates (Europe)

(*Source*: JPMorgan Credit Index Europe)

All of a sudden, which means within hours, the large continuous stream of funds normally available became congested and arrived at our balance sheet as a meagre stream. The funding crisis had become effective, and it turned out to relate to us specifically.

In a name-related stress the institution affected should not be taken by surprise. One element of the contingency plan is to get to a level of 'alert' when circumstances exceed certain risk levels. And this level was exceeded in about late September.

7.4.3.1 Analysis

Having analysed continuously the comments from analysts and newspapers, we recognised the heightened risk of a stress, especially if we should be subject to a downgrading by one of the rating agencies. The new and lower rating assigned by Standard & Poor's on 8 October simply confirmed the existing anxiety in the markets and seemingly proved right the steps already taken 3 days before. Being on the receiving end, we soon concluded that a proactive stance was the best remedy to counteract the attack.

The main concerns of the market and further participating groups can be summarised as follows:

- Very low earnings at that time.
- Detrimental effects on our shareholdings due to falling equity markets.
- Relatively low regulatory capital ratios compared with many peers, although well above the required minimum.
- The bank being faced with a serious liquidity problem. Whether it was seen as a problem in itself or derived from anxiety about the bank's solvency was not clear.
- A potential downgrading of Commerzbank (we were on the watch list) would increase spreads to be paid by us well above the already high levels applicable for the whole market, with the effect of burden our earning outlook even further.

With the benefit of inside knowledge we were in a position to distinguish between false rumours and facts: solvency was not in peril, neither did we envisage a crisis in liquidity, quite the contrary. Our core business was solidly financed and buffers were replenished to withstand a severe stress – not for ever, but at least for some time without severely reducing 'assets at risk', and for 1 year if the latter were given up in total. The question was whether we could transmit the message to the markets and be believed. As various former vigorous attempts had failed to produce a positive impact, management decided to keep up the effort but not to base strategy on succeeding in this respect.

We adopted an old Chinese proverb: an intelligent banker accepts that some occurrences can be changed while others cannot; however, it takes a wise banker to know which of them can be changed. We at least tried to act sensibly and address the crisis in its entirety, which for us meant:

- At least addressing the key concerns of the markets, i.e. solvency, earnings and securing liquidity for a very prolonged market crisis, including further worsening of general market conditions and an additional, non-name-related stress.
- Tackling issues which can be changed quickly, visibly, immediately and vigorously.
- Analysing interdependences of issues to arrive at a coherent approach.
- Not falling into the trap of short-term activism but continuing to follow the bank's strategic goals.
- Assuring transparency and communication with all relevant internal and external groups.

The task of developing a concept along these lines was given to a small group, consisting of the departmental heads for Group Planning and Strategic Controlling, Finance and Group Treasury. The proposal was presented to the full board and contained the following key elements:

- Regulatory capital ratios: Although being well above minimum requirements (around 6% compared with 4% required) and with no danger of falling well below, we need to increase them in order to put markets at ease. This can be achieved rapidly and it is visible. As we do not know what the future will bring, we have to be prepared to reduce risk weighted assets (RWAs) by about €23 bn by the end of 2003, with intermediary goals as per year end 2002 and per middle and end 2003.
- Liquidity-related measures: Liquidity is secured for 'core' business. Reducing RWAs has to be accommodated by 'assets at risk'. In order to assure planned effects on generating liquidity to pay back liabilities in case of a long-lasting funding squeeze, we have to be prepared to reduce funding requirements by €47 bn by the end of 2003, with intermediary goals set in the same sequence as for RWAs.
- Net earnings: Reducing RWAs inevitably is accompanied by falling earnings. They need to be counter-balanced by cost reductions. Further steps are to be taken to improve the present and unsatisfactory levels of net earnings.

The proposal was accepted by the board on 15 October with the proviso that details being finalised at a special meeting with all heads of regions and business units be brought to the board for review and decision. The respective meeting took place on 29 October at Head Office in Frankfurt.

7.4.3.2   *Tactical response*

The normal sequence lists strategic before tactical issues. Under duress some tactical decisions should get priority, however. Firstly, the bank is to be moved from a mode of 'normal business' to 'stress'. Secondly, tactical measures can be implemented faster; strategic issues take longer until they become visible and the process of decision making is more complex. However, both of them need to be embedded in the general direction derived from the analysis.

The issues to be tackled can be segregated into two basic groups: technical and behavioural elements. We will not expand on all details but emphasise the vital points related to our experience. Not all of them belong to the hard-core items and distinctions between 'shock' and 'chronic' stresses will become quite obvious.

Technical issues

- Keep the technical and organisational infrastructure basically unchanged. They are tested and have reached a level of routine in the understanding defined in the contingency plan.
- Integrate the head of communications into the team. The function needs first-hand information to do the job successfully for internal and external addressees. Over and above this, however, the head knows best how messages will be received and which channels and levels to use for specific purposes.
- Set up a detailed plan concerning the reduction in RWAs and funding needs for all operating units per sector and location. The supervisory body controls adherence to instructions; the escalation process in case of deviation from the goals as well as the body granting exceptions

has to be reconfirmed and communicated. This is already laid down in the contingency plan, but will not be common knowledge to all managers in a large group. Furthermore, it sends a message to take the decision seriously.

- Adjust all effected limits. Individual employees take them as authority to do business. In addition, it is an effective controlling mechanism as any violation shows up in the excess reports.
- Shorten the intervals of reporting and add new reports as and when required. They have been catered for in the contingency plan.
- Define for Group Treasury the line of defence. In our case Group Treasury was to use a portion of its liquidity buffer to ease pressure on 'assets at risk' with good margins, but was required to hold a minimum enabling the group to withstand any further stress and secure orderly payment execution (the balance of daily in- and outflows can be volatile and substantial). The hard-core reserves are to be kept in instruments 'eligible' with central banks.
- Watch closely the funding capability of conduits and other units financing themselves independently, but rely on Group Treasury as the internal lender of last resort. In our case, one conduit could keep its funding capacity while the other one had to be wound up in an orderly fashion.

Behavioural elements

- Do not panic but take a considered and firm stance and act accordingly. Indecisive behaviour will be taken as an indication that reality is worse than what official data show.
- Do not be influenced by external forces but act in a proactive manner. We need to believe in the facts and analyses available to us and not in rumours and 'what if' scenarios.
- Group Treasury is to take ways and means to demonstrate to the markets that Commerzbank is liquid and will stay liquid. Due to rumours, market perception fell far short of reality and market behaviour did not return to normal even after the statement by BaFin (9 October) and the assessment of Merrill Lynch (14 October). It took till the early part of the following year until we were in a position to receive interbank funds up to 3 months, but with hardly any inflows with maturities beyond.
- Communicate within the defined guidelines.

As stated at the beginning, we limited ourselves to what we believed to be the key issues in the stress experienced. One should not take it as a 'fix for all' agenda. Stresses and banks experiencing them do differ, and so should the response seen as appropriate.

7.4.3.3 Strategic response

Not all types of stresses require strategic responses. A name-related one does, however. The perception of the markets has to be turned. Even without taking all of the above actions, we would have overcome the mistrust concerning solvency and liquidity (both Tier 1 and Tier 2 were about 2 percentage points above legal requirements and fulfilling payment obligations was never in peril). On 14 October, Merrill Lynch stated in its report: 'Recent market fears of liquidity problems at German banks have been very much overdone, in our view.' Thus, we could have concentrated exclusively on net earnings. Improving this item on a solid basis is a longer-term process in general, and in the economic conditions prevailing at that time in particular. Under these conditions markets would be on alert until financial success was visible and viewed as sound. Management assessed as too high the risk of being at the mercy of any future rumours the market might come up with and believe in, however unfounded they may be. Commerzbank at that time was in the process of implementing its newly defined strategy, named 'CB 21', under the leadership of the new CEO, K.-P. Müller, who was elected the year before. Three measures were deemed necessary to keep the strategic initiative in hand.

Aiming for a larger buffer in regulatory capital   Although solvency was never in peril and regulatory ratios were well above the minimum required, management accepted that markets viewed things differently.

RWAs were the leverage to achieve the aim. Figure 7.6 gives an overview with respect to the development of both the core and total capital ratios according to BIS rules. There are two interesting findings we will have a closer look at: capital ratios do respond fast. We indicated this before, but actual developments confirmed it. More revealing is the second observation: in October when all types of downside scenarios circulated, starting with a base of 5.9% for Tier 1 capital, Commerzbank actually had already moved up and ended September closer to 6%, in line with the strategy formulated in 'CB 21'.

Great care was taken not to end up killing the endeavour. Reducing RWAs improves capital ratios but at the same time it depresses earnings, assuming everything else stays equal. Turning the screw on RWAs to improve capital ratios has therefore to be performed with perceptiveness, otherwise it could end up replacing one evil with another. In our case management targeted a specific level within a band. Any forecast level above was taken as freedom to grant exceptional increases in strategic and profitable businesses.

Cutting cost   Reducing cost was one of the key items of 'CB 21' and was already somewhat advanced in implementation. Reducing RWAs did not alter the concept but had implications on the speed and areas affected. Conclusions had to be drawn on whether activities should be reduced only temporarily or for good. The review extended over the whole bank. The strategic business concept served as a yardstick.

Straightening the balance sheet   The severe downturn in equity prices, especially in the second half of 2002, had left its mark on the balance sheet. Several shareholdings in participations fell below book level and did not fully recover by about mid-2003. Although the portfolio would have fully recovered accepting a longer period, management preferred to clean up the balance sheet. With value at September 2003 all assets of the balance sheet were valued at prevailing market rates and adjustments amounting to €2.3 bn were taken against the profit and loss account. In order not to jeopardise capital ratios, a share issue producing €760 million of new capital was launched. It was well received and oversubscribed four times. The measure was an important step towards greater strategic flexibility for the bank, in the form of either in-house expansion or acquisition.

7.4.4   Technical handling

Technical in our present context is not restricted to technique but refers to a wide range of activities and considerations within the management of liquidity. As such it is the continuation of strategy/policy which determines the frame within which to act.

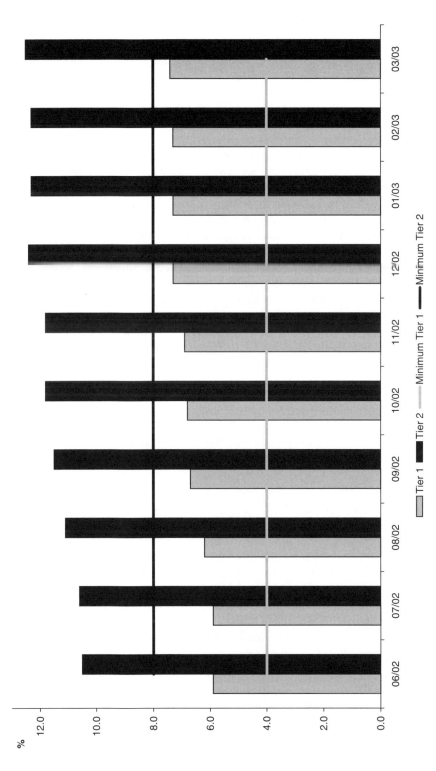

Figure 7.6 BIS regulatory capital ratios: actual against minimum

(Reproduced by permission of Commerzbank AG)

7.4.4.1 Dealing with imminent issues

Being faced with a 'shock' liquidity stress requires responding fast as time is at a premium. Most likely it will be over within a few days at most and the bank either can keep on fulfilling its obligations or has failed; it is the first 24 hours which are most critical. Cash in this case has to be ready and in hand; using markets to create it instantly is of no avail since cash in the account is not a phone call away, due to the timespan between trade and payment day. On the other hand, a shock-type stress is very much a focused event and encompasses very few groups in the bank.

A name-related stress is extremely public, in contrast. Your partners on the liability side of the balance sheet see their risk shooting sky high and wish to secure their exposure with you; anxious borrowers need to know whether the signed loan agreement and overdraft facilities are still valid and can be upheld by the bank; supervisors in charge of head office and operations all over the world want to be briefed on the liquidity status; the media wish to get first-hand information, just to mention the most likely groups addressing the bank after the news has broken. All channels to the bank are used to get the information required: members of the board, heads of operating units, the communication department, relationship managers, dealers, down to your own staff. In the end all information centres on the treasurer, whether given or taken. To deal with all requests and secure the liquidity of the bank in parallel, sound preparation is paramount. The considerations and decisions dealt with in the section covering contingency planning have to completed beforehand, written down and understood by managers and staff directly involved in a name-related liquidity crisis. Whatever is not done is missed, as there is no time to make it up, at least not in the first 24 hours or so, the most dangerous phase.

This is not the time for elaborate and long meetings. Yet the 'stress' team has to meet, analyse, consider and decide on the immediate steps to be taken, give orders to people responsible for specific subjects, decide on delegated authority, fix the next meeting and establish the information flow about progress made and special events.

In our case, the first day was spent primarily dealing with departmental matters. Changing the mode from normal business to 'stress' brought about three issues which had to be decided on immediately.

The use of reserves   We kept two kinds of reserves with the following characteristics: securing payment obligations and 'eligible' with central banks; protecting the franchise and either 'eligible' with central banks or for use in markets.

As we kept sufficient collateral at the central banks there was no need to replenish them at this time. Expected balances for the next few days were assessed and the needed collateral was allocated to the respective central banks in good time, i.e. in advance. At that point we did not rely on 'non-eligible' instruments to create cash. We assessed the market as being too nervous and taking a normal daily business action as confirmation of a very severe liquidity problem. At a later date and in less highly strung markets, we reversed the priority in order to safeguard the most liquid assets in our hands.

The attitude towards the markets   The funding capacity dropped immediately and sharply. If maturing liabilities were renewed at all the amount was definitely smaller and very short term; that is to say, a big share of it was overnight money. The question was how to behave in these circumstances: should all possible ways and means be applied to get as much as possible?

For staff in contact with financial institutions our considerations went along the following line. Immediate cash was not the problem, and cash was also secured for the period of 'buying time'. However, in order to reduce the burden on 'assets at risk' we had to stimulate confidence in the markets. 'Confidence building' in fact was a pillar of the market-related strategy. It was decided upon and communicated to all units with the following behavioural guidelines:

- Quote our standard spreads.
- If declined, do not improve to get it.
- If you get funds but do believe the amount or maturity is too small and short, do not ask for improvement.
- If a deal is struck, behave as in the months before (and do not go for the equivalent of a 'mental bow').
- If asked about our liquidity 'problem', tell the truth: we have no liquidity shortage.

Dealing with relationship customers   For both retail and corporate customers the bank had dedicated relationship officers in place. Then we decided on a proactive stance by contacting the major ones directly. On our side we employed all available channels from board members down to relationship officers and customer traders. Our core customer base was contacted at all levels, large customers at multiple levels. The message was unison: the business continues on its normal course and all commitments will be honoured; we are not facing any liquidity crisis at all.

Informing central banks   Central banks were immediately contacted at board level or by the regional managers in or responsible for the respective region, after they had been briefed. The treasurer who had visited them periodically in the past, briefing them about the concept, the status of liquidity and the head office function as internal lender of last resort, was not involved in the very early stage, except for the BaFin/Bundesbank with which the contact was ongoing. Foreign supervisors were briefed personally and in detail as soon as possible. One observation is specifically worth mentioning. Two supervisors of smaller foreign operations of ours demanded a report and documentation with respect to liquidity flows between the unit and head office. Their concern centred on head office using liquidity from the foreign operations to their detriment. As we could prove this was not the case, they were satisfied (Figure 7.7).

Further immediate issues   Further issues concerned adjusting the limits to secure acting within the new frame; changing the reporting intervals and ordering additional reports in line with the rules set down in the Contingency plan; and cancelling the authority of regional centres to act within the previously granted band, just to mention the key decision. The last issue served as a precaution against an uncoordinated approach towards the market. In fact, acting only with permission became the rule rather than the exception in the first week or so.

Building up trust   Other related issues had to be dealt with differently and not on the first day. A few corporate and bank CROs decided immediately to cut the lines fully. Some corporates made use of their borrowing lines; at least one corporate treasurer drew the full amount available under the committed line, although he already had a perfect hedge in his overall position with us. Corporates were dealt with by board members and high-ranking relationship managers. The CEO contacted his banking colleagues and we used our contacts

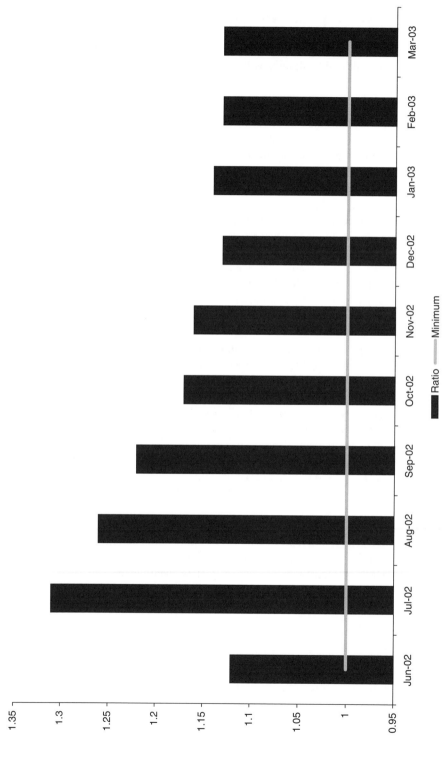

Figure 7.7 Fulfilling German liquidity requirements (Principle II, required minimum 1.0) (Reproduced by permission of Commerzbank AG)

at the treasurer level. Having previously established a network of professional friends turned out to be extremely helpful. In our case the contacts derived from our membership of the Treasury Management Committee of the Bundesverband Deutscher Banken (Association of German Banks) on a German level, and from the European Bank Treasurer Group (EBTG) on a European level. The latter was particularly important as contacts were not as intense as with German colleagues. Based on the principle of open discussions at the semi-annual meetings, concerning treasury matters we knew more about each other than any analyst ever deemed. The communication was built on the following structure: you know the rumour; it is unfounded as I have reserves in excess of €30 bn, most of them in central bank 'eligible' instruments; I cannot certify it, but trust me. And they did. These phone calls have become the author's most treasured events in his whole professional life. The lines stayed open in Frankfurt as well as at EBTG banks, and where necessary, the contacts managed to convince their CRO and their management to open the lines again. True, the amount was cut and the period granted shortened, but the lines were established again, although some of the banks had to accept buying back Commerzbank-issued papers from their customers and taking them on their books. Convincing other banks to continue business, although on a much lower level, was not a question of 'going or gone concern', it was part of the approach to inspire confidence in the markets.

7.4.4.2   Addressing and implementing policy decisions

Assessing and deciding on policy issues and in particular their implementation on a group level take time. Therefore, as far as the treasury is concerned, they are not the first priority but still important. The treasury was entrusted with three major tasks, apart from being on standby for presentations to key customers on request.

Establishing a detailed plan for reduction in RWAs and liquidity utilisation   On 15 October the board decided on the reduction for RWAs and liquidity utilisation. The same team (Heads of Group Planning and Strategic Controlling, Finance and Group Treasury) was entrusted to agree the details for each business segment and foreign unit at a meeting with the respective heads and regional managers, called for 29 October in Frankfurt. We invited them for 2 days.

None of them had ever experienced a stress like the one we were in. The team decided that a meeting without proper information beforehand would most probably start with a long debate. The meeting was not a cold call, as all of them had been informed continuously. Nevertheless, detailed consequences were not available to each of them, following the board's decision. Consequently, we composed a letter of several pages in which background information, considerations and conclusions were expounded and sent it in good time to allow for internal discussions with their experts. As strategic guidelines had been given and the information letter pre-empted any long debate, the meeting was concluded after 1 day.

To remain in line with the strategic business concept, the brunt had to be taken by the units abroad when measured in relative terms; Asia especially was reduced significantly. For investment banking, the formerly and provisionally granted excess over and above core business was cancelled, and the treasury was to invest part of its reserves into the present stress but ordered to keep sufficient means to be in a position to counteract a potential further stress.

Since the agreed outcome could be kept within the guidelines and was judged sensible, the board agreed on it on 13 November. All affected limits were adjusted and supervision of adherence and possible adjustments were delegated to the functions in charge within the organisational setup in the bank. The task was therefore relieved of its 'stress' status and dealt with as a normal business item for most of 2003.

Checking behavioural attitudes of lenders   As concluded previously, banks have great control over most parts of the asset side, but when it comes to the liability side, they are very much at the mercy of lenders and investors. The latter's behaviour under stressed conditions is simulated and forms a decisive part of the contingency plan. It was, however, paramount for us to compare expected and actual behaviour as the steps taken were very much founded on the expected behaviour side.

Regarding the groups we labelled as 'volatile' in their behaviour, although to different degrees, we had no illusions at all, and we were right:

• Institutions with a rating-triggered behaviour ceased lending after the last downgrading, as expected.
• Funding from rating-related markets like the one for US CPs dried up, as expected.
• Funding from areas where we did not have an operating unit dried up as well and as expected, yet the amounts were negligible, as had been our focus on them.
• Banks with whom we had no established personal relationship through head office or the local unit responded sharply, as foreseen.
• Corporates abroad responded in a relatively modest way, less than expected. Most probably, keeping a source for their own funding requirements and being hedged by larger borrowing are explanations for their behaviour.
• Banks with which we had close personal relationships and communications reduced the amount and even the length of maturity, but less than we expected.

A vital but open question related to our German customer base; we assessed its response as relatively moderate: −10% for retail (Figure 7.8), in line with the supervisor; and −20% for corporates (Figure 7.9).

Both retail and corporate funds kept up very well, even exceeding our expectations. Partly, this may be attributable to the deposit insurance fund, at least for retail deposits, as in the case of Germany the former is covered rather generously compared with other countries. It is not inconceivable to link the astonishing stability in corporate funds to a combination of being hedged vis-à-vis the bank through borrowing and slightly improved spreads (2–3 basis points as from October). On the other hand, according to Matz (2002, page 140), several banks in the past had experienced a run involving even federally insured depositors. Thus, we like to believe that our attempts to approach our customers actively and keep them informed were not fruitless and might have added to the stability.

Demonstrate being liquid!   Here again, fostering confidence in the markets was the prime goal. In an environment of perceived high risk, statements made by the banking supervisor do help, yet the institution in question should not contradict them by insensitive behaviour but rather take steps which confirm the declaration. Based on this belief, we acted immediately. Excess cash was available but often invested in secondary market papers with an extremely short tenor till maturity. Although invested in international banks, the latter were not aware of it due to the anonymous character of the investments. The point was to make them visible. As a consequence, we sold them or did not prolong the investment at maturity and placed the cash as an interbank deposit with particular banks. Picking the names was done on a combination of

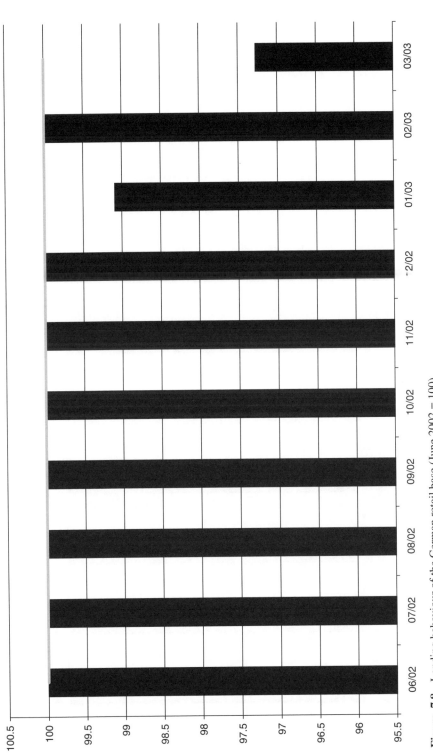

Figure 7.8 Lending behaviour of the German retail base (June 2002 = 100)
(Reproduced by permission of Commerzbank AG)

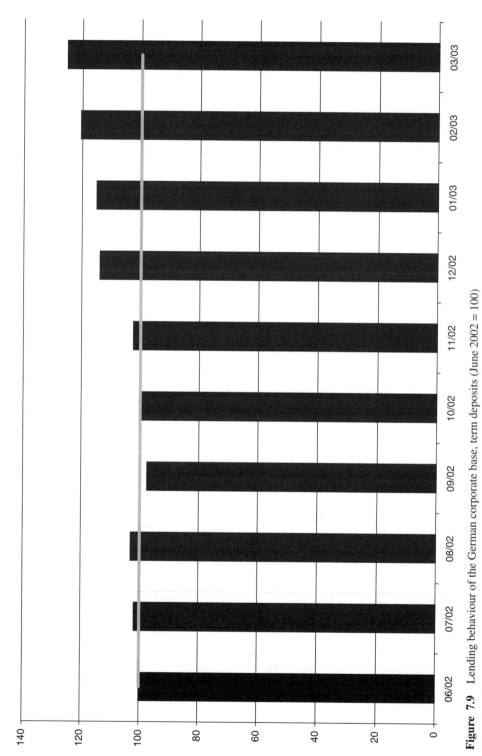

Figure 7.9 Lending behaviour of the German corporate base, term deposits (June 2002 = 100) (Reproduced by permission of Commerzbank AG)

three criteria: Did they still fund us? Do we achieve a geographical diversification? Can they serve as multipliers of our attempt to demonstrate being liquid? We started with about €1 bn and increased the amount gradually to an excess of €3 bn. And word got around.

7.4.4.3 Keeping the line of defence

It would be misleading to believe that an existing stress could not coincide with a second one, both of them being totally separate occurrences: if 9/11 had happened 1 year later, Commerzbank would have been dealing with two stresses at the same time. On the other hand, if the worst scenario is happening one needs to employ reserves kept for this event. Taking both arguments into consideration, we arrived at the following conclusion: a minimum, for covering daily negative balances with the clearers and providing the means to withstand a further potential but less severe stress, needed to be kept as a line of defence. In our case it amounted to about €20 bn. The remaining share was to be employed to reduce pressure on 'assets at risk'. On a sequential basis, for each period under consideration the net outflow was calculated, made up of maturing liabilities and adjusted for most likely prolongations. The result was compared with the expected liquidity inflow according to the programme decided by the board. A negative difference was to be financed by treasury reserves. The overall plan assumed that over the full period treasury reserves would not fall below the line of defence, which turned out to be correct. Had they fallen below the threshold according to the sequential forecast, the decline in 'assets at risk' would have been speeded up. Actually, over time our performance in prolongations exceeded the assumptions. The excess in liquidity was employed to foster profitable business, which was not necessarily in the section 'assets at risk'.

7.4.5 Behavioural attitudes

In this section we will not repeat subjects dealt with before but limit ourselves to some additional items believed to be important for a comprehensive understanding.

7.4.5.1 Nursing relationships

Immediate actions relating to the subject have been described above. We will limit ourselves to rounding it up and adding conclusions drawn from the experience. Information, whether internal or external, has been a constant feature throughout the whole process. Back in April 2002, the CEO addressed shareholders directly, and staff of the bank indirectly, by copying them in. The key elements of the strategy formulated in 'CB 21' were presented and their meaning and consequences explained. KPM (Klaus-Peter Müller), as he is called affectionately by staff and management, engaged in a tireless manner to motivate internally and to put the status of the bank straight externally. Good communication does not make the problem disappear, but is of great help within the frame of a diligent preparation and sensible execution. The level of communication was kept up throughout the stress; in its worse days, KPM was omnipresent, both internally and externally.

Although customer deposits were kept stable during the culmination of the stress and even increased later on, we decided to improve on this. In March 2003 the board agreed to strengthen the segment further. As a result, regional board members added fostering funding from the customer base to their agenda applicable for corporate visits; the private client department since then has been formulating specific funding goals in the budgeting process. Coordinating goals and assessing progress is performed by the treasury. The subject has become a standing quarterly item on the agenda of the central ALCO.

7.4.5.2 *Commerzbank is liquid! The message to the capital market . . .*

During the very early stage of the stress, measures were taken with a view to demonstrate to the markets our true liquidity condition by way of placing deposits with selected banks. While we were able to muffle their most extreme reservations, reserved they remained; quoted spreads for our (unsecured) Senior Debts remained stubbornly high in the capital markets. Quotations had already come down somewhat from peaks between 180 and 200 basis points and were hovering at about 140. A deeper analysis revealed the market to be somewhat in a deadlock.

When the rumours about liquidity problems at Commerzbank started, and in the days to come, market makers quoted sufficiently defensively to avoid having to take Commerzbank debts onto the books. There was no reason for any of them to change their attitude, although lower spreads were needed later on to avoid 'being given'. Within our endeavours to foster confidence in us, the picture of Commerzbank in the capital markets was not acceptable. Thus, we had to take the initiative if we wanted to break the deadlock.

We tested the market and offered to buy back Senior Debts at 130, with no limitation on quantity. (Internally, we had put aside a 'buy-back fund' to the tune of €1 bn.) The market was astonished but hardly took up the offer, while according to market logic our spreads were lowered to 130. The next day we offered 120. Again, the market hardly took up the offer; nevertheless, our debts quoted 120. We continued the process for many days.

What was the logic behind our attempt on the one hand and the investors' response on the other hand? We tried to understand the position of investors with Commerzbank debts in their portfolio. The market price was below purchasing price and the investors were sitting on an unrealised loss. In their risk assessment they must have concluded it to be worthwhile to keep our debts in their portfolio, otherwise they would have sold them already. Yet there had been only negligible turnover in our debts. If we offered a better price, the investors had two options: either they were relieved at being in a position to sell the paper at a reduced loss or their confidence was improved further to hold onto Commerzbank debts in their portfolio, with the aim of redeeming them at issue price on maturity at the latest. We assessed the second option as close to reality, especially against the background of some cautiously positive remarks concerning our liquidity status. Our assessment turned out to be correct.

We continued the process till we reached a spread level of 80 basis points, a mark which we assessed as 'fair' given our rating and compared with our peers. At the end of the action less than half of the 'buy-back fund' needed to be employed to reduce the spread by 60 basis points. Both parties benefited: the investors could confidently hold onto the debts and saw the unrealised loss disappear over time; and Commerzbank had surmounted one highly visible obstacle potentially counteracting the endeavour to foster trust in the markets. Several months later we had replaced all Senior Debts in the market again.

7.4.5.3 *. . . and its limitation*

Spread conditions for Subordinated Debts and Participation Certificates (*Genussscheine*) were not dissimilar. They also were priced too high in our view. It was primarily the latter we had in focus. According to German capital rules, they do not qualify as 'eligible' as Tier 2 capital in the last 2 years before maturity. Buying back 'non-eligible' Participation Certificates could have had a smoothing effect on spreads in general, without affecting our capital ratio according to KWG (German Banking Law) and with moderate and relatively short-term implications on the BIS ratios.

By law, maintaining own issues in the balance sheet is permitted for the sake of market making but is restricted to 3% of the total outstandings. Our intention was to exceed the threshold in order to secure a long-lasting stabilising effect. The request for a temporary and restricted exemption was not granted at the time. This shows that ways and means to assure 'fair' price conditions are very much limited when products are linked to capital adequacy rules.

7.5   'SUBPRIME' CRISIS: A STRESS IN PROGRESS

The third example contrasts with the previous ones in two ways: the subprime crisis has undoubtedly produced shock waves that we have not experienced in the last 60 years or so, even shaking and endangering the fundamentals of financial stability. Furthermore, for many, even well-known names in the banking industry, the impacting forces were too stern a test for the level of protection built against shortages in liquidity. Had it not been for political intervention, some of the biggest banks in various countries would have failed, and in this way speed up the avalanche just started.

At the time of writing, the stress may have reached its climax; nevertheless, uncertainty about further developments and the final outcome prevails. Naming this section a 'case' would thus not be appropriate. A case study requires not only the event to be fully concluded, but the outcome and its implications to be factual and known as well. Equally important are independent in-depth analyses of the causes of bank failures. Both sets of requirements are not available at this time, and many a bank chairperson or CEO still reveals their lack of understanding of why they and their colleagues failed to detect all this – it may even be true and not an excuse.

Despite the shortcomings just mentioned, it would not be appropriate to suppress the most severe liquidity crisis in our lifetime so far. We will thus attempt to get a preliminary understanding of the nature of this crisis, based on available information, observations and experience related to market structures and the behavioural attitudes of market participants. What we will apply is our best assessment, with all the uncertainties built in, so we will not take it as the final analysis.

7.5.1   An attempt to reconstruct causes and processes leading to the global infection of a local problem

The subprime crisis is not the first blow to the banking industry causing severe losses and needing prolonged efforts to overcome. The observation includes the United States where about a quarter of a century ago the whole sector of Loan and Savings Associations had to be restructured at high cost and energy to the country and its industry. Nevertheless, it remained a national event. In sharp contrast, the problems in the subprime mortgage segment, although of US origin, could not be kept on a national level but infected wide areas of the global industry.

According to Gorton (2008), the reason for the 'internationalisation' of a local event is to be found in the specific structure of subprime mortgages, their securitisation and integration into wider-defined asset-backed portfolios, which allowed for global distribution and led to the creation of derivatives for hedging purposes. (His paper was prepared for the Federal Reserve Bank of Kansas City, Jackson Hole Conference, in August 2008.)

As in the previous two examples, we do not intend to expand on all relevant aspects but will restrict ourselves to those elements essential to our liquidity task.

7.5.1.1 The 'creative' structure of a new mortgage facility

Subprime mortgages were an instrument created with the intention of allowing poorer people access to mortgage financing, necessary to establish themselves as house owners. Under the terms applied for prime mortgages, the group to be addressed would not qualify as borrowers. The characteristics of a subprime status may include a relatively high probability of default; a debt service-to-income ratio of 50% or more; or repossession in the last 24 months. Under any of these terms prime mortgages are out of reach.

If lending to a clientele with such characteristics were to become feasible, other criteria than creditworthiness of the borrower had to be found. The best protection for the lender turned out to be the house. This time not as backup in case of worsening income conditions of the borrower, as in case of prime mortgages, but as the prime and sole health criterion. Two variables needed to be considered by the lenders: development of house prices and early repayment behaviour of the borrower in case of more attractive borrowing rates. (The US market for prime mortgages usually contains in its packages an embedded option to repay mortgage borrowings early without repayment fees.) In order not to be exposed for too long to the variables, two alterations to the general practice relating to prime mortgages were introduced. The typical long-term contract of up to 30 years was drastically shortened to a few years, in order to get in line with expected forecasting capabilities about the future development of house prices. To discourage early repayment, significantly higher prepayment penalties compared with prime mortgages had been built into the contracts. See Gorton (2008, page 12f.).

As a result, at comparatively short intervals mortgage contracts fall due and need replacement at the then prevailing market conditions, including the level or expected development of house prices. In case of a downturn in house prices, conditions might change in such a way that a large part of this customer segment will not be in a position to keep the house financed. Whatever problems the housing market and the economy might develop from such a fall in house prices, it would still be a national issue, however.

7.5.1.2 Transforming local mortgages into an international product

In line with our general approach, here again we will not enter into details but outline the structure and mechanism of the internationalisation process to the extent necessary for our purpose.

Subprime mortgages were not intended to be kept on the balance sheet by the original lenders. Based on the statistics from the Joint Economic Committee displayed by Gorton (2008, page 20), growth became too dynamic for single institutes. The amount of origination rose from $190 bn in 2001 to $600 bn 5 years later, meaning that its share of total mortgage origination rose from 8.6% to 20.1% in the same period. For a wider distribution of subprime mortgages, but still within the United States, individual house loans were packed into portfolios of subprime Residential Mortgage-Backed Securities (subprime RMBS). The securitised portion within the subprime mortgage issuance reached a level of 50.4% in 2001, increasing to 80.5% in 2006. Based on the enhancements and structures chosen, it was not uncommon to get a share of up to 85% of a specific issue AAA rated. Yet, according to Gorton (2008, page 34): 'They [securitised subprime RMBS] are not at all like standard securitisation transactions. In particular, the difference illustrates how the "option" on house prices implicitly embedded in the subprime mortgages has resulted in very house price-sensitive behaviour of the subprime RMBS.'

In a next step subprime RMBS found their way into CDOs (Collateralised Debt Obligations). A CDO is an SPV (Special Purpose Vehicle) collecting cash against which it holds a portfolio of fixed income assets. Cash is received through the issuance of tranches grouped into rating classes ranging from senior (AAA), through mezzanine (AA to BB), down to unrated. In our context, we will focus on ABS CDOs which consist of asset-backed securities (ABS), including RMBS and CMBS (Commercial Mortgage-Backed Securities). Higher-grade ABS CDOs tend to allocate better-rated subprime Mortgage Bonds while mezzanine ABS CDOs took a bigger share of BB tranches. CDOs are often managed within guidelines, which in the course of required reinvestments gives the manager some leeway when selecting the quality level. CDO managers became attracted to BBB tranches of subprime RMBS. Having difficulty in establishing their own market, spreads offered by the issuer had to widen. 'By 2005 spreads on subprime tranches appeared to be wider than other structured products with the same rating, creating an incentive to arbitrage the ratings between the ratings on the subprime and the CDO tranches', according to Gorton (2008, page 37). In its publication 'Mortgage and ABS CDO Losses' (13 December 2007), UBS indicates that out of a sample of 420 ABS CDOs, the share of the two lowest-rating groups had increased from 65% to 83% in the years 2003 to 2006.

For many years and into the turn of the millennium subprime risk was cash based. In the following years derivatives start to play a growing part of significance, leading in January 2006 to the launch of an index (ABX). In addition to the overall index with reference to 20 equally weighted RMBS bonds, sub-indexes were created including those for subprime bonds and segregated into different rating categories. Taken as such, derivatives can be used either to reduce or increase the cash exposure in a specific segment. Based on data given in Gorton (2008, page 42), the picture for BBB-rated subprime RMBS and exposures to them by mezzanine ABS CDOs presents itself as follows: while physical issuance of BBB-rated subprime RMBS increased from $12.3 to $15.7 bn in the period 2004–2006, the respective exposure to the category in mezzanine ABS CDOs issued in the same timespan had risen from $8.0 to $30.3 bn, suggesting 'that the demand for exposure to riskier tranches of subprime RMBS exceeded supply by a wide margin. The additional risk exposure was created synthetically.' In addition, as demand for investments in ABS CDOs was growing faster than the physical market, new types of CDOs were created: the 'synthetic CDO' consisting of an entirely synthetic portfolio; and the 'hybrid CDO' with a combination of cash and derivatives. Both of them will have contributed to the remarkable growth in the synthetic risk exposure.

7.5.1.3 Evaluating subprime mortgage risk in structured portfolios

As has been shown in condensed form above, subprime RMBS are taken into further portfolios until they end up as a tranche within a CDO bond. And an additional layer is added when a CDO owns other CDO tranches. If subprime mortgage risk is to be evaluated within a CDO bond, one has to pass through all the layers backwards and follow all the strings until the contents of the originating portfolios are detected and then assess whether house prices will rise, stay stable or fall, and by how much. If derivatives are integrated in the creation of CDO portfolios: 'It is literally not possible for a buyer of a CDO tranche . . . to determine, say, the extent of subprime exposure', concludes Gorton (2008, page 45). Thus the respective quality stamp of a rating agency was generally taken as the quality and risk yardstick. Yet rating agencies were faced with the same problems just mentioned and obviously believed in being able to make a true qualitative assessment. Recent events reveal this was a misconception.

7.5.2 The downturn of the US housing market and the infection of the global financial sector

As stated previously, it is not our intention to cover the subprime crisis in detail. Such a task cannot be performed while the event is still going on, neither is it required to deal with the aspect of liquidity. On the other hand, its severity has surpassed anything experienced within the economic and financial frames set up after the Second World War. It raises the question of the qualitative dimension, or to put it in another way: we will analyse if the segregation of stresses into 'shock' and 'chronic' still covers the whole range of occurrences, or whether we are experiencing something emerging which is outside our defined understanding of liquidity risk and cannot be managed with the concepts and instruments presented. The implications on liquidity policy in case of a positive verdict could be fundamental. It is for this reason that we are going to enlarge this section. We will start with a chronology of events, limited to those occurrences that enable us to get a picture of the origins and looking for thresholds which, once broken, triggered a further escalation of the crisis. Subsequently, we will investigate the most likely mechanisms transforming a severe local problem into a global crisis, bringing the financial system close to collapse. Finally, the implications on liquidity policy for banks are evaluated, with emphasis on the question of whether we have to redefine our understanding of liquidity risk for a banking institution.

7.5.2.1 *A selective chronology of events*

2006
December   Ownit Mortgage Solutions files for bankruptcy.
2007
March   Data show: In Q.4 2006 late or missing payments on mortgages rose to 4.95% and to 13.3% in subprime market.
      Subprime lender Accredited Home Lenders loses about 90% of value within 2 days.
April   Mortgage originator New Century Financial Corporation fails.
May   UBS closes its hedge fund Dillon Read Capital Management.
June   Moody's and S&P downgrade or put on review billions' worth of subprime RMBS as well as CDOs.
      News that Bear Stearns managed hedge funds engaged in subprime mortgages close to being shut.
July   Moody's reviews 184 mortgage-backed CDO tranches for downgrading. Other agencies follow.
      The NAHB index indicates new home sales fell 6.6% y-on-y in June.
      IKB of Germany warns of losses related to US subprime market.
      American Home Mortgage Investment Corp. announces its inability to fund lending obligations and files for bankruptcy within 1 week.
      Sowood Capital lost 57% on $3 bn in 1 month and announces closure.

August	Further losses at IKB require €3.5 bn rescue fund provided by state-owned KfW and group of public and private sector banks.
	Losses at 'quant' hedge funds due to massive deleveraging.
	BNP freezes redemptions for three investment funds, caused by inability to value them appropriately in current market conditions.
	Coventree, a large sponsor of Canada's asset-backed CP market declares being unable to place AB CPs on behalf of its conduits.
	The ECB injects €95 bn of liquidity into interbank market. Similar steps by other central banks.
	After Countrywide had to draw its entire credit line of $11.5 bn the bank faced a run by customers. Bank of America injected $2 bn cash.
September	Run on UK's Northern Rock, £1 bn withdrawal of retail deposits.
	Cheyne Finance is the first SIV to go into receivership.
	Dollar overnight Libor at 6.7975%, highest level since LTCM crisis.
	Bank of China seemingly lost $9 bn in subprime investments.
	Several high-profile CEOs had to leave due to repeated high losses.
October	IKB of Germany concludes SIV Rhinebridge Plc is unable to repay debts.
	Citigroup: additional write-down of $5.9 bn.
November	BoA, Legg Mason, SEI Invest. and Sun Trust Banks prop up their money market funds against possible losses to debts issued by SIVs.
	HSBC takes $41 bn in SIV assets onto its balance sheet.
	Citigroup gets capital boost of $7.5 bn from Abu Dhabi.
December	German West LB and HSH Nordbank $15 bn bailout of their SIVs.
	Citibank takes $49 bn on balance sheet from its seven SIVs.
	BoA shuts $12 bn MM mutual fund; losses in subprime sector.
	Added write-downs of around $10 bn each by UBS and Morgan Stanley.
	Citigroup Q.4 loss $18 bn; partly due to write-downs on mortgage-related exposure.
2008	
January	Hedge fund Peloton Partners liquidated.
February	Northern Rock: UK government steps in.
March	Thornburg Mortgage Asset Corp. cannot meet margin calls.
	Bear Stearns faces liquidity crisis 4 days after a funding injection of $30 bn by JPMorgan, taken over by the latter.
April	New Century files for bankruptcy.
July	Mortgage lender IndyMac Bank seized by federal regulators.
	The NY Fed gets lending authority to Fannie Mae and Freddie Mac.
August	UBS, Citigroup and Merrill Lynch agree to buy back Auction Rate Securities of $36 bn (18.6, 7.3 and 10 respectively).
	The US FDIC assesses 117 US banks as critical (90 a quarter earlier).
September	US government takes over Fannie Mae and Freddie Mac.
	Lehman Brothers bankrupt; collapse of Washington Mutual (to JPMorgan) and Wachovia (to Wells Fargo). FDIC takes stakes to protect customers.
	Merrill Lynch in last-minute action taken over by BoA.
	US insurer–bank AIG bailed out by government.
	UK bank HBOS to be taken over by rival Lloyds Bank.

Fortis (Belgium) needs government support and gets downsized: government of the Netherlands buys Dutch part; BNP Paribas acquires units in Belgium and Luxembourg.

France, Belgium and Luxembourg take stakes in Daxia and guarantee all borrowings. (Losses from US Sub Financial Security Assurance.)

Spanish bank Santander buys UK Alliance & Leicester and sound part of UK Bradford & Bingley as well as US Sovereign Bankcorp.

State of Ireland guarantees interest-related liabilities of six local banks.

October   US Congress approves $700 bn rescue package for banks. In a second step mentions an amount of $250 bn for taking stakes in selected banks.

Several European states declare guarantees for customer deposits.

German government and banks rescue Hypo Real Estate.

Island takes over control of Kaupthing-Bank.

Swiss government takes stake in UBS and takes over assets of $54 bn put into a special unit.

Member banks of the ECB place up to €100 bn with it overnight at penalty rates in order to avoid counterparty risk.

Following the IMF meeting in Washington, EU ministers of finance agree to implement the principles defined in a common plan but with national specifications:

1. Lift minimum of guaranteed customer deposits to €50 000 for 1 year. Examples: UK £50 000; Germany unlimited.
2. Restriction on present mark-to-market accounting rules to avoid loss absorption for 'going concern' assets.
3. If required, all banks relevant for 'systemic risk' are to be saved. Examples of liquidity fund: UK £400 bn; Germany €400 bn.
4. To agree on common principles for banks' recapitalisation. Examples of planned fund: UK £37 bn; Germany €80 bn.

(*Sources:* Information from Gorton (2008), *Financial Times, Frankfurter Allgemeine Zeitung, Die Welt, Welt am Sonntag*)

The chronological overview shows a clear pattern of internalisation of a local problem. What it does not show is the mechanism leading to the global infection, which we will try to distil.

The subject is a difficult one by any standard. In the midst of an ongoing crisis, it would resemble 'mission impossible' if one were to aim to reach answers based on proven facts. Getting a full picture that is up to academic standards will take years. Practitioners cannot wait that long. In our case, too much is at stake. There is the question of whether the understanding of liquidity stress events needs to be altered, thus requiring significant adjustments to liquidity policy and management, or whether we stay with the defined and explained patterns, but with higher intensity, expanded duration and more pronounced global infection than experienced before. Out of need, and not out of belief in superior insight, we will attempt to extract the most likely mechanism leading to the global infection, which in turn brought down even large banks in many countries and necessitated government intervention on an unprecedented scale.

7.5.2.2   The initial stage

Based on present knowledge we can firmly establish a link between falling house prices in the United States and the start of the present crisis, initiated in the subprime mortgage markets. After about a decade of stable or increasing house values, in about September 2006 they started to dive. For the majority of prime mortgage borrowers (PMBs), the turn in trend was not pleasant but not threatening either. According to statistics from the Office of Federal Housing Enterprise Oversight, prices increased slightly over 50% in the period from Q.4 2000 to the same period in 2005, not in each region and neither for each property, but on average. Depending on the time of purchase and the level of restraint in taking out created value, the house owner enjoyed some cushion. Furthermore, for prime mortgages, the house value is of subsidiary importance as long as mortgage-related payments are fulfilled.

The subprime mortgage sector contrasts markedly in this respect. The financial status of home owners in this segment would not qualify them for prime mortgages. The design of securing the lender's exposure rests solely on the value of the house, which needs to increase in value within relatively short periods. As house prices started to fall and continued to do so, more and more subprime borrowers failed, and through growing supply in the housing market fed the negative trend even further.

As explained above (7.5.1.2) subprime mortgages were not intended to stay with the original lender till maturity. In a market of such volume and growth, amounts in the process from origination, warehousing to issuance of CDO bonds are substantial at any time. The perceived characteristics that the securitised tranches through all the steps of the process were easily marketable and thus highly liquid determined a specific form of funding in the CP market. We have addressed borrowing in this segment on various occasions before in the context of contingent liabilities towards corporate customers, whereby the bank acts as guarantor in case the former is no longer in a position to replace maturing borrowing in this segment. Due to the perceived high liquidity status of the assets, the advantage of short-term funding was taken, not least in the CP market. As the asset represents a value in itself, it was replacing the bank as guarantor and funding was done on Asset-Backed Commercial Paper (ASCPs). According to Federal Reserve statistics, the volume outstanding peaked in the third quarter of 2007 at a level of about $1200 bn, almost double the level 3 years before. Three months later the amount had shrunk to about $800 bn.

In line with growing insolvencies in the subprime mortgage sector and their negative effects on the value of asset-backed portfolios, lenders gradually hesitated to replace funding becoming due. Thus, real and expected losses reduced the available liquidity, forcing portfolio managers to sell assets in order to meet funding; forced sales by a growing group of portfolio managers then depressed prices and produced new losses, which in turn reduced the willingness of lenders to provide further funding – a vicious downward spiral.

Before we look at the wider picture, it may be helpful to look at two aspects within the vicious cycle, as they seem to play a vital role again in the global context of the crisis: perception/uncertainty and accounting rules.

The pressure on institutions in the front line of subprime mortgage lending can be no surprise. In the months after the downturn in house prices, Ownit Mortgage Solutions filed for bankruptcy in December 2006; so did mortgage originator New Century Financial Corporation in April of the following year; and subprime lender Accredited Home Lenders lost about 90% of its value in 2 days (March), for example. What cannot be explained in a straightforward way is the run on SIVs (Structured Investment Vehicles). According to Gorton (2008, page 59), who refers to a study of Standard & Poor's, the average distribution of SIVs looked very balanced, based on data of August 2007. The biggest share of investment was with financial institutions (around 40%) and RMBS (about 20%). Subprime did not exceed 3% on average. Why then did SIVs come under such pressure? Was it financials or was the market not in a position to distinguish 'subprime' from 'prime' RMBS and assessed the risk on the overall mortgage exposure? Of course we are talking about an average SIV within deviations on both sides. Two vehicles were 'significantly above-average exposure to home equity and subprime assets. On Aug. 28, Standard & Poor's took a rating action on Cheyne (it went into receivership the following month). The other vehicle, Rheinbridge . . . received an infusion of capital', according to Gorton (2008, page 59); however, its parent, IKB, later needed to be bailed out. Yet excesses above require levels below to get an average. Leaving the reasoning behind for the moment, the fact was that relatively few SIVs actually collapsed, but most were saved by the sponsors who took them onto their balance sheets to secure funding, like Citibank, HSBC, Bank of Montreal or Standard Chartered, just to list some names with large volumes. As mentioned before, locating a risky subprime RMBS within a CDO bond is a serious challenge. In the meantime, some names failed; faltering funds have been saved and taken over by other institutions; and a substantial portion in amount has been transferred to banks' balance sheets. Under these circumstances, even meticulous and diligent investors most probably had no chance to locate the particular subprime mortgage risk anymore. And against a background when substantial amounts of subprime RMBS bonds and large numbers of CDOs were subject to potential and actual downgrading by the rating agencies, investors wanted to get out of anything and anybody related to housing, and subprime in particular, without looking for nuances such as instruments and names. Bearing in mind that SIVs, for example, included a whole range of investments of which subprime mortgages were a small part, the price pressure started to spread beyond the actual problem area.

Now to the second point. The respective accounting rules are governed by the US Financial Accounting Standard Board which states that as a principle (with some exceptions) positions are to be 'marked-to-market'. The aim is to value positions at actual prices at which they could be turned in the market in order to come to an up-to-date valuation of a portfolio or vehicle like an SIV etc. It is thus assumed to always get a fair quote in the market, reflecting the 'real' value of the instrument. Yet, Gorton (2008, page 64), limits the market's capability for fair price assessment to conditions not characterised by extreme anxieties. If uncertainties are mounting, 'no one wants to trade, there are no markets. And hence there are no fair market prices.' Quotes are no longer a statement of execution levels but defensive measures, with the view of not being hit by any potential seller. The subject was expanded on in the above case related to the 'name' stress experienced by Commerzbank in late 2002. The defensive quotes could easily be broken without any material purchases in comparison with the total outstandings. But with no liquidity cushion established, subprime-related vehicles had to sell, and in this way depressed prices even further. Trying to make liquidity ends meet, portfolio managers had to shed from the balance sheet assets that were sellable, which were the prime tranches with a still functioning market. The overall quality of the portfolio thus deteriorated further.

7.5.2.3 Global infection

As stated at the beginning, there is hardly any research which addresses the point of infection in depth at the present time. This should not come as a surprise, since we are at the height of the crisis, just after governments in almost all industrialised countries and beyond have taken stern and unprecedented measures to stem the flood which was about to overwhelm the financial system. We will therefore have to rely on observations and knowledge gained about markets and their behaviour.

On this basis, we suggest looking at three elements in particular: losses, liquidity and uncertainty/perception. All three elements have become rather familiar to us. It may be helpful to refer back to our graph in Figure 3.9. There, growth was declared as the most important initiating element with respect to the downside as well as liquidity risk potential. Capital was defined as the buffer to withstand losses when they become effective, and liquidity level was described as the level of liquidity buffer set by management, since loss of liquidity can only be compensated by liquidity (buffers) again. The rating expresses the financial health of a bank, which can be assessed formally (rating agencies, in-house) or simply perceived. For investors, the financial health, even the perceived one, is taken as a first indicator for determining their lending attitude. After taking investment/lending alternatives into consideration, the decision on actual lending to a particular counterparty or segment is taken. Should their willingness to lend not match the expected funding gap of the particular bank, growth has to be adjusted, either by forgoing planned expansion or by reducing the asset side on the balance sheet.

Losses started at an early stage in the US markets, especially in the segment lending directly to the subprime clientele. In the course of the third quarter of 2007, pressure was mounting, however. Within a few days, starting in late July, Countrywide Financial Corp. warned about difficult conditions; Sowood Capital shut down after losing 57% in 1 month; and American Home Mortgage Investment Corp announced its inability to finance lending obligations, leading to bankruptcy. The expansion and concentration of failures seem to have escalated cautiousness in lending. Based on Gorton (2008, page 62), the 3-month Libor–OIS (Overnight Indexed Swap) spread 'had a multi-year average of 11 basis points, and was 15 basis points on August 8, 2007. On August 10 it was over 50 basis points and it was over 90 basis points by mid-September'. As we are not discussing funding spreads for subprime mortgages but the rates applicable for the whole banking sector, the basic attitude towards the industry as a whole must have altered, including the banking members of the industry in relation to other members, as both of the rates are very much determined by the participants of the interbank markets.

Our best assessment is that markets got nervous, as implications of the problems in the subprime housing market exceeded their anticipated degree of severity. And the markets reacted. As mentioned earlier, outstanding AB CPs dropped heavily in the months following the peak in July 2007, due to a severely curtailed supply. Yet assets did not evaporate into thin air; financing was primarily taken over by the sponsoring banks, thus depressing their liquidity status. Internationally experienced banks with a respective network tapped international markets for funding and brought about a first pressure on spread widening also in the eurozone, for example. There is, however, the second route of internationalisation.

Starting in the third quarter of 2007, all of a sudden some European banks had to bail out their SIVs with sometimes substantial amounts when compared with their own capital base. The German bank IKB was probably the first that had to be rescued; others, however, like the two large Swiss banks, several of the German state-owned Landesbanken, and many further banks in Europe started to declare losses, blaming difficult circumstances in the US subprime mortgage market. Only then did it dawn on European bankers not directly involved in this type of asset: the subprime crisis had extended to their zone. The run on the UK bank Northern Rock confirmed the new perception.

(a) Germany

Distribution by product

Jumbo Pfandbriefe 35%

Registered Pfandbriefe 34%

Domestic Pfandbriefe 31%

Euro 841 bn*

*as of August 31, 2008

Pfandbrief issuance by product

■ domestic Pfandbriefe ■ Jumbo Pfandbriefe ▪ registered Pfandbriefe

In Euro bn

Subprime and liquidity crisis

Jun-07, Jul-07, Aug-07, Sep-07, Oct-07, Nov-07, Dez-07, Jan-08, Feb-08, Mar-08, Apr-08, May-08, Jun-08, Jul-08, Aug-08

(b) Europe

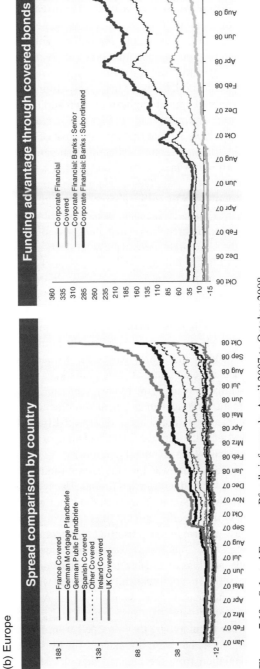

Figure 7.10 Selected European Pfandbrief spreads, April 2007 to October 2008
(Reproduced by permission of Commerzbank AG)

The reaction was swift. Figure 7.10 illustrates the point made extremely well. We take the spread developments in the Pfandbrief sector (mortgage-secured debt issues) from six European countries.

Until the end of August 2007, spreads between the national Pfandbriefe hardly differed, almost neglecting differentiations in market circumstances and the security levels of the respective national instruments. Liquidity in the eurozone was abundantly available and fallout risk in this segment perceived as almost negligible. With the mortgage crisis accelerating in the United States and recognising potential if not likely backlashes into the European housing markets, investors started to press for a risk-adjusted return. Pressure became most intense for countries having enjoyed large price increases within the last decade, namely the UK and Spain. The UK Pfandbrief spread might have been additionally burdened by the difficulty of Northern Rock, demonstrating that the higher risk is real and not potential only. That is, till the end of September 2008. At that time, irrespective of the prior differentiated assessments, all spreads jumped without exception, reflecting that panic had taken over.

Cautiousness, born out of lack of trust, had started well before panic prevailed. An acceleration of announcing write-offs, blamed on adverse market conditions in the US subprime markets, took the community by surprise. Since the original cause of the problem could hardly be located in the banks' balance sheets after having become portions of CDOs, health assessment of banks turned into perception – and a negative one, at that. When even banks with no strategic focus on the US market were heavily hit (IKB and several Landesbanken in the case of Germany), some of which failed, what horrors might be looming for all other banks was the question among the community at large and across borders. Bank-to-bank lending dropped sharply as a consequence, and so did the level at which non-sovereign tradable assets were liquefiable through the repo market or provided as collateral. Yet mistrust of any asset not state secured was one factor only (flight to quality), in our opinion.

In this context, we refer to our discussions on the liquidity balance sheet in general and the role of risk appetite in particular. Three aspects are primarily significant for our hypothesis. On the basis of the expected behavioural attitude of market participants, we first assessed the level of protection for the bank by applying a 'base scenario'. Protection was provided by funding all assets with a maturity longer than 1 year (contractual long-term obligations; short-term franchise and tradable assets not sellable or not qualifying for covered funding) with stable funding. In a second step, the gap was quantified under a 'worst-condition' scenario. The level of risk appetite decided by management determined the level of the buffers required to get to the protection envisaged. That was the concept in a nutshell. To the best of our knowledge, banks would not have worked with such a formal concept in general. Nevertheless, intuitively, that is what they would have done. Why then did it not work for many of them?

We will not deal with a specific case but filter the critical factors for the banking community as a whole. Some assets have failed, thus affecting income (which is part of capital) as well as liquidity negatively. We assume losses exceeding planned for and anticipated write-offs. The liquidity status under stress as to tradable assets and the ones qualifying principally for covered funding has been assessed too optimistically compared with reality. As a consequence, funding was kept short term, not least for cost saving reasons. As mentioned above, conditions in the market turned the market-dependent instruments and portfolios less liquid or even illiquid for some time. In our terminology, they dropped from asset at risk to the bucked long-term obligations and franchise, but were not catered for by stable funding. As concluded earlier, such a negative deviation from the planned liquidity structure can be tolerated for a short period of time, provided it can still be financed short term; the originally decided status needs to be rectified swiftly, especially as the bank is without protection for a new or prolonged event. Unfortunately, banks could not even keep up short-term funding to the extent required, and those without a large retail base suffered more. Under these circumstances, many banks struggled for cash and collected as much as they could get hold of in a problematic environment with a bleak outlook. To the extent that liquidity still could not cover keeping present assets on the books, assets had to be sold. With the interbank markets becoming less liquid every day, only two routes were open: exchange-traded instruments and assets eligible with central banks. The choice for banks was extremely limited when it came to selecting dispensable assets: sell what still has a functioning market, even at lower prices than hoped for. The widespread effort to create cash had a compounding effect on these market prices, thus reducing the health status of the banks even further. The liquidity problem became even more pronounced when banks kept part of the liquidity buffer in market-dependent assets, or even worse, and this is not unheard of, in subprime bonds. The shortage in this case was not only due to a high-risk appetite as far as funding gaps were concerned; it was also the buffer and thus the element of security which was melting away before it could be put into use and perform its function.

7.5.3   Financial system in jeopardy

The crisis continued for the remainder of 2007 and into the next year, characterised by significant write-downs by several well-known banks in the United States and Europe and their mostly successful endeavours to replenish the reduced capital stock. Central banks gradually increased their level of cash facilities in order to ease the liquidity shortage felt by the system as a whole and by banks with no substantial retail segment in particular. With hindsight, indications of a further escalation and a new dimension could be drawn from Northern Rock (February 2008), where the UK government stepped in, and the failure of Bear Stearns (March), which was taken over by JPMorgan. Yet, at that time, the market most probably judged the two incidents as isolated cases and not as a signal of a storm brewing up. Several experts and high-profile bankers indicated that the crisis might have passed the zenith, although with some difficult times still ahead.

A relatively quiet period of about 4 months followed, with no bankruptcy of any internationally known bank. The underlying health of many banks continued to deteriorate, however. In September of the same year, the US deposit insurance body (FDIC) published a further increase to 117 US banks assessed as critical, compared with 90 institutes one quarter earlier. The underlying causes were still at work: the value of equity or interest-related assets eroded further, triggered by the liquidity-induced need to produce cash in whatever way possible and thus deteriorating the institutions' health at the same time; as time passed without the hoped-for normalisation in interbank lending behaviour, any shorter-term financing was coming close to the maturity date and with little chance of getting the whole amount prolonged, even on a secured basis; and last but not least, a new quarter end was approaching fast, requiring the accumulated losses of the previous 3 months to be taken into account, calculated on a mark-to-market basis against capital. What specific role each of the three causes played for individual institutes will only transpire once research has been done. Nevertheless, the causes have been at work and with a terminal effect for many financial institutions.

September 2008 will be remembered as the time in recent history when the financial system was on the brink of collapse. Although the US government's takeover of its state-sponsored mortgage lenders Fannie Mae and Freddie Mac was first, in the view of most bankers and banking commentators it was Lehman Brothers which signalled the turning point in an already highly endangered market. The decision by the authorities not to take it over, after endeavours to get a prime shareholder and an accompanying substantial injection of funds failed, brought about an avalanche of bank collapses in many countries. Political authorities had to step in to prevent the financial system from breaking down (see also the chronology of events in 7.5.2.1). Although the sequence of events supports the generally held opinion about the bankruptcy of Lehman being the trigger for the bank collapses or near collapses following swiftly, we should not neglect the possibility of a coincidence in timing.

To form at least a somewhat qualified opinion of the question, we will look at the few facts available some weeks after the event. From what can be gathered from discussions and expert statements made in newspapers, markets and their highest representatives in banks had formed an assessment along the following lines. Lehman is a big bank and one of the few top investment banks in the world. Based on this position, its activities are linked to many financial sub-markets at home and abroad. In many of these segments the failure of Lehman would cause severe disturbances. The latter would affect the behaviour of participants in the respective sub-market, with the effect of negative impacts on further sectors of the financial industry. The strong linkage between Lehman and various segments on the one hand and the tight connections of financial segments among themselves on the other hand put the investment bank in the following category: a potential systemic risk if it fails. From this line of deduction, it followed logically that Lehman could not be allowed to fail and as a consequence, the authorities would not let it go bankrupt. Business policy vis-à-vis Lehman was conducted in accordance with this view.

When Lehman actually failed and was not saved by the state authorities, this established market view was shattered. Although impacts of psychological shocks should not be under-estimated, the failure had severe consequences for specific market segments. We will select three which we believe had the utmost relevance for global markets, apart from the losses experienced by shareholders and the intensified downward pressure on financial equity prices: namely, the money market; the long-term debt market and the hedge fund sector.

The US money market fund industry managed at that time about $3500 bn and was tapped by banks and companies worldwide for their short-term financing. Debts issued by Lehman into this segment amounted to $785 million at the time of collapse (see also *Financial Times*, 13 October 2008). Although a very small amount in relative terms, the implication was severe. Within 5 days $200 bn were withdrawn by private and institutional investors. In order to fulfil their obligations and in an attempt to bolster the cash element, money market funds had to sell assets into a market already rather illiquid and/or curtail renewals. Both actions were damaging to the short-term funding capacity of borrowers in the United States and abroad. Also, when comparing the Lehman share of $785 million in the affected Reserve Primary Fund ($62 bn), the severity experienced by the financial community was not explained by the loss in absolute or relative terms. Write-offs of financial institutions in many instances have amounted to a multiple of it. And this for a single institution; in several cases in one quarter, followed by further losses. The reasons are to be looked for in the change of the behavioural attitude of lenders towards banks. Yet, for such circumstances, the remedy applied in case of losses is not available. A shortage in liquidity cannot be closed by replenishing the reduced capital base, as liquidity reduction can only be compensated by (than lacking) liquidity reserves.

The volume of long-term debts outstanding was in a different category. It amounted to about $130 bn (*Financial Times*, 13 October 2008). After declaring bankruptcy, the value of bonds in the secondary market dropped from the prior level at around 95 cents in the dollar down to 10% of face value. Whether the recovery rate at the end will turn out to be comparable with the 30–40% of the historical average remains to be seen. In any case, the losses to be borne by private, financial and institutional bondholders will be substantial. The immediate implication exceeded this range, however. The value of Lehman bonds trading at 9% of face value 1 or 2 weeks before failing supports our previous view with respect to market assessments: whatever may happen, Lehman will be saved; and if necessary, the state authorities will come to the rescue. Suddenly, bankruptcy of any bank failing to maintain the status of going concern was a possibility. The waves travelled through all markets with negative effects on price and (already meagre) availability of liquidity.

Hedge funds were affected in two ways. Many of those who had used Lehman as a prime broker had to keep collateral with it. With the declaration of bankruptcy, their collateral was frozen and thus not available for some time. More severe was the growing trend of lending to banks on an unsecured basis. After having had the risk profile of such transactions reassessed, they shied away from unsecured bank lending, accelerating the reduction in funding capacity of the banking sector as a whole.

In our opinion, the fall of Lehman Brothers was definitely a blow to the market and triggered an escalated shortage of liquidity well beyond the borders of the United States. Such an implosion might have pushed several banks over the brink. On the other hand, keeping liquidity status at a level capable of withstanding the failure of a large counterpart had already become 'best practice' some time ago. But even without the demise of Lehman, the underlying forces explained above would still have been at work. For many of the banks that needed to be saved in the aftermath of the Lehman bankruptcy, problems over a shorter or longer period would have become insurmountable, we deduce. If our assessment holds true, Lehman and its handling by the authorities were not the cause of further banks failing, but rather played the role of a catalyst for the avalanche experienced in such a short timeframe.

7.5.4   Reflections and outlook

In our discussion above (7.5.2.1) we considered the question: in the light of the subprime crisis, should the understanding of liquidity stress events need to be altered, requiring significant adjustments to liquidity policy as defined in this book, or should we stay with the defined and explained pattern, but at higher intensity, expanded duration and more pronounced global infection than experienced before?

According to our personal assessment, banks in this crisis have been endangered on three fronts: losses, strongly diminishing funding capacity and rapidly growing incapacity to turn tradable assets into cash. If we refer back to causes of liquidity stresses (Figure 3.5), describing the present liquidity crisis does not leave out nor add one single possible source listed there. It is a unique combination that market participants have not faced before, at least within the present world financial system. A crisis in which all three elements exert their pressure at the same time, and with a high level of severity has not been neglected in the assessment of potential events, but only addressed with a very low probability not catered for.

The concept presented in this book does not focus too much on a single event or combinations of it. The aim is to give bank management time for measures to counteract the pressure and bring the bank through the periods of danger, irrespective of the cause. Whether the bank is then affected by a single cause or a combination of them does not really matter. The remaining question to address is whether the subprime crisis is outside the advanced understanding of liquidity risk as described before. We do not think it is. Losses, diminishing funding capacity and growing incapacity to turn tradable assets into cash are traditional elements which any liquidity policy and its management have to address. We therefore see no need to alter or enhance our concept in any way.

There are four critical factors we should not neglect, however, although they apply to any stress scenario and not just the present crisis:

- Loss potential needs to be reflected correctly. In the present case, downside risk in new products with little to hardly any historic track record apparently has been grossly underestimated. Based on our findings that a bank can be solvent and illiquid at the same time but can never be illiquid and still solvent, it is not liquidity policy which should be the focus in this respect. Being liquid is only one condition for remaining solvent, but it is never able to replace loss capacity.
- In the case of any liquidity crisis, buying time for management is the key purpose of liquidity policy. The latter cannot solve the underlying problem, but a sound policy can assure that the problem and its rectification are not aggravated by unnecessary pressure from lack of liquidity. For how long protection is bought is decided by the bank's management. We have recommended 1 year, and as it is performed on a rolling basis, it turns out to be between 18 and 24 months, in order to avoid capital market borrowing at too short intervals.
- Special focus needs to be put on fast and drastically changing circumstances as caused by a large acquisition, for example. At the date when the deal becomes effective, actually overnight, the liquidity structure might present itself as drastically changed and not necessarily to the benefit of the purchasing institute. If both acquisition and liquidity stress coincide within a short period, there is not sufficient time to rectify the imbalance. As a consequence, taking measures to secure liquidity status from day 1 is as paramount as preparing the finance for the acquisition – a point which may have applied to RBS and Fortis.
- For risk appetite and its dimensions, in a wider sense, deciding on the length of 'buying time' is already part of them. In a narrower definition, management expresses its risk appetite in four areas: the portion of assets defined as assets at risk; the percentage by which assets not liquid within 1 year are covered by stable funding; the level of severity chosen to determine the level of the buffers; and deciding on the level of adding non-eligible assets at the central bank to the buffers.

In this chapter three types of liquidity crises have been viewed from a practitioner's point of view. The first two incidences – a shock and a name-related stress – have been prepared as case studies. Since we are still in the midst of the subprime crisis, the third example has been set up as an illustration of applying the liquidity concept in a period of uncertainty, with the outcome still not known. Testing the concept under three different and severe scenarios has demonstrated its robustness, we believe. It also clearly transpired, so we hope, that the human factor cannot be neglected. The concept is an instrument but requires critical input from management, as summarised above. Yet applying the liquidity balance-sheet approach produces the benefit of having the facts and the most likely implications clearly and expressly stated. How solid protection will be is dependent on following internally set rules and the willingness of management to spend even comparatively modest amounts as insurance premiums.

Management of many banks is presently faced with a further and unprecedented challenge linked to liquidity but exceeding its boundaries at the same time. In our assessment, banks applying the concept will not face any serious liquidity problem, as long as their management sticks to the rules set out. Even if the crisis were prolonged for some time, liquidity status would not be endangered. Yet events in the first half of October 2008 have brought about an alteration related to the function of governments within the frame of the banking industry, and this on a level exceeding national boundaries.

Mounting losses and/or a further escalation of the liquidity squeeze after the bankruptcy of Lehman Brothers brought many banks to the brink of failure. In order to safeguard the financial system, the governments of a large group of countries stepped in. Without going into nuances, three lines of action were taken:

- The amount secured by the deposit insurance scheme was improved, either by an increase in the individual sum or without limit. The action intended to avoid further runs on banks, as experienced by Northern Rock and Washington Mutual, for example. Ireland on the other hand extended the guarantee to all lending, irrespective of status.
- Substantial portions have been allocated by many state authorities to provide loans to banks with funding problems, as the mechanism of injecting liquidity through the central bank no longer produced the effects experienced in the past. In Europe, for example, in the second half of October special bank refinancing through the ECB amounted to more then €300 bn on average, of which two-thirds was redeposited again with the central bank. In other words, €200 bn provided for funding the system was not employed accordingly, but kept on account with the ECB, at a cost of 0.5%.
- Additional facilities have been allocated to bolster the capital ratios of banks, with mostly governments becoming (quasi-)co-owners of the respective institutions. Apart from quasi-nationalisation to avoid straightforward bankruptcy, governments have chosen one of two different approaches: in countries like the United States and the UK, state capital participation was enforced on selected banks, while countries like Germany left the decision on whether or not to use the facility to individual banks.

There is no room for management considerations and decisions when state support and participation are part of a political act; in addition, everybody affected is in the same boat. Other authorities took a different route. They left the decision to the individual banks but stated at the time provisional conditions which may still be adjusted: securing the banking sector by providing support via several channels, like full security for private investors; state guarantees for other liabilities to third parties at an insurance premium related to present short-term funding costs and credit swap rates for the institution concerned; capital injections with the condition of forgoing dividend payments to shareholders and capping enumeration to board members. The political goal of the government to put banks into a position of not needing to curtail previous lending volumes to German customers was not directly linked to the package, but needs to be taken into consideration. For a bank with a solid liquidity structure there is no actual need to ask for state support. Considerations will primarily concern two issues, of which one subject goes to the heart of liquidity policy.

The key element of general liquidity policy has always been to secure the fulfilment of payment obligations when, and in whatever currency, they fall due. In contrast to the general definition, which is shared by the Basel Committee on Supervision as well as national supervisors, we extended the definition by also securing the franchise for a predefined period. Our definition is in the interest of the bank and thus (or by coincidence?) also favourable for the economy as a whole. The concept applied in this book and exceeding supervisory requirements by far, however, also allows for letting the franchise lending decline in case a crisis turns out to be more severe or prolonged than anticipated and secured for in a conservative manner. Fulfilling payment obligations has always been the prime yardstick. At present, when too many banks struggle for funding, negative implications on lending behaviour cannot be excluded on a national level. And, as personally observed, public opinion makers tend to take a shortcut: even if an institution can keep up its lending power, if the credit volume overall is shrinking, the blame will be on the ones which have not asked for state support.

The second issue relates to financial health in the form of capital ratios. State ownership on the one hand and capital participation combined with state-guaranteed funding on the other hand have altered the relative value of capital ratios. All of a sudden, core capital ratios of about 7.5%, with 4% as a minimum, are judged by markets as no longer 'solid'. The floor for solid has been lifted to 9% and more in the meantime. Depending on the national authority, banks with a lower ratio have either been forced (UK) or been given the opportunity (Germany) to increase capital through state shareholding in different forms.

The question now arises of whether the steps taken make the liquidity concept obsolete or put it at least in a position of relative value. According to Figure 5.4 we have had 14 international crises in the last 20 years. Any one of them could have led to the bank's failure, if handled in an inappropriate way, or at least damaged the franchise. And although authorities will again tighten the regulatory frame, liquidity will still be subject to new turmoil. On top, even nationalised banks have to manage liquidity. But quite apart from these considerations, the concept will permit bank management to decide on the liquidity component, and keeping the power for decision making is one of the indispensible elements of solid management.

7.6 FINAL REMARKS AND CONSIDERATIONS

In the present chapter we intended to provide an insider view when in the midst of stressed conditions. Inevitably, the character of such an undertaking is bank specific and personal at the same time – bank specific in the sense that different economic environments and business structures of institutions allow for many alternative conditions, of which only one has been presented; and personal because it is people who analyse, consider, decide and implement, individuals with all their specific cultural background, professional experience and business philosophy. We tried to overcome the restriction at least partly by presenting three incidents and broadening the aspect of actions taken as far as the reasoning behind it has been explained.

Leaving particularities aside, from the illustrated cases we can draw some basic conclusions that are independent of the structure of the bank and the environment in which it operates.

'Shock' event:

- In a shock event a relatively small group within the bank is effectively involved in handling it.
- Time is extremely precious as a shock event will neither announce itself, nor allow time for additional preparations.
- Sufficient cash needs to be readily available. In our terms, 'a phone call away'.
- We cannot necessarily rely on markets to create liquidity, even if tradable papers not 'eligible' with central banks are held abundantly.
- Most probably the shock is triggered by 'technical' causes, although the origin of the occurrence may not be 'technical'.
- Such an event is generally over within a short time.
- Being of a relatively frequent nature, although on various degrees, shock events should not disrupt the bank's normal business.
- A pure shock event does not undermine confidence in markets and institutions.
- If not properly handled, it may develop into a 'chronic' scenario.

'Chronic' events:

- A chronic event affects the bank as a whole.
- It can develop from a 'shock' event that is not handled well, or relate to systemic and institute-specific circumstances.
- In the latter case, with insider knowledge at hand, management ought to recognise the critical danger level that the bank is in and put itself on higher alert.
- The stress is market or name related. In the first case it may remain confined or change to a name-related occurrence – not generally but regarding specific banks, a statement which still holds in the light of the subprime crisis.
- In a chronic incident all business and financial segments are affected.
- Impacting on the bank in total, a chronic event has to be faced with a pre-formulated business strategy and policies.
- Such an incident is probably made up of two phases: initiation and continuation.
- The phase of initiation is not unlike a 'shock' event; being properly prepared for the event buys time.
- The second phase, continuing until cruising level is reached again, may last for quite some time.
- Continuation requires a management technique not unlike strategic planning: one will have to deal with 'magic' polygons, i.e. goals will partly conflict.
- If lasting over a longer term, the principle of the three Cs applies: commanding, controlling and correcting. It is a continuing process till 'end of stress' is declared.
- Ensuring that the actions taken turn out to be transparent, coherent and visible is decisive.
- Communication is most important: internally to get staff at all levels on board; externally to counteract rumours with facts.

On a more general level, we wish to put one or two further conclusions forward. Today, too much emphasis is still put on elaborating funding cost implications in case of stress. It is an issue, no doubt, yet the real risk concerns the danger of getting no cash whatever price one is willing to pay. It is important to distinguish between purely stress-related actions on the one hand and policy decisions taken during a stress event on the other hand. The second set is most likely a response to the stressed condition, but, being a business element that will continue even after the stress, it should be shifted to the 'business as usual' organisational setup as soon as possible. In other words, in a crisis there is a dedicated team to deal with the specific circumstances; nevertheless, there is still a bank to manage with a timely view of reaching beyond the crisis, and this cannot be the job of a special committee.

Although in 2002 it took quite some time at Commerzbank until we were back to more or less normal conditions, once the pressure abated and policy decisions were made on the succeeding path, we started work on developing and integrating measures into normal business which were based on conclusions drawn from the recent experience. The central ALCO today gets all relevant information, analyses and comments on them, either directly or indirectly linked to liquidity, including forecasts on capital ratios and P/L, changes in business policy, etc. A preliminary ALCO meeting was set up to tune issues among the experts; the allocation of liquidity cost was altered from a transaction- and product-related approach to a concept of net funding requirements per business segment; the liquidity concept was adjusted to integrate recent findings; an updated set of stress scenarios and responses to them was presented to the central ALCO for review and acceptance by the board of directors; and a strategic initiative was started with the aim of augmenting and furthering secure stickiness of customer funds. Due to continuing general upheavals in the markets we prolonged this beyond the minimum date. In June 2003 the board declared 'end of stress'. Despite having acquired the large mortgage and public finance sector bank Eurohypo at the end of 2006, by applying the liquidity concept without delay and vigorously, Commerzbank managed to withstand the mounting worldwide turbulences and still increase its lending volume to franchise customers at least until the financial system was about to collapse.

8

Acting Within the Supervisory Frame

In our previous dealings with liquidity aspects we abstained from referring in detail to supervisory rules and regulations. The decision to exclude them was taken on purpose as risks do exist irrespective of external and binding rules, and the duty of management is to deal with any risk in an appropriate manner anyway, being answerable to shareholders, the owner of the bank. Thus, the focus has been put on the requirements deemed necessary to establish liquidity as a policy element within a 'magic' polygon and supporting the endeavour to reach optimal results for the company as a whole.

Having completed the task in the first six chapters and illustrated the concept in action in the previous one, it seems appropriate now to widen the scope. Widening does not imply changing the stance we have taken so far. In other words, it is not our intention to enter into a comparative study of supervisory policies and central bank rules, as this would entail an undertaking fully dedicated to the subject. Our aspiration and need is limited and contains primarily three aspects. Firstly, we will outline presently predominating schemes applied by supervisors. Secondly, we will assess whether the view on liquidity policy and management presented in the book is compatible with adherence to supervisory rules. Thirdly, if the concept applied exceeds the supervisory and regulatory requirements, we need to evaluate the rationality of our actions.

8.1 HIGH-LEVEL RISKS

In line with the general understanding we recognised downside as well as liquidity risks as being fundamental items of banking risk. Taking into consideration our advanced understanding of liquidity risk and extending the scope to encompass supervisory restrictions, the elements of the 'circles' (Figure 8.1) can be named and presented in the following manner: endurance risk, authorisation/regulatory risk and business continuation risk. Although each one is a separate item, they are strongly interlinked with each other. (Endurance and business continuity represent solvency and liquidity respectively. As the latter terms are loaded with a variety of definitions, especially liquidity, we prefer to use more neutral expressions.)

Endurance means protecting the risk-adjusted value of the bank. Extreme levels of downside risk can eliminate the capital base if the former becomes fully effective and cause the bank to fail. The risk is a potential one and needs not to materialise or at least not to its full extent. If it does, however, and in a substantial manner, then it is not only shareholder capital which is in peril: depositors and investors may face substantial losses, and with the increasing size of the institution a failure poses growing threats to the stability of the financial system as a whole.

Endurance or standing power is a precondition for conducting business, even at the lowest level. The understanding with respect to protecting business that we have developed in the meantime is much more specific. The protection against liquidity problems of any kind has been made high, securing all core activities as defined by management for at least one full year.

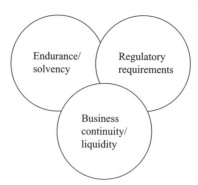

Figure 8.1   The interlinking of banking risks with supervisory requirements

Fulfilling payment obligations is a requirement to be adhered to under any circumstances, but with the additional condition that core business is to be protected.

The duties of management to protect at least the value of their shareholders, and to further it to the extent possible, are strong incentives to keep downside as well as liquidity risk within appropriate levels. Failing to do so despite the incentives cannot be excluded. To reduce the danger of such an occurrence is thus deemed necessary, especially in light of damaging implications for stakeholders as well as the stability of the financial system. A set of strict rules has been set up by national regulators for banks, with respect to both downside as well as liquidity risk. In 2002, the European Central Bank concluded for the first issue: 'In the area of market risk, the value-at-risk (VaR) concept has become the industry standard, and VaR is now also widely accepted by bank supervisors as a technique for calculating regulatory capital requirements' (ECB, 2002, page 29). Consequently, we will not follow up on this subject, having dealt with it in detail already.

The ECB then continues:

> There is still no such mechanism for liquidity risk, although some of the major banks are working on probabilistic liquidity-at-risk models, with the parallel aim of replacing supervisory liquidity ratios with a set of requirements determined on the basis of such models. However, these still seem to be at an early stage of development. Complicating factors in liquidity modelling are that a normal distribution cannot be assumed for cash flows and that historical data do not adequately capture the stress-dimension of liquidity risk.

Since then only limited progress has been made in applying probabilistic models. In our section dealing with securing payment obligations, recent research was evaluated resulting in the conclusion that more advanced mathematical concepts allow maximum gaps to be assessed with a high probability, under the proviso of staying within 'normal' conditions. Predicting the effects under various forms of stress is still outside the reach of such modelling. In this respect it continues to be scenario analysis qualifying for best practice, which is also the basis of our liquidity concept.

The presently low state of research concerning liquidity gives central banks room for choosing concepts when defining liquidity rules for the banking sector. Generally speaking, the choice refers less to principles such as the responsibility of top and senior management, adequate financial resources, scenario analysis, stress testing, contingency plans, etc. They are derived from Basel II and thus show significant similarity when applied nationally. It is the part not regulated by Basel II which gives room for alternative handling, i.e. reporting requests. In this respect two sets of approaches can be distinguished:

- Quantitative versus qualitative
- Mismatch versus stock.

The focus in the coming sections is on supervisory policies and their meaning for bank management in the light of business, financial and liquidity policy as defined in the previous chapters. Whenever points are exemplified, we will refer to the supervisors of Germany (BaFin) and the UK (FSA) for illustrative purposes.

8.2   THE REGULATORY FOCUS SET BY SUPERVISORS

As we stated at the beginning, we will not enter into a comparative study of central bank liquidity policies. It would be beyond our scope and also not appropriate since the regulatory sector does not have a unanimous approach and is partly in a process of formulating new concepts and rules whereby the level of implementation differs among the national bodies. Our aim is limited to the essentials of the present developments relevant to our discussion. We will, however, refer to specific statements regarding policies and rules for illustrative purposes if we feel they reflect a more general understanding among major supervisors.

As regulators do set rules in respect to downside and liquidity risk, we will address both of them. Yet the first item will be touched very restrictively, and limited to some key elements that are highly relevant for liquidity policy and management.

8.2.1   Downside risk and capital requirements

For downside risk, i.e. potential losses stemming from credit, market and operational risks, the protective counter-balance is set up in the form of capital. Supervisory rules are clearly defined and well established. Principles and methods to be applied for determining potential losses in 'normal' conditions and circumstances of stress are widely accepted and have become an instrument used by supervisors for calculating capital requirements. The minimum ratios based on risk potential (losses) and risk capacity (capital) are defined in a somewhat granulated manner known as Tier 1, Tier 2 and Tier 3. According to the BIS standards for example, Tier 1 and Tier 2 ratios are not to fall below 4% and 8% respectively. Any violations of the minimum requirements are subject to strong penalties, including the loss of the banking licence. The regulatory frame thus defines minimum requirements for solvency of the banking industry beyond national borders, with the view to enhance security for stakeholders and the financial system.

Stakeholders include retail depositors and further investors. Internationally accepted minimum standards controlled by supervisors help them to assess the level of risk involved if they engage in any form of dealing related to a bank. Although the assessment process is further supported by adding additional criteria relevant for the financial health of an institution and ranking them in a specific order, not all of them are key points regarding supervisory rules. The aim of sufficient capital in relation to risk of loss is to assure minimum levels commensurate with the strength to withstand strong financial pressures related to losses in difficult times.

The risk-adjusted capital strength, a part of financial health, has been declared as a vital element (Figure 3.9) when it comes to investor attitude. This is not the only element but clearly a strong one, otherwise supervisors would not have chosen it as the centre of focus for downside risk. However, what role does it really play for liquidity in special and thus exceptional circumstances? We will limit ourselves to three topics: two observations and one issue of recent high-level discussions.

8.2.1.1 The question of full risk integration

When calculating segmental downside risks in order to get to the total risk potential of the bank, two questions arise: are all potential risks taken into consideration and are they assessed correctly?

When it comes to the first point we may have to distinguish between internal and external (or regulatory) practices. For internal purposes, getting a full picture of risk taken is a must, for two reasons. Starting with a total volume of risk viewed as acceptable by the management, it needs to be broken down into segmental shares in the form of delegated limits. Upholding management control requires all of them to be subject to review concerning adherence to the defined restrictions. In addition, accepting downside potential demands a benefit on the other side of the equation, i.e. producing a return in line with the particular ratio defined for each risk-taking unit. In order to fulfil both of the management principles, full coverage of all risk-producing activities is indispensable.

Regulatory requirements are necessarily not so strict. It is common practice not to include balance-sheet-related interest rate risk in the calculation of capital ratios. The ratios according to the BIS (Tier 1 and Tier 2) are just one example in which they are excluded. Furthermore, calculating potential losses has always been a challenge, even at times when products were rather simple in their construct. The past, taken as a basis for the prediction, may be as tangible as we can hope for. Nevertheless, it does not limit the pattern for future events. And the growing popularity of more complicated structured deals and constructs have not eased the challenge of predicting losses in specific stressed circumstances; quite the contrary, as has become visible once more in the case of the subprime crisis, but not limited to it.

The examples may suffice to illustrate the point: although covering the vast part of the bank's downside risk, regulatory capital ratios do not necessarily cover the full risk position of the institutions, neither is there any guarantee that the risks are reflected precisely. As the size of the uncovered difference can vary greatly from bank to bank, it allows room for speculation. This leads to the next point.

8.2.1.2 Market perception

Markets and their participants assess risk individually. Although having information from independent sources in hand, like capital ratios from supervisors or ratings from internationally known agencies, the attitude towards an institution does not rely exclusively on this information. The mind-set is often very much affected by additional elements of non-formal assessment, leading to a perception concerning the actual circumstances of the bank's health.

The possible consequences of perception have been shown in the previous chapter when dealing with the Commerzbank name-related stress in 2002. Perception has also played its part during much of the US subprime mortgage crisis, and this on an even larger scale encompassing not one but a multitude of institutions. Uncertainties about the actual loss effects still to come over and above the published ones affected the spread to be asked and in many case the amount ready to be invested, even in banks with a very comfortable core capital ratio up to double digits.

Without doubt, risk-adjusted capital ratios are an important pillar of financial strength and supervisors putting an emphasis on them makes perfect sense. Yet, although the concepts endeavour to integrate all relevant risk into the ratio, there is still room for unexpected negative surprises. It is this element of uncertainty which leads market participants to be dissatisfied with the minimum BIS ratios of 4% and 8% when engaged in funding third-party banks. If it were not the case, managing liquidity would primarily be derived from adherence to regulatory capital requirements.

8.2.1.3 Liquidity risk and capital adequacy

On several occasions the point was made about integrating liquidity risk into the capital adequacy concept. It refers to the Basel II requirement for the purpose of pillar 2 (see IIF, 2007, page 42). The main issues of the subject have been touched on in various instances within the book. We will therefore limit ourselves to a few main considerations.

Within the present capital adequacy rules, capital serves as a buffer to absorb potential losses initiated by credit, market and operational risks becoming effective. As all these risks result in an adverse impact on profit and loss, given a severe stress capital will be reduced accordingly. We described the relationship as being of a one-dimensional character: risk–loss–capital.

Liquidity risk is multi-dimensional and can be related to at least four sources:

- Name-related reduction in funding capacity.
- Liability-market-related reduction in funding capacity.
- Deterioration in asset quality and/or asset-market-related reduction in absorption capacity.
- Drawings connected to optionalities.

Only name-related liquidity risk is largely related to the financial health of the bank. Here a link to capital exists, whereby capital stands at the beginning as a precondition for financial health and not as a buffer at the end of the chain. We concluded in this context that a bank can be solvent and illiquid at the same time. It refers not least to and is exacerbated by the further three sources of liquidity risk. For this type of scenario, the conditions are not ruled by capital level or ratio but emerge from specific circumstances.

All the same, capital reduces dependences from external funding sources at least. If liquidity is treated like the elements of downside risk, capital augments and becomes available for financing assets without referring to markets. For banks, the sum of all capital-related items compared with balance-sheet size usually turns out to be a lower one-digit figure. Assuming it is 4% and that one is going to double the capital for covering liquidity risk within the capital adequacy regime, what safety level has one achieved in the liquidity segment?

The answer depends on the assumptions. If the bank uses the additional (capital) funds to replace financing in the markets, dependency on them will decrease, yet the safety level may improve to a negligible degree only. Why is that? When capital is allocated to finance assets it cannot be employed again to compensate for any liquidity shortage. Only if liquidity-related capital is taken up to increase marketable assets on and above the present level does it improve the safety level. Yet the price to be paid by reducing ROE by half is very high, and a low return on capital may become a new source of concern to the markets. We therefore cannot see any benefit in following the suggestions but assess the concept proposed in the previous chapters as a more efficient way to achieve the goals.

8.2.2 Supervisory rules on liquidity

Compared with capital, supervisory policy on liquidity is diverse and new rules to better grasp the increased complexity of the matter are at various stages of preparation and implementation. Nevertheless, general trends can be observed. In line with the approach applied before, we will try to distil the essence and analyse the implications for banks in general and for the concept presented here in particular.

8.2.2.1 Underlying assumptions

From a bank's point of view, knowing and understanding the underlying assumptions on which regulators and supervisors base their policies and rules are essential. To illustrate the point we take two scenarios.

In the first instance the rules set up by the regulator cover a wide range of banking institutions of which the vast majority consists of small regional and savings banks. The regulator having opted for one rule for all, we assume that the liquidity framework is strongly geared towards the small institutions but also applicable to a few large and internationally oriented banks. Alternatively, the regulator may have opted for a two-tier ruling: a plain one for banks of a smaller size and with less complicated instruments and portfolios; and an advanced concept for larger and rather complex banks with respect to international presence, legal structure and portfolios managed.

For the management of a large international bank, the regulator's choice between the two approaches is significant. Although adhering to the rules is indispensable in any case, when living in the environment of the first instance the bank will not come close to securing liquidity based on the valid framework. The bank's own endeavour has to reach well beyond the official standard, with the effect that supervisory rules have to be adhered to within the category 'high external priority but negligible for internal use'. In a two-tier scheme, differences between banks are catered for and the regulatory ruling actually supports the endeavour of prudent bank management.

The question of the underlying assumptions enters even deeper fields. As a starting point we refer to the BIS and its statement:

> Liquidity is the ability of a bank to fund increases in assets and meet obligations as they come due, without incurring unacceptable losses. The fundamental role of banks in the maturity transformation of short-term deposits into long-term loans makes banks inherently vulnerable to liquidity risk, both of an institution-specific nature and that which affects markets as a whole.

This concludes: 'Liquidity risk management is of paramount importance because a liquidity shortfall at a single institution can have system-wide repercussions' (BCBS, 2008, page 1).

The focus is thus less on a single bank and its potential to fail, but more on the impact of such a case on the financial system. The interpretation is supported by advising supervisors to 'more carefully scrutinize banks that pose the largest risks to the financial system and hold such banks to a higher standard of liquidity risk management' (BCBS, 2008, page 31). Avoiding any hazard to the financial systems seems to be an overriding goal, not only with regard to preventive measures, but also in the midst of a crisis when a large bank is about to fail. Respective interventions by state authorities or agencies in the cases of Northern Rock (UK), Bear Stearns, Fannie Mae and Freddie Mac (United States), UBS (Switzerland), Hypo real Estate (Germany), Fortis (Belgium) and Kaupthing (Iceland) during the subprime mortgage crisis are just a few prominent examples substantiating the interpretation. Letting Lehman Brothers go bankrupt can most probably be qualified as a mistake, at least with hindsight.

One could conclude that a further two-tier system of a different kind has emerged somewhere along the line. Depending on whether or not collapses are a hazard to financial stability, authorities either intervene or abstain. Or, to put it in a more common way, some institutions are 'too big to fail'. While the statement seems correct, one still needs to interpret the term 'fail'. The subject is not generally addressed within the scope of regulatory or supervisory policies as it belongs to the area of 'rare and extraordinary exceptions'. However, we will not be far from the truth if we refer to a remark made in a speech by Vincent Baritsch (FSA, 2006): 'Aim is to promote orderly winding down in a crisis by ensuring sufficient liquid resources are available.' This most probably reads: 'Regulators to take necessary steps to allow bank management at least to go through a process of "smooth liquidation" in case of severe and prolonged stresses.' The actions taken during the subprime crisis do not contradict the interpretation. If it had not been for the danger of seeing the financial system crash, winding down would have been the policy to follow, and will be so in the future on an individual basis. Lehman was thus an exception.

Although the view of 'smooth liquidation' contradicts our expressively formulated understanding of securing liquidity, whereby protecting the franchise, however defined, is included, regulators do not believe in 'self-responsibility' of bank management. On their view, determined from past experience and reconfirmed in the subprime crisis, setting rules and controlling adherence to them are necessities to make the banks change their attitude in the direction envisaged by the authorities. The ECB alludes to two examples: on Germany, 'When the supervisory authority in DE changed its liquidity requirements (2000), this resulted in a new composition of banks' portfolio of highly liquid assets as well as other short-term investments immediately convertible into cash'; and on the UK, 'Following the introduction of the "sterling stock regime" in the UK, one of the liquidity requirements imposed by the Financial Services Authority (FSA), firms were observed to substantially increase their holdings of sterling certificates of deposits (CDs)' (ECB, 2002, page 18).

8.2.2.2 Regulating liquidity

When it comes to the implementation of the concepts, by design they are mainly rather short-term orientated. The core frame hardly exceeds a period of 1 month and sometimes has a specific focus on the first five working days (stock approach, FSA). The main consideration is given to a drain on funding capacity under severe conditions. As a starting point, flows of contractual maturities are taken. Yet it is not uncommon to come across a built-in component of behavioural attitudes: wholesale funds are clearly distinct from retail deposits. While the former is judged as extremely volatile – thus possible renewals at maturity are usually excluded from the calculation – retail deposits are assessed as having a high level of intrinsic stickiness. Depending on the regulator, the degree of stability can be put up to 90 or 95%. In case of a negative balance of the underlying (business-induced) flows, depending on the regulator, either a 'stock' or a 'funding' approach is applicable for fulfilling the requirement of a zero balance for the period defined. The latter obliges banks to adjust the funding volume to meet the regulatory target. If a 'stock' approach is applicable, there are unencumbered marketable assets which can close the gap, provided they qualify for defined 'eligibility'. Irrespective of the chosen scheme, the goals envisaged are comparable: setting up and enforcing a regulatory frame for liquidity with the aim of securing the fulfilment of payment obligations of the banks for the period defined.

An important benefit of this type of scheme is the clarity of the method and simplicity of its handling. Yet there is a price to be paid for the advantages:

- The rules usually do not segregate exposures per currencies but define ratios or stocks in the legal tender of the supervisor. Smaller regional banks should hardly be affected by the restriction, while large international banks have their reality very much distorted.
- A short-term frame of 1 month or so does not imply securing liquidity in the periods beyond. Internally, at Commerzbank we added calculations for further periods up to 1 year on the basis of present transactions. The aim was to detect sharp deteriorations in funding at an early stage.
- Rules deciding not to integrate behavioural attitudes on the asset side (what we call franchise) will have repercussions on the bank's business concept in the case of a severe stress; alternatively, substantially over-fulfilling the regulatory requirement will be the effect if banks wish to secure their franchise.
- According to BCBS (2006, page 10), banks 'commonly assume that they will roll over loans as they mature in order to protect their franchise'. This applies for regional and international institutions. Opting internally to protect the franchise, Commerzbank substantially over-fulfilled the minimum requirements during all the severe name-related stress in 2002.
- Since the scheme is primarily based on rather deterministic flows – with a few exceptions like retail deposits – it does not or may not sufficiently consider potentially negative implications from 'optionalities'. In some instances they can turn out to be substantial.
- All in all, adhering to the minimum of basic liquidity rules set by regulators gives a chance of surviving a stress for at least 1 month, provided the bank has no complex instruments and business structure, no substantial engagements in optionalities and is rather locally orientated.

Supervisors became aware of the limited effects of short-term focused rules years ago and started to define further regulations with the aim of controlling liquidity risk better. Apart from enhancing the regulatory scheme by a two-tier approach – as done for example by Germany in 2007 – minimum requirements to be observed by banks have been defined and implemented on a wide geographical basis. The Basel Committee on Banking Supervision has addressed the subject related to 'Sound Practices' since the year 2000 (BCBS, 2000) and published its latest recommendations concerning sound liquidity risk management and supervision in 2008 (BCBS, 2008). The banking community, represented by the Institute of International Finance (IIF), formulated wide-ranging recommendations the year before (IIF, 2007). Many of the suggestions raised in previous documents and by various bodies have been integrated into the latest analysis of the Committee of European Banking Supervisors and its recommendations (CEBS, 2008). Although the proposals also deal with the nature, environment and management of liquidity risk, we will concentrate on their view of the 'Supervisory Approach to Liquidity Risk Management and Internal Methodologies' (Section IV).

8.2.2.3   'Best Practice' for (European) regulators

As a starting point, the Committee states: 'The role of supervisors is to ensure the safety and soundness of individual institutions and, more broadly, of the financial system' (CEBS, 2008, page 55). Based on its analysis the Committee concludes:

- Institutions are facing a competitive disadvantage if they mitigate liquidity risk solo but not in line with their competitors.

- Availability of central bank emergency liquidity assistance, deposit insurance schemes and implicit government guarantees may reduce managers' and shareholders' incentives to build in much resilience to liquidity stress 'as the wider costs of failure to the economy at large would justify'.
- Solvency problems or perceived ones can be a source of liquidity pressure. Vice versa, capital as one key element of solvency may not be an appropriate buffer in times of difficult circumstances.
- The ongoing turmoil (referring to the subprime mortgage crisis), which to a large extent is characterised by loss of confidence in supervised institutes as well, indicates a lack of full trust in supervisors.
- It is for these reasons why supervisory actions are called for.

The Committee concludes with three lines of recommendations: namely quantitative, qualitative and organisational ones (CEBS, 2008, page 55f.):

- Quantitative: An appropriate liquidity buffer is needed as a first line of defence. The buffer is seen as a vital instrument in stressed situations which we call 'shock'. Especially banks with greater dependence on wholesale funding are more vulnerable in these circumstances. Consequently, emphasis has to be put on the actual and future liquidity status of instruments making up such buffers. The qualitative resistance in turmoil, a possible reduction in the absorptive capacity leading to market congestion as well as contagion effects like flight to quality are all assessed to be critical points to be considered. To evaluate them, appropriate tools need to be developed.
- Qualitative: Setting rules to assess the adequacy of banks' internal methodologies as to liquidity risk. Being mainly of a static nature, quantitative rules should be complemented with qualitative elements. As a growing number of institutions depend on funding sources which respond sensitively to other risk categories (what we presented graphically in Figure 3.9), evaluating liquidity implications from those sources cannot be neglected. Also in this view, sound management of market, credit, operational and further risks support the endeavour but do not fully mitigate liquidity risk. Further measures are required such as: segregation between operational and monitoring functions; personnel, methodological and technical setups to be in line with the level and complexity of risk taking; the allocations of funding cost being appropriate debited to the initiating unit and reflected in their performance, including in the planning phase; insisting on and reviewing the appropriateness of stress tests, whereby liquidity implications stemming from on-balance-sheet as well as off-balance-sheet instruments, non-contractual support (e.g. majority holdings) and covenants vis-à-vis the bank's own SPVs and conduits need to be included; and not the least a complete and coherent contingency plan based on conservatively applied governance and sound methodology.
- Organisational: Close coordination at an international level. The committee suggests that national supervisors develop and perform macro stress-test scenarios to detect possible origins of systemic risk leading to unsettling the financial stability as a whole. Cross-sectoral analysis could encompass financial segments such as insurers, pension funds, banks and investment firms and indicate primary as well as second-round effects. The findings, provided to the segments involved in the supervisory test, could be used to review the set of measures taken by the latter. On a wider aspect, from recent and ongoing events (the subprime mortgage crisis) the committee concluded swift and coordinated actions to be necessary beyond borders and in close coordination between supervisors, central banks

and finance ministries. Furthermore, the Committee suggests a distinction between 'credit institutions and investment firms that merit close attention and those allowing a lighter approach' (CEBS, 2008, page 56).

The proposals addressing the national European supervisors are very much in line with the principles as suggested by the IIF (2007). From a practitioner's point of view, the mind-set of the proposals is highly welcome. But how are they applied? For illustrative purposes we will restrict ourselves to the approaches of the supervisors in Germany and the UK, thereby sticking to our intention not to enter into a comparative study of central bank policy. For further discussions we refer to BaFin (2006b) and FSA (2007).

Regarding the overall frame, both supervisors derived their rules and regulations from the second pillar within Basel II. The key elements like banks taking reasonable steps to withstand a name- or market-related liquidity stress, defining principles for scenario analysis, stress testing, the setting up of a contingency plan, etc., are comparable, although specific national characteristic in the national banking sector are accommodated within the specific rules. The approaches differ when it comes to reporting – not generally, but in part.

Both of them apply a mismatch approach as a standard instrument. In order to secure sufficient means to fulfil payment obligations, outgoing payments are deducted from incoming flows and put into a time sequence. The latter has at least to match outflows. Although the reporting requires information on balances up to 1 year, the 100% coverage applies in both cases to the first month only. Supervisors in both countries allow for behavioural adjustments with regard to retail deposits, for example, whereby the 'stickiness' is put at 90% and 95% by the BaFin and the FSA respectively. Marketable assets are viewed as cash provided the required conditions are met. A significant difference relates to committed lines provided to a bank: the FSA admits a portion of the lines established while the BaFin actually stresses the inherent danger of non-fulfilment by the third party in the case of a severe condition.

Both the BaFin and FSA distinguish between a standard approach applicable in general and a further or 'advanced' approach for larger banks characterised by a higher complexity level. In the UK, this is known as the 'sterling stock regime' and applied for 17 banks. The stock held by the bank in sterling liquid assets needs to match the wholesale sterling net outflow over the next five working days, minus allowable CDs, plus 5% of sterling retail deposits contractually withdrawable over the next five working days. According to the FSA, 'the sterling stock regime should not be considered as one component of a wider crisis management regime' (FSA, 2007, page 32). The aim is to gain time in order to define measures to be taken appropriate to the respective circumstances.

The BaFin follows a different route. Although applying a mismatch concept for the standard approach as well, an advanced approach (the opening clause) is offered but not imposed on any bank – so the official version – while applying the sterling stock regime is 'agreed' with the banks, according to the FSA. The advanced approach in Germany is based neither on stock nor on any other quantitative measurement, but relates to qualitative criteria. Considering that the FSA is in a process of reviewing its concept, the focus will now be on the approach taken by the BaFin.

8.2.3 Internal liquidity risk measurement and management systems: the case of Germany

As of 1 January 2007, the German supervisory authorities changed the legal frame related to liquidity from Basic Principle II to the Ordinance on Liquidity (*Liquiditätsverordnung*).

The new frame contains an 'opening clause' permitting institutions to use internal liquidity risk measurement and management systems (advanced approach) in place of the standard requirements as per the *Liquiditätsverordnung*. The regulation brought about a two-tier supervisory systematic to liquidity, taking into consideration marked differences in complexity of instruments and structure between the vast group of regional banks and the relatively small group of internationally orientated banks. The segregation into the two groups largely follows the above-described suggestion of the CEBS to distinguish between firms that merit close attention and those allowing a lighter approach. Although the opening clause permits firms to opt for an internal approach, the supervisor expects institutions beyond a certain level of inherent complexity to apply for permission to use the advanced concept.

8.2.3.1   National adoption of Basel II

As stated by Rehsmann and Martin (2008, page 56), liquidity in the second pillar within the frame of Basel II is dealt with in the context of capital adequacy and the capability of a bank to fulfil payment obligations even in the time of a crisis in 2005. In the later revised 'Core Principles' of 2006 the management of liquidity risk was declared as being a separate basic principle of supervision. The Federal Financial Supervisory Authority, hereinafter referred to as the BaFin, and the Bundesbank (BUBA) with which audits are performed jointly, derive their functions from two nationally legal frameworks: the 'German Ordinance on Liquidity' (referred to as LiqV) and the 'Minimum Requirements for Risk Management' (referred to as MaRisk). The first one applies a basically quantitative approach and the latter a qualitative one. We will address the qualitative part here.

MaRisk applies to all institutions within the confine of the German regulator. It covers a wide range of subjects, including minimum requirements for trading activities (MaH), credit lending (MaK) and internal audit (MaIR). Furthermore, MaRisk refers expressly to interest rate risk on a group level, operational risk and, not least, liquidity risk. MaRisk is structured in a modular manner, distinguishing between general and specific requirements. As a starting point the general requirements will be addressed, but limited to liquidity (see also Rehsmann and Martin, 2008, page 61f.).

The primary principle related to any form of risk and the quality of procedures is defined as the responsibility of the executive board or board of directors. According to MaRisk, the responsibility extends to:

- Risk strategy for liquidity: The focus is on orderly management of a bank with respect to liquidity risk in general and the practical application regarding the frame of liquidity risk management as well as the development of risk measurement and management procedures appropriate for the respective institution. Appropriate signifies to be in line with type, complexity and risk level of the respective organisation and its business concept: establishing rules for dealing with liquidity risk in general; determining the sources of liquidity and their limitation in quantity; setting rules for a diversified funding policy and setting up a contingency plan may all serve as examples.
- Controlling the systematic: An adequate liquidity controlling system includes a proper segregation of duties into managing and controlling functions with separated reporting lines; assessing liquidity implications for alternative stress scenarios and periodic reporting to the board on status, potential threats, measures taken or proposed, etc., just to mention some relevant points.

- Internal audit: This contains, for example, examining adherence to set rules and regulations as well as correctness and completeness of data collected and utilised. Furthermore, risk processes are to be evaluated in respect of methodological and technical soundness.
- Auxiliary points: These cover written organisational directives (e.g. related to the risk management and controlling processes); appropriate documentation of data; allocation of personnel and technical resources in quantity and quality fitting the tasks to be performed; appropriate assessment and integration of new products/markets into liquidity management; a limit and controlling frame as well as contingency planning.

While general requirements formulate the obligations of top management, the specific ones concentrate on liquidity management, focusing on elements relevant for securing the fulfilment of payment obligations. The requirements can be segregated into five spheres, to which we add some examples:

1. Markets/products: Is there a liquid market for individual products or are they to be considered illiquid? What haircut is to be applied for liquid products, and if the former changes over time is it updated? To what degree (time and volume) can potentially liquid assets be turned into cash in the market (collateral, repo transactions, etc.) or with central banks?
2. Flow of cash balance: This instrument gives an overview of expected in- and outflows of cash over a specified period of time. Retail funds like saving deposits etc. are assessed as relatively 'sticky'. Such behavioural attitudes on liabilities are taken into account in the calculation based on historic experience. For complex products with embedded options (what we call optionalities) a historic view is not seen as appropriate. More sophisticated and forward-looking analyses are required. Implications of stressed situations should reveal whether the obligation to fulfil payment obligations can be upheld on the basis of various scenarios.
3. Degree of liquidity: This item concerns the means available for fulfilling payment obligations. Avoiding dependency on unreliable sources is at the forefront. Risk-reducing measures such as limiting unsecured interbank funding or tapping distant markets where the bank is not operatively present are endeavours in this direction. Taking steps to reduce negative daily balances gradually along the timescale towards the payment date and creating surpluses for the very short-term dates are further possible steps. On the assets side, tradable instruments with a liquid market can serve as a buffer to compensate shortages, provided haircuts and possible quantitative restrictions in a congested market are taken properly into consideration.
4. Acting under liquidity stress: Actions to be taken in stress conditions have to be prioritised in advance. The organisational setup under stressed conditions, the authorities and responsibilities of individuals, teams and groups throughout the hierarchy as well as the channels of communication and command need to be determined in advance as well.
5. Internal information: The board of directors is to be informed at all times about developments under stressed conditions. Given the severe implications of a liquidity stress, the board has to be informed periodically about the liquidity status of the bank, potential threats and measures taken or proposed.

As stated earlier, the set of qualitative rules is derived from the second pillar within Basel II. The regulatory frame and its relatively precise formulation of actions, responsibilities, controlling mechanisms, etc., will lead over time to a level of 'best practice' adhered to by banks and could turn into a comfort building measure for the banking industry as a whole. It is the inherent characteristic of qualitative measures taking into account the specific complexity of individual banks when applied. The regime is thus not uniform but individualised for the respective institution within the generally applicable frame. Consequently, requirements on risk measurement and management will vary and increase in line with the complexity of the bank's structure and business performed. These factual circumstances were expressed when reformulating the quantitative reporting requirements.

8.2.3.2 The ordinance on liquidity (LiqV)

The LiqV is the successor of the old Principle II and entered into force on 1 January 2007 (BaFin, 2006b; see also Rehsmann and Martin, 2008, page 68f.). When applying the standard approach, changes to the old rules are limited. The method is defined by the supervisor based on a combination of maturity mismatch and stock approach. The reporting is pre-structured and standardised for all banks concerned, based on a scenario of normal conditions or 'going concern'.

The rule applied demands that cash outflow has to be covered by cash available. The latter exists of inflows created by maturing assets and non-maturing cash producing assets by means of collateral, repo transactions, etc. The reporting form distinguishes four bands: the first band up to 1 month, the remaining bands covering 1–3, 3–6 and 6–12 months. For deterministic contracts the remaining time till maturity applies. A deviating treatment is given to short-term liabilities with no contractual maturity, for which a specific 'stickiness' is assumed. Securities traded at official exchanges and cash at the central bank are all allocated to the first band irrespective of the remaining maturity. The first band requires a liquidity ratio ≥ 1, while the other bands are only 'observed', with no ratio requirements defined. Furthermore, changes in the liquidity structure caused by derivative obligations and drawings of unutilised short-term committed lines, for example, are not considered in the scheme.

According to the regulator, the shortcomings and its implications (see 8.2.2.2) are not accidental but part of the design. For those banks with a higher complexity level and thus advanced risk measurement and management requirements within MaH, an opening clause was established within the LiqV, giving the respective banks the right to apply to use an internal liquidity model for calculation and reporting purposes, where the term 'model' stands for 'liquidity risk measurement and management procedure' (BaFin, 2006b, page 1).

8.2.3.3 The 'advanced' approach

The advanced approach requires the use of internal models within the frame of adhering to liquidity rules within MaH and reporting to the supervisor. For the internal model no directives are given. The bank has the freedom to design a structure, defining its risk appetite, setting up procedures and control mechanisms fitting its business model, complexity of structure and instruments employed. Individual circumstances and business models will be taken into account. The emphasis is thus on: consistency, clarity, completeness and appropriateness. Qualitative criteria as presented before are put into the frame of internal models and adequate fulfilment of them is checked in the application process. The elements checked and evaluated are:

• Adequate investigation and supervision of liquidity risks.
• Appropriate presentation of the liquidity risk

- Procedures covering expected short-term net cash outflows and capacity for obtaining unsecured funding.
- Setting quantitative limits for individual liquidity risk elements under normal and scenario-related stressed conditions.
- Identifying ratios indicating a lack of sufficient liquidity.
- Defining the level at which the institution judges itself to be at medium and high risk concerning liquidity.
- Documentation as to measures to be taken if predefined thresholds are reached or exceeded.
- Application of the internal model and its limit systematic with respect to liquidity and business management.

Furthermore, liquidity management and thus the internal model are put into a wider frame, encompassing sectors which can impinge on it. It contains the examination of technical systems, analysis of procedures and their embedding in an appropriate management and controlling environment; integration of modelled results (use tests) into scenario analyses of risk management and controlling; the setting up of limit systems and the respective escalation procedures; reporting channels and frequency in normal and stressed conditions; predefined measures in case of stress; and last but not least, the soundness of computer systems, their links to other systems and the quality of their reports.

The opening clause endeavours to produce benefits in two areas. For the financial system it is seen as a step towards greater stability, as banks with a higher degree of complexity are supervised on a more diligent and sophisticated level. For banks, supervisory reporting falls more into line with their internal measures when fulfilling MaH rules: there is no one-for-all reporting requirement, but it is set individually in the course of the application process, to see consequently requests for internal and external reporting narrowing. Assuming that the concept of internal models gains ground on an international basis, which means that home and host regulators can agree on a common concept as to internal models, duplication in preparing reports on different rules and regulations could one day be a thing of the past. One would also assume that internal models validated by the supervisor would enhance trust within the banking community (Rehsmann and Martin, 2008, page 66f.).

8.3   CONSIDERATIONS AND CONCLUSIONS FOR BANK MANAGEMENT

It would be a severe misconception if management were to believe that liquidity risk is primarily a concern that could be handed over to its specialists and the respective supervisors. No doubt, both are indispensable: the specialists in the bank to apply and manage controlling, measuring liquidity risk, setting up and administering procedures as well as taking all necessary further steps to secure the fulfilment of payment obligations in a professional manner; the supervisors in order to give each bank a level playing field by applying appropriate rules to all institutions within their jurisdiction. Yet, in the end, for both shareholders and supervisors alike, it is top management which carries the ultimate responsibility for securing the proper management of all banking aspects, including liquidity risk. The latter could actually be reduced to an operational task delegated to a professional were it not for the severe implications under conditions of a crisis, starting from damaging core business and ranging to illiquidity and then insolvency of the bank. Market-related severe negative impacts are relatively rare, but intervals have become very short, as we can detect from Figure 5.4, and a name-related stress can still be called an exception within rare occurrences, although, if hit by it, more often than not the bank concerned is likely to fail. The categories sensibly include all the cases in which, for example, a cooperative of saving banks steps in and takes over all assets and liabilities, when the state authorities guarantee potential losses with the view to finding a buyer or outright nationalisation.

For bank management, liquidity is part of the triangular relationship with business and financial policies (Figure 8.2). In our presentation in Figure 3.9, we identified growth as the driving element affecting most internal parameters directly and the remaining parts indirectly. Business policy needs to be brought into equilibrium within what we called the magic polygon. As the respective elements do not necessarily act in a complementary way but often in a contradictory manner, the relationship is not one way but takes the character of interaction. Planned growth may lead to a level of downside risk potential outweighing risk capacity in the form of capital. Or an inappropriate business concept may lead to losses over a prolonged period and thus drain the capital base. In both examples the aspect of liquidity is affected negatively and in the first case in an extremely serious way.

In a first round, bank management needs to concentrate on keeping the VAR circle in balance. This is a critical task due to the strong implications of the rating, defined as the market assessment regarding the financial strengths of the institution. It is a starting point but requires further measures, of which two should be emphasised: underestimating risk potential and market perception.

Assessing risk potential is a forward-looking process. Assumptions are made to arrive at the result. In traditional businesses and environments historic data provide a sensible basis of what potentially to expect. Product innovation with respect to type of instrument, packing individual assets into portfolios or structured instrument/portfolio enhancement with optionalities do not provide the benefit of experience. Even if such 'contracts' have become standard business in a market foreign to the bank, for the latter they are innovative products due to lack of experience. For innovations in particular, assessments can turn out to be wrong and actually exceed the calculated risk potential by a large margin, as painfully experienced in the subprime crisis. The risk, when investing in packages and other securitised assets, has not been underestimated for the first time in the US subprime mortgage crisis. Actually, it is only one event in a long chain of such occurrences.

When it comes to the markets, assessing the financial health of an institution is a forward-looking process as well. Capital ratios and rating grades are taken by the market as a first

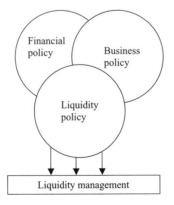

Figure 8.2   Liquidity within the strategic triangular relationship

indication. Yet both of them are lagging indicators. Any underestimated risk potential and thus losses, in the event of actually materialising, are not incorporated in the indicators. The perception of markets may therefore differ from the results reached by using past data and internal risk assessments. And markets will always act on perception, whether or not it coincides with formal financial health assessments.

For both somewhat related circumstances, supervisory rules do not provide a remedy. They define the process and methodology of evaluating risk, demand adherence to minimum procedures (e.g. MaH) and determine the coverage through capital (capital adequacy rules) but do not enter into elements of assessment. That stays with the management, the people responsible for managing the bank. The latter may avoid the risk or minimise it by taking smaller stakes in comparison with the overall risk potential. Alternatively, a larger capital buffer than legally required may be set up to withstand unexpected losses in the area where experience is lacking. Neglecting such a cautious attitude increases the danger of capital-related insolvency or could, in less severe circumstances, cause a stress on liquidity which could lead to insolvency through illiquidity. This brings us to the second circle: the liquidity risk.

We concluded that liquidity is of a multi-dimensional nature. For downside-risk-related stresses – the major cause for name-related ones – management has means at hand to reduce the likelihood of their occurring; not fully, as we have seen, but to some extent. When it comes to market-related stresses affecting assets or liabilities, the causes are determined externally to quite an extent, although to different degrees.

The bank's funding represents the opposite to lending by market participants. The decision to invest in a particular bank is theirs. A sound level of financial strength increases the probability of getting funds even in a severe market-related liquidity crisis. There is no guarantee of such market behaviour, however, and even less a chance to assume being provided with funds at the present level; cost expressed as liquidity spread will augment in any case. Counteracting measures are mainly limited to fostering more stable funding, tapping markets on a diversified basis, keeping in close contact with fund providers, etc., as listed in 4.4.

Assets are in the books because of a conscious decision by management to do so. Thus, the decision lies with the bank, in contrast to liabilities. Choosing the quality of tradable assets with respect to the creditworthiness of the issuer, marketability of the instrument and depth as well as reliance of markets are key items determining their potential capability to be turned into cash. Although all assets can be turned into cash – at maturity – with the proviso of 'securing the franchise', tradable assets employed for liquidity management need to fulfil a further requirement: being able to be exchanged against cash immediately or within a very short timeframe. In making up the buffers to secure the bank's liquidity status for payments and the defined franchise, the condition related to timing is of paramount importance. In case of a mistaken judgement, instruments in the buffer may not be exchangeable into cash in time to secure payments, thus requiring the utilisation of assets falling due now.

If the latter happens to be part of the franchise, a portion of core business needs to be used to secure payment obligations, with corresponding detrimental impacts on business strategy. Even if conservative criteria are employed for choosing instruments in buffers, the market may contradict experience and logic. For example, in Germany a type of mortgage-backed security exists called 'Pfandbrief', which could be called a gilt-edged investment. The collateral for the issue should not exceed the first 60% of the underlying property value, adherence to which is controlled independently. Furthermore, house prices have not ballooned over the last 10 years or so; in fact they have stayed rather stable. In any previous banking or liquidity crisis they have been a pillar of relative stability. This time, however, markets had become destabilised and even 6–9 months after the subprime crisis started, the absorptive capacity of the market had been way off normal conditions, with the consequence that investors saw their liquid capacity reduced. The author's friend John Reilly in New York, when asked for an explanation, replied dryly: 'Looks like a duck, walks like a duck, quacks like a duck – it surely must be a duck', and this even for insiders. Experiences like these are the reason for the advice to keep the largest part of buffers in instruments 'eligible' to central banks; luckily for the banks, it was eligible.

A further source of uncertainty relates to drawings in excess of expectations which are anticipated. We called them optionalities, consisting of various forms of contingent liabilities such as backup lines for CP issuers and acting as lender of last resort for SPVs, conduits and units with the right to fund themselves independently in the markets. In the case of a liquidity crisis, demands from these corners can be substantial. The latter being part of the bank in the understanding of the market, the head office, as the internal lender of last resort, has to take precautionary steps irrespective of the legal status of the relationship. There is often a misconception when it comes to legally independent units. From a market point of view they are part of the group, and limits are set for the highest level before being broken down. Any problem anywhere within the limit frame will have repercussions on the group assessment and will affect the overall limit and thus the funding capacity of the bank.

Supervisors do not and cannot solve the dilemma that management is in with regard to asset or liability liquidity. The second pillar of Basel II requires appropriate steps to be taken in this respect. Their content is very much left to bank management, although some general guidelines are given in the national rules.

The BIS states: 'Supervisors should assess the risk tolerance of a bank to confirm that it ensures sufficient liquidity, given the bank's role in the financial system'; it continues: 'Supervisors should assess whether the board of directors and senior management are taking full responsibility for the guidance to line management and staff' (BIS, 2008, page 31). The first point refers to avoiding hazards to the financial system and thus is purely supervision focused, giving the basis to employ for example a 'standard' as well as an 'advanced' approach, as in the case of Germany. The second recommendation is expressed in more detail later on and found its way into national regulations in the form of concrete instructions. It may even include views on specific issues, as in the case of the German regulator not to overestimate the value of 'committed funding lines': in case of perceived high risk the counterpart may prefer potential litigation to comprehended losses. Nevertheless, regulations stop before going as far as addressing how to assess the actual risk on assets or liabilities in respect of liquidity. In these areas, the ball is clearly in the court of bank management. The subprime crisis has made that abundantly clear. To the best of our knowledge, no supervisor has been – at least not sufficiently – alarmed by the degree of leveraging liquidity by financing subprime or subprime-infected tradable assets with short-term funds.

Today, a wide range of national supervisory approaches within the frame of BIS recommendations can be observed, even within the system of the ECB. Depending on the type and degree of supervisory approaches – standard or advanced, with emphasis on qualitative or quantitative elements – the room within which bank management has to act on its own responsibility and without further guidance can vary significantly. But even in the best of all worlds, there is one vital divergence between supervision and bank management interest: securing the franchise. The supervisory endeavour is on avoiding any hazard to the financial system, although with little avail in this crisis. Rules defined for banks thus accept preparations which eventually can lead to what we called 'smooth liquidation', i.e. winding up a bank without hazard to the financial system. The recently observed concentration of interventions by the authorities with regard to some banks about to fail is to be seen as a consistent application of the rules set by the authorities themselves.

For bank management answerable to shareholders the frame needs to be wider: securing the franchise during any type of liquidity stress is a task to be fulfilled. As the task reaches beyond supervisory requirements, it has to be properly communicated to the specialists on liquidity management. Their endeavours naturally will concentrate on serving the bank in the best way by securing adherence to regulatory requirements. Yet, for the regulator, it does not matter whether the next payment is obtained through a payback from an 'asset at risk', by employing the buffer securing the franchise or maturing asset belonging to core business. For management it makes all the difference, however. Taking up the business requirements as well, liquidity management is not only protecting the liquidity-related solvency of the bank, but supporting and contributing to the long-term business goals of the institution. Since management and policy are strongly interlinked, both parties need to work together. Successful liquidity management, therefore, demands a learning process that both members of the board and liquidity managers must be willing to take on.

In the aftermath of the subprime crisis with its near collapse of the financial system, there is no doubt that state authorities will tighten their rulings, not only by speeding up plans already designed or in the process of implementation, but well beyond the schemes presently planned and worked on. In the heat of the moment, politicians in all countries and irrespective of political party castigated greed; the attitude of a short-term view; the intentional policy of investment banks to buy junk, securitize it and sell it as subprime with a high-grade label stamped by the rating agencies. The remedies proposed were then in accordance with the analysis. The heat of the moment is a bad time to offer advice; what is needed is an analysis regarding the causes, the mechanisms as well as the behavioural attitudes at all stages of the process leading to the near crash of the financial system. Such a task is well beyond a single person and definitely exceeds the purpose of this book. We concentrate on liquidity and some findings gained in the previous chapters and leave out macroeconomic considerations such as the influence of over-proportionate money supply for a much extended period, with interest rates kept artificially low compared with average rates in the comparable past. The findings in the midst of a crisis cannot be judged as final but have to be seen as an intermediary assessment by a practitioner forced to evaluate the implications for a bank.

Grave losses have definitely played a key role in the initial stage of the crisis. A specific group of assets has been assessed to contain a much lower potential for downside risk as actually experienced, and by a wide margin. Three causes present themselves as explanations: the value of the asset was the only cover for the mortgage loan; borrowers had the right to withdraw book gains at maturity of the short-term loan, thus keeping the debt level high; and house prices were assumed to increase continuously or to stay stable at least. The effect was not necessarily due to any single component in isolation but to all of their full effects in combination and featuring through all portfolios containing loans. Because of the underestimation of the loss potential, capital ratios were too favourable compared with the risk and overstated the health of the respective bank. What led to the underestimation of the risk potential has still to be analysed, yet lack of historic track records has surely played its part.

Short-term financing of assets is another area to focus on. Liquefiable assets can be financed with maturities in accordance with the speed at which assets can be turned into cash. Yet it is not a (short) track record which can be taken as the basis. If we do so, we most probably assess implications under 'normal' conditions, to use the technical term. Assessing the liquidity status demands a forward-looking attitude: up to yesterday we were liquid or we would be out of work today. Especially with no long-term track record, but not limited to it as there are other vagaries of market conditions like the fallout of a large bank or the drying up of asset or liability liquidity, the future can be worse than the past. We referred to this point when dealing with basic principles at the end of Chapter 1. Has the banking community at large steered liquidity while looking in the rear mirror and thus saved cost in the short run? The question is not just directed at institutions in the first and second lines of the subprime mortgage business but refers also to banks which experienced a severe liquidity squeeze in the second and third rounds.

Conduits and similar constructs have seemingly become a surprising liability for many owner banks. If such a bank cannot detach itself liquidity-wise from a subsidiary company, and based on market behaviour it cannot whatever the legal status, any unit not integrated into the parent bank, whether legally or organisationally, poses a risk which likely stays hidden for bank management and supervisors alike. In this respect, non-banking subsidiaries are of ungraded risk, so they fall through the supervisory grid. It is the ultimate (liquidity) lender of last resort who needs to see the full picture and demand adherence to the basic rules, including the authority to enforce them. An alternative handling may be acceptable if potential liquidity demands on the parent company are negligible related to the overall picture, and allow for putting aside a cushion for any extreme case. A similar effect can be caused by a large acquisition. Actually, the liquidity structure is changed overnight. Even if appropriate the day before, it may have turned for the worse. Under normal market conditions regarding liquidity, there is time to re-establish the set of appropriate rules. But who knows with certainty the market conditions of tomorrow? Taking respective steps in advance has to be as high a priority as securing the financing of the acquisition.

Without doubt, the selection just presented and discussed is not complete. Know your customer, and if you have no customers but a share of a portfolio, know the ultimate customer behind the portfolio. Or, if your capital is vastly in excess of genuine client business, reduce the capital, and if it is not feasible because the customer base is too low to justify running a bank, close it. But these points belong to general banking, are not liquidity specific and will thus not be addressed in our context.

What is striking, however, when looking at the three sets of points discussed, is that in most instances supervisors cannot do much to solve the potential problem. They could increase the minimum capital ratios. But most banks have not failed or needed state support because the ratio for core capital amounted to between 4 and 5%. Some of them were in the double-digit area. Where then is the safe haven mark if banks can get the fallout rate totally wrong? As for assessments of the degree to which tradable assets are liquefiable, who should know better than the institution specialising in these markets? The same is true for the level of funding capacity in general and related to a specific institution. Where supervisors can impact best is on reducing the leveraging of liquidity, i.e. less gapping between long and short liquidity positions, to increase liquidity buffers and demand that a substantial portion of the latter qualifies for central bank eligibility. The essence of assessments has been and should remain the duty of bank management. There are good reasons why supervisors have only set basic rules and tightened requirements on processes but not entered into defining the degree of actual risk. Over centuries, banks have established themselves as intermediaries between lenders and borrowers, as both of these groups wish to avoid the transformation risk and uncertainty about availability and repayment respectively. It is the genuine business of banking, but needs proper leadership.

While the subprime crisis escalated, the question came up frequently of whether the book had to be rewritten because of the unprecedented developments, not least with regard to liquidity. The answer must have been disappointing: the banking industry knows all there is to know about liquidity, at least since Leonard Matz, but may have forgotten about it or was distracted and no longer remembered that liquidity is the twin of downside risk and equally dangerous if neglected. Adding the 'subprime' section was thus only for illustrative purposes.

Bibliography

BaFin (10 October 2002) Untersuchung möglicher Kursmanipulationen gegen Commerzbank: Es gibt keine Zweifel an der Liquidität der deutschen Banken, Presse-mitteilung.

BaFin (2006a) Mindestanforderungen an das Risikomanagement (MaRisk), Rundschreiben 18/2005, Bonn.

BaFin (2006b) Verordnung über die Liquidität der Kreditinstitute (LiqV), Bonn.

Bardenhewer, Martin. M. (2007) Modeling Non-maturing Products, in Matz, Leonard and Neu, Peter (eds), *Liquidity Risk: Measurement and Management*, John Wiley & Sons Singapore, pages 220–256.

Bartetzky, Peter (2008) Liquiditätsrisikomanagement, in Bartetzky, Peter, Gruber, Walter and Wehn, Carsten (eds), *Handbuch Liquiditätsrisiko: Identifikation, Messung und Steuerung*, Schäffer-Poeschel Verlag, Stuttgart, pages 1–27.

Bartetzky, Peter, Gruber, Walter and Wehn, Carsten (eds) (2008) *Handbuch Liquiditätsrisiko: Identifikation, Messung und Steuerung*, Schäffer-Poeschel Verlag, Stuttgart.

BCBS (2000) Sound Practices for Managing Liquidity in Banking Organisations, Bank for International Settlement, Basle.

BCBS (2006) The Joint Forum: The management of liquidity risk in financial groups, Bank for International Settlement, Basle.

BCBS (2008) Principles for Sound Liquidity Risk Management and Supervision, Bank for International Settlements, Basle.

Bernstein, Peter L. (1996) *Against the Gods – The remarkable story of risk*, John Wiley & Sons, Inc., New York.

Brandenburg, Dierk (2007) Sound Liquidity Management as an Investment Criterion, in Matz, Leonard and Neu, Peter (eds), *Liquidity Risk: Measurement and Management*, John Wiley & Sons Singapore, pages 310–323.

CEBS (2008) Second Part of CEBS's Technical Advice to the European Commission on Liquidity Risk Management, June.

Comptroller of the Currency (2001) Liquidity, *Comptrollers' Handbook*, February.

Copeland, T., Koller, T. and Murrin, J. (1995) *Valuation – Measuring and Managing the Value of Companies*, John Wiley & Sons, Inc., New York.

Die Welt (1 October 2008) Bonitäts-Gerüchte belasten Commerzbank, page 11.

Die Welt (14 October 2008) Wie eine halbe Billion die Finanzbranche retten soll, page 10.

Die Welt (4 November 2008) Commerzbank lässt sich vom Staat helfen, page 9.

Duttweiler, Rudolf (1991) The Money Desk: Functions, risks and limits, in Weisweiler, Rudi, *Managing a Foreign Exchange Department* (2nd Edition), Woodhead-Faulkner, Cambridge, pages 86–119.

Duttweiler, Rudolf (2007) Die Finanzierung als möglicher Begrenzungsfaktor für die Geschäftspolitik einer Bank – und Wege zu seiner Überwindung, Speech at the Schmalenbachgesellschaft (Arbeitskreis Strategieentwicklung und Controlling in Banken), Eschborn, 5 October.

Duttweiler, Rudolf (2008) Liquidität als Teil der bankbetriebswirtschaftlichen Finanzpolitik, in Bartetzky, Peter, Gruber, Walter and Wehn, Carsten (eds), *Handbuch Liquiditätsrisiko: Identifikation, Messung und Steuerung*, Schäffel-Poeschel Verlag, Stuttgart, pages 29–50.

Duttweiler, Rudolf and Moez, A. Jamal (1991) Euro-Currencies, in Weisweiller, Rudi, *The Foreign Exchange Manual* (2nd Supplement), pages 13/1–13/49, Woodhead-Faulkner, Cambridge.

ECB (2002) Developments in Banks' Liquidity Profile and Management, May.

ECB (2007) Liquidity Risk Management in the EU for Cross-Border Banking Groups, Working Group on Developments in Banking within the Banking Supervision Committee of the ECB, March.

Elkenbracht, M. and Nauta, B.-J. (2006) Managing Interest Rate Risk for Non-Maturing Deposits, *Risk*, **19**(11): 82–87.

Fiedler, Robert (2007) A Concept for Cash Flow and Funding Liquidity Risk, in Matz, Leonard and Neu, Peter (eds), *Liquidity Risk: Measurement and Management*, John Wiley & Sons Singapore, pages 173–203.

Financial Times (1 October 2002) Commerzbank raises risk provisions again, page 17.

Financial Times (5 October 2002) Weekend edition: the Lex Column, page 22.

Financial Times (5 October 2002) Weekend edition: Merrill e-mail casts doubts on strength of Commerzbank, page 1.

Financial Times (8 October 2002) Bad loans fears hit European bank shares, page 1.

Financial Times (9 October 2002) S&P cuts Commerzbank's long-term rating, page 15.

Financial Times (10 October 2002) German banks get official vote of confidence, page 1.

Financial Times (13 October 2008) UK poised to pump £37 bn into four banks in recapitalisation, page 10.

Frauendorfer, Karl and Schürle, Michael (2007) Dynamic Modeling and Optimisation of Non-maturing Accounts, in Matz, Leonard and Neu, Peter (eds), *Liquidity Risk: Measurement and Management*, John Wiley & Sons Singapore, pages 327–359.

Frankfurter Allgemeine Zeitung (4 November 2008) 8,2 Milliarden Staatshilfe für die Commerzbank, page 11.

FSA (2006) Liquidity Risk – Regulatory Framework, Presentation by Vincent Baritsch, Wholesale and Prudential Policy Division, London, 8 August.

FSA (2007) Review of the Liquidity Requirements for Banks and Building Societies, December.

Gorton, Gary (2008) The Panic of 2007, Prepared for the Federal Reserve Bank of Kansas City, Jackson Hole Conference, August. Available online at: www.kc.frb.org/publicat/sympos/2008/Gorton.08.04.08.pdf (accessed January 2009).

Greenspan, Alan (2007) *The Age of Turbulence*, Allen Lane, London.

Gruber, Walter (2005) Praxisorientierte Bepreisung von einfachen und strukturierten Credit-Default-Swaps, *Handbuch Asset-Backed-Securities und Kreditderivate*, Schäffer-Poeschel Verlag, Stuttgart, pages 93–117.

Handelsblatt (2 October 2002) Vertrauen in deutsche Banken ist brüchig.

Heidorn, Thomas and Schmaltz, Christian (2008) Neue Entwicklungen im Liquiditätsmanagement, in Bartetzky, Peter, Gruber, Walter and Wehn, Carsten (eds), *Handbuch Liquiditätsrisiko: Identifikation, Messung und Steuerung*, Schäffer-Poeschel Verlag, Stuttgart, pages 141–170.

Heuter, Henning, Schäffler, Christian and Gruber, Walter (2008) Einbettung der Liquiditätssteuerung in die Gesamtbanksteuerung, in Bartetzky, Peter, Gruber, Walter and Wehn, Carsten (eds), *Handbuch Liquiditätsrisiko: Identifikation, Messung und Steuerung*, Schäffer-Poeschel Verlag, Stuttgart, pages 193–229.

Ibel, Korbinian Dominic (2001) *Bankenkrisen und Liquiditätsrisiko*, Schriftenreihe Wirtschafts- und Sozialwissenschaften, Band 45, Verlag Wissenschaft & Praxis, Sternenfels.

IIF (2007) Principles of Liquidity Risk Management, March.

Jarrow, Robert A (2007) Liquidity Risk and Classical Option Pricing Theory, in Matz, Leonard and Neu, Peter (eds), *Liquidity Risk: Measurement and Management*, John Wiley & Sons Singapore, pages 360–375.

Joint Forum (2007) The Management of Liquidity Risk in Financial Groups, BCBS, IOSCO and IAIS, Basle, May.

Kalkbrener, M. and Willing, J. (2004) Risk Management of Non-Maturing Liabilities, *Journal of Banking & Finance*, Vol. 28 (7), pages 1547–1568.

Knies, Karl (1876) Geld und Credit II, Abteilung Der Credit, Leipzig.

Küpper, Hans-Ulrich (2005) *Controlling*, 4th Revised Edition, Schäffer-Poeschel, Stuttgart.

Leistenschneider, Armin (2008) Methoden zur Ermittlung von Transferpreisen für Liquiditätsrisiken, in Bartetzky, Peter, Gruber, Walter and Wehn, Carsten (eds), *Handbuch Liquiditätsrisiko: Identifikation, Messung und Steuerung*, Schäffer-Poeschel Verlag, Stuttgart, pages 171–192.

Mason, Bruce W. (2007) Managing a Funding Crisis: Citizens First Bankcorp, a Case Study 1989–1994, in Matz, Leonard and Neu, Peter (eds), *Liquidity Risk: Measurement and Management*, John Wiley & Sons Singapore, pages 268–292.

Matz, Leonard (2002) *Liquidity Risk Management*, Thomson/Sheshunoff, Austin, TX.

Matz, Leonard (2007a) Scenario Analysis and Stress Testing, in Matz, Leonard and Neu, Peter (eds), *Liquidity Risk: Measurement and Management*, John Wiley & Sons Singapore, pages 37–63.

Matz, Leonard (2007b) Monitoring and Controlling Liquidity Risk, in Matz, Leonard and Neu, Peter (eds), *Liquidity Risk: Measurement and Management*, John Wiley & Sons Singapore, pages 67–99.

Matz, Leonard (2007c) Contingency Planning, in Matz, Leonard and Neu, Peter, *Liquidity Risk: Measurement and Management*, John Wiley & Sons Singapore, pages 121–145.

Matz, Leonard and Neu, Peter (eds) (2007a) *Liquidity Risk: Measurement and Management*, John Wiley & Sons Singapore.

Matz, Leonard and Neu, Peter (2007b) Liquidity Risk Management Strategies and Tactics, in Matz, Leonard and Neu, Peter (eds), *Liquidity Risk: Measurement and Management*, John Wiley & Sons Singapore, pages 100–120.

Matz, Leonard and Neu, Peter (2007c) View from the Mountaintop, in Matz, Leonard and Neu, Peter (eds), *Liquidity Risk: Measurement and Management*, John Wiley & Sons Singapore, pages 379–389.

Merrill Lynch (3 September 2002) Commerzbank: Shaken and Stirred, Germany/Banks – Multinational/Universal/ADR.

Merrill Lynch (23 September 2002) German Banks: Turning Japanese, Pan Europe.

Merrill Lynch (14 October 2002) German Banks, Banks – Multinational/Universal.

Müller, Kai-Oliver and Wolkenhauer, Klaas (2008) Aspekte der Liquiditätssicherungsplanung, in Bartetzky, Peter, Gruber, Walter and Wehn, Carsten (eds), *Handbuch Liquiditätsrisiko: Identifikation, Messung und Steuerung*, Schäffer-Poeschel Verlag, Stuttgart, pages 231–246.

Neu, Peter (2007) Liquidity Risk Measurement, in Matz, Leonard and Neu, Peter (eds), *Liquidity Risk: Measurement and Management*, John Wiley & Sons Singapore, pages 15–36.

Neu, Peter, Leistenschneider, Armin, Wondrak, Bernhard and Knippschild, Martin (2007) Market Developments in Banks' Funding Markets, in Matz, Leonard and Neu, Peter (eds), *Liquidity Risk: Measurement and Management*, John Wiley & Sons Singapore, pages 146–169.

Probst, Gilbert and Gomez, Peter (eds) (1989) *Vernetztes Denken: Unternehmen ganzheitlich führen*, Gabler Verlag, Wiesbaden.

Raffis, Louis. D (2007a) The Liquidity Impact of Derivatives Collateral, in Matz, Leonard and Neu, Peter (eds), *Liquidity Risk: Measurement and Management*, John Wiley & Sons Singapore, pages 204–219.

Raffis, Louis D. (2007b) The Net Cash Capital Tool in Bank Liquidity Management, in Matz, Leonard and Neu, Peter (eds), *Liquidity Risk: Measurement and Management*, John Wiley & Sons Singapore, pages 257–267.

Rappaport, Alfred (1986) *Creating Shareholder Value: The New Standard for Business Performance*, Macmillan, New York.

Rehsmann, Stefan and Martin, Marcus R. W. (2008) Neuerungen in der aufsichtsrechtlichen Behandlung des Liquiditätsrisikos, in Bartetzky, Peter, Gruber, Walter and Wehn, Carsten (eds), *Handbuch Liquiditätsrisiko: Identifikation, Messung und Steuerung*, Schäffer-Poeschel Verlag, Stuttgart, pages 51–76.

Reichmann, Thomas (2006) *Controlling mit Kennzahlen und Management Tools*, 7. Aufl., Munich.

Reitz, Stefan (2008) Moderne Konzepte zur Messung des Liquiditätsrisikos, in Bartetzky, Peter, Gruber, Walter and Wehn, Carsten (eds), *Handbuch Liquiditätsrisiko: Identifikation, Messung und Steuerung*, Schäffer-Poeschel Verlag, Stuttgart, pages 121–140.

Sauerbier, Peter, Thomas, Holger and Wehn, Carsten (2008) Praktische Aspekte der Abbildung von Finanzprodukten im Rahmen des Liquiditätsrisikos, in Bartetzky, Peter, Gruber, Walter and Wehn, Carsten (eds), *Handbuch Liquiditätsrisiko: Identifikation, Messung und Steuerung*, Schäffer-Poeschel Verlag, Stuttgart, pages 77–120.

Schierenbeck, Henner (2003a) *Ertragsorientiertes Bankmanagement, Band I: Grundlagen, Marktzins-methodik und Rentabilitäts-Controlling*, 8. Aufl., Gabler Verlag, Wiesbaden.

Schierenbeck, Henner (2003b) *Ertragsorientiertes Bankmanagement, Band II: Risiko-Controlling und integrierte Rendite-/Risikosteuerung*, 8. Aufl., Gabler Verlag, Wiesbaden.

Schröter, Dirk and Schwarz, Oliver (2008) Optimale Strukturen und Prozesse für das Liquiditäts-risikomanagement, in Bartetzky, Peter, Gruber, Walter and Wehn, Carsten (eds), *Handbuch Liquiditätsrisiko: Identifikation, Messung und Steuerung*, Schäffer-Poeschel Verlag, Stuttgart, pages 247–278.

Schwartz, Robert and Francioni, Reto (2004) *Equity Markets in Action*, John Wiley & Sons, Inc., Hoboken, NJ.

Spremann, Klaus (1996) *Wirtschaft, Investition und Finanzierung*, 5. Aufl. vollständig überarbeitet, Verlag Oldenbourg, Munich.

Spremann, Klaus and Zur, Eberhard (eds) (1992) *Controlling*, Gabler Verlag, Wiesbaden.

Spremann, Klaus, Pfeil, Oliver P. and Weckbach, Stefan (eds) (2001) *Lexikon Value-Management*, Verlag Oldenbourg, Munich.

Stützel, Wolfgang (1959) Liquidität, in Beckerath, Erwin von (ed.), *Handwörterbuch der Sozialwis-senschaft*, Stuttgart, pages 622–629.

Stützel, Wolfgang (1983) *Bankpolitik heute und morgen*, 3. Aufl., Frankfurt am Main.

Suedeutsche Zeitung (11 October 2002) Gerüchteküche London, page 19.

Taleb, Nassim N. (2005) *Fooled by Randomness – The hidden role of chance in life and in the market*, Random House, New York.

Taleb, Nassim N. (2007) *The Black Swan – The impact of the highly improbable*, Random House, New York.

UBS (2007) Mortgage and ABS CDO losses, 13 December.

Volkart, Rudolf (2003) *Corporate Finance: Grundlagen der Finanzierung und Investition*, Zurich.

Vormbaum, Herbert (1995) *Finanzierung der Betriebe*, 9. Aufl. aktualisiert, Gabler Verlag, Wiesbaden.

Weisweiller, Rudi (ed.) (1991a) *The Foreign Exchange Manual* (2nd Supplement), Woodhead-Faulkner, Cambridge.

Weisweiller, Rudi (ed.) (1991b) *Managing a Foreign Exchange Department* (2nd Edition), Woodhead-Faulkner, Cambridge.

Witte, Eberhard (1964) Zur Bestimmung der Liquiditätsreserve, in *Zeitschrift für Betriebswirtschaft*, Heft 12, pages 763–772.

Wondrak, Bernhard (2008) Bilanzielle Aspekte des Liquiditätsmanagement, in Bartetzky, Peter, Gruber, Walter and Wehn, Carsten (eds), *Handbuch Liquiditätsrisiko: Identifikation, Messung und Steuerung*, Schäffer-Poeschel Verlag, Stuttgart, pages 305–322.

Zeranski, Stefan (2005) *Liquidity at Risk zur Steuerung des liquiditätsmäßig-finanziellen Bereichs von Kreditinstituten*, GUC Verlag, Chemnitz.

Zimmermann, Heinz, Jaeger, Stefan and Staub, Zeno (1995) *Asset und Liability Management*, Verlag Neue Zürcher Zeitung, Zurich.

Index